International and Development Education

The *International and Development Education Series* focuses on the complementary areas of comparative, international, and development education. Books emphasize a number of topics ranging from key international education issues, trends, and reforms to examinations of national education systems, social theories, and development education initiatives. Local, national, regional, and global volumes (single-authored and edited collections) constitute the breadth of the series and offer potential contributors a great deal of latitude based on interests and cutting-edge research. The series is supported by a strong network of international scholars and development professionals who serve on the International and Development Education Advisory Board and participate in the selection and review process for manuscript development.

SERIES EDITORS
John N. Hawkins
Professor Emeritus, University of California, Los Angeles
Senior Consultant, IFE 2020 East West Center

W. James Jacob
Assistant Professor, University of Pittsburgh
Director, Institute for International Studies in Education

PRODUCTION EDITOR
Heejin Park
Project Associate, Institute for International Studies in Education

INTERNATIONAL EDITORIAL ADVISORY BOARD
Clementina Acedo, *UNESCO's International Bureau of Education, Switzerland*
Philip G. Altbach, *Boston University, USA*
Carlos E. Blanco, *Universidad Central de Venezuela*
Sheng Yao Cheng, *National Chung Cheng University, Taiwan*
Ruth Hayhoe, *University of Toronto, Canada*
Wanhua Ma, *Peking University, China*
Ka Ho Mok, *University of Hong Kong, China*
Christine Musselin, *Sciences Po, France*
Yusuf K. Nsubuga, *Ministry of Education and Sports, Uganda*
Namgi Park, *Gwangju National University of Education, Republic of Korea*
Val D. Rust, *University of California, Los Angeles, USA*
Suparno, *State University of Malang, Indonesia*
John C. Weidman, *University of Pittsburgh, USA*
Husam Zaman, *Taibah University, Saudi Arabia*

Institute for International Studies in Education
School of Education, University of Pittsburgh
5714 Wesley W. Posvar Hall, Pittsburgh, PA 15260 USA

Center for International and Development Education
Graduate School of Education & Information Studies, University of California, Los Angeles
Box 951521, Moore Hall, Los Angeles, CA 90095 USA

Titles:

Higher Education in Asia/Pacific: Quality and the Public Good
Edited by Terance W. Bigalke and Deane E. Neubauer

Affirmative Action in China and the U.S.: A Dialogue on Inequality and Minority Education
Edited by Minglang Zhou and Ann Maxwell Hill

Critical Approaches to Comparative Education: Vertical Case Studies from Africa, Europe, the Middle East, and the Americas
Edited by Frances Vavrus and Lesley Bartlett

Curriculum Studies in South Africa: Intellectual Histories & Present Circumstances
Edited by William F. Pinar

Higher Education, Policy, and the Global Competition Phenomenon
Edited by Laura M. Portnoi, Val D. Rust, and Sylvia S. Bagley

The Search for New Governance of Higher Education in Asia
Edited by Ka-Ho Mok

International Students and Global Mobility in Higher Education: National Trends and New Directions
Edited by Rajika Bhandari and Peggy Blumenthal

Curriculum Studies in Brazil: Intellectual Histories, Present Circumstances
Edited by William F. Pinar

Access, Equity, and Capacity in Asia Pacific Higher Education
Edited by Deane Neubauer and Yoshiro Tanaka

Policy Debates in Comparative, International, and Development Education
Edited by John N. Hawkins and W. James Jacob

Increasing Effectiveness of the Community College Financial Model: A Global Perspective for the Global Economy
Edited by Stewart E. Sutin, Daniel Derrico, Rosalind Latiner Raby, and Edward J. Valeau

Curriculum Studies in Mexico: Intellectual Histories, Present Circumstances
William F. Pinar

Internationalization of East Asian Higher Education: Globalization's Impact
John D. Palmer

Taiwan Education at the Crossroad: When Globalization Meets Localization
Chuing Prudence Chou and Gregory S. Ching

Mobility and Migration in Asian Pacific Higher Education
Edited by Deane E. Neubauer and Kazuo Kuroda

University Governance and Reform: Policy, Fads, and Experience in International Perspective
Edited by Hans G. Schuetze, William Bruneau, and Garnet Grosjean

Higher Education Regionalization in Asia Pacific: Implications for Governance, Citizenship and University Transformation
Edited by John N. Hawkins, Ka Ho Mok, and Deane E. Neubauer

Post-Secondary Education and Technology: A Global Perspective on Opportunities and Obstacles to Development
Edited by Rebecca A. Clothey, Stacy Austin-Li, and John C. Weidman

Education and Global Cultural Dialogue: A Tribute to Ruth Hayhoe
Edited by Karen Mundy and Qiang Zha

The Dynamics of Higher Education Development in East Asia: Asian Cultural Heritage, Western Dominance, Economic Development, and Globalization
Edited by Deane Neubauer, Jung Cheol Shin, and John N. Hawkins

The Quest for Entrepreneurial Universities in East Asia
By Ka Ho Mok

The Quest for Entrepreneurial Universities in East Asia

Ka Ho Mok

THE QUEST FOR ENTREPRENEURIAL UNIVERSITIES IN EAST ASIA
Copyright © Ka Ho Mok, 2013.

Softcover reprint of the hardcover 1st edition 2013 978-1-137-32210-4

All rights reserved.

First published in 2013 by
PALGRAVE MACMILLAN®
in the United States—a division of St. Martin's Press LLC,
175 Fifth Avenue, New York, NY 10010.

Where this book is distributed in the UK, Europe and the rest of the world, this is by Palgrave Macmillan, a division of Macmillan Publishers Limited, registered in England, company number 785998, of Houndmills, Basingstoke, Hampshire RG21 6XS.

Palgrave Macmillan is the global academic imprint of the above companies and has companies and representatives throughout the world.

Palgrave® and Macmillan® are registered trademarks in the United States, the United Kingdom, Europe and other countries.

ISBN 978-1-349-45828-8   ISBN 978-1-137-31754-4 (eBook)
DOI 10.1057/9781137317544

Library of Congress Cataloging-in-Publication Data is available from the Library of Congress

A catalogue record of the book is available from the British Library.

Design by Newgen Knowledge Works (P) Ltd., Chennai, India.

First edition: December 2013

10 9 8 7 6 5 4 3 2 1

To God, in whom I faithfully trust,
Who is the origin of wisdom and faithfulness
Also to Jasmine, Esther, and Lucinda

Contents

List of Illustrations xi
Acknowledgments xiii
Introduction xv
List of Acronyms xix

1 Globalization and Higher Education: Major Trends and Challenges 1
2 Policy Context for the Quest for Innovation and Entrepreneurial Universities in East Asia 19

Part I Questing for Entrepreneurial Universities and Promoting Innovation

3 Diversifying the Economic Pillars and Enhancing Innovation and Research Development: Hong Kong Experiences 33
4 Promotion of Innovation and Knowledge Transfer: South Korean Experiences 47
5 After Massification of Higher Education: Questing for Innovation and Entrepreneurial Universities in Taiwan 59
6 Asserting Its Global Influence: The Quest for Innovation and Entrepreneurial Universities in Singapore 75
7 Promoting Entrepreneurship and Innovation: Enhancing Research and Reforming University Curriculum in China 91

Part II Internationalization and Transnationalization of Higher Education and Student Learning

8 The Call for Internationalization: Questing for Regional Education Hub Status and Transnationalizing Higher Education in Malaysia, Singapore, and Hong Kong — 121

9 Transnationalization of Higher Education in China: Development Trends, Salient Features, and Challenges for University Governance — 139

10 Transnationalization and Student Learning Experiences — 161

11 Changing Regulatory Regimes and Governance in East Asia — 191

Part III University Performance, Changing University Governance and Policy Implications for East Asia

12 Questing for Entrepreneurial Universities in East Asia: Impacts on Academics and University Governance — 201

Conclusion — 217

Notes — 225

References — 243

About the Author — 261

Index — 263

Illustrations

Figure

9.1 Typology of CFCRS Programs in China (Based on Curriculum Offered and Degree/Certificate Awarded) 145

Tables

2.1 Asian Four Little Dragons GDP Growth: Ten-Year Forecasts 24
5.1 Number of Companies Stationed at the Hsinchu, Central, and Southern Taiwan Science Parks by Industry, as of 8 April 2013 61
5.2 Taiwan's Expenditure on Industry-Academia Collaboration, 2007 and 2010 69
6.1 SPRING Singapore's Innovation and Entrepreneurship Supporting Schemes 80
7.1 Funding for China's First Nine Project 985 Universities 96
7.2 China's Vice-Ministerial Universities and Project 985 Universities 97
7.3 A Comparison of University-Run Enterprises before and after Structural Reform 105
9.1 Wuhan University's International Joint Programs 152
10.1 Schedules of Focus Group Discussions with Students Enrolled in TNHE Programs 162
10.2 Summary: Focus Group Discussions by Region 166
10.3 TNHE in Hong Kong, Mainland China, Singapore, and Malaysia: A Comparison 186
11.1 Varieties of Regulatory Regimes 192

12.1 *Times Higher Education* University Rankings,
      2011/12–2012/13   203
12.2 Asia University Rankings 2013 Top 100,
      Times Higher Education World
      University Rankings   204

Acknowledgments

This volume would not have been possible without the generous help of several organizations, starting with the Research Grants Council of the HKSAR government for providing funding support to two competitive research project grants, awarded to me in the last few years. One of the grants is a public policy grant entitled "A Comparative Study of Transnational Higher Education Policy and Governance in Hong Kong, Shenzhen China and Singapore" [HKIED 7005-PPR-6], and the other is a general research grant entitled "Fostering Entrepreneurship and Innovation: A Comparative Study of Changing Roles of Universities in East Asia" [HKIEd GRF 750210]. With the grant support, I have been able to conduct research activities to conduct fieldwork and appoint research assistants to support me during the process of writing and publishing this volume. Particular thanks go to the Research Grants Council of the HKSAR government. Throughout the last few years, I have been traveling to different East Asian societies to talk to students, academics, government officials, and policy analysts to explore how they evaluate the recent transformations taking place in major universities and how far such transformations, along with calls for strengthening university-industry-business cooperation, have affected the academic community and university governance. Meanwhile, I am thankful to all students whom I met in the last few years when examining the development of transnational higher education and student learning. This volume owes much to these ongoing discussions and to the institutions that made my research activities possible. Deep gratitude goes to all organizations, universities, and research institutes that I have visited for providing support and coordination during my research trips.

Through participating and presenting in different international conferences and symposia, I received much positive and constructive feedback on the preliminary findings generated from these two projects, while my earlier drafts of the present volume benefited tremendously from comments received from my peers in the international academic community. I could not name all of the colleagues who have provided me with suggestions and insights for improving this book. But I would like to dedicate this volume to those who have offered me advice and support throughout the writing process. I would also like to express my thanks to my research staff, including Dr. K. C. Ong,

Dennis Leung, and Evi Liu for offering me assistance during the last few years in my research activities. Particular thanks also go to Joey Lee of the Centre for Greater China Studies, Hong Kong Institute of Education, for organizing different international and regional research activities during the past few years for allowing me to engage with the academic community to share my research.

Last but not least, I would like to thank my beloved wife, Jasmine, for bearing with me over many sleepless nights and as I hid myself in preparing the manuscript, while supporting me and taking care of the family during my different trips the last few years. Gratitude also goes to my two daughters, Esther and Lucinda, for providing joy and love to enrich my life, through which I am very much energized to keep going with my research and scholarship even though I have taken up very heavy university administration duties. I also want to extend my thanks to editors Professor John Hawkins and James Jacob for encouraging me to publish this piece in their very distinguished book series. Finally, I would like to thank our friends at Palgrave Macmillan, New York Office, for turning the project into a reality with the publication of this volume.

Introduction

Globalization, rising costs of public services in general, and the evolution of the knowledge-based economy have caused dramatic changes to the character and functions of higher education in many countries around the world (Burbules and Torres 2000; Mok and Welch 2003), although the local dimension also remains important (Deem 2001; Marginson and Sawir 2005). Higher education systems across different parts of the globe have recently been going through significant restructuring processes to enhance their competitiveness and hierarchical positioning within their own countries and in the global market place (Nelson and Wei 2012). One major consequence of this is the intensified competition among universities to prove their performance through global university league tables or ranking exercises (Dill and Soo 2005; Guarino, Ridgeway, et al. 2005; Liu and Cheng 2005; Merisotis and Sadlak 2005; Marginson 2006). University ranking and league tables, including various measures of quality, which are increasingly used in other kinds of organizations too (Jarrar and Mohamed 2001), are becoming highly influential in shaping how contemporary universities are governed and what core activities they undertake, especially as many universities worldwide come under pressure to become more entrepreneurial (Clark 1998; Marginson and Considine 2000; Anderseck 2004; Mok 2005a; Zaharia and Gilbert 2005).

Universities in East Asia, experiencing similar challenges as their counterparts in other parts of the globe outlined above, have adopted different measures for enhancing their global competitiveness by concentrating funding on only a select few universities to groom them to compete globally in the quest for higher rankings in global university leagues. Meanwhile, university governance has been undergoing significant changes in the last decades, especially as universities in East Asia are increasingly affected by the ideas and practices of neoliberalism, resulting in the privatization, marketization, and corporatization of universities. In order to enhance research capacity and advance technology and innovation, many governments in East Asia have driven universities to expand the third mission, that is, to support social and economic development by making universities more enterprising and entrepreneurial through deepening their cooperation with industry and business. Under the heavy pressure to become "world class" no matter how we define it, performance evaluations of the contemporary university are increasingly guided by criteria such as readily quantifiable (and commercializable) research, and emphasis is being placed on postgraduate and professional over undergraduate education, often through international partnerships and with the help of internationally mobile students and scholars, as Nelson (2012) has rightly suggested. In addition, the global university is assumed to promote internationalization and to foster a spirit of entrepreneurialism, advancing private enterprises for economic growth. In many ways, the global university, as Nelson (2012) has argued, resembles a multinational corporation. Therefore, it is not surprising to witness the rise of private universities and transnational higher education flourishing across different parts of the world, including those in East Asia and Pacific.

This book sets out in the context briefly outlined above to critically examine what major strategies governments/economies in East Asia have adopted in promoting innovation, advancement, research, and development for fostering knowledge transfer, as well as enhancing national higher education systems to become more internationally competitive through transnationalization of academic programs, curriculum design, and student learning. This volume is based on the author's recent research projects, with major focuses on transnationalization of higher education and promotion of innovation and knowledge transfer in East Asia. The book is divided into three major parts. The first part provides the wider socioeconomic and political economy context for the quest for entrepreneurial universities in East Asia, with particular focus on critically examining major trends taking place in higher education systems during recent decades as they have been under significant pressure from global competition. More specifically, we look at what major strategies the universities in East Asia have adopted in coping with globalization challenges by supporting research and promoting innovation through strengthening university-industry-business cooperation. Our five case studies of Hong Kong, Taiwan, South Korea, Singapore, and China offer comparative perspectives that enable us to understand how universities in these East Asian societies are becoming more entrepreneurial.

The second part of the book focuses on major strategies adopted by selected East Asian countries/economies in transnationalizing and internationalizing academic programs and student learning. Based on field interviews with students enrolled in different forms of transnational higher education program in East Asia, either through participating in overseas university branch campuses or various forms of academic program cooperation like distance learning or on-site study programs, the discussions in part 2 provide policy backgrounds, key program features, and student reflections on their learning experiences. The last chapter of part 2 also reflects the changing regulatory regimes and university governance under which transnational higher education is flourishing in

East Asia, as well as what major implications we can draw to manage the challenges resulting from the proliferation of education providers, especially when higher education is no longer provided in the conventional manner, with the growth of transnational corporations offering programs for higher learning. This shows us the sorts of regulatory frameworks that will develop in assuring the quality and enhancement of student learning when higher education provision is no longer confined to any geographical space.

The third part of the book discusses how the quest for entrepreneurial universities in East Asia has affected the academic community in general and university governance in particular. The chapters presented in parts 1 and 2 critically examine how universities and governments in selected East Asian societies have responded to the growing challenges of globalization by promoting innovation and research development, driving new initiatives in knowledge transfer and engaging in internationalization and transnationalization of higher education. After adopting these measures, have universities in these East Asian societies enhanced their global competitiveness? The third part of the volume focuses on assessing how universities in East Asia have performed through the international benchmarking exercises like university league tables and other major forms of international competitiveness studies. In addition, chapter 12 in this part will also reflect upon how the quest for entrepreneurial universities has affected the academic community and university governance in East Asia. The present volume will conclude by drawing major policy implications for management and governance of universities in East Asia against the context in which universities in East Asia are under continued pressure to become more entrepreneurial.[1]

Acronyms

ACYF	All China Youth Federation
ADCSC	Academic Degrees Committee of the State Council
A*GA	A*STAR Graduate Academy
AITD	Angel Investors Tax Deduction Scheme, Singapore
A&M	Agricultural and Mechanical
APAS	Automotive Parts and Accessory Systems
ASEAN	Association of Southeast Asian Nations
A*STAR	The Agency for Science, Technology and Research, Singapore. A statutory board under the Ministry of Trade and Industry of Singapore.
APEX	Accelerated Program for Excellence
ASTRI	Applied Science and Technology Research Institute
AVP-RI	Associate Vice President for Research and Innovation
BAS	Business Angel Scheme, Singapore
BK21	Brain Korea 21 Project
BPC	Business Plan Competition
BSA	Biomedical Science Accelerator
CAS	China Academy of Science
CAST	China Association of Science and Technology
CCJS	Center of Chinese and Japanese Studies, Nanjing University
CCP	Chinese Communist Party
CCYL	Central Committee of the Communist Young League
CDHAW	Chinesisch-Deutsche Hochschule für Angewandte Wissenschaften
CEO	Chief Executive Officer

CEPA	Closer Economic Partnership Arrangement
CFCE	Chinese-Foreign Cooperation Education
CFCRS	Chinese-Foreign Cooperation in Running Schools
CINTEC	of CUHK Centre for Innovation and Technology of the Chinese University of Hong Kong
CLEVO	A Taiwan computer manufacturer
CN	China
CNY	Chinese yuan
COIN	Chinese University of Hong Kong Open Innovation Network
CQT	Centre for Quantum Technologies
CREATE	Campus for Research Excellence and Technological Enterprise
CRF	Collaborative Research Fund
CRP	Competitive Research Program
CSI	Cancer Science Institute Singapore
CUEP	Committee on University Expansion Pathways
CUHK	Chinese University of Hong Kong
CPR	Cohort Participation Rate
DBS	A leading financial services group in Asia, with over 200 branches across 15 markets. Headquartered and listed in Singapore.
DDS	Doctor of Dental Surgery
DfES	Department of Education and Skills
DGIST	Daegu Gyeongbuk Institute of Science and Technology
ECNU	East China Normal University
EDB	Education Bureau
EDB	Economic Development Board
EI	Engineering Index
EMBA	Executive Master of Business Administration
EOS	Earth Observatory of Singapore
ESSEC	École Supérieure des Sciences Économiques et Commerciales, France

ETP	Enterprise
EU	Europe
EYB	Expand Your Business
FDI	Foreign Direct Investment
FPD	Flat Panel Display
GATS	General Agreement on Trade in Services
GDP	Gross Domestic Product
GERD	Gross Domestic Expenditure on Research and Experimental Development
GIST	Gwangju Institute of Science and Technology
GRF	General Research Fund
GYB	Generate Your Business
HEIs	Higher Education Institutes
HKBAN	Hong Kong Business Angel Network
HKBU	Hong Kong Baptist University
HKCAA	Hong Kong Council for Academic Accreditation
HKCAAVQ	Hong Kong Council for Accreditation of Academic and Vocational Qualifications
HKPU/ PolyU	Hong Kong Polytechnic University
HKRITA	Hong Kong Research Institute of Textiles and Apparel
HKSAR	Hong Kong Special Administrative Region
HKU	University of Hong Kong
HKUST	Hong Kong University of Science and Technology
HRBNU	Harbin Normal University
HRD	Human Resource Development
HSBC	Hong Kong and Shanghai Banking Corporation
HSK	Hanyu Shuiping Kaoshi, Chinese Proficiency Test
HUST	Harbin University of Science and Technology
IATA	International Air Transport Association
IDP	Incubator Development Programme, Singapore
IGOs	Intergovernmental Organizations
IIE	Institute of Innovation and Entrepreneurship

iLEAD	Innovative Local Enterprise Achievement Development
ILO	International Labor Organization
IMU	International Medical University
INSEAD	Institut Européen d'Administration des Affairs
IP	Internet Protocol
iPass	Information Portal for Accredited Post-secondary Programmes
IPO	Initial Public Offering
IPR	International Patent Registration
IRENE	Institute for Research and Education
IT	Information Technology
ITC	Innovation and Technology Commission
ITF	Innovation and Technology Fund
ITRI	Industrial Technology Research Institute
JCU	James Cook University, Singapore
JQRC	Joint Quality Review Committee
JTC	Jurong Town Corporation, Singapore's principal developer and manager of industrial estates and their related facilities
KAB	Know about Business
KAIST	Korean Advanced Institute of Science and Technology
KE	Knowledge Exchange
KEDI	Korean Educational Development Institute
KRW	Korean Won
LAN	Lebgaba Akreditasi Negara, Malaysia
LED	Light Emitting Diode
LG	Electronics Life's Good Electronics
LNU	Liaoning Normal University
LSCM	Logistics and Supply Chain Management
Ltd.	Limited Company
MA	Master of Arts
MBA	Master of Business Administration
MBI	Mechano-Biology Institute

MD	Medical Doctor
MedTech	Medical Technology
MEST	Ministry of Education, Science and Technology
MIT	Massachusetts Institute of Technology
MNCs	Multi-National Companies
MOE	Ministry of Education
MOEL	Ministry of Employment and Labor
MOST	Ministry of Science and Technology
MQA	Malaysian Qualifications Agency
MQF	Malaysian Qualifications Framework
MSU	Missouri State University
MTI	Ministry of Trade and Industry
NAMI	Nano and Advanced Materials Institute
NCTU	National Chiao Tung University
NEC	National University of Singapore Entrepreneurship Centre
NEC	New Era College
NEI	National University of Singapore Enterprise Incubator
NFIE	National Framework for Innovation and Enterprise
NGO	Non-Governmental Organization
NHG	National Healthcare Group
NIFA	National Innovation Framework for Action
NIS	National Innovation System
NJU	Nanjing University
NRF	National Research Foundation
NRL	National Research Laboratories
NSA	National Science Council
NSC	National Science Council
NSTB	National Science and Technology Board
NTHU	National Tsing Hua University
NTU	National Taiwan University
NTU	Nanyang Technology University
NUC	Nilai University College

NUS	National University of Singapore
ODL	Open Distance Learning
OECD	Organisation for Economic Co-operation and Development
OTC	Over-the-Counter
PAA	Program Area Accreditation
PDR	People's Democratic Republic
PDT	Photodynamic Therapy
PET	program PhD Entrepreneur-in-Training Program
P&G	Procter & Gamble Company
PhD	Doctor of Philosophy
PIC	Productivity and Innovation Credit, Singapore
PISA	Program for International Student Assessment
PRD	Pearl River Delta
QF	Qualifications Framework
QR	Qualifications Register
RAE	Research Assessment Exercise
R&D	Research and Development
REF	Research Endowment Fund
RFIC	Radio Frequency Integrated Circuit
RFID	Radio Frequency Identification
RGC	Research Grants Council
RIE	Research, Innovation, and Enterprise
RIEC	Research, Innovation and Enterprise Council
RISs	Regional Innovation Systems
R2M	Platform Research to Market Platform, Singapore
RMB	Renminbi
SAS	An American founded private software company
SBC-USST	Sino-British College, University of Shanghai for Science and Technology
SCELSE	Singapore Centre on Environmental Life Sciences Engineering
SCE	School of Continuing Education
SCI	Science Citation Index

SDIBC	Sino-Dutch International Business Center
S&E	Science and Engineering
SEC	State Education Commission, China
SEEDS	Start-up Enterprise Development Scheme, Singapore
SHNU	Shanghai Normal University
SICA	Students' International Communication Association
SINGA	Singapore International Graduate Award
SIYB	Start and Improve Your Business
SMA	Singapore MIT (Massachusetts Institute of Technology) Alliance
SMBA	Small and Medium Business Association
SMEs	Small and Medium-Sized Enterprises
SMEA	Small and Medium Enterprise Administration
SMU	Singapore Management University
SMUEA	Singapore Management University Entrepreneurship Alliance
SPRING	Singapore An agency under the Ministry of Trade and Industry responsible for helping Singapore enterprises grow and building trust in Singapore products and services
SSA	Sector Specific Accelerators
SSC	SPRING SEEDS Capital Pte. Ltd., Singapore
SSCI	Social Science Citation Index
S&T	Science and Technology
STCSM	Science and Technology Commission of Shanghai Municipality
STEFG	Shanghai Technology Entrepreneurship Foundation for Graduates
TECS	Technology Enterprise Commercialization Scheme, Singapore
TIMSS	Third International Mathematics and Science Study
TNCs	Transnational National Corporations
TNHE	Transnational Higher Education`
TSSCI	Taiwan Social Science Citation Index
UCNs	Upconverting Nanoparticles
UGC	University Grant Committee`
UIC	United International College

UK	United Kingdom
UM-SJTU	Joint Institute University of Michigan–Shanghai Jiao Tong University Joint Institute
UNESCO	United Nations Educational, Scientific and Cultural Organization
UNIST	Ulsan National Institute of Science and Technology
UNN	University of Nottingham Ningbo
UNSP	University National Science Parks
UOB	United Overseas Bank Limited
URIs	Universities/Research Institutes
USA	United States of America
USM	Universiti Sains Malaysia
USN	Ubiquitous Sensor Network
UW	University of Waterloo
VTC	Vocational Training Council
WCHE	World Conference on Higher Education
WCU	World Class University
WEF	World Economic Forum
WTO	World Trade Organization
YA	Year of Assessment
YES!	Schools Young Entrepreneurs Scheme for Schools, Singapore
ZFYEE	Zhejiang Foundation for Youth Entrepreneurship and Employment
ZUNSP	Zhejiang University National Science Park
ZUT	Zhongyuan University of Technology

Chapter 1

Globalization and Higher Education: Major Trends and Challenges

Introduction

The rise of the knowledge economy has generated new global infrastructures, with information technology playing an increasingly important role in the global economy. Such a development has huge implications for different stakeholders in a national innovation system. For the government, how to make the country thrive in a competitive knowledge economy has become an important national development agenda. That it is often hard-pressed to orchestrate strategic research and development (R&D) activities with higher education has increasingly been seen as one key component of the national innovation system (Edquist and Hommen 2008; Etzkowitz 2008; Lundvall et al. 2006; Nelson 1993). For entrepreneurs, an era of "open innovation" is argued to have emerged, where firms, rather than conducting in-house R&D, have been increasingly outsourcing their research activities to diverse external units, including universities, so that innovation can be achieved in a more efficient manner (Chesbrough 2003; Perkmann and Walsh 2007).

As for universities, apart from performing their traditional missions of teaching and academic research, they are now under tremendous pressures to acquire the third mission of serving economic and social development. The new mission opens up lots of opportunities for universities to establish linkages with the industry sector, namely through setting up university spin-off companies, conducting licensing activities and contract research, providing consulting services, and exploring graduate and researcher mobility between the two sectors. As higher education has become more associated with social and especially economic development, R&D activities in universities can no longer be regarded as purely academic pursuits within the ivory tower. Therefore, structurally, universities are required to build a "university-based entrepreneurship ecosystem" (see Fetters et al. 2010) where "academic entrepreneurship" flourishes (see Wong 2011). In a nutshell, the conception of many countries, especially in the minds of policy makers, is that a closer, interactive cooperation among the government, industry, and academia will lead to sustainable economic growth and enhanced competitiveness in the knowledge economy, where innovation is the key factor supporting such goals.

In order to enhance their national competitiveness in the globalizing economic context, the governments of East Asia have tried to transform their higher education systems to become more responsive and proactive to rapid social, economic, and political changes by not only serving the traditional missions of teaching and research but also supporting economic growth through engaging in entrepreneurial activities such as the promotion of knowledge transfer activities in the last few decades. The major objective of this chapter is to identifying major trends and challenges that the higher education sector in East Asia is facing, particularly when universities are increasingly influenced by the growing impacts of globalization. More specifically, the following discussion focuses on identifying the major trends and challenges confronting higher education development in the selected East Asian societies of Hong Kong, Taiwan, South Korea, Singapore, and Mainland China. In addition, this chapter also examines how and what strategies universities and governments in East Asia have adopted in addressing the growing challenges of globalization.

Globalization: Contested Concepts and Unfinished Debates

In the last decade or so, scholars and writers have repeatedly discussed the nature and impact of globalization at political, economic, social, and cultural levels (see, for example, Held and McGrew 2000; Schirato and Webb 2003). Despite the contested concepts and heated debates on globalization, some scholars have attempted to categorize such discussions into three major schools of thought, namely hyperglobalists, skeptics, and transformationists (Held and McGrew 2000). For hyperglobalists, they strongly believe the global economy is dominated by uncontrollable global forces in which nation-states are structurally dependent on global capital, which is primarily determined by transnational corporations (TNCs). To believers in this strong globalism, the globalizing economy means a drastic shift in structural power and authority away from the nation-state toward nonstate agencies and from national political systems to a global economic system (Held, McGrew, Goldblatt, and Perraton 1999). Unlike these strong globalists, those who oppose the convergence theory think that globalization is overstated and overgeneralized. According to skeptics, nation-states are more heterogeneous and independent in action than they are given credit for. Since they have never responded to external changes in the same fashion, there are a wide variety of local and regional responses to globalization. In this regard, skeptics argue that contemporary levels of economic interdependence are not historically unprecedented. In contrast, the global economy is less global in its geographical embrace, especially when compared with the former world empires. Somehow taking a stand between the hyperglobalists and the skeptics, the transformationists believe that globalization is unprecedented, but there is no convergence. Instead, they believe the globalizing world has resulted in a kind of global stratification, a new international division of labor. It is against this wider context that some nations succeed at the expense of others, and even within nations there are winners and losers. Therefore, the old terms such as the North and the South and the division between the first, second, and the third world are no longer relevant (Held and McGrew 2000).

The diverse views on globalization outlined above have clearly demonstrated the disagreements among academics and researchers on many aspects of the form, direction, definitions, and significance of globalization. Nonetheless, no matter how we assess the impacts of globalization on the contemporary world, no one can deny that the intensification of worldwide social relations, which link distant regions in such a way that local happenings are shaped by events occurring many miles away and vice versa, is a reality (Hirst and Thompson 1999). Held has said, "We live in a world of overlapping communities of fate, where the trajectories of countries are deeply enmeshed with one another" (Held 2004, 2). Held's statement clearly suggests that we are living in an increasingly interdependent world, and therefore we are not immune from the growing influences of the market and the ideas and practices of neoliberalism on many different dimensions of the contemporary world. Yang has succinctly summarized the impacts of globalization:

> Globalization is the result of the compression of time and space that has occurred since advanced technology allowed the instantaneous sharing of information around the world, leading to a cross-border flow of ideas, ideologies, people and goods, images and messages, capital and financial services, knowledge and technologies, creating a borderless world economy. It has a material base in capitalism and an ideological genesis in neo-liberalism. (Yang 2005, 28)

While some see globalization as an inexorable process of global economic integration (Fukuyama 1992), others see it as a deliberate policy project, which celebrates the market as economic savior (Yang 2005, 28). However, Jill Blackmore (2000) reminds us that globalization is far more complicated. She describes it as

> increased economic, cultural, environmental, and social interdependencies and new transnational financial and political formations arising out of the mobility of capital, labor and information, with both homogenizing and differentiating tendencies. (Blackmore 2000, 467)

Central to the ideas and practices of neoliberalism is a shift in the balance between the state and the market, strongly in favor of the latter (Fukuyama 2006, 121). The neoliberal philosophy, with its roots in an intellectual movement promoted by scholars like von Mises and Hayek, advocates the reduction of the role of the state, the opening of national markets, free trade, flexible exchanges, deregulation, the transfer assets from the public to the private sector, and an international division of labour. This political-economic agenda is often referred to as the Washington consensus although some may argue that it is more an ideology than a consensus (Bayliss and Smith 2001; Stiglitz 2002). In recent decades, a major emerging trend from such a political-economic aspect of globalization has been the increased significance of competition. Jessop (2002), Cerny (1990), and Ball (2007) also argue that modern states are struggling to become "competition states," which aim to "secure economic growth within its borders and/or to secure competitive advantages for capitals based in its borders" (Jessop 2002, 96). In order to enhance the national competitiveness in the globalizing world, higher education is seen to be performing a very important function. Nelson (2012), in his recent volume titled *The Global University*, asks questions related to the nature, functions, purposes, and missions of being a global university. Does it refer only to ranking in global league tables? What distinguishes its approach to teaching, to research, to knowledge? Whose interest does it serve, and how? The present book is set out against the wider context in which universities in East Asia have been increasingly challenged by globalization, to critically examine how they respond to and what strategies are being adopted in addressing both homogenizing and differentiating tendencies resulted from the processes of globalization.

Challenges of Globalization and University Responses

The Quest for Global Competitiveness and University Governance

In order to enhance their global competitiveness, governments in different parts of the world have started to conduct comprehensive reviews of and implement plans to restructure their higher education systems (Mok and Welch 2003). In response to the growing pressures generated by globalization forces, modern states have attempted to reinvent themselves by moving beyond the welfare state to become the competition state (Gill 1995; Moran 2002; Jordana and Levi-Faur 2005). Governments across different parts of the globe, facing similar competitive pressures, have undertaken regulatory reforms such as privatization or corporatization of state-owned industries or publicly owned organizations such as post offices and universities, opening up new markets to multiple providers and the introduction of new regulatory regimes under the control of independent regulators (Drahos and Joseph 1995; Levi-Faur 1998; Scott 2004). To enhance the efficiency of public policy/public management, modern states may deregulate some areas while enforcing competition in others, hence becoming a facilitator or even a generator of markets. Thus, it is common to witness that the extent of reregulation or recentralization in the processes of market restructuring is accompanied by the emergence of strong regulatory states and by the entrepreneurial role that states play (Chan and Tan 2006; Ng and Chan 2006; Hawkins 2005). Unlike Cerny's (1997) characterization of the competition state as a basically liberal state, Levi-Faur argues that the state (particularly in the intensified global competitive environment, the emphasis of this book) faces a paradox: "The greater the commitment of the competition state to the promotion of competition, the deeper its regulation will be" (Levi-Faur 1998, 676). More importantly, the actions and mission of the competition state do not necessarily result in the retreat of the state from the market but rather a reassertion of the role of the state under changing social and economic circumstances (Levi-Faur 1998, 676).

In order to promote basic national interests through the creation and enforcement of competition, the developmental states in Asia have taken the opportunity offered by the fundamental economic restructuring processes to transform them into "*market-accelerationist states*" by proactively shaping the market institutions for the benefits of market creation (Mok 2006a; Lee 2004). Unlike the regulatory state in America that evolved against a liberal market economy context, the regulatory state in Asia has emerged from a context of a combined strong state and a free market economy, by which the state ideologically commits to an "authoritarian mode of liberalism." As Jayasuriya has rightly pointed out, "this authoritarian liberalism presupposes the existence of a strong (or better described as politically illiberal) state with a capacity to regulate the economy" (Jayasuriya 2000, 329). In order to promote competition in the markets against the context of authoritarian liberalism, a market-accelerationist state is forming (Mok 2006a). The market-accelerationist state has the features of a "dualistic state" as Fraenkel (1941) has described: a strong state combined with a liberal market economy. With this kind of state architecture in place, the success of the markets rests heavily upon the presence of strong regulatory institutions. It is against such a wider sociopolitical context that far more procompetition policy instruments are adopted by modern states to transform the way the public sector is governed. Hence, the higher education sector, like other public policy domains, has gone "private," while ideas and strategies along the lines of neoliberalism and economic rationalism are increasingly influencing the way public policy is managed (Brehony and Deem 2005; Neubauer 2006).

The socioeconomic and sociopolitical environments outlined above have inevitably affected the way higher education is governed. In order to become globally competitive, governments and universities in Asia have started to search for new governance strategies to improve university governance by the adoption of corporatization and incorporation strategies. In order to become more globally competitive, Asian universities have taken world university ranking very seriously and therefore have engaged in a quest for "world-class" university status.

University Restructuring: Incorporation and Corporatization

To survive in this highly competitive world, universities have to become customer-focused business enterprises (Currie and Newson 1998). As the nation-state acts as a player in the new global marketplace (Currie et al. 2003), universities are encouraged to act in market-like ways, and therefore changes begin to emerge in funding, management, and function (Yang 2005; Mok 2006a; Hawkins 2005). Being unsatisfied with the conventional model along the lines of "state-oriented" and "highly centralized" approaches in higher education, coupled with the pressure to improve the efficiency of university governance, a growing number of Asian governments have recently tried to "incorporate" or introduced "corporatization" and "privatization" measures to run their state/national universities, believing that these transformations could make national universities more flexible and responsive to rapid socioeconomic changes (Mok 2006a; Oba 2006; Hawkins 2007). Instead of being closely directed by the Ministry of Education or equivalent government administrative bodies, state universities in Asia are now required to become more proactive and dynamic in looking for their own financial resources. Similar to their Australian and British counterparts, universities in Asia are now under constant pressure to become more "entrepreneurial," to look for alternative funding sources from the market, strengthening their partnerships with industry and business (Olsen and Gornitzka 2006; Marginson and Considine 2000).

Inclining more toward market and corporate principles and practices, universities in Hong Kong are now run on a market-oriented and business corporation model. Universities in Hong Kong have experienced corporatization and privatization processes, whereby higher education institutions (HEIs) have proactively engaged in fostering entrepreneurship to search for additional revenue sources from the market (Mok 2005b; Lee and Gopinathan 2005). In order to enhance the efficiency of university governance, the University Grant Committee (UGC), the organization that shapes the direction of higher education development in Hong Kong, has recently subscribed to the notion of "deep collaboration" among universities, believing that synergy could be pulled together if universities in the city-state could better integrate. The UGC even supports university merging or other forms of restructuring to further establish Hong Kong as a regional center for excellence in research and scholarship (Chan 2007). Turning universities into enterprises and entrepreneurial institutions is becoming increasingly popular in Hong Kong, while the university presidents or vice chancellors have been heavily involved in fund-raising activities (Chan and Lo 2007).

Similarly, the Ministry of Education in Taiwan has decided to change the statutory position of state universities into an independent judicial entity by adopting principles and practices of corporatization. In order to reduce the state burden in higher education financing, all state universities in Taiwan have to generate additional funds from nonstate sectors, such as the market and enterprises. In order to generate sufficient funds to finance their institutions, various kinds of market-driven strategies have been adopted. More recently, the Taiwan government has attempted to restructure its state universities by passing a new University Act to make state universities independent legal entities. Influenced by the Japan model, state universities in Taiwan have to establish new governance structures; at the same time they are under immense pressure to search for additional financial support from nonstate channels, especially since the Taiwan government has significantly reduced core funding (Lo and Weng 2005; Mok, Yu, and Ku 2013).

In facing a new market economy context, the Chinese government has also found the old way of "centralized governance" in education inappropriate (Yang 2002; Hawkins 2000). Acknowledging that overcentralization and stringent rules would kill the initiatives and enthusiasm of local educational institutions, the Chinese Communist Party (CCP) called for resolute steps to streamline administration and devolve powers to units at lower levels so as to allow them more flexibility to run education. In the last decade or so, higher education in the post-Mao era has experienced structural reforms ranging from curriculum design, financing, and promotion of the private/*minban* sectors in higher education provision, to adopting strategies to develop world-class universities. In order to promote the competitiveness of its higher education in the global marketplace, the Chinese government has introduced various kinds of restructuring exercises to merge universities or to streamline the stubbornly sustained bureaucratic university systems. With strong intention to identify and develop a few Chinese universities into world-class universities, the government has implemented various reform measures such as the "211 Project" and the "985 Project" to concentrate state resources on a few selected top-tier national universities for boosting them to become leading universities in the world (Min 2004; Lo and Chan 2006; Chou 2006).

Like societies in greater China, Japan is not immune from the impact of neoliberalism, managerialism, and economic rationalism, three major ideologies underlying the tidal wave of public sector reforms and reinventing government projects across the world. With the intention to make its state university system more responsive and flexible in coping with intensified pressures generated from the growing impact of globalization, the Japanese government has incorporated all state universities since 2004. Central to the transformation of the existing national universities into "national university corporations" are three major reform aspects: increased competitiveness in research and education, enhanced accountability together with the introduction of competition, and strategic and functional management of national universities (Hawkins 2007; Oba 2006). Moreover, some universities in Japan are selected as part of the "Flagship University" project, an initiative to promote a select few to become world-class universities.

Higher education restructuring is popular not only among East Asian states but also among Southeast Asian societies. Having reflected upon changing university governance models and having evaluated the recent experiences of Singapore Management University (SMU), the Ministry of Education in Singapore has decided to change the governance models of the existing state universities, namely the National University of Singapore and Nanyang Technological University, by making them independent legal entities through the process of "corporatization" (Mok 2005b; 2006b). By "incorporatizing" these state universities, the Singapore government hopes that universities in the island state will become more entrepreneurial. Similarly, public universities in Malaysia have started a similar project of "incorporation" and "corporatization" of national universities since 1998. In the last few years, private universities have grown in number, while the public universities are run like corporations. According to Molly Lee, "the structural changes in the corporatized universities show that collegial forms of governance have been sidelined, entrepreneurial activities have increased, and corporate managerial practices have been institutionalized" (Lee 2004, 15).

Privatization and Marketization of Higher Education

Historically, education has been essential to East Asia. In East Asia, education is crucial to nation building—an instrument to create a sense of belonging and nationhood and to build up the government's political legitimacy by enhancing economic growth through educational improvement (Bray and Lee 2001; Gopinathan 2001). In recent decades, when responding to the growing pressures generated by globalization forces, many governments have attempted to reinvent themselves by moving beyond the welfare state to become the competition state. Facing fiscal pressures, governments are hard-pressed to undertake neoliberal reforms, such as deregulation and privatization or corporatization of state-owned industries or publicly owned organizations. More private providers are introduced into the market. In the arena of higher education, many East Asian governments have on one hand enhanced the autonomy and flexibility of universities to run their own businesses and on the other hand have devised strategic planning to guide the development of universities in ways that align with the national development agenda. For example, governments have devoted more financial resources to the higher education sector as a whole as incentives and have set benchmarks for universities to compete for funding. Another approach is the "concentration and selection" strategy, under which governments have allocated resources for certain special projects that involve only the best and most suitable universities in order to boost their R&D capacities and international recognition (see discussions in part 2 of the present volume).

Parallel to the call for more government financial commitment to higher education, higher education funding sources have been diversified in the Four East Asian Tigers, which has given rise of private higher education, as in many countries in the world (see Altbach and Levy 2005). According to 2011 World Bank statistics, the number of private higher education institutions had the highest share of the market in Malaysia, Indonesia, and the Philippines respectively, while Korea, Japan, and Taiwan had the largest enrollment rate in private higher education. It also emerged that open distance learning (ODL) has had an increasing share in China, India, Indonesia, and Thailand. In the case of China, government subsidy of this type of learning was the highest at 75 percent of the budget; while Thailand's government subsidy of ODL stood at 26.5 percent.[1]

In the Four Little East Asian Tigers, with the rise of private HEIs, the division of labor between private higher education and public higher education has become clearer. While the former will shoulder the responsibility of massification of higher education by offering more higher education seats to aspiring students, the latter, with the aid of government subsidy and the favor of public policy facilitation, will engage in more R&D and entrepreneurial activities. While the majority of universities/higher education institutions in Hong Kong and Singapore are either run by the government or are heavily state financed, there is a clearer private-public mix in South Korea and Taiwan, where the proportion of private HEIs is higher. But in recent years the Hong Kong and Singapore governments have made efforts to increase the number and share of private education institutions to make use of the market to fulfill the policy goals of the massification of higher education (Mok 2006a).

Private higher education is becoming more and more important in Asia, and there is a trend of a public-private mix, with public higher education institutes transforming into entrepreneurial universities. The conventional conception of the public-private distinction is no longer appropriate in understanding the nature of higher education, as it has become a "hot product" for both public and private pursuits, that is, for both the government to advance the national development agenda and the private sector to sustain business growth (Mok 2012a).

The Quest for "World-Class" Status and University Ranking

With strong intentions to enhance their global competitiveness, governments and universities in Asia have taken global university ranking exercises very seriously. Recent studies have repeatedly shown that universities in East Asia are increasingly under pressure to co mpete internationally, and research has obviously become one of the major yardsticks in measuring university performance. University league tables are not only popular in the UK and Canada; various university ranking exercises have also been launched by academic institutions in Taiwan and Mainland China (Liu and Cheng 2005; Mok and Hawkins 2010; Altbach 2010).

Positioning itself as a regional hub of higher education, Hong Kong has placed heavy weight on research performance, and this has been reflected in the research performance–led funding formula adopted by the government. Since the 1990s, Hong Kong higher education has gone through several research assessment exercises (RAEs), modeling the UK approach to monitoring research performance. Universities in Hong Kong have gone through major review exercises, and they have been asked to differentiate themselves in terms of roles and missions, identifying major strengths and developing their centers of excellence. Academics currently working in Hong Kong are confronted with increasing pressures from the government to engage in international research, commanding a high quality of teaching and contributing to professional and community services. As Hong Kong universities have tried to benchmark with top universities in the world, they are struggling very hard to compete for limited resources, just as are universities in Central Europe (Kwiek 2004). Under a "publish or perish" context, academics in Hong Kong are becoming more "instrumental" when choosing publication venues, and therefore international journals indexed in Social Science Citation Index (SSCI) and Science Citation Index (SCI) are major targets for getting their works published, while university presidents/vice chancellors in the city-state are concerned with their institutions' rankings in the global university league (Mok and Cheung 2011).

In Taiwan, the government has realized that globalization has accelerated competition among higher education institutions globally. With intentions to improve the global competitiveness of Taiwan's institutions, the Executive Yuan set out a policy target to develop at least one university in Taiwan as one of the top 100 universities in the world, and at least 15 key departments or cross-university research centers will become the top in Asia within the next five years (Lu 2004). With these policy objectives, the Ministry of Education and the National Science Council have jointly launched the "Programme for Promoting Academic Excellence of Universities," primarily aiming at improving universities' infrastructure and invigorating research (MOE Taiwan 2000).

Well aware of the importance of its international position, higher education institutions in Taiwan have attached far more weight to university ranking exercises. For instance, the Research Institute of Higher Education at Tamkang University has conducted university assessment studies in the last few years. University league tables have been produced, and subsequent reports have aroused lively debates in Taiwan (Lo and Weng 2005; Research Institute of Higher Education and University Evaluation 2005; Lo and Chan 2006). Similar to Hong Kong, research assessment has dominated academic life in Taiwan. Despite the fact that the university sector in Taiwan has established the Taiwan Social Science Citation Index (TSSCI) in order to counterbalance the pressures to publish only in SSCI journals, academics confront the reality that special weight is still attached to international publication venues in terms of promotion and research evaluations (Chen and Lo 2007). A study related to academic evaluations in Taiwan in the context of the quest for world-class university status clearly suggests a strong sentiment commonly shared among university academics that their academic freedom is being undermined, while universities are under great pressure for restratification since special funding support would attach to the few universities selected by the government for strategic development purposes (Mok 2012a).

In order to enhance the international competitiveness of Chinese universities in the globalizing world, the Chinese government has implemented a few major projects such as the 211 Project and the 985 Scheme to enable some higher education institutions to become world-class universities. For the 211 Project, the government has attempted to develop 100 key universities and key disciplines in the twenty-first century with additional funding allocated to improve their teaching and research facilities, while the 985 Scheme is intended to transform Beijing University (Peking University) and Tsinghua University to be world-class universities by 2015 and 2011, respectively. Realizing the intensified global competition among leading universities and feeling the pressure for better ranking in the global university league, the Chinese government has strategically identified key national bases for humanities and social sciences research, and major national laboratories have been established to promote scientific research (Huang 2006a). More recently, a research institute of higher education based in Shanghai has published a report titled *The Academic Ranking of World Universities*, which has drawn a great deal of attention and sparked considerable debate among academics in China (Liu and Cheng 2005). In the context of the quest for world-class universities in China, other research institutions such as the Research Centre of Chinese Scientific Evaluation of Wuhan University and the College of Education, Zhejiang University, have also conducted research of similar kinds to promote university assessment and performance (Research Centre of Chinese Scientific Evaluation of Wuhan University 2005; Zhejiang University 2006). Most recently, Ngok and Guo have critically reviewed the quest for world-class universities in China, pointing out the gap between government policy goals and the reality. They also report some malpractice and even corruption among academics resulting from the strong drive to obtain world-class status (Ngok and Guo 2007).

In Japan, academics are becoming increasingly aware of the ranking exercises, and therefore they have launched a "Flagship Universities" project to identify a few major Japanese universities and develop them as world-class universities. According to Yonezawa (2006), consistent and protracted development of Japan's higher education system has long been driven by strong national initiatives since the late nineteenth century. Heavily invested in its university systems, Japanese universities long dominated the top echelons in Asia Week's annual "Asian University Ranking." Nonetheless, Japanese universities have recently found their positions declining in both the regional and global university league tables. After benchmarking with the world university rankings, the Japanese government has become very concerned about how to reposition Japanese universities in the rapidly changing global environment. Therefore, the government has allocated additional resources to promote internationalization, and students and academics are strongly encouraged by the government to engage in international collaborations and exchanges (Furushiro 2006; Yonezawa 2006). Like other Asian societies, universities in Japan have also experienced different forms of restratification under the increasingly competitive environment, the development of which has led to different classes of university students and graduates.

Similarly, universities in Singapore are becoming increasingly aware of their international standing. To strengthen Singapore as a regional hub of higher education, the government strategically identified major top universities internationally and invited them to set up their branch campuses in the city-state. In addition, the government has attempted to attract leading academics to collaborate with local scholars (Mok and Tan 2004). Similar situations can be found in other Southeast Asian societies such as Malaysia, especially since the university system there has been going through restructuring along the lines of neoliberalism and the present government is very keen to make Malaysia a regional hub of higher education. More overseas academics will be appointed to the system, and international collaborations with overseas institutions in terms of research and teaching have received strong support from the state (Mok 2007a).

After putting serious efforts into questing for world-class status, a growing number of universities in East Asia have obtained increasingly good international reputations, which has clearly been indicated by some international university benchmarking exercises. According to the *Times Higher Education* University Rankings, 11 elite universities in Asia ranked among the top 100 universities in the world. And 5 of them were even among the top 50 in the world, many of them from the Four Little Dragons. In the 2012/13 ranking, the top 20 Asian universities included 5 from Japan, 4 from Hong Kong, 4 from South Korea, 2 from Singapore, and 1 from Taiwan.[2]

In the 2012/13 *Times Higher Education* World University Ranking of the top 50 engineering and technology universities, the National University of Singapore was number 12, the Hong Kong University of Science and Technology was 23, the Pohang University of Science and Technology was 24, Nanyang Technology University was 26, the University of Tokyo was 28, Seoul National University was 37, the University of Hong Kong was 43, the Korea Advanced Institute of Science and Technology was 44, Kyoto University was 47, and the Tokyo Institute of Technology was 50.[3]

In the 2012/13 *Times Higher Education* World University Ranking of the top 50 life sciences universities, Japan was the only Asian country in the world top 50, with the University of Tokyo at number 30 and Kyoto University at 32.[4]

According to Shanghai's Jiao Tong University's Academic Ranking of World Universities by region in 2012, although universities in East Asia are still lagging behind their counterparts in the United States and Europe, those from Japan, South Korea, and Singapore are already among the top in Asia.[5] Although the Asian universities are latecomers in the quest for running world-class universities, the above global ranking exercises clearly demonstrate how fast they are trying to catch up. In the context of the global financial crisis, American scholars are issuing warnings to their countrymen worrying about the loosening of global competitiveness of American universities as a result of significant budget cuts, while Asian scholars are more optimistic about the prospect for Asia's innovation and improvement. For instance, in *The New Asian Hemisphere*, Singaporean scholar and former diplomat Kishore Mahbubani (2008) argues that one of the factors contributing to the irresistible shift of global power from the West to the East is exactly the gigantic improvement of education in Asia.

Transnationalizing and Internationalizing Higher Education and Student Mobility

In the last decade or so, we have witnessed the rise of transnational higher education in Asia, especially when some Asian countries have begun the quest to become regional education hubs by establishing university cities, inviting overseas universities to offer offshore programs or set up offshore campuses. Against the backdrop of an increasingly borderless world, Chapman, Cummings, and Postiglione (2010) witnessed transformations in higher education in Asia for crossing borders and bridging minds. Perceiving education as trade and industry, a few Asian economies have started their hub projects, such Bangalore in India, Singapore, Hong Kong, Malaysia, South Korea, and other economies in the Middle East (Shields and Edwards 2010). Obviously, the emerging regional education hubs in Asia have inevitably transformed the patterns of international student mobility and induced intensified competition for students among these regions (Rivza and Teichler 2007). The international flow of students is not a new phenomenon, but student mobility has become increasingly frequent in recent years, particularly when Asian universities are expanding. Unlike the patterns of international student mobility in the 1970s and 1980s, when most international students chose their study destinations in Europe, the UK, and North America, students have begun to study in the Asia and Pacific region since the late 1980s, especially after the 1996/97 Asian financial crisis (Mok and Ong 2011). Analyzing the changing patterns of international student mobility in the light of Phillip Altbach's conceptual framework (Altbach 1989), we have witnessed that there has been a fundamental shift from students moving from "periphery" (developing economies) to "core" (developed economies) for overseas learning experiences to "periphery" to "semi-periphery" (emerging economies).

In more recent years, we also observe that students from the core have chosen their study destinations in China, Taiwan, Hong Kong, Singapore, Malaysia, and South Korea. According to the British Council, two-way travel has begun when a growing number of students from the developed economies in the West have gone to the less-developed economies for further studies, while students from Asia have diversified their destinations for overseas study. With the expansion of higher education in the Asia and Pacific region in recent years, more students choose to stay home or join universities in the region for pursuing their studies in higher education (Kingston and Forland 2008). The rise of new destinations for international students is unlikely to usurp the global dominance of traditionally preeminent universities overnight; nonetheless, student movement toward these emerging economies does suggest that competition will increase for the revenues associated with foreign student enrollment. According to Alison Wride, a professor at the University of Exeter's School of Business and Economics, there has been a downturn over 10 to 15 years in the international student market in the UK as China and Pakistan further develop their own infrastructures. In view of the emerging regional education hubs, Wride points out the importance of reasserting the international/world-class standard of universities in the UK and developed economies (Wride 2008).

Wride's remarks are particularly true when we have found that more students in Asia have chosen their study destinations in the Asia and Pacific region at a time when Singapore, Hong Kong, Australia, Malaysia, and South Korea are rapidly expanding their transnational higher education programs to attract students from the region for further studies.

In the last decade, higher education in the Asia-Pacific region has expanded rapidly, with the number of students enrolled in higher education growing year by year. There were over 3 million tertiary students enrolled outside their home country in 2007, an increase of 3.3 percent compared to 2006 (*Education at a Glance 2009: OECD Indicators*, 309). In 2009, 70 percent of international students primarily came from Asia, particularly from China and India. The most preferred places for overseas learning for these Asian students are still the United States, the UK, Germany, and France, but there is an emerging trend showing that students from the Asia-Pacific region have begun to choose to study within the region rather than going to the traditional countries as outlined above in the western developed economies.

Massification of Higher Education and Social Mobility

Globalization and the evolution of the knowledge-based economy have caused dramatic changes in the character and functions of education in most countries. In order to enhance their national competitiveness in the global marketplace, higher education in East Asia has experienced a significant expansion in terms of an increase in higher education enrollment. However, the regional financial crisis in 1996/97 and the global financial crisis in 2008 has clearly suggested that there is no longer any guarantee of the steady economic growth that the East Asian Tigers experienced before the 1996/97 era. According to Mok and Green (2013), the global economic crisis is the deepest and longest in the West since the 1930s and has affected all groups in society, but the worst affected have been young people. The problems faced by higher education are part of the bigger economic crisis and, in particular, the unfolding crisis for youth, manifested in rapidly declining opportunities for work and housing. Moreover, the crisis has not spawned growing anticapitalist movements among youth. It has also intensified intergenerational conflicts which have been rising for some time in Europe. Similarly, the Asian financial crisis of 1996/97 and the 2008 global financial crisis have inevitably interrupted continued and rapid economic growth in East Asia as had been the case before the crises. Countries undergoing the expansion of higher education, particularly those higher education systems in East Asia experiencing massification over the last two decades, have begun to confront challenges similar to their counterparts in Europe, such that university graduates now experience insufficient job opportunities or a mismatch of jobs with their expertise. In his recent comparative studies about university student perceptions of graduate employment and social mobility in Hong Kong, Taipei, and Guangzhou, Mok (2012) finds that university students being interviewed are very concerned about their future career development, especially when they are now facing a highly competitive world for high-skilled labor but with growing supplies from different parts of the world. Against this context, university students in these Chinese cities do not find themselves highly competitive, since higher education systems in Asia have continued to graduate highly qualified young professionals competing for jobs not only in the region but also in the global marketplace. Therefore, it is not surprising to hear the comments that university students are worried about their future and are not confident about upward mobility, particularly when some of the students (particularly in Taiwan) have found that their salary level has declined rather than increased when compared with their counterparts decade ago. Similar to Europe, the changing political economy in East Asia, especially when the labor market confronts the global auction as Brown, Lauder, and Ashton (2011) argue, is also facing a crisis for young people. According to Green (2012), there are some major parameters of the crisis for young people, including the following:

- rapidly declining job opportunities;
- rising unemployment;
- stagnant graduate incomes;
- unaffordable housing;
- paying higher education contributions and working longer for smaller pensions, and
- encountering poorer prospects relative to their parents than at any time during the last century.

In assessing the youth crisis in Europe in light of the major parameters outlined above, Mok and Green (2013) discover that the youth unemployment rate in EU27 is over double the overall unemployment rate. Meanwhile, the percentage of young people aged 15 to 24 in September 2011 who were without jobs but looking for work in EU27 was 21.4 percent and the Eurozone was 21.2 percent, with the lowest rates in Austria (7.1 percent) and the Netherlands (8 percent), while the highest rates were reported in Spain (48 percent) and Greece (43.5 percent). All these data clearly suggest that the massification of higher education in Europe has created significant social and political problems if youth unemployment continues unresolved. What makes the above situation even worse is when there is increasing cost competition for high-skilled professional jobs due to the routinization of many graduate jobs (known as "digital Taylorism") and the outsourcing of many high-skilled jobs to lower-wage countries. For example, China's advancements in key fields such as nanotechnology, supercomputers, genomics, and stem cell research would attract major transnational corporations to outsource such jobs to them in order to maintain competitiveness and cost reduction. It is against this context that some scholars estimate that up to 29 percent of US jobs could be outsourced, while the increased global supply of highly skilled graduates would certainly intensify competition in graduate employment globally.

In Brown et al.'s (2011) book, they argue that the "neo-liberal opportunity bargains," which promised high salaries to highly trained western graduates outsmarting workers from other nations, has been broken. It is particularly true when Europe and the United States have experienced economic downturns or financial difficulties in the post-2008 global financial crisis. Therefore, the global auction is more than a competition for knowledge and ideas; it is also a competition based on price. What is revolutionary about the globalization of high skills is that it has been combined with low-cost innovation; such a development would challenge many of the beliefs about the social foundations of economic success. The rise of high-skill but low-paid jobs is due to the intensification of cost competition for high-skilled professional jobs when many Asian countries are able to supply high-skilled labor. For example, the participation rate of higher education in Mainland China reached 24 percent in 2012, while higher education admissions rates are up to nearly 98 percent in Taiwan and around 70 to 80 percent in South Korea and Japan. In addition, 41 percent of science and engineering doctorates in the United Sates and UK were awarded to foreign students in 2012. By 2000, graduates made up 35 percent of immigrants to OECD countries (up from 30 percent in 1990). In the UK, an estimated 80 percent of new doctors and 73 percent of nurses hired between 1997 and 2003 were foreign born (Mok and Green 2013). All these observations point to the potential challenges that East Asian higher education systems would face in the near future if increasing numbers of higher education graduates cannot find jobs because of the global auction and "neoliberal opportunity bargains" becoming more popular in the Asia-Pacific region.

Conclusion

This chapter has made attempts to outline a few major trends and challenges confronting higher education development in East Asia. In addition, the present chapter also discusses how universities have tried to respond to these challenges by engaging in different forms of governance reforms. In order to enhance their national competitiveness in the context of a globalizing economy, the governments in East Asia have tried to transform their higher education to become more responsive and proactive to rapid social, economic, and political changes by not only serving the traditional missions in teaching and research but also supporting economic growth through engagement in entrepreneurial activities such as the promotion of knowledge transfer activities. The following chapters in part 1 will focus on how governments in East Asia have encouraged universities to work closely with industry and business for promoting innovation and entrepreneurship. In addition, part 2 will examine how universities have made attempts to "transnationalize" and "internationalize" higher education in order to prepare students for the globalizing world, while part 3 will discuss the impacts of different types of university transformations to be discussed in the following chapters on academic community and university governance.

Chapter 2

Policy Context for the Quest for Innovation and Entrepreneurial Universities in East Asia

Introduction

This chapter aims at setting out the wider policy context for examining how and why East Asian states (more specifically, the East Asian Tiger economies, namely Hong Kong, South Korea, Taiwan, and Singapore) have tried to engage in the quest for innovation and entrepreneurial universities. With particular reference to reviewing the major policies and strategies adopted by the Four East Asian Tigers in fostering and advancing an innovational mindset, universities in these Asian economies have placed significant emphasis on enhancement of innovation, promotion of research, and entrepreneurship in the past decades, especially after the 1997/98 Asian financial crisis. Before examining how the Four East Asian Tiger economies have made attempts to promote innovation and entrepreneurial universities, this chapter provides a macro context that explains the need to transform the role of universities in East Asia, particularly discussing the reasons underlying the recent drive for strengthening university-industry-business cooperation in promotion of innovation and technological advancement. In addition, the second part of the chapter will discuss how these East Asian Tiger economies perform when compared to other developed economies in terms of international innovation and global competitiveness indexes. With the discussions and analyses of the present chapter, we hope readers will develop a better understanding of the particular context for the quest for innovation and entrepreneurship through strengthening university-business-industry cooperation in East Asia, with more detailed case discussions in part 2 of the present volume.

Policy Context for Promotion of Innovation and University-Industry-Business Cooperation

Conflict Between Global and Local Needs in University Transformations

Compared to western economies like their European and North American counterparts, the selected Asian economies (Hong Kong, Taiwan, Singapore, South Korea, and Mainland China) have started the promotion of university-industry cooperation late. There are a few factors that account for such late development because economic growth was heavily based on a low labor costs formula by engaging in manufacturing production instead of depending on production based on high technology. The Four East Asian Tiger economies (and even Mainland China) were very successful in the past few decades in producing cheap products exported to overseas markets for generating economic growth. However, this growth model is no longer sustainable, especially when continuously confronted with the challenges of the knowledge economy. The late participation in research and development and serious knowledge transfer activities would have given them relatively lower rankings in terms of global competitiveness or knowledge economy indexes.

Moreover, all these Asian economies were colonies of some kind during the First and Second World Wars. Only after the end of the Second World War, these Asian economies began to start economic development in a relatively peaceful environment until the late 1960s and early 1970s. Singapore became an independent state in the 1950s but still experienced significant internal and external rivalries, while Hong Kong was still a British colony until 1997. Although Taiwan and South Korea have been independent political entities (Taiwan's independent status is still controversial) since the end of the Second World War, there were various kinds of warfare between South Korea and North Korea and between Mainland China and Taiwan in the late 1950s and early 1960s. Starting in the 1970s, these Asian economies began to experience significant economic growth with the rise of industrialization and manufacturing activities. In this regard, the Four Asian Tiger economies developed the so-called East Asian Miracle in the 1980s and 1990s. Before the 1990s, these Asian countries still relied upon secondary rather than tertiary production to drive their economic growth. Realizing the coming of the knowledge-based economy, these East Asian Tiger economies have begun to expand their higher education and invest in research and development. Being latecomers in the enterprise for innovation advancement, it is self-explanatory that they have not ranked well when compared to the developed economies.

Apart from the different stages of development that these Asian economies have experienced, the relatively lower international ranking in knowledge economy indexes and global competitiveness indexes is closely related to underdevelopment of a conducive environment for facilitating collaboration between the state, industry, and universities until recent decades. Our above analysis has clearly shown that the US model in innovation advancement is, to a certain extent, represented in the cases of Taiwan and South Korea where the promotion of innovation is more driven by the firm-led approach. Being ex-colonies of the United Kingdom, the tiny city-states of Hong Kong and Singapore have not taken up the tradition in promotion of innovation and technology until recent years with the growing emphasis being place on this particular front. But we must realize that the different governance philosophies between Hong Kong and Singapore have clearly shown the variations and patterns in innovation promotion, with a more firm-led approach in Hong Kong and a government-led regime in Singapore. Hence, when comparing the innovation advancement experiences of these Asian states, we cannot discard the governance style, the ex-colonial and postcolonial influences, the changing economic needs in these societies, and the changing university-industry-business relationship.

Balancing Economic Determinism and Globalist Inclusion Forces

Analyzing the changing role of the university in promoting entrepreneurship and innovation in East Asia in line with the contestable hypotheses outlined above, we have noted that the economic, social, and cultural development of higher education in these selected Asian societies is driven by multiple sources of influence rather than by a single force. Aspiring to become more globally competitive, we have witnessed that universities in East Asia are trying very hard to benchmark with their western counterparts (Altbach 1989), especially when the global university leagues are dominated by universities based in the UK and the United States. Our above discussion has clearly shown how these East Asian university systems have tried to engage in different forms of enterprising activities by developing closer cooperation with industry and business, not only within their own countries/societies but also with multinational corporations for promoting knowledge transfer activities. Such moves clearly suggest that universities in East Asia cannot be excused from the highly competitive globalizing market context. The growing emphasis being placed on the economic and social functions of universities as their third mission would suggest that the higher education development trend in East Asia is going along with the global pathway. Regardless of whether we would agree that there is any "emerging global model," the quest to become enterprising and entrepreneurial universities has clearly shown how universities in East Asia are under the shadow of the "western model" with a mix of European and American forms and values (Morhman 2008).

One of the contested hypotheses accounting for social, economic, and cultural development in higher education is "economic determinism"; basically it argues that higher education development is primarily driven by economic needs. According to this school of thought, Asian countries were either pursuing an industrial model in their transition from dominant agricultural societies (traditionally elite dominated) to industrial modes of production or reindustrializing from the ravages of the war, and this has become doubly true in the long transition to postindustrial, knowledge-based societies, where it is argued that "innovation capital" and along with it the notion of the "innovative university" has come to play the role previously played by land-based capital, industrial capital, and financial capital (Christensen and Eyring 2011). In response to the changing needs driven by the knowledge-based economy, universities are under pressure to transform the way they are managed, and hence the knowledge structure and curriculum design have also undergone significant restructuring to be able to engage students to promote innovation creation, innovation exploitation, and implementation. With a strong push to energize innovation and knowledge transfer, modern governments proactively steer universities to work with industry and business to maximize the nexus of innovation shifts from purely making the knowledge product to perfecting its use within "soft" structures (Pillay 2011).

When reflecting upon the linkage between education and economic development, tertiary education especially has become a fundamentally reductionist or (alternatively) determinative force. As Deane Neubauer (2013) has rightly pointed out, if one can argue that (a) the primary policy objective of Asian governments is development, and specifically economic development, and (b) widespread effective tertiary education is a necessary precondition for such development (even while it might be a sufficient condition), then it would seem that (c) the degree to which higher education institutions produce the necessary conditions for development become their essential common factor. Analyzing the current higher education development in the region in line with the "economic determinism" thesis, one could argue that such might be the case whether or not the "proof" of the relationship is drawn from the relative success of a country with respect to market forces, or from the perspective of governmental priority setting within policy.

Even we have to accept the fact that higher education development is never far away from economic drives, since nation building in terms of sustaining economic growth is extremely important. Higher education, being one of the most important institutions preparing people to support economic development, plays a very important role during the economic transformation process. However, we should not overstate the case of economic determinism. Thought our above discussion has clearly shown that the hypothesis of economic primacy "trumps" that of either western emulation or cultural values as an explanatory frame that accounts for the shape, scope, and trajectory of Asian higher education, we should appreciate that the reality is far more complex since Asian governments are tactical enough to override the global and local forces. Packaging reform agendas with strong globalization justifications, these governments have successfully taken away resistance embedded locally for educational changes. Meanwhile, these Asian economies are able to guard against excessive forms of global "penetration" as proposed by the globalist inclusion hypothesis to lift the national border and allow transnational education to grow beyond borders. Our above analysis has clearly demonstrated that the unique feature of the Asian governments in dealing with the global market is to perform the role as a "market-accelerationist state," taking an active role to interfere in the market to reduce inefficiency in order to create a more conducive market environment (Mok 2008). The strong steering role of these Asian governments in facilitating university-industry-business cooperation clearly shows that the globalist inclusion thesis is not sufficiently convincing to the East Asian economies to entirely open up their education sectors (Mok 2011).

Latecomers and the Drive for Catching Up

The need for innovation, which rests on the development of human capital and the fostering of entrepreneurial spirit, is always included in the national economic development agenda of many countries. For example, in recent years there have been increasing worries in the United States as to whether it will lose its competitive edge in innovation to other competitive economies, especially in regard to the shortfalls of nurturing local talent at home and attracting foreign talent from abroad (Florida 2005; Kao 2007; Porter 2008). For instance, amid the global financial crisis in late 2008, the management studies guru Michael Porter, renowned business scholar and author of the seminal book *The Competitive Advantage of Nations* which elucidates the importance of human capital for nations to compete, wrote an article titled "Why America Needs an Economic Strategy" in *Businessweek*, urging the American government to devise sound policies for long-term economic prosperity. He listed a set of competitive strengths that made America great in the past and will continue to back it up in the future:

1. A friendly environment for entrepreneurship and business start-ups.
2. Entrepreneurship is supported by the best science, technology, and innovation in the world.
3. America has the best universities to equip students with advanced skills and to attract foreign talent.

4. The existence of and the commitment to free markets and competition.
5. A decentralized federal system that gives autonomy to regional economies.
6. The most efficient capital markets for entrepreneurs to raise capital.

His detailed prescriptions aside, Porter's core argument is that technological development, innovation, and education (especially higher education) are the keys to a nation's competitiveness (Porter 2008). While American scholars are issuing warnings to their countrymen, Asian scholars are more optimistic about the prospect for Asia's innovation improvement. For instance, in *The New Asian Hemisphere*, Singaporean scholar and former diplomat Kishore Mahbubani (2008) argues that one of the factors contributing to the irresistible shift of global power from the West to the East is exactly the gigantic improvement of education in Asia.

Even with the rise of optimism about Asia's prospects, Asian countries are in fact latecomers in the innovation and R&D endeavor compared to developed economies like OECD countries. The fact is that many Asian economies were colonies of some kind during the First and Second World Wars, and it was only after the end of the Second World War or even in the late 1960s and early 1970s that many of them began to develop their economies in a relatively peaceful environment. In the 1950s, Japan was still in the recovery process after being heavily defeated in the Second World War. Taiwan was in constant confrontation with Mainland China after the loss of the civil war between the Nationalist Party and the Communist Party. South Korea was fighting a civil war with communist North Korea. Singapore was seeking independence from Britain, while Hong Kong was a British colony where the living conditions of the public were poor. But starting in the late 1960s and 1970s, these Asian economies began to kick off an industrialization boom that lifted the countries to a higher economic development level.

From 1992 to 2002, the GDP of the Four Little Asian Tigers had grown from 3.6 to 5.6 percent. Table 2.1 shows that the forecast annual growth of

Table 2.1 Asian Four Little Dragons GDP Growth: Ten-Year Forecasts

	GDP US$ billion	GDP per capita	Historic 10-year annual growth (%)	Forecast annual growth (%)	Forecast GDP US$ billion	Forecast GDP per capita $
	2003	2003	1992–2002	2013	2013	2013
HK	160	23,990	3.6	4.0	237	35,512
Taiwan	290	12,719	5.0	5.0	472	20,718
Singapore	90	22,676	6.4	5.5	154	38,734
South Korea	600	10,478	5.6	5.0	977	17,067

Source: Asian GDP Growth: 10-year Forecasts. http://www.zanran.com/q/GDP_growth_rate_forecasts_for_Asian_Economies.

Singapore is 5.5 percent, Taiwan 5.0 percent, South Korea 5.0 percent, and Hong Kong 4.0 percent, respectively. In dollar terms, the forecast GDP of South Korea in 2013 is US$977 billion, Taiwan US$472 billion, Hong Kong US$237 billion, and Singapore US$154 billion.

The economic success story of these East Asian Tigers, known as the "East Asian Miracle," has gained more currency since the World Bank's 1993 publication of a seminal report with this title. The research leading to the report was sponsored and heavily advocated by the Japanese government to showcase the success of its unique state-steered developmental path, as compared to the Washington Consensus's liberal free market model spearheaded by the United States. However, as East Asian economies began to slow in the 1990s, a number of researches started to question the so-called Japanese-led East Asian developmental model, saying that its success in driving industrialization over the past few decades relied more on increased capital investment, improved educational levels, and more labor participation than on the advance of technological developments, innovation, and economic productivity (see, for example, Baer et al. 1999; Krugman 1994; Stiglitz 1996; Stiglitz and Yusuf 2001; Vogel 1991; Wade 2004; Young 1995).

However, the admission that East Asia has not been adept at technological innovation does not suggest that the countries in the region did not attain any technological developments. Past research indicates that in the process of industrialization, East Asian firms have mainly enhanced their entrepreneurial capabilities by absorbing knowledge and acquiring technologies from the more industrialized and developed economies (see, for example, Hobday 1995a, 1995b; Kim and Nelson 2000). For instance, in his 1990s study on how the latecomer electronics firms in East Asia built up their technological capabilities, Michael Hobday (1995a, 1188) concluded that "the competitive advantage of East Asia's latecomers is low-cost, high-quality production engineering, rather than software or R&D." He concluded that firms in East Asia, in face of obstacles such as technologically weak universities and poorly equipped technical institutions, have overcome the barriers to acquiring complex technologies and to entering the market through several mechanisms, such as foreign direct investment, joint ventures, licensing, subcontracting, informal means (overseas training, hiring, returnees), overseas acquisitions/equity investments, strategic partnerships for technology, and more (Hobday 1995a, 1177). Therefore, for East Asian latecomer firms to upgrade themselves, Hobday emphasized the need for R&D: "Without stronger product innovation capabilities they will continue to rely on a mixture of catch-up, imitation-based growth and incremental innovation in electronics. Lacking R&D capabilities and a strong capital goods sector in electronics, the technological roots of the four dragons remain shallow" (Hobday 1995a, 1189).

In fact, for firms to succeed and catch up with the market trend, they need to do more than technological learning and technology acquisition. Apart from developing hard infrastructures, the capabilities of harnessing and managing physical and human resources are also at stake. According to the World Business Environment Survey conducted by the World Bank in 1999 and 2000, which interviewed more than 10,000 firms in 80 countries, firms in the three newly industrialized East Asian countries (China, Singapore, and Malaysia) identified that the biggest constraints facing them were the high cost of labor, lack of skilled technicians, and lack of skilled production workers, followed by government regulations and taxes and lack of machinery (Batra and Stone 2004, 11). The provision and successful implementation of managerial and business skills training, vocational and technical training, and on-the-job training are not just important to firms' technological capability but to the national technological capability (Rodrigo 2001, 99–120).

That East Asia is lagging behind the developed West in innovation is a well-explained problem that the countries in the region have to overcome in order to stage the economic great leap forward that it experienced in the 1970s and 1980s. In the past decade or so, some international organizations having been emphasizing the importance of higher education to the technological innovation and economic development of developed and developing countries alike. For instance, the Organisation for Economic Co-operation and Development (OECD) values the importance of innovation to the long-term prosperity of developed and high-income economies, such as Japan and South Korea (for example, see OECD 1998 and 1999). In its recent report in 2010, *The OECD Innovation Strategy: Getting a Head Start on Tomorrow*, the OECD urges that searching for new sources of growth is important in face of the 2008/09 global financial crisis, which has led to declining output growth, and innovation will play a crucial part in the searching process. Therefore, it warns that for countries and firms to recover from the crisis and build sustainable economic growth, it will be too shortsighted to ignore the importance of investments in education, infrastructure, and research. Therefore, even in the face of budget crises, there has been a stronger call for an increased government role in OECD countries to promote R&D, especially in advancing the demand-side factors "such as smart regulations, standards, pricing, consumer education, taxation and public procurement that can affect innovation" (OECD 2010, 2).

Apart from the OECD, the World Bank, which is more concerned about developing countries than the OECD, also had a number of publications about the relationships between higher education, innovation, and economic growth in the past decade, such as *Constructing Knowledge Economies: New Challenges for Tertiary Education* (World Bank 2002b), *Building Knowledge Societies: Opportunities and Challenges for EU Accession Countries* (World Bank 2002a), *How Universities Promote Economic Growth* (Yusuf and Nabeshima 2007), *Accelerating Catch-Up: Tertiary Education for Growth in Sub-Saharan Africa* (World Bank 2009), and *Putting Higher Education to*

Work: Skills and Research for Growth in East Asia (World Bank 2012). Besides this, the Asian Development Bank also highlighted in its 2008 report, *Education and Skills: Strategies for Accelerated Development in Asia and the Pacific*, that the advancement of working skills of the populace has become an imperative for developing Asian countries to achieve economic growth (Asian Development Bank 2008). In Asia, countries with higher degrees of market openness (marked by exports and foreign direct investment) and technological innovation have greater demand for skilled labor. While low-income economies and low-technology clusters (such as Vietnam, Cambodia, and Lao PDR) are still specialized in producing low-skill intensive goods, firms in middle-income countries have already become more skills based, let alone those in high-income countries such as Japan and the Four Little Dragons (Almeida 2010; World Bank 2012). Therefore, education, especially higher education, has never been more crucial.[1]

To enable higher education to achieve these goals, Singaporean scholar Wong Poh-Kam and his colleagues conclude three urgent reasons for universities in East Asia to move away from a traditional model (e.g., with emphasis on teaching and academic research) to an entrepreneurial model: First, East Asian economies are latecomers in technology, which for a long time has been receiving technology transfers from more technologically advanced countries rather than conducting indigenous innovation. Second, many university faculties in East Asia are former or current state employees, and they have less bureaucratic autonomy and commercial sense to engage in R&D competition compared to their counterparts in Europe and America. Third, the private sector has less experience and capability in commercialization of knowledge and technology transfer. In this regard, universities have to be more proactive in entrepreneurial activities to complement the weakness of the private sector (Wong et al. 2007, 942). Ultimately, higher education is essential to the competence building of a national innovation system. Apart from engaging in entrepreneurial activities in the form of academic-industry R&D cooperation, now universities are also urged to foster a sense of entrepreneurship and innovation through teaching in order to foster an S&T-savvy and innovative citizenry and to produce a capable workforce equipped with required knowledge and skills. Chapters in part 2 of the present volume will focus on how selected East Asian economies like Hong Kong, Taiwan, Singapore, South Korea, and Mainland China have made attempts to transform their universities by strengthening the link between the university and industry for promoting innovation and entrepreneurship. These detailed case studies offer more comparative insights and international perspectives in understanding how universities in East Asia have tried to honor not only the first and second missions of universities, namely teaching and research, but now drive for the third mission: supporting social and economic development through research and knowledge transfer activities.

How the East Asian Tigers Perform in Innovation and Global Competitiveness Indexes

Advancing Innovation and Enhancing Research Performance

Before the examination of how the Four Asian Little Tigers foster R&D and innovation as individual case studies, it is important to gauge the general picture of the technological performance of East Asia vis-à-vis the world. In the twenty-first century, many East Asian economies have stepped up as significant producers and consumers of higher-technology products. For example in 2007 Asia accounted for 27.9 percent of the world share of imports of high-tech products and 2.9 percent of the world share of exports of high-tech products. China was the biggest exporter in the Asian region, and Japan was the biggest importer. South Korea was also a big importer and exporter of high-tech products

In 2007, China, Japan, and South Korea were among the ten leading importers and exporters of high-technology products in the world. In terms of exports, Mainland China was top in Asia, only behind the United States in the world. In 2010, the Four Asian Tigers were among the top six leading importers and exporters of high-technology products in the world, and China was the biggest importer and exporter.

The favorable business environments of the "Asian Four Little Dragons/Tigers" are conducive to entrepreneurial activities and R&D innovation. For instance, in 2012, according to the World Bank's analysis, Singapore and Hong Kong were the best two places in the world to do business, followed New Zealand, the United States, and Denmark. South Korea ranks number 8, while Taiwan ranks number 25. Besides the importance of a sound macroeconomic environment, the willingness of the people to engage in entrepreneurial activities and R&D is also crucial. According to a report of the Global Entrepreneurship Monitor, although there are fewer people in South Korea, Singapore, and Taiwan who thought that there were perceived opportunities for starting their own businesses than in Nordic countries like Finland, Sweden, and Norway, there are more of them who had entrepreneurial intentions and also who thought entrepreneurship was a good career choice. The people in the Four Asian Tigers are favorable to the idea of starting their own businesses.

Despite the fact that the Four Little Dragons are hailed as a desirable place to do business, America and European countries are still commonly regarded as the leading and the most competitive knowledge economies. Statistics show that the euro area has attained better R&D performances in publishing scientific and technical journal articles, filing patent applications, and earning royalty and license fees than East Asia and the Pacific. To explain why East Asia is losing to US and some European countries, apart from the difference of R&D capabilities due to the difference in the size of the countries, low R&D investments by East Asia may also be another reason. Over the years, the gross expenditures on R&D (GERD) in East Asia (except Japan) have generally been lower than in America and Europe (Germany and some Nordic countries).[2]

In view of the above statistics, it is clear that the United States and many European countries are still ranked as the most competitive economies despite the fact that they have experienced economic recession against the context of the global financial crisis. However, the 2012/13 Global Competitiveness Ranking shows that seven out of the top ten are western countries, while some of the Asian countries/societies perform comfortably well, such as Singapore, which was ranked number 2, Hong Kong at number 9, and Japan at number 10, respectively. If we take the top 20 into consideration, we can see that Taiwan and South Korea also performed well as top-20 countries in the Global Competitiveness Ranking of 2012/13. When comparing the knowledge economy index of some of the Asian economies/countries with the rest of the world in the last two decades, it is clear that their performance has improved despite the fact that such performance varies across years.

Discussion and Conclusion

As we said, the major objective for the present chapter is to set out the wider policy context for examining how and why East Asian states (more specifically, the East Asian Tiger economies, namely Hong Kong, South Korea, Taiwan, and Singapore) have tried to engage in the quest for innovation and entrepreneurial university. More specifically, this chapter discusses the reasons behind the recent drives for strengthening university-industry-business cooperation in promotion of innovation and technological advancement, through which efforts the East Asian states hope to enhance their global competitiveness. This chapter has also compared how the East Asian Tiger economies have performed in terms of international comparative data like innovation and global competitiveness indexes. With the discussions and analysis in the present chapter, coupled with the observations generated from chapter 1 regarding major trends and challenges that East Asian higher education systems have confronted and responded to, we hope readers have developed a better understanding of the unique context for the quest for innovation and entrepreneurship through strengthening university-business-industry cooperation in East Asia and will be in a better position when reading the case discussions in subsequent chapters examining how different East Asian economies have tried to enhance their global competitiveness.

Part I

Questing for Entrepreneurial Universities and Promoting Innovation

Chapter 3

Diversifying the Economic Pillars and Enhancing Innovation and Research Development:
Hong Kong Experiences

Introduction

Hong Kong has successfully relied upon "four traditional economic pillars," including financial services, trade and logistics, tourism, and professional and other producer services. Yet these industries are facing ever-mounting challenges from regional competitors like Shenzhen, Shanghai, and Singapore in recent years. The striving for a knowledge economy has become even more acute after the 1997 handover and the Asian financial crisis in 1997/98, when Hong Kong's finance-centered economy was questioned for its sustainability. Being too heavily dependent on finance and trade, the role of the government in promoting research and development (R&D) has been criticized for being insufficient to compete with other nearby countries. The Hong Kong Special Administrative Region government (the Hong Kong government, hereafter) used to assume that technological development was a straight linear process and that innovation would spread from upstream scientific research by universities to downstream commercialization processes by enterprises. Hence, it simply acted as an infrastructure builder and funding provider without playing an importance role in the process (Baark and Sharif 2006). However, since the last decade, there has been more government participation in R&D activities, especially in promoting more regional innovative cooperation with Mainland China. Most recently, the Hong Kong government has reiterated its ambition to restructure its economy in response to growing challenges after the global financial crisis. It therefore proposed the development of six new industries—education services, medical services, testing and certification services, environmental industries, innovation and technology, and cultural and creative industries. This chapter sets out against the brief context outlined above to examine how the Hong Kong government has tried to encourage its public universities to engage with industry and business to promote innovation and research development, knowledge transfer, and research capacity in universities of the city-state.

Promotion of Innovation

In the colonial period, the government put less emphasis on industrial development than on the service/financial industry because of the fiscal conservatism adopted by the British rulers (Tsui-Auch 1998). The major economic drives came from banking and service sectors instead of industries, while businessmen and bankers were reluctant to engage in long-term industrial investment. Thus before the 1990s, the Hong Kong government's role regarding industrial development was mainly as a provider of infrastructure (e.g., support of industrial land, trained manpower, transport and communications, water, electricity, fuels and raw materials, financial and business services) and a facilitator (e.g., supply of technical information and advice, laboratory and bureau services that help entrepreneurs to enhance their productivity, quality, and innovation) (Yeh and Ng 1994, 460). At that time, R&D linkages among manufacturers, governmental supportive organizations, and HEIs were underdeveloped (Leung and Wu 1994). It wasn't until recent years that the government became more serious in developing strategies to support innovation and technological development.

In the past decade, Hong Kong's innovation system has expanded. Trade statistics show that the exporting activities of high-technology products have become more active in the past decade. The research capacity of Hong Kong also increased as shown in the increase of R&D personnel and R&D expenditures. As illustrated, the higher education sector and the private sector were the biggest spenders and employers, which shows that the government barely conducted its own research. Yet the government is important in its role as funder, contributing over 40 percent of the total R&D expenditures.[1]

More importantly, since the 2000s, the government has become more active in formulating public policies and launching public projects to promote innovation and technology. Inspired by the successes of South Korea and Taiwan, the government completed the construction of the Hong Kong Science Park in 2000. Like many other science parks across the world, the Hong Kong Science Park, located next to the Chinese University of Hong Kong, also emphasizes "industry-university collaboration," establishing networks to facilitate partnership among enterprises, strengthening the talent pool, bringing expertise together into universities and industry, organizing training and seminars, as well as promoting successful research outputs and developing products.

One of the key functions of the Hong Kong Science Park is to incubate business start-ups. Since 1992, the incubation programs have nurtured 277 start-ups, nearly 80 percent of which (216 out of 277) were still in operation as of 2011. Since April 2003, angel/venture capital investment has amounted to HK$699 million, 444 IP registration applications filed, 204 technical/design and management awards, and 16 IPO/merger/acquisition/joint-venture/spin-off transactions (Hong Kong Science and Technology Parks Corporation 2011, 30–31). As of March 2011, the Hong Kong Science Park housed 258 companies, with 31 percent of them specializing in electronics, 29 percent in IT and telecommunications, 14 percent in biotechnology, 11 percent in green technology, 9 percent in precision engineering, and 6 percent in professional services. Most of the companies residing in the science park were local companies (60.2 percent), followed by those from the United States and Canada (13.6 percent), Europe (10.6 percent), Asia-Pacific (8.6 percent), and Mainland China (7 percent) (Hong Kong Science and Technology Parks Corporation 2011, 27).

The Hong Kong Science Park also aims to serve as a platform linking the academy and industry. To help enterprises search for R&D personnel, it organized recruitment talks and set up an online Talent Pool Career Platform to help job seekers and students to better locate desirable jobs in partner companies as well as at the Science Park. In 2010, recruitment day attracted 2,000 candidates to apply for 400 jobs offered by 60 partner companies in the park, and the Talent Pool Career Platform registered over 1,000 job opportunities. Besides, the park also aims at building talent pool networks through its partner universities, such as the Chinese University of Hong Kong's MBA program, the Hong Kong University of Science and Technology's business school, and the final-year program of the University of Ontario Institute of Technology, to get access to experienced pools of working executives (Hong Kong Science and Technology Parks Corporation 2011, 39). In terms of liaising with potential entrepreneurs and capital investors, in 2010 the science park co-established the Hong Kong Business Angel Network (HKBAN) with four local universities (i.e., HKU, HKUST, CUHK and HKPU) and the Hong Kong Venture Capital and Private Equity Association, which aims to conduct funding matching between entrepreneurs and investors for potential R&D projects.[2]

After forming the Hong Kong Science Park, the government continued to put more efforts in R&D promotion in the 2000s. In 2000, it established the Hong Kong Applied Science and Technology Research Institute (ASTRI) as the public research institute of Hong Kong. By 2010, the tenth anniversary of its establishment, ASTRI has completed over 360 technology transfers and has 130 patents granted. More than HK$160 million income was received from industry. The Industry Collaborative Project scheme, which at that time involved ten projects, was expected to receive a committed income of about HK$47 million (Applied Science and Technology Research Institute 2011, 2). Also in 2000, the government established the Innovation and Technology Commission (ITC) to devise and implement government policies to promote innovation and technology, as well as to run the Innovation and Technology Fund (ITF), which comprises a number of financial supporting programs and training schemes. Since the majority of companies in Hong Kong are small and medium-sized enterprises, their needs should be core to the government's innovative policies. Hence the Hong Kong government has set up various research funds for which SMEs can apply. By 31 January 2012, ITF had already approved HK$6,292.1 million for 2,708 projects, many of which are related to electronics, as well as information technology.

Since the inception of these programs, the government has continued to invest in them in order to help more SMEs. Taking the Small Entrepreneur Research Assistance Program as an example, it relaxed the eligibility of applicants from companies of less than 20 employees to less than 100 in 2007 so that the program could cover up to 99 percent of the companies in Hong Kong (Legislative Council Panel on Commerce and Industry 2007). Approved projects will be offered a grant of up to HK$6 million on a dollar-for-dollar matching basis. The government's support measures offered to SMEs include not only more funding for their own research but also training schemes to upgrade their employees, and incentive measures to encourage them to cooperate with the universities. In regard to the upgrading of employees, ITC launched the New Technology Training Scheme, which is administered by the Vocational Training Council (VTC), to assist companies in training their staff to acquire skills in using new technologies. The different forms of support include overseas training courses or working attachments, preapproved local training courses, and tailor-made training courses for individual companies.

Since 2009, to help SMEs hire new employees after the global financial crisis, the ITC internship program, which previously only covered universities and research institutes, has been extended to cover those private companies that engage in R&D projects funded by the ITF. Monthly allowances for first-degree graduates and those with masters or higher degrees are HK$10,000 and HK$12,000 respectively. With regard to encouraging private-public R&D partnerships, the government also allocated about HK$200 million to launch the Research and Development Cash Rebate Scheme in 2010. Under the scheme, businesses are offered a cash rebate equivalent to 30 percent of their R&D expenditures in projects under the ITF, or projects funded by the companies and conducted by designated local research institutions, including six public universities,[3] the R&D centers under the ITF,[4] the Hong Kong Productivity Council, and the Vocational Training Council.

Besides organizational infrastructures like the science park and the ITC, the government also considered establishing public research institutes. Apart from the ASTRI, in June 2004, the Innovation and Technology Commission issued a consultation paper titled "New Strategy of Innovation and Technology Development," which put forward a new direction for Hong Kong's innovation system, emphasizing a focus on selected strong industries, market relevance, industry participation, and leverage on Mainland China, as well as better coordination among stakeholders. Two proposals in the consultation paper are worth highlighting. First, the paper proposed 13 technology focus areas[5] to which Hong Kong should direct enough resources to develop. Secondly, the paper proposed to set up five research centers under the Hong Kong R&D Centers Program,[6] some of which are hosted by leading universities in Hong Kong. Together with the Hong Kong Jockey Club Institute of Chinese Medicine, these six government-university-industry cooperation centers are among the leading research centers in Hong Kong. Finally, the government has allocated HK$358.7 million from the Innovation and Technology Fund to pursue the plan.

The founding of these research centers in 2006 was a breakthrough for R&D in Hong Kong, especially demonstrating the fact that the Hong Kong government was willing to set aside its conventional "noninterventionist" industrial policy and take up a more proactive role. The government explains that the government-led initiative has "the aim to harness Hong Kong's advantages in applied research, intellectual property protection, business-friendly environment, and proximity to the manufacturing based in the Pearl River Delta (PRD), to thrive as a regional technology service hub."[7] The establishment of the five R&D centers—(1) the Automotive Parts and Accessory Systems R&D Centre (APAS); (2) the Hong Kong R&D Centre for Information and Communications Technologies under the Hong Kong Applied Science and Technology Research Institute (ASTRI); (3) the Hong Kong Research Institute of Textiles and Apparel (HKRITA); (4) the Hong Kong R&D Centre for Logistics and Supply Chain Management Enabling Technologies (LSCM); and (5) the Nano and Advanced Materials Institute (NAMI)— was a significant step forward for closer R&D co-operation among the government, industry, and university.

After a few years of operation, the government further allocated HK$369 million from the Innovation and Technology Fund in 2009 for the continued operation of the four R&D centers up to 2013/14. However, the government was not satisfied with the performance of these centers and hinted that its longer-term commitment would be contingent upon several factors: cost-effectiveness, the performance in technology transfer and commercialization, and whether the centers could meet the targeted level of industry contributions. Originally, the government set the target at 40 percent in 2005; however, it lowered the expectation to 15 percent in 2009 because of the unsatisfactory performance of the centers (Legislative Council, Panel on Commerce and Industry 2011b). The government proposed that unless the centers could achieve the industry contribution target, it will consider ceasing the funding (Legislative Council, Panel on Commerce and Industry 2011a). Therefore, it is clear that the Hong Kong government has taken a more active role to invest in R&D activities in the past decade and has acted as an initiator to promote R&D activities by building a platform for the private sector to run their own businesses. In addition to the promotion of innovation, the Hong Kong government has made attempts to enhance higher education development to raise the research profile and level of innovation of universities in the city-state.

Higher Education Development

Over the last decade, the government has become eager to develop the city-state into an education hub, both in terms of academic and research capacities. In 1996, the University Grants Committee (UGC), the statutory body responsible for advising the government on higher education, issued a report that encouraged staffs and students of HEIs to engage in pure research and to develop closer research collaborations with the various government agencies, the industrial sector, and the sector of social services. In 2002, the UGC issued an important consultant report titled *Higher Education in Hong Kong*, reiterated the need for HEIs to engage with local industry and community, and meanwhile also encouraged applied research and the commercialization of research outputs. On the one hand, the proposal aims to enable university research to contribute to the society more directly, while on the other hand, universities can also extend their pools of research money by working closer with the industrial sector.

Hong Kong universities are vital to the overall innovation system since they are big R&D spenders. In this respect, the government is concerned about how taxpayer money can be used effectively. In order to make Hong Kong universities more accountable and efficient, two policy reports, *Integration Matters* and *Hong Kong Higher Education: To Make a Difference, to Move with the Times*, were published by the UGC in 2004. The two reports suggested the government expand its role in evaluating and monitoring the "performance," "mission," and "differentiation" of each HEI. In short, the Hong Kong government is strengthening its role in the strategic development of the higher education sector. At the same time, the government aims to develop Hong Kong into an education hub. In the *2009–10 Policy Address*, the government made its education hub ambition very explicit, stating, "On the development of education services, our objective is to enhance Hong Kong's status as a regional education hub, boosting Hong Kong's competitiveness and complementing the future development of the Mainland" (Tsang 2009, 11). It is hoped that, by being an education hub, Hong Kong could attract foreign talents to stay and work there, who could provide new impetus to drive future economic growth.

Although the Hong Kong government is considered a novice in building the national innovation system through S&T policies and programs, its role is more active in developing the higher education sector. In Hong Kong, the higher education sector is heavily funded by the government. Hong Kong now has a total of 15 degree-awarding HEIs: eight of them are government-funded HEIs and six are self-financing institutions, while the remaining Hong Kong Academy for Performing Arts is also publicly funded. In terms of financing, the government has been the dominant stakeholder in Hong Kong's higher education sector.

Compared to its counterparts in South Korea and Taiwan, the universities in Hong Kong are latecomers in engaging in S&T entrepreneurial activities.

Therefore, its major contribution to the city's innovation system lies in the development of human capital. In Hong Kong, undergraduate students comprise the largest part of the enrollments in public HEIs. Among the overall public higher education student population of Hong Kong, S&T students (students in the disciplines of science, engineering, and technology) constituted more than 35 percent. With the expansion of students in the past few years, what is particularly encouraging has been a modest increase in the number of research postgraduates, who are the potential R&D talents. In view of this, the government invested HK$300 million per year to provide 800 additional places for postgraduate research programs (all fields, not exclusively for S&T-related programs) from 2009/10 to 2011/12, hoping that this would enhance the R&D manpower in Hong Kong.[8]

Apart from nurturing local talents, Hong Kong intends to expand the talent pool by recruiting more foreign students. In the past few years, there has been a rise in the number of nonlocal students enrolling in public HEIs, with most of them studying in the disciplines of science, engineering, and technology. In view of this positive development, in 2009 the Research Grants Council (RGC) launched the "Hong Kong PhD Fellowship Scheme." The RGC chairman explained that that "the main objective of the Fellowship Scheme is to broaden the breadth and depth of Hong Kong's postgraduate learning environment and raise global awareness of Hong Kong's attractiveness as a key research hub." Although he said the scheme had no targeted disciplines or research areas, he highlighted Hong Kong's close proximity to Mainland China as an attraction to those interested in China studies and high-tech manufacturing (Research Grants Council 2009). In the first two years of operation, the scheme selected more than 100 recipients each year. Most of the recipients were Asian, especially Mainland Chinese students, and most of them were enrolled in S&T-related disciplines (i.e., engineering, physical sciences, biology, and medicine).[9] In terms of research, which is also closely related to innovation, coupled with the increase in public HEIs' departmental expenditure on research, the research performance has also improved. The number of total research outputs increased from 21,530 in 2001/02 to 25,773 in 2011/12 in all subject areas. At the same time, the number of prizes and awards also increased from 200 in 2001/02 to 772 in 2011/12.

Promotion of Knowledge Transfer

In the face of improvements in R&D activities, the government has in recent years recognized the need for knowledge transfer, which aims to extend the benefits of research outputs to the community. In November 2007, the UGC co-organized the Knowledge Transfer in a Knowledge-Based Economy Symposium with the City University of Hong Kong and the Hong Kong

University of Science and Technology. Representatives from prestigious overseas universities, such as Stanford University, Oxford University, and the University of Leeds, and venture capital firms were invited to share their technology and knowledge transfer experiences with Hong Kong stakeholders. In 2009, the UGC set up a HK$50 million annual fund to support public universities to promote knowledge transfer activities. The UGC has incorporated "knowledge transfer"—the UGC definition of which includes capacity building, frontline knowledge transfer activities, and knowledge generation—into its mission statement and the institutional role statements of its funded public universities.[10] According to the UGC, knowledge transfer refers to "the systems and processes by which knowledge, including technology, know-how, expertise and skills are transferred between higher education institutions and society, leading to innovative, profitable or economic or social improvements."[11] This means that knowledge transfer includes but is not limited to the commercialization of R&D products in the S&T fields. Under the auspices of the UGC to carry out knowledge transfer, public HEIs in Hong Kong have to submit annual reports to the UGC to report the accomplishments made in the previous year.

The government's commitment to knowledge transfer activities has huge impacts on the universities' organization structures, finances, rules and regulations (particularly those regarding R&D activities), and the promotion of entrepreneurship education. However, compared to their counterparts in South Korea and Taiwan, universities in Hong Kong were relatively late in engaging in entrepreneurial activities. It wasn't until the 1990s that some of them started to seek ways to explore the potential for university-industry partnerships, mainly through setting up spin-off companies and technology transfer offices (Sharif and Baark 2008). For example, HKU set up the Technology Transfer Office and a company called Versitech. In 1998, HKU revisited its vision and mission, which pledges to place more emphasis on applied research from then onward. In the 2000s, the University of Hong Kong incorporated knowledge transfer as a key pillar in its Strategic Development Plan 2009–2014. In the academic year 2010/11, all ten faculties of HKU have set up their own knowledge exchange units as a formal structure, which are led by the faculty dean or associate dean. In the face of more knowledge exchange activities, the university council approved the intellectual property rights policy to set a framework for knowledge exchange activities, especially for those conducted with outside parties. As for incentives to induce knowledge transfer, in 2010/11 a competitive funding scheme was launched to encourage faculty members to undertake innovative projects that have social, economic, environmental, or cultural impacts for industry, business, or the community. The Faculty Knowledge Exchange (KE) Award Scheme was also launched to recognize faculty members' achievements in knowledge transfer. In terms of entrepreneurship education, the Technology Transfer Office established the Entrepreneurship Academy to organize workshop series in entrepreneurship for research staff, research postgraduate students, and alumni of related postgraduate programs (University of Hong Kong 2011). As for CUHK, with the UGC funding for knowledge transfer, it set up a Knowledge Transfer Project Fund for staff to apply to carry out technology-based or nontechnology-based knowledge transfer activities. In 2009/10, there were 45 applications, while in 2010/11, the number jumped to 62. Besides, the Technology Transfer Office launched the Patent Application Fund to encourage investors to apply for intellectual property rights protection, and also the Technology and Business Development Fund to explore the commercial potential of their research outputs. The number of patents filed increased from 109 in 2009/10 to 148 in 2010/11, and the number of patents granted also increased from 36 to 68 in the same period. The increases in the number of licenses and intellectual property rights income were most notable in the fields of biomedicine, health care, and life sciences. In 2010/11, CUHK's overall income was more than HK$248 million, and the income generated from intellectual property rights have accounted for HK$18.67 million (Chinese University of Hong Kong 2011). In 2010, the Centre for Innovation and Technology (CINTEC) of the Faculty of Engineering launched the CUHK Open Innovation Network (COIN) to offer industrial companies free consultancy on technical subjects, organize regular seminars to disseminate CUHK innovations, issue a newsletter announcing CUHK innovations, and provide free assistance to employers to conduct recruitment activities on campus. The CINTEC director explained that,

> in the past, connections between the Faculty of Engineering and the industry mainly took the form of industry seeking advice from the Faculty or research collaborations. It's neither comprehensive nor proactive. COIN enables CUHK to systematically and proactively build a network with the industry.

Within a year of inception, COIN recruited about 100 industry members. COIN anticipates that as the number accumulates, the collected information can be used for the construction of a database for industrial contacts shared with university members (Chinese University of Hong Kong 2011, 12–13).

Like HKU and CUHK, the Hong Kong University of Science and Technology is also a comprehensive university but with a stronger emphasis on S&T research and entrepreneurial activities. Since the 1990s, HKUST has established three key units to promote innovation and entrepreneurship within the campus, namely the Technology Transfer Center, the Entrepreneurship Center, and the HKUST R and D Corporation Ltd. Through the Technology Transfer Center, from 1991/92 to June 2011, HKUST has obtained a cumulative number of 279 granted patents and has 1,222 pending patent applications. About 30 percent of the patents/patent applications are used by private companies in new products development or technology integration.[12] In recent years, with the auspices of the government's Knowledge Transfer Fund, the

Technology Transfer Center introduced the Proof-of-Concept Fund to enable university staff to develop technology projects with commercial potential.[13] In 2000, the Entrepreneurship Center was established to promote entrepreneurial knowledge and activities to university staff and students and to encourage them to participate in the commercialization of new technologies.[14] And the HKUST R and D Corporation Ltd. is the business arm of HKUST which seeks partnership with the industrial sector through R&D, consultancy, licensing and technology transfer, analytical and testing services, joint ventures, and model agreements.[15]

In the past decade, HKUST has made some remarkable achievements in industry-academia collaboration. From 1999 to 2010, HKUST has received HK$573.9 million from the Innovation and Technology Fund. In the same period, it received HK$577.3 million in funding from industry partners for contact research and collaborative R&D (Honk Kong University of Science and Technology 2009). Taking the period of 2008/09 as an example, collaborative projects were conducted with different local and foreign industry partners, such as the Mass Transit Railway (MTR) in Hong Kong, the Hong Kong International Terminals, the Boeing Company in America, and Motorola Inc. USA, in which HKUST staff participated as researchers. Apart from some one-off projects, there were some cooperative efforts on building research infrastructures. For example, HKUST received funding from the telecommunications company Huawei to set up the Huawei-HKUST Innovation Laboratory to conduct R&D projects on wireless communications (Hong Kong University of Science and Technology 2009).

Taking knowledge transfer more seriously, HKUST has created a new senior management position, associate vice president for research and innovation (AVP-RI), to assist the vice president for research and graduate studies in the planning and execution of knowledge transfer activities. With regard to funding support for staff, under the support of knowledge transfer funding by government, the Technology Transfer Center launched the Proof-of-Concept Fund to steer mid-to-downstream research toward commercialization. In addition, to better promote knowledge transfer and technology marketing, HKUST conducted a number of exhibitions, sharing sessions, seminars, conferences, delegations, and visits (Hong Kong University of Science and Technology 2011).

Networking with Mainland China

Apart from knowledge transfer initiatives, the R&D activities of Hong Kong universities have also undergone profound changes under the closer relationship between Hong Kong and Mainland China. In the 1990s, it was commonly envisaged that Hong Kong's innovation system would be increasingly integrated with Mainland China's after handover. In fact, Hong Kong's proximity to Mainland China has always been an attraction for overseas companies based in Hong Kong. According to a consultancy report on the Hong Kong Science Park conducted in the early 1990s, out of the 560 tech-based firms interviewed in 17 countries, 63 of them (mainly from Mainland China, the West Coast of the United States, and the strongest European economies) expressed interest in establishing firms in the park, citing the possibility of exploring the market, manpower, and technological potential of China as one of the main reasons (Yeh and Ng 1994).

Since the 2000s, aiming to develop Hong Kong's innovation capacity, the government has tried to position Hong Kong as a regional service hub for the Pearl River Delta (Baark and So 2006). This vision became a reality when Shenzhen and Hong Kong signed the Shenzhen-Hong Kong Innovation Circle cooperation agreement in May 2007. The newly developed Innovation Circle aims to establish innovation bases, service platforms, and major research and development projects. One of the goals is to set up a Shenzhen–Hong Kong Industry-University-Research Base for Hong Kong's universities. The Innovation Circle has three key pillars—innovation foundation (provision of laboratories or facilities), service platform (sharing of technological resources and provision of a technological services platform), and major research and development (R&D) projects (cooperation in particular technological areas, such as solar batteries) (Hong Kong Information Services Department 2009). In 2008, the government successfully made a deal on the first megaproject under the concept of the Innovation Circle. The US firm DuPont has agreed to establish the Global Thin Film Photovoltaic Business/R&D Center in the Hong Kong Science Park while setting up its production line in Shenzhen.

At the same time, the Hong Kong higher education sector has also been strengthening its ties with Mainland China after the handover, but more so in recent years. The increasing cooperation between Hong Kong and Mainland China in higher education is propelled by Hong Kong universities' own demands to expand the operation scale and harness more resources and also by Mainland China's policy needs. For instance, in December 2008, the National Development and Reform Commission of the Chinese government promulgated *The Outline of the Plan for the Reform and Development of the Pearl River Delta (2008–2020)*, proposing a cross-border higher education collaboration with the region. It is stated that "the prestigious universities of Hong Kong and Macao will be encouraged to establish cooperative institutions of higher education in the Pearl River Delta, the authority for undertaking cooperative education with overseas organizations will be expanded, and the all-sided, multidisciplinary and multiform cooperation on intellect introduction and talent cultivation will be encouraged, so as to optimize the structure of talent development" (Civic Exchange 2009, 65). The outline therefore expects that by 2020, the cities of Guangzhou, Shenzhen, and Zhuhai in the Guangdong Province will establish joint HEIs with three to five famous foreign universities.

In 2011, China launched its twelfth Five-Year Plan, which stresses the need for developing technology-based strategic industries. All these policy plans are viewed by Hong Kong policy makers as opportunities for Hong Kong R&D to groom. The ASTRI chairman commented that the launch of China's twelfth Five-Year Plan would provide a golden opportunity for Hong Kong to increase R&D investments (Applied Science and Technology Research Institute 2011, 6). In fact, back in 2008, ASTRI already set up the ASTRI Science and Technology Research (Shenzhen) Co. Ltd, a wholly owned subsidiary, on the mainland.

As for the higher education sector, HKUST is among the first HEIs in Hong Kong to establish strong ties with Mainland China. The cooperation between HKUST and government agencies and higher education institutions in Mainland China, especially in South China (i.e., Nansha), dates back to late 1990s. In 1999, the Nansha Information Technology Park was approved by the Ministry of Science and Technology to be a key component of Guangzhou high-technology industries. In 2007, Fok Ying Tung Graduate School was established, which was named after Fok Ying Tung, a close friend of the Chinese government and a prominent "red capitalist" in Hong Kong. In 2010, the HKUST LED-FPD Technology R&D Center was established at Foshan with financial support from the Foshan government. HKUST hopes that the center "will strengthen HKUST's research infrastructure and activities in the Pearl River Delta region and provide HKUST with a platform to reach out for collaboration opportunities and funding sources in the Mainland"(Hong Kong University of Science and Technology 2010). Other prominent projects of HKUST in the mainland include the HKUST Shenzhen Research Institute and the HKUST R and D Corporation (Shenzhen) Ltd.

Joining the bandwagon, HKU and CUHK have also started to deepen their ties with Mainland China, especially in R&D. For HKU, some landmark initiatives include the Hong Kong–Shenzhen Institute of Research and Innovation, the Hong Kong–Guangdong Stem Cell and Regenerative Medicine Research Centre co-established with the Chinese Academy of Sciences, Guangzhou Institute of Biomedicine and Health, and the HKU Shenzhen campus which is expected to be in operation in 2013. As for CUHK, it is also establishing a new campus in Shenzhen.

Despite the trend of increasing higher education cooperation between Hong Kong and Mainland China, many difficulties abound that remain to be solved. A Hong Kong government-commissioned report finds that the major difficulties include a lack of research talent due to government restraints on Hong Kong HEIs' independent ownership and independent student recruitment, the lack of Chinese government policy and financial support to commercialize the research, the need to pay taxes for equipment acquisition, and the lack of a technology transfer platform due to the immaturity of the alliance between government, industry, and higher education in China (Central Policy Unit, HKSAR Government 2011). Besides this, the difficulties in transferring research talents and research money between Hong Kong and Mainland China also hinder cooperation (Bauhinia Foundation Research Centre 2009, 52).

Discussion and Conclusion

This chapter has reviewed major initiatives that the Hong Kong government has adopted to support the higher education sector to work with industry in promoting research, knowledge transfer, and innovation advancement. In order to further enhance the higher education sector in Hong Kong to become regionally leading and globally competitive, the Hong Kong government has continued its support for research and development via its executive arm, the University Grant Committee (UGC), to allocate funding support to higher education institutions in the city-state. In recent years, the UGC has supported institutions' academic research activities through different kinds of grants and funding, such as the Theme-Based Research Scheme, Areas of Excellence Scheme, General Research Fund, Collaborative Research Fund, and Joint Research Schemes with the mainland and overseas countries. The UGC also encourages institutions to strengthen and broaden their endeavors in transferring knowledge, technology, and other forms of research outputs into real socioeconomic benefits and impacts for the community and society. Moreover, the UGC established a research group to advise on the strategy for promoting excellence in research and to review the research assessment and funding methodology.

In response to calls from the UGC for excellent research, the aggregate expenditure on research in 2010/11 amounted to HK$6,948.3 million, representing 41 percent of the total expenditure in academic research for the institutions, and 0.38 percent of Hong Kong GDP. UGC and RGC funding, in the form of block grants and competitive research grants respectively, constituted the bulk of research funding for the institutions. The various funding schemes administered by the RGC represent the largest single source of funding for supporting academic research in Hong Kong's higher education. These funding schemes are managed by the RGC based on competition and peer review. Annual research funding to be distributed by the RGC will amount to about HK$1.1 billion starting in 2012/13.[16]

The RGC distributed HK$795 million through the Earmarked Research Grant for 2011/12; there are four main funding schemes under the RGC Earmarked Research Grant: the General Research Fund (GRF), the Collaborative Research Fund (CRF), the Direct Allocation, and the Joint Research Schemes. The HK$18 billion Research Endowment Fund (REF) was established in February 2009 after approval was granted by the Legislative Council. The fund has been set up as a trust under the Permanent Secretary for Education Incorporated. Its investment income replaces a large portion of recurrent subvention originally allocated to the RGC as the Earmarked Research Grant, thus providing greater funding stability and certainty. A portion of its investment income will also support theme-based research, thus allowing the institutions to work on research proposals on themes of a more long-term nature and strategically beneficial to the development of Hong Kong. An injection of HK$5 billion into the Research Endowment Fund was approved by the Legislative Council in January 2012. Of that, a portion of the injection will provide research funding to the self-financing tertiary institutions on a competitive basis.[17]

In conclusion, there are various forms of funding support to higher education institutions in the city-state, through which research performance has improved and research capacity has been enhanced in Hong Kong. Nonetheless, depending upon the government alone would not be sufficient to promote innovation, research, and development; higher education and industry have therefore partnered closely in advancing innovation and research / development. The Hong Kong case clearly shows how universities/higher education institutions are becoming more entrepreneurial, and this strengthened university-industry relationship will eventually affect the way universities are managed in Hong Kong.

Chapter 4

Promotion of Innovation and Knowledge Transfer: South Korean Experiences

Introduction

South Korea has caught up very fast in science and technology (S&T) since its inception of industrialization. Throughout this process, the state has played a proactive role, particularly during the 1970s and 1980s, by setting up government research institutes and science parks. Since the 1980s, the national innovation system of South Korea has evolved from one that was public-institutes centered to one that is private-companies centered (Lee 2006), and the trend continues up to the present. This private-driven national innovation system is "bipolarized" in nature, referring to the dual structure of strong *chaebols* (big corporations) on the one end and weak SMEs on the other (Lim 2008). Unlike Taiwan and Hong Kong where SMEs acquire a core role in the economy, the South Korean economy has been dominated by *chaebols* (big corporations) with the state's strong support. Because the *chaebols* have abundant resources to set up their own in-house research units, their reliance on university-industry linkages is rare. In light of this, the government has actively pushed for university-industry collaboration and has expanded the roles of Korean universities from teaching and research to entrepreneurial activities. In South Korea, the *chaebols* are the driving force of innovation, followed by government-funded research institutes. Meanwhile, universities are gaining momentum in R&D by partnering with SMEs and are playing an increasingly important role in the country's regional innovation systems. However, university-industry research collaborations are still limited with the lack of government funding for universities. Hence, the future development of South Korea's national innovation system depends on whether the government will increase its support for universities and SMEs as well as on the cooperation between them. This chapter critically examines how the South Korean government has promoted the innovation and research capacity of the country by engaging the universities and industries for cooperation.

Promotion of Innovation

After the 1997/98 Asian financial crisis, South Korea has committed to catching up with the technologically advanced countries by expanding its innovation system. In 1999, the government laid out the "Vision 2025" plan. Not only did the plan aim to improve the efficiency of national R&D investments and benchmark the R&D system with international standards, but it also aimed to transform the national innovation system structurally from being government led to private led. Under the Vision 2025 plan, the government established the first Five-Year S&T Principal Plan, enacted the Science and Technology Framework Law, and launched the 21st Century Frontier R&D Program and invested a total of US$3.5 million over a period of ten years in new frontier R&D areas such as bioscience, nanotechnology, and space technology.[1] In 2000, to encourage universities to engage in entrepreneurial activities, the government enacted the Technology Transfer Promotion Act, which would enable universities and public research organizations to deal with issues related to technology transfer.

Since the 1990s, South Korea's R&D expenditures have continued to increase. And R&D expenditures as share of GDP also rose simultaneously from 1.68 percent in 1990 to 3.37 percent in 2008. In South Korea, private companies were the biggest spenders in R&D (over 70 percent), while public research institutes (over 13 percent) and universities (about 10 percent) only spent less than 30 percent combined. In the private sector, R&D expenditures were highly concentrated in top companies. In 2005, 55.6 percent of the R&D expenditures were spent by the top 20 companies. The private sector was not only the biggest spender but also the biggest funder. In terms of R&D funding, the total amount of R&D funding continued to increase from 2000 to 2005. The ratio of government and public to private, in terms of funding, maintains a stable pattern since 2000. As of 2005, the percentage ratio of government and public to private was 24:76.

In addition to the increase in R&D investments, South Korea also witnessed an expansion of R&D talents in the past decade. The number of R&D personnel increased from 212,510 in 1999 to 436,228 in 2008, and most researchers work for private business companies. The private sector is a very important driver of innovation in South Korea. In this regard, the government has to rely on it to foster innovation. In terms of cultivating R&D talents, the Korea Research Foundation, the core government agency in South Korea to support scientific research, has launched a number of programs to cultivate R&D talents nationwide, such as the Human Resources Development Plan, the Regional University Researchers Program, the Women Scientists Program, Support of High-Class Knowledge Expansion, Next-Generation Academic Researchers, and Medical Scientist Training (MD/DDS-PhD Program). But the government also offered some incentives to the private sector to nurture their own R&D talents. For example, in 2004, the Ministry of Commerce, Industry and Energy introduced the "Foreign R&D Human Resource Development Program" as an investment incentive program to nurture R&D talents by providing financial support to foreign R&D centers (or host companies) which have operations in South Korea. The aims of the program are to attract foreign R&D centers (or host companies) to invest in South Korea, and through them to nurture local R&D talents. Host companies which possess a state-of-the-art R&D capacity (more than 100 R&D personnel or overseas branches in more than ten countries), a global marketing and distribution network, and an advanced in-house R&D training program can apply for the program. The program supports the awarded foreign companies to hire local research staff and to subsidize those foreign R&D personnel who come to South Korea for work. For hiring research staff, the support is up to 50 percent of the annual salary per research worker who are Korean national with a BA or higher degree in S&T fields. The cap of the support is KRW 30 million per recruit per year. For R&D training, the support is up to 50 percent of accommodation expenses for foreign R&D personnel (foreign educators and trainers) dispatched to South Korea to perform instruction/training. The cap of the support is KRW 50 million per recruit per year.[2]

In addition to doubling the efforts to invest in R&D activities, the government has to induce the private sector to expand its R&D expenditures through deregulation of corporate research institutes and expansion of tax deduction rates for R&D facility investment. Even though large companies have dominated the market, SMEs are in fact important to the South Korean economy in terms of their number and the numbers of their employees. In 1994, there were about 2.4 million firms in South Korea; SMEs accounted for 99.3 percent of them. And there were about 10 million employees; those working in SMEs constituted about 75.1 percent. In 2009, the number of SMEs increased, constituting about 99.9 percent of about 3 million firms, and SME employees constituted about 87.7 percent of the workforce of about 12 million.[3] In this regard, the government has also been giving special attention to innovative small and medium-sized enterprises.

In South Korea, SMEs are largely categorized into three categories—venture businesses, management-innovative businesses, and "inno-biz" (technologically innovation businesses), the number of which increased significantly in recent years, from 11,526 in 2007 to 16,243 in 2010. With regard to "inno-biz," the government aimed to boost their technological capability by promoting the tripartite cooperation of industry, academia, and research institutes.[4] As of 2009, the Small and Medium Business Administration had managed 28 business incubators, mostly at universities and research institutes, to help the SMEs to innovate. In 2008, these incubators have helped produce about 4,500 enterprises, which generated revenue of KRW 2.3 trillion (Small and Medium Business Association 2009, 9). In 2009, the SMBA selected 1,473 SMEs to carry out joint R&D with 245 universities and research institutes, involving 1,400 professors from 217 universities and 530 researchers from 28 research institutes nationwide. As revealed by an SMBA official, SMEs' lack of R&D manpower was a reason SMEs were interested in open-type R&D with other parties (Small and Medium Business Association 2009, 22). While the *chaebols* have their own resources to conduct in-house research, the SMEs have to team up with universities for applied and development research. After the 1997/98 Asian financial crisis, when *chaebols* started to cut their R&D expenditures, SMEs seized on the opportunity to jump-start innovation. The number of venture firms increased exponentially from 100 before the crisis to more than 7,000 in the mid-2000s (Kim 2001, cited in Shapiro 2007, 176). A study by the Korean Research Foundation found that in 2006, 51.6 percent of the university-industry research collaborations by the 12 leading universities were with SMEs with a size of less than 300 employees (Hemmert et al. 2008, 167).

Another support given to SMEs is the matching of R&D talents. To facilitate SMEs to search for talents and employees, universities were also encouraged to participate in students' field experience at innovative SMEs (Small and Medium Business Association 2009, 15–16). In addition, specialized high schools were called upon to strengthen their field education through SME-employment classes. It is hoped that the specialized high school graduates would get prepared to become competent SME employees.[5]

While recognizing the need to support the private sector, the government put forth the effort in setting up the strategic development of national R&D activities. The latest milestone was set by the Lee Myung Bak Administration in 2008, which aims to develop South Korea into an "S&T Power Nation" with the launch of the "577 Initiative." The "5" stands for the goal that the government aims to increase the proportion of GDP the government spends on R&D (GERD) from around 3 percent in 2006 to 5 percent in 2012, which means the Lee administration would commit KRW 66.5 trillion over the five-year period from 2008 to 2012, while the previous administration only committed KRW 40.1 trillion. The two "7s" stand for the seven major technology areas, (1) key industrial technologies (cash cow), (2) emerging industrial technologies (green Ocean), (3) knowledge-based service technologies (knowledge-based S&Ts), (4) state-led technologies (big science), (5) national issues-related technologies (risk science), (6) global issues-related technologies (mega trend), and (7) basic and convergent technologies (national platform tech), it wants to focus on, and the seven major S&T systems, (1) cultivation and utilization of world-class human resources in S&T, (2) promotion of basic and fundamental research, (3) support for SMEs' innovation, (4) S&T globalization, (5) enhancement of regional innovation capacity, (6) advancement of S&T infrastructure, and (7) spread of S&T culture, it wants to advance.[6] At the same time, the Ministry of Knowledge Economy identified 22 new growth engines in 6 sectors, including (1) energy and environment—clean coal, maritime bop fuel, solar cell, utilizing captured CO2 to produce chemical products, fuel-cell power systems, nuclear power plants; (2) new IT—semiconductors, display panels, wireless communications, LEDs, REID/USN; (3) knowledge services—software, design, healthcare, cultural contents; (4) bio—pharmaceuticals and biomedical devices; (5) convergence of industries—robotics, new materials and nanoconvergence system, IT convergence system, broadcast communications convergence system; and (6) transportation system—green vehicles, ship and maritime system.

Park Geun-hye has taken up the presidency of South Korea since December 2012. Many people are paying keen attention to what specific policy will be implemented by the new government. Some of the anticipated policies are those for the promotion of creativity-oriented small and midsize enterprises and start-up firms led by young businessmen, expansion of national R&D investment, establishment of a new concept of cultural contents industry, revitalization of the information communications industry, and advancement of science technologies and the culture industry.

For the first goal, the government is planning to foster young entrepreneurs by providing colleges with more start-up assistance functions. Tax incentives and financial supports are beefed up in accordance with the Special Tax Treatment Control Act so that more young company founders can benefit from angel investment while the government raises funds to that end in conjunction with major corporations. Further, the government is going to come up with A&M support measures to help venture firms increase their presence and strength in the industry.

In the meantime, the president promised during her campaign that she would raise the proportion of national R&D investment to the GDP to 5 percent by 2017. The percentage had been 4.03 percent in 2011. The new investment will concentrate on SMEs and long-term research and development projects. Also, some of the budgets of government-funded research institutes are invested in R&D projects of SMEs in a quota system to be newly introduced.[7]

Higher Education Development

Apart from launching national R&D projects, the government's commitment to fostering innovation is clearly supported by its measures in enhancing the capacity of higher education. Since the 1990s, South Korea has accelerated its education reforms. From 1995 to 1997, the government launched the Education Reform Scheme for a New Education System. The reform mainly aimed to diversify and privatize education generally. In regard to higher education, university establishment requirements were relaxed to enable expansion and "universalization" of higher education. Apart from expansion, higher education has also been reformed along the lines of autonomy, specialization, quality enhancement, and assurance (Choi 2010, 31). The expansion of the higher education sector was accompanied by an increase in government expenditures in education. Since the 2000s, the government has continued to expand the budget for the Ministry of Education. From 2001 to 2007, the share of the MOE budget increased from 16.1 percent to 17.9 percent.[8]

In order to cultivate more human capital besides formal education, in 1999 the government enacted the Lifelong Education Law. Many policy programs, such as the credit bank system, corporate university, and cyber-university, were introduced to encourage adults to continue lifelong learning while at work. After two decades of expansion, the number of tertiary education institutions in South Korea has increased from 265 in 1990 to 372 in 2007.[9] At the same time, the enrollment rate of higher education institutions increased from 23.6 percent in the 1990s to 70.5 percent in 2008.[10] In South Korea, students in science and technology fields are the core group of the student population. For example, in 2004, S&T students (in engineering, medicine and pharmacy, and natural science) constituted 42.6 percent and 32.2 percent of the whole student population in universities, colleges, and graduate schools.[11]

South Korea's growing concern with education was also illustrated by the restructuring of the government bureaucracy. In the 2000s, the government agency overseeing educational development underwent several changes. In 2001, the South Korean government expanded the Ministry of Education to the Ministry of Education and Human Resources Development. Human resources development, which used to be an issue of private organizations or companies, has become a matter of great importance at the national level. In 2008, the government combined the Ministry of Science and Technology and the Ministry of Education into a new Ministry of Education, Science and Technology (MEST). This merger was a clear signal that the government foresees the vital role of education in S&T development in the future.

Apart from the expansion of higher education, another major higher education reform since the late 1990s is to build up the research capabilities of public universities. The landmark initiative in this respect is the 1.4 trillion won "Brain Korea 21 Project" (BK21) initiated in 1999. Only top universities in the country were selected and highly subsidized to excel in two key academic areas—natural/applied S&T and the humanities and social sciences—in order to become world-class HEIs (Moon and Kim 2001). The first phase of the project was carried out between 1999 and 2005 with a US$1.34 billion budget. In total, 564 centers/teams and 89,366 students participated over the seven-year period, with US$400 per month for masters, US$600 for doctoral, and US$1,250 for postdoc researchers, and US$2,500 for contract professors.

The second phase was carried between 2006 and 2012. This time 74 universities, with a US$2.3 billion budget, 244 centers, 325 project teams, 20,000 graduate students participated per year, with US$500 per month for masters, US$900 for doctoral, and US$2,000 for postdoc researchers, and US$2,500 for contract professors.[12]

The project contributed significantly to the nurturing of research talents, building up of research institutes, and increase in research outputs. The official statistics shows that the first phase of BK21 has produced 6,602 S&T PhD students. From 1998 to 2005, the number of S&T SCI-level papers increased from 3,765 to 7,281, and South Korea's world ranking in SCI-S&T papers improved from sixteenth to twelfth. Moreover, the quality of these papers also improved, with the impact factor per article increasing from 1.9 in 1999 to 2.4 in 2005. With these good achievements, the MEST set more ambitious goals for the second-phase project, which includes developing ten top research-oriented universities in the key fields, developing South Korea to become one of the top-ten countries in SCI-paper publication, and also to become one of the top-ten advanced countries in university-industry technology transfer. The target goal is to increase the technology transfer rate from 10 percent in 2004 to 20 percent in 2012 (Korean Ministry of Education, Science and Technology [MEST] South Korea 2007). As of 2009, the second-phase BK21 has devoted 265.9 billion won to support 565 project teams at 71 participating universities. It is required that a minimum of 70 to 80 percent of project funds should be allocated to support graduate students and new research personnel. According to estimates, 20,000 graduate students and 3,000 new research personnel were subsidized (MEST 2009a). Apart from supporting research talents, research outputs were also boosted by BK21. As of 2010, the share of South Korean papers among globally published papers was 3.37 percent, up from 1.13 percent in 1998 (Korean Educational Development Institute [KEDI] 2010, 25).

Apart from the BK21 Project, other projects have been implemented to advance the nurturing of talents and R&D activities. For example, the New University for Regional Innovation Project was launched by MEST from 2004 to 2008 to encourage universities to play the role of knowledge provider to local industries. The government had devoted around US$1.3 billion into the project, and a total of 109 local universities, 130 project units, and 170,000 students have participated. As a result, the graduate employment rate has increased from 60.2 percent in 2004 to 68.1 percent in 2006, and about 20,000 trainees participated in on-site training at major companies (MEST 2007). In addition, South Korean universities were also mobilized to participate in the building and development of regional science parks (Kim 2007). In 2009, the Ministry of Education, Science and Technology and the Korea Research Foundation further announced a support project for University National Research Laboratories (NRL) with a budget of KRW 34 billion. The project aims to support University NRL to establish research centers in universities and to develop them into world-class research centers. Resources are concentrated on supporting selected high-quality research centers, especially S&T-related ones. Selected science and technology institutes are eligible for KRW 500 million per year for science and engineering, KRW 300 million per year for convergence, and KRW 230 million per year for social sciences. The funding period is up to nine years.[13]

While South Korea has achieved notable achievements in developing R&D capacity in higher education since the late 1990s, more drastic changes were to happen under the former Lee Ming-Bak administration beginning in 2008. The former Lee Ming-Bak administration focused on three policy objectives for higher education: to maintain and reinforce the educational capacity of HEIs, to raise the autonomy and accountability of HEIs, and to increase the research capacity of HEIs. To achieve these goals, the government launched the "Formula Grant Project for Enhanced Higher Education Capacity," a competitive grant scheme, to induce competition and financial efficiency of HEIs. The beneficiary universities will be given autonomy to devise and implement their own improvement strategies. The government will act as consultant during the process and as performance evaluator upon the termination of the grant period (MEST 2009a). Speaking overall, the strategy adopted by the former Lee Ming-Bak administration is "concentration and selection, and specialization."

For the strategy of "concentration and selection," alongside the BK21 Project initiated by the previous administration, the former Lee administration launched the national World Class University (WCU) project in 2008, which aims to concentrate resources on top universities to enhance their teaching and research capacity by recruiting top academics around the world. There are three types of WCU project:

1. To recruit foreign scholars to help establish new academic departments or specialized majors.
2. To employ foreign academics as full-time professors to provide lectures and conduct joint research with local Korean scholars.
3. To invite world-class scholars (e.g., Nobel Prize laureates) to conduct joint research with local scholars and conduct lectures as visiting professors.

The government has reserved KRW 825 million, funding the project from 2008 to 2012. Selected universities will be heavily subsidized by the government, which will provide full wages for foreign scholars, fees for their joint research with local scholars, and lab establishment expenses (MEST 2009a). In 2009, the first operational year of the WCU project, the budget was set at KRW 160 billion. A total of 284 top academics (including two Nobel Prize winners) around the world were recruited in different forms: 35 research teams at Korean universities established new academic departments or specialized majors in future growth-generating fields. Another 36 universities employed foreign scholars at existing academic programs, and 76 universities invited distinguished world-class scholars to teach and conduct research in Korea (MEST 2008).

With regard to human capital development, in 2010, MEST designated 19 universities to lead human resources development programs. They were given a subsidy of KRW 100 billion to help create 500 new jobs. The ministry also designated 32 universities to promote academy-industry collaboration and allocated resources to subsidize projects for the Innovative Local HRD Program to link regional SMEs with the science and engineering departments of local universities to conduct joint research (MEST 2009b).

For the strategy of specialization, the government attempts to identify the key development areas and to establish a clear and efficient division of labor system among the universities. For example, in 2009, MEST intended to extend the scope of professional graduate school from the fields of law, business administration, and medicine/dentistry to include three "growth-generating fields"—green growth industry, new fusion technology, and high value-added service industry (MEST 2008). In 2010, it designated four S&T universities to be responsible of a specialized research area:

- Korean Advanced Institute of Science and Technology (KAIST)
  o (Specialized areas: emphasis on national strategic areas including cutting-edge converged and compound technology, etc.)
- Gwangju Institute of Science and Technology (GIST)
  o (Specialized areas: photomics, IT-based converged technology, etc.)
- Daegu Gyeongbuk Institute of Science and Technology (DGIST)
  o (Specialized areas: medical/new medicine, intelligent vehicles, etc.)
- Ulsan National Institute of Science and Technology (UNIST)
  o (Specialized areas: advanced biomaterials, nuclear energy, etc.) (MEST 2009a).

Strengthening University-Enterprise Cooperation in Education

In order to facilitate more cooperation between universities and enterprises, the Science and Technology Ministry of Education in South Korea recently announced "Contract Program Operations," encouraging enterprises and universities to communicate with each other to tailor programs and subjects for students. For example, Sung Kyun Kwan University engages in cooperation with Samsung Electronics Company Ltd. to offer the Semiconductor Systems

Engineering Program for students, whereby the facilities and funding are provided by Samsung. Similarly, Pusan National University also cooperates with Samsung to open the refrigeration and air conditioning energy faculties. In fact, this is a win-win situation: the enterprises can nurture professional employees while the universities can guarantee students with job opportunities. Currently, there are 46 universities in South Korea cooperating with enterprises to offer "contract programs" for enhancing university-industry cooperation.

In order to encourage more universities to work with enterprises, the Science and Technology Ministry of Education has lowered the standard requirements of university-enterprise co-operation. Nowadays, not only large enterprises, but middle- and small-size enterprises, unions, and local governments can also provide funds for universities. In addition, the universities and enterprises engaged in cooperation are not restricted to being in the same city or province, if only less than 100 kilometers away. Enterprises are not required to pay up to 100 percent of funding in support of the contract program; they can contribute only 50 percent or above of the funding. Moreover, the schemes are not only confined to local universities but now extend to all universities that located in Seoul to cooperate with enterprises.[14] The following discussion highlights a few enterprise-run education institutions offering training for students.

Distribution University of Hyundai Department Store

Following the Corporate University of LG Electronics, Korea's first corporate university established on 9 October 2010 with the support of the Ministry of Employment and Labor (MOEL), the second corporate university, called the "Distribution University of Hyundai Department Store," was launched on 20 November 2012. MOEL provides active support for companies to voluntarily set up and operate a corporate university for high school graduates. This is aimed at realizing inclusive employment and creating an environment that enables workers to combine work and learning.

The Distribution University of Hyundai Department Store provides students with systematic education and training ranging from technical knowledge about distribution to basic education covering humanities, global competencies, social contribution, and so forth (869 hours for two years). Although the Distribution University gives no degree, it guarantees its graduates equal treatment as that enjoyed by university graduates, and thus leads the way in establishing a corporate culture where workers are evaluated based on practical skills rather than educational attainment.[15]

Yeungjin College

Yeungjin College is the most famous specialist university in Korea, which has 10,000 students, mainly offering practical technology education. Yeungjin College's graduates can enroll as year three students at Kyungpook National University, Sung Kyun Kwan University, Kon Kuk University, Han Yang University, Hongik University, and American Purdue University. With a special focus on technology education, Yeungjin is ranked as the number-one specialist university by the Ministry of Education in South Korea, and has become a role model for other specialist universities. Yeungjin College has the most advanced teaching and practice equipment, greatly improving students' practical ability and innovation ability. Yeungjin College graduates are highly praised by enterprises in Korea; therefore enterprises sign employment agreements with the college, entrusting them to nurture outstanding talents. Enterprises such as Samsung, LG, Modern, and Hynix have cooperated with Yeungjin College.

From 2001 to 2010, 2,000 enterprises cooperated with Yeungjin College, and the college also obtained great support from the Korean government, the Ministry of Education, the Ministry of Commerce and Industry, and the Ministry of Labor. With a strong practical and work-related orientation, students enrolling in Yeungjin certainly benefit from experiential learning through participating in practice-oriented classes. Moreover, the government has set up an "Expert Park" in Yeungjin College, all the test products production, determination of the finished product, product processing, authenticate, new product development, and all other processes are conducted in "Expert Park" with the operating money paid by the government. In recent years, Yeungjin College received 2.2 billion won from Samsung, LG, and Hynix. Other enterprises also donated expensive training equipment to Yeungjin. Obtaining both support from the government and enterprise, Yeungjin College is becoming a leading specialist college in Korea, making a unique contribution to support the university-enterprise cooperation mission.[16]

South Korea and Kazakhstan: Strengthened Cooperation Between Universities and SMEs

Recently in September 2012, the ex-president of South Korea Lee Myung-bak and Kazakhstan president Nursultan Nazarbayev held a press conference stating that both the government and enterprise had reached a consensus on strengthening cooperation between universities and small and medium-sized enterprises. President Lee Myung-bak also emphasized that the two sides would establish a model of mutually beneficial cooperation between the two countries, and Korea and Kazakhstan would develop a long-term cooperation in the field of atomic energy, the production of high-speed trains, and railway modernization. As in the field of information exchange, both sides would carry out the Nazarbayev University Technology Park project.[17]

Discussion and Conclusion

In conclusion, this chapter has critically examined how the South Korean government has made serious attempts to strengthen the global competitiveness of the country by encouraging enterprises to work with the university sector, inducing small and medium enterprises to engage with universities/colleges for promoting entrepreneurial education to prepare students for future industrial and business developments. With a strong conviction to enhance the regional and global position of the country, the South Korean government has also invested hugely in the expansion of higher education, cultivating a more conducive environment to enhance the research capacity of the university sector. All these efforts have begun to obtain returns, especially when we have seen an increasing number of universities from South Korea steadily move up their ranking in various forms of international benchmarking and ranking exercises.

Chapter 5

After Massification of Higher Education: Questing for Innovation and Entrepreneurial Universities in Taiwan

Introduction

In order to enhance its national competitiveness in the global marketplace, the Taiwan government has followed the US model by expanding higher education through the establishment of a significant number of private universities to fulfill pressing higher education learning needs. In the last two decades, more than 160 universities have been founded in Taiwan, and a higher education enrollment rate of nearly 100 percent has been achieved. The rapid increase in private universities in Taiwan has undoubtedly created an abundant supply of education opportunities; however people in Taiwan have begun to doubt the quality and standard of the graduates. The Taiwan government, making serious efforts to model itself after the US experience when transforming its higher education sector, has now found that the massified university system has created an immense pressure for the Taiwan society to absorb the "oversupply" of graduates into the labor market. This chapter critically examines how universities in Taiwan have made attempts to enhance their global and regional competitiveness through advancing research, development, and innovation.

Taiwan has been a strong high-tech product exporter in East Asia. Its semiconductor industry was particularly praised as the "Silicon Valley of the East" (Mathews 1997). Since the start of its industrialization in the 1960s, the Taiwanese government has actively pushed for the development of industry, based on the conviction that industrial and technological latecomers like Taiwan urgently need the state's solid support to jump-start and secure a fast development process. In Taiwan, the government, universities, and industry (especially SMEs) are interacting very closely and dynamically in areas like curriculum design, technology licensing, and incubation centers.

While universities and industries have been actively strengthening ties with each other by themselves, the government always lends its very visible hands through national programs, facilitative policies, and funding.

In recent years, especially after the 2008/09 global financial crisis, Taiwan has launched a new national development plan that hopes to jump-start the economy and further consolidate its leading edge in innovation and entrepreneurship in East Asia. The plan envisions that Taiwan's future success will hinge on the development of six emerging industries, four intelligent industries, and ten key service industries. Particularly related to innovation are the four intelligent industries, which are electric cars, cloud computing, green architecture, and the commercialization of patents. It can be expected that the success of these areas will depend on the innovation and entrepreneurship of Taiwan. With particular reference to examining how universities in Taiwan have made attempts to enhance their global and regional competitiveness through advancing research, development, and innovation, as well as engaging in an internationalization agenda to enhance students' global competence, the present chapter also critically examines the significance of the strong emphasis placed on R&D in Taiwan.

Advancing Research and Technological Innovation

As a technology latecomer compared to the developed western countries, the Taiwan government ceaselessly plays a great role in jump-starting and initiating R&D activities, as well as cultivating an enabling environment. This effort started as early as the 1960s, for example, the duty-free policy for the production and exportation of products resulting from innovation and technological advancement. A dozen industrial estates were also built by the government to accommodate more laborers. In addition to these was the low wages of Taiwanese laborers. All these factors have created a favorable environment for foreign direct investment (FDI) (Cheng 2001). Not only that, but right from the very outset of industrialization, the government has dabbled directly in R&D activities; the National Science Council (NSC) and the Industrial Technology Research Institute (ITRI, the most important public research institute in S&T) are two of the most important responsible bodies. The NSC was established in 1959 as a branch of the Executive Yuan, playing the role of the Ministry of S&T in Taiwan.[1] Under its supervision, science parks like the Hsinchu Science-Based Industrial Park, which was established in 1980, have achieved world-class status. As of April 2013, the three Science Parks—Hsinchu Science Park, Central Taiwan Science Park, and Southern Taiwan Science Park—hosted more than 755 companies, many of which were specialized in integrated circuits R&D and production. Table 5.1 clearly shows the large number of companies stationed in Hsinchu, Southern, and Central Taiwan.

Table 5.1 Number of Companies Stationed at the Hsinchu, Central, and Southern Taiwan Science Parks by Industry, as of 8 April 2013

Science Parks	Statistics Item	Integrated Circuits	Optoelectronics	Computer and Peripherals	Telecommunications	Precision Machinery	Biotechnology	Other	Grand Total
Hsinchu Science Park	Effective number of approved companies	204	106	53	50	40	57	6	516
	Number of companies in the parks	196	97	52	50	37	47	3	482
	Number of enterprises reporting administrative fees	0	0	0	0	0	0	0	0
Central Taiwan Science Park	Effective number of approved companies	7	39	14	1	49	23	11	144
	Number of companies in the parks	5	32	8	1	39	15	10	110
	Number of enterprises reporting administrative fees	0	0	0	0	0	0	0	0

Continued

Table 5.1 Continued

Science Parks	Statistics Item	Integrated Circuits	Optoelectronics	Computer and Peripherals	Telecommunications	Precision Machinery	Biotechnology	Other	Grand Total
Southern Taiwan Science Park	Effective number of approved companies	13	51	2	11	45	56	6	184
	Number of companies in the parks	10	46	2	9	43	50	3	163
	Number of enterprises reporting administrative fees	0	0	0	0	0	0	0	0
Grand Total	Effective number of approved companies	224	196	69	62	134	136	23	844
	Number of companies in the parks	211	175	62	60	119	112	16	755
	Number of enterprises reporting administrative fees	0	0	0	0	0	0	0	0

Source: National Science Council, Taiwan, https://nscnt12.nsc.gov.tw/WAS2/English/AsScienceParkEReport.aspx?quyid=tqindustry01.

In terms of the governance of R&D activities, inspired by the United States' Bayh-Dole Act and the UK's Patent Law in the 1990s, the Taiwan government enacted the Fundamental Science and Technology Act in 1999 to lay down broad principles and future directions for S&T development. The act stipulates that the government should issue the National S&T Development Plan and the White Paper on S&T periodically to document the progress of S&T development in Taiwan. As required by the act, the Taiwanese government has released the *National Science and Technology Development Plan (2001–2004)* and *National Science and Technology Development Plan (2005–2008)*; both of these are four-year development plans that outline the missions, strategies, and specific measures of technological and innovation policies. In order to closely monitor and evaluate the execution and feedback of programs outlined by the plan, the government also released the *White Paper on Science and Technology (2003–2006)* and the *White Paper on Science and Technology (2007–2010)* respectively. These white papers can be conceived as the midterm progress reports of the plan. According to the National Science Council, Indicators of Science and Technology 2011, the sales of companies stationed in various science parks in Taiwan increased steadily from 2001 to 2010 and formed a very important part of national incomes.

Moreover, it is worth noting that the three major science parks in Taiwan together generated over NT$2 trillion (US$67.7 billion) in revenues in 2012. Among them, the Hsinchu Science Park generated the most at NT$1.05 trillion in sales in 2012, a 2.3 percent increase from a year earlier. The Central Taiwan Science Park posted the largest annual growth in revenues at 11.1 percent, reaching NT$323.3 billion. Meanwhile, the Southern Taiwan Science Park created NT$622 billion in sales in 2012, up 7.3 percent from the previous year. Notably, Taiwan Semiconductor Manufacturing Company, the world's largest contract chip producer, and United Microelectronics Corporation are expanding their operations in the Southern Taiwan Science Park, with planned investments projected to top NT$740 billion and new job openings expected to reach 9,600 in the next five years. In 2013, the Hsinchu Science Park is expected to recruit 3,600 staff, the Central Taiwan Science Park 2,000, and the Southern Taiwan Science Park 6,000, thanks to expansions and new investments. Combined exports from the three science parks grew 8.8 percent in 2012, better than the 1.6 percent contraction in Taiwan's overall exports that year. By country, China was the top destination for exports from the three science parks in 2012, accounting for NT$562.2 billion worth of exports, or 45 percent.[2]

In order to enhance global and regional competitiveness, the Taiwan government stated explicitly its ambition of becoming a "technologically advanced nation," especially in the midst of the Asian financial crisis in 1997/98. On 2 April 1998, the Executive Yuan of Taiwan proposed the "Action Plan for Building a Technologically Advanced Nation" (Executive Yuan, Taiwan 1998). The plan stated that S&T development in Taiwan means to:

1. Raise the standards of S&T as a whole;
2. Promote economic development;
3. Raise the standard of living; and
4. Establish an autonomous national defense capability.

Accordingly, the government is very eager to make Taiwan into an "academic research and knowledge creation hub in the Asia-Pacific region" (NSC, Republic of China 2003, 14). Unlike Hong Kong which was severely affected by the Asian financial crisis of 1997/98, the strategic vision of the Taiwan government was to make R&D and advancement in technology very core to its economic and industrial policies. Against this policy context, Taiwan's national innovation system has continued to expand in terms of increased R&D expenditures and the size of the R&D workforce, even given the Asian financial crisis. For research input, the amount of R&D expenditure has increased in the past decade. Business enterprises and the government are the biggest R&D spenders and funders. The majority of expenditures (over 70 percent) were invested in engineering and technology research. At the 2012 National Science and Technology Conference, President Ma Ying-jeou announced that the island's R&D spending in 2011 reached 3.02 percent of its GDP, which fulfilled his promise during the 2008 election to increase R&D spending to 3 percent of GDP by 2012.[3] Besides the expansion of quantity, the quality of Taiwan's R&D manpower also improved, with more R&D personnel obtaining an educational level higher than a bachelor's degree.[4]

The strategic role attached to R&D has undoubtedly made Taiwan's high technology stand out among the neighboring Asian economies. R&D has considerably sustained the labor market in the island state since it has created steady employment opportunities. Even though the government has a significant role in steering and shaping the rules and regulations for R&D activities in Taiwan, the scientific community and the private sector are not dictated by the government (Chen 1997; Hsu and Chiang 2001; Mahmood and Singh 2003). Especially, the SMEs are the driving force of innovation in Taiwan's economy, and they have constituted nearly 98 percent of all enterprises and about 30 percent of total sales value.[5]

Recognizing the dynamics of SMEs, the Small and Medium Enterprise Administration (SMEA) of the Ministry of Economic Affairs has undertaken a series of programs to assist SMEs over the past decades. Examples are the Small Business Innovation Research Program, the Industrial Technology Development Plan, the Innovative Technology Applications and Services Program, the Conventional Industry Technology Development Initiative, and the Assist Service Sector Technology Development Plan. These programs aim to facilitate the start-up of SMEs and their technical upgrading through university-industry collaborations. Unlike the vertically integrated big corporations in South Korea that aim at economies of scale, the horizontally networked SMEs in Taiwan have more organizational flexibility to adapt to changing export demands. Yet because of their small sizes, they have to depend on state and university support for R&D. A recent statistical study indicates that SMEs tend to cooperate with public universities, which have more resources than private universities to help SMEs in emerging industries like biotechnology and nanotechnology (Hu and Mathews 2009).

The SMEA also assisted the SMEs in training up their manpower, including R&D personnel. For example, in 2003, the SMEA launched the SME e-Learning Project to establish Taiwan's SME Online University. From 2003 to 2009, the five online colleges of the university (Information Technology College, Finance College, Marketing and Channel Management College, General Knowledge College, and Human Resource College) have offered 900 free online courses to 350,000 SME employers and employees. Apart from courses, the online university also contains e-books, online lectures, and book reviews to meet the diverse demands of SME members. In 2006, the SMEA launched the Incubation Center Knowledge Service Environment Construction Project to not only help business start-ups maximize their profits and enhance their effectiveness, but also to groom professionalism and incubate key talents (i.e., through the establishment of professional services and incubation support centers).6 The ultimate aim of Taiwan, as the government pronounced in the 2008 National Development Plan, is to become an "Asia Entrepreneur Center." Our discussion above has pointed out how the Taiwan government has tried to enhance its economic development through investments and developments in R&D-related activities. The following section will examine how the Taiwan government has attempted to engage the university sector to work and cooperate with industry in advancing science and technology development and promoting entrepreneurial universities in that island state.

Education Reforms and Enhancement in Science and Technology

In addition to supporting research and development to foster advancement in industrial development, the Taiwan government has strongly encouraged universities to engage in deep cooperation with industry and business to enhance economic growth. Believing that education is key to the enhancement of national competitiveness in a globalizing world, Taiwan immediately kicked off higher education reform right at the turn of the twenty-first century. In the 2001 *White Paper on Higher Education*, which was the first white paper on higher education in Taiwan issued by the Ministry of Education, the Taiwan government envisioned that the twenty-first century would be the era of the knowledge-based economy, and higher education would be expected to play an important role in knowledge innovation and cultivating human capital, both of which are essential to national competitiveness. It was stated in the document that innovation, relearning, online learning, and technological literacy would be key indicators of increasing national competitiveness. From 2000 to 2005, the government carried out numerous higher education reform programs, including the Program for Promoting Academic Excellence of Universities (2000), the Program for Improving Basic Education in Universities (2001), the Program to Promote International Competitiveness of Universities (2002), the Research University Integration Project (2002), the Program for Cultivating Science and Engineering Talents at Universities (2002), the Program for Improving Research University Infrastructure (2002), the Program for Expanding Overseas Student Recruitment (2003), the Project for Developing Top-Notch Universities (2004), the Program for Rewarding Teaching Excellence of Universities (2005), and the Program for Promoting Teaching Excellence of Universities (2005). In addition, the Top University Project was started in 2006 and will go on until 2016.[7]

One major theme of these programs is to advance the teaching and research excellence of universities. For example, the Program for Promoting Academic Excellence of Universities was launched by the MOE together with the National Science Council in 2000, aimed at encouraging large-scale intra- and inter-university cooperation with a budget of NT$13 billion. A group of prominent local and international scholars would host the review panel to safeguard the research standard. Moreover, this screening process would favor proposals that were innovative, international, and have the potential to meet the needs of national development (Song and Tai 2007, 328–329). It is thus shown that at the moment, establishing hallmark universities and research centers has become the top agenda item of higher educational reform in Taiwan.

In Taiwan, the cultivation of S&T talents has always been one of the top priorities for national S&T development. For example, the National S&T Development Plan (2001–2004) outlines a proposal for "strengthening the training, recruiting, and utilization of technological manpower" as one of the S&T development strategies (National Science Council [NSC] 2001). The midterm goal of this strategy was to increase the number of research personnel with a bachelor's degree to 80,000, and for at least 60 percent of all personnel to have an MS or PhD by 2004. The long-term goal for 2010 was to increase the number of the former to 100,000, and the proportion of the latter to at least 65 percent (NSC 2001). The second National S&T Development Plan (2005–2008) also vowed to do the following:

1. Implement "macro planning of higher education."
2. Encourage "the development of interdisciplinary courses, shrinking the gap between university education and industrial S&T manpower needs."
3. Strengthen "cooperative work-study programs involving industry, academia, and research organizations in order to boost S&T manpower development." (NSC 2005, 14)

Further, in 2009, amid the global financial crisis, the Ministry of Education launched a one-year Research Talent Recruitment Program in Colleges and Universities in order to seize on the moment to retain R&D talents in universities, when graduates were having a hard time finding jobs in the private market. Two types of researchers—postdoctoral research fellows and research assistants (who held master's degrees and above)—were recruited to perform full-time research work (Ministry of Education, Taiwan 2009).

Moreover, the Top University Project Phase II (April 2011–March 2016) is meant to further help recipient universities attain the goal of topping the world. In addition to assisting local universities in resource integration and upgrading teaching and research competence, special emphasis is to be placed on fostering closer cooperation with esteemed international counterparts and broadening the world outlook of students and instructors alike. Guidance is to be extended to universities for them to better meet the needs of local industry by turning themselves into R&D hubs that excel in both academic research and practical applications. Last but not least, top-tier universities will be called upon to help recruit and cultivate leaders for the future so that Taiwan can be justifiably recognized as a land inhabited by global citizens who have a well-rounded world outlook and the capacity to pursue self-improvement constantly. The ultimate goal is to make possible the world's best universities in Taiwan with an unwavering dedication to the pursuit of excellence in both teaching and research.

Nearly half of students enrolled in higher education institutions in Taiwan choose to study S&T disciplines. The percentage of S&T students was even higher in advanced studies, as about 70 percent of PhD students are S&T students.[8] But apart from cultivating local talent, in the past decade, the Ministry of Education was concerned with attracting foreign talent to Taiwan. In 2004, the MOE issued a report on the increased numbers of international students, which was later absorbed in the Executive Yuan's National Development Plan. In 2008, the Executive Yuan initiated the so-called "Ten Thousands Horses stampeding" program, which aims to subsidize 10,000 local students for foreign exchange and to attract 20,000 international students in four years. The program not only aims at broadening the horizons of the students, but also at internationalizing Taiwan's higher education sector. At the same time, the government launched the Southern Sunshine Scholarship Program to attract students from Southeast Asia. As a result, the number of international students increased from 9,600 in 2004 to 24,732 in 2010.

In addition, the majority of international students in Taiwan were coming from Asian countries. For example, in 2010, 74.59 percent of international students were from Asia, followed by 15.31 percent from the Americas, 5.11 percent from Europe, and 4.99 percent from other regions. In terms of these international students' contribution to the economy, which includes tuition and miscellaneous fees, living expenses, the travel expenditures of their parents, their contribution rose from NT$788,397 to NT$1,716,209 from 2007 to 2010 (Ministry of Education, Taiwan 2011a).

In terms of disciplines, S&T in Taiwan is the most popular to foreign students. In 2007, 34 percent of foreign students in Taiwan enrolled in S&T programs, followed by 33 percent in business management, and 17 percent respectively in both social sciences and the humanities and arts (Ministry of Education, Taiwan 2011b).

In view of this, like many countries aspiring to become technologically advanced economies, Taiwan has also paid special attention to S&T talents. As mentioned above, the Taiwan government has put effort into helping companies train up their talents, but it does not fully leave the task of cultivating, recruiting, and rewarding sci-tech talents to the private sector. Over the years, the NSC has created various awards and incentives for S&T research excellence, such as the Presidential Science Prize, the Outstanding Achievement in Science and Technology Award, the Ta-You Wu Memorial Award, and the Outstanding Industry-University Cooperation Award.[9] The Academia Sinica, the most prestigious public research institute in Taiwan, also engages in the development of human capital. For instance, in 2002 it launched the Taiwan International Graduate Program to attract talented S&T students worldwide. In collaboration with seven top universities in Taiwan, qualified candidates would be enrolled in the PhD programs offered by these universities with a scholarship of NT$32,000 per month. As of 2011, 328 students coming from 33 countries were enrolled in the program, among which 136 were international students (Ministry of Education, Taiwan 2011a).

Fostering Entrepreneurial Universities: Deepening University-Industry Cooperation

Apart from the development of R&D manpower, Taiwan is also keen on fostering industry-academia cooperation. As Hu and Mathews (2007, 1017–1018) rightly note,

> While university R&D in the advanced countries plays a role of linking a country's innovation infrastructure and industrial cluster, the impact of academic R&D in the latecomer country like Taiwan is shifting from building the national innovation infrastructure (i.e., training the well-educated manpower of help targeting on high-tech industrial clusters) in the earlier years to now acting as a knowledge platform to link innovation infrastructure and industrial clusters (through technology licensing and incubator centers) beginning in the 2000s.

In Taiwan, the government is the main source of funding for R&D activities of the higher education sector, which has been consistently over 80 percent, but the share of contribution of business enterprise has increased in the past decade, from 3.2 percent in 2001 to 6.7 percent in 2010. The government's important role in financing is also shown in the area of industry-academia collaboration. As in 2010, the government provided NT$7,276 million to support industry-academia collaboration, while the nongovernment funding was about NT$4,068 million.[10]

Moreover, table 5.2 shows Taiwan's expenditure on industry-academia collaboration in the last decade, indicating the government's strong commitment to research and development. In the last decade or so, the government has also launched a number of state-led national sci-tech research projects that involve academic-industry cooperation, for example, the National Research Program for Genomic Medicine (2002), the National Program on Nano Technology (2003), the National Science and Technology Program for Telecommunications (2005), the Development Program of Industrialization for Agricultural Biotechnology (2008), the National Science and Technology Program for Biotechnology and Pharmaceuticals (2000), the National Science and Technology Center for Disaster Reduction (2003), the National Science and Technology Program—Energy (2007), the Networked Communications Program (2008), and the National Program for Intelligent Electronics (2011).[11]

In regard to academic-industry cooperation, from 2006 to 2010, the total amount of money involved in academic-industry cooperation with participating universities was NT$93.5 billion, with an annual growth rate of 17.61 percent. The annual growth rate of intellectual property revenues was 138.73 percent. Built upon these foundations, the second phase of the initiative, now renamed the Toward World Class Universities Project, was launched in 2011

Table 5.2 Taiwan's Expenditure on Industry-Academia Collaboration, 2007 and 2010 (in NT$1,000)

	Year	Government Funding	Nongovernment Funding
National higher education	2010	3,844,982	1,542,875
	2007	4,314,859	1,119,492
Private higher education	2010	1,495,248	917,834
	2007	1,100,521	531,524
National professional education	2010	1,000,744	586,770
	2007	944,272	352,543
Private professional education	2010	935,050	1,020,952
	2007	614,488	657,455
Total	2010	7,276,024	4,068,431
	2007	6,974,140	2,661,014

Source: Higher Education Evaluation and Accreditation Council of Taiwan. http://uice.heeact.edu.tw/zh-tw/2011/Page/Fund%20Comparison.

to further support the selected elite universities. With strong conviction to foster closer collaboration between the university and industry, not only has the government encouraged the establishment of adequate hardware, like incubation centers, to facilitate exchange and collaboration, but it has also provided software, like research incentives for the university's R&D personnel. For instance, the National Science and Technology Development Plan (2005–2008) suggests revising regulations to allow instructors to participate in industry-academic cooperation incentive mechanisms (National Science Council 2005, 21). Also, to train industry-needed manpower, the government suggests expanding implementation of "final mile" preemployment courses, allowing industry personnel to participate in course planning (National Science Council 2005, 22).

In 2007, the Ministry of Education passed rules that promote and govern industry-academia collaboration. The rules stipulate that the Ministry of Education would include industry-academia collaboration performance as one of the criteria for school evaluation, and that teachers and students who have performed well in the collaboration should be awarded (Ministry of Education, Taiwan 2007b). In addition, the Ministry of Education has planned to relax restrictions on professors' temporary employment in the computation of years of service. In 2007, the Minister of Education noted, "We would like to encourage the universities to put equal emphasis on education and internship, and enhance the cooperation between enterprises and schools." He added, "Besides the tasks of research and teaching, the universities should also be engaged in social service. . . . Their graduates should contribute talents and skills to industry. . . . This means that the universities should be managed with a spirit of entrepreneurship; the programs of the institutes and colleges should be designed based on the principle of pragmatism" (Ministry of Education, Taiwan 2007a).

In addition, setting up an incubation center is another common form of industry-academia collaboration in Taiwan since the government finds it hard for SMEs to establish their own research departments. Seen in this light, support from the government and academic institutions is significant and pivotal to SMEs' growth and competitiveness. In 1997, SMEA launched the Innovation Incubation Program. As of 2008, there were 104 incubation centers with more than 3,380 incubated enterprises in Taiwan; 84 of them (80.8 percent) were administrated in universities. Overall, an amount of NT$51.9 billion has been invested, and 45 incubated companies have been listed as OTC (over the counter) or on the Taiwan Stock Exchange (Ministry of Economic Affairs, Republic of China 2008). As a recent statistical study indicates, SMEs in Taiwan are deeply involved in university-industry linkages and have transformed their innovation activities from process innovation to product innovation through these linkages. The study also shows that SMEs tend to cooperate with public rather private universities, since the resource-rich former are more capable of helping SMEs in the emerging industries like biotechnology and nanotechnology (Hu and Mathews 2009). As of 2013, the top ten categories of incubation center in Taiwan are (1) IT and Electronics (distribution: 22.08 percent), (2) biotechnology (16.67 percent), (3) Machinery and Electric Machinery (10.09 percent), (4) others (9.06 percent), (5) tourism and recreation (8.91 percent), (6) education and cultural art (6.80 percent), (7) environmental protection industry (4.90 percent), (8) medical industry (4.77 percent), (9) multimedia and broadcasting (4.47 percent), and (10) livelihood industry (3.93 percent).[12]

Being strongly encouraged by the national government to foster more cooperation between the university sector and industry/business, universities have taken a more proactive approach in reaching out to industry and business in order to transform into entrepreneurial universities. For instance, the National Chiao Tung University (NCTU) is noted for its long engagement in entrepreneurial activities. Back in the 1980s, NCTU was selected by the government to oversee R&D in microelectronics and computer science to help Taiwan cultivate R&D talent. NCTU also engaged in entrepreneurial activities on its own, especially with the establishment of the Technology Licensing Office[13] and the Innovative Incubation Center.[14] Since 1997, the Incubation Center has incubated 108 companies and housed 1,200 employees of these companies, with 79 percent of them being information technology and electronics entrepreneurs.[15] The most important initiative in recent years to boost R&D and entrepreneurial activities is the Diamond Project launched in 2010, which sets as its goal the development of NCTU into the MIT of Asia.[16] The primary strategy is to provide specialized research staff with more generous job benefits and a more stable job environment. Their stable job environment is maintained by setting up permanent laboratories in cooperation with the industry. Apart from raising benefits for research staff, a scholarship called the "Wiki Partnership Fund" was established to help qualified students participate in laboratory projects.[17] Yet the greatest strength of NCTU is its historical roots in the Hsinchu Science Park. For example, in February 2012, NCTU signed a cooperative agreement with the Indian Institute of Technology Kharagpur to explore cooperation in talent nurturing and R&D activities. The Indian school cited the close ties between NCTU and the Hsinchu Science Park and the former's rich experience in commercializing academic research as one of the reasons to forge a relationship with NCTU. Apart from internship programs, the two schools aim to launch a joint PhD degree program.[18]

The National Tsing Hua University is another top university excelling in research and entrepreneurial activities. From 1999 to 2009, the number of SCI journal articles increased from 847 to 1,472, and the number of Engineering Index (EI) journal articles also increased from 317 to 1,056.[19] In 2008, it set up the Office of University-Industry Collaboration, which was later renamed as the Operations Center for Industry Collaboration, which is responsible for industry collaboration administration, innovation incubation, and intellectual property management and technology licensing.[20] Due to the achievements that since 2007 NTHU have been issued more than 20 US patents per year, the Division of Intellectual Property and Technology Licensing has been given the Outstanding Technology Licensing Center Award by the National Science Council for four consecutive years from 2007 to 2010.[21] Apart from patent acquisitions, NTHU also engaged in providing incubation services.

As of 2010, the NTHU incubation center has successfully incubated 103 companies, 49 of which were founded together by faculty staffs and students. The investment amounted to NT$3.11 billion; the cumulative sales volume is about NT$8.2 billion. To further promote academic-industry cooperation, in 2010 NTHU revised the incentive mechanism. Apart from the traditional method of granting an outstanding academic-industry cooperation award, NTHU increased the proportion of technology transfer licensing fees granted to the inventor to 70 percent. In addition, faculty staff members' achievements in patent acquisition, technology transfers, and academic-industry cooperation are included in their performance evaluations. Similarly, the National Taiwan University, the top university in Taiwan, also set up the Office of Research and Development, which comprises the Division of Industrial-Academic Cooperation and the Division of Technology Transfer. Besides this, NTU also runs the NTU Innovation Incubation Center.[22]

Discussion and Conclusion

With deepening cooperation between enterprise and universities in Taiwan, more than 22 enterprises recruited employees from National Taiwan University during the 2010–2012 period. Examples include HSBC Holdings plc (a British multinational banking and financial services company); Cosmos Bank (the oldest urban cooperative bank in India); Proctor & Gamble (an American multinational consumer goods company); Macquarie Capital Securities (a global investment banking and diversified financial services group, founded in Australia); Morgan Stanley Private Wealth Management (an American multinational financial services corporation); Wan Hai Lines (a Taiwan shipping company); Lung Yen Group (a Taiwan undertaking company); Unilever (a British-Dutch multinational consumer goods company); Standard Chartered plc (a British multinational banking and financial services company); Janssen Pharmaceutica (a pharmaceutical company established in Belgium); Deloitte Touche Tohmatsu Ltd. (a professional services firms, founded in London); SAS (an American-founded private software company); DBS Bank (a Singapore-based bank); and the L'Oréal Group (the world's largest cosmetics and beauty company, found in France). In addition, TSMC (the world's first semiconductor foundry, founded in Taiwan), the French Trade Commission, and CLEVO (Taiwan computer manufacturer) offer practical training for students.[23]

In order to offer better job opportunities for university graduates, the Taiwan government is actively promoting entrepreneurship education. Currently, entrepreneurship education programs offered in universities in Taiwan are mostly combined with the existing resources of the university, and they are generally the most valued area of the university. For example, Donghua University, the National Taiwan University, Zhongshan University, and Southern Taiwan University are planning more professional courses in the universities' important areas. Yuan Ze University places much emphasis on entrepreneurship courses, and Union University has courses that emphasize entrepreneurship as part of business management and financial planning. This shows that different universities have different entrepreneurship education programs and focus on different subjects. Donghua University has 48 different entrepreneurship programs while Yuan Ze University has 9. Most universities believe that legal courses should also be included in the program planning, for example commercial law, patents, property rights, and other law-related courses. Moreover, Donghua University adds many economic-related subjects into the program planning, such as the basis of economics, the economic life of the commercial economy, and Taiwan's economic development. The Global Institute of Technology adds team management skills, interpersonal skills, communication skills, and other practical applications courses into the program planning. As we can see, different universities add different course as they need.[24] To cope with the consequences of an oversupply of graduates resulting from the massification of higher education, this chapter critically reviews how the Taiwan government has adopted different means to strengthen university-enterprise cooperation, reforming its curriculum in offering more work-related and work-relevant education experiences to students. How far these reform measures will really enhance the innovation of the country and the global competitiveness of university students in the island state is still open for further discussion and evaluation in the future.

Chapter 6

Asserting Its Global Influence:
The Quest for Innovation and Entrepreneurial Universities in Singapore

Introduction

Singapore's successful industrialization has always been attributed to its effective industrial policy to attain a desirable macroeconomic environment for industrial development (Goh 2005; Hu and Mathews 2005). Since independence, in face of a scarcity of natural resources, Singapore directed its industrial policies toward employment creation, using favorable incentives to attract foreign direct investment and multinational companies (MNCs) to increase productive capacity. Gradually, a vibrant manufacturing sector was formed and dominated the economy. Unlike other "Asian Miracles," Singapore primarily relied upon MNCs to produce the knowledge spillovers and technology transfers necessary to develop its national technological capability rather than indigenous R&D. For example, the initial intention of the government to establish a Singapore Science Park was to attract foreign direct investment (FDI) and MNCs. The 1997/98 Asian financial crisis and the 2008/09 global economic crisis led to the Singaporean government's realization that overreliance on FDI and MNCs had constrained the country's ability to resist external economic crises as global competition intensifies, and thus has recognized the importance of diversifying its national investment (Goh 2005). Establishing a dynamic innovation hub that supports high-tech manufacturing and R&D has become a national development agenda in Singapore. This chapter critically examines how the Singapore government has attempted to transform its higher education sector to make it more entrepreneurial while adopting different measures to promote innovation by encouraging more university-enterprise cooperation.

Promotion of Innovation

In 1989, the Singapore government created the first Small and Medium-Sized Enterprise (SME) Master Plan to introduce measures and assistant schemes for SME development and to improve entrepreneurial infrastructure. Moreover, the entrepreneurial mind-set was introduced in civil services through the Public Service for the 21st Century in 1995, a deliberate exercise aimed at nurturing an entrepreneurial attitude of excellence and fostering an entrepreneurship-friendly environment in the public service. In 2000, the Enterprise Challenge (a branch under the Prime Minister's Office) even set up an S$10 million fund to sponsor innovative projects which may improve the provision of public service. Hit by the 1997/98 Asian financial crisis, the government released the Second Master Plan (SME21) in 2001, calling for urgency to inspire entrepreneurship yet again in Singapore. Meanwhile, it also actively promoted spending in the private sector through various incentives. To maintain its attractiveness as a place for businesses of the future, in recent years Singapore has gradually switched its developmental focus from a large manufacturing base for MNCs to a dynamic innovation hub that supports high-tech manufacturing and R&D.

Back in the 1990s, Singapore had already realized that it was overdependent on foreign MNCs for technological upgrading and its indigenous technology development was weak. Therefore the government planned to increase R&D investment in the coming years, targeting primarily long-term strategic research (Koh 2006). In 1991, it launched the first five-year National S&T Plan (1991–1995). Under the plan, the government would invest a total of S$2 billion to develop key resources in technology, manpower, and skills to meet the needs of industry. During the plan, the National Science and Technology Board (NSTB) was assigned to develop new research institutes for a number of identified key research areas, including biotechnology, food and agrotechnology, information technology and telecommunications, microelectronics and semiconductors.

In the second plan (1996–2000), the government envisioned "an innovative and enterprising society that embraces science and technology to develop a thriving knowledge economy and good quality of life," and therefore shifted its developmental strategy to domestic capacities in applied and basic scientific researches. In order to meet the world-class science and technological capacities, it had been set that by the end of this period, government's R&D expenditure should reach 2.6 percent and the research talent pool should be strengthened to achieve the level of 65 research scientists per 10,000 workers. These targets were achieved two years ahead of time with S$4 billion of investment funding. A number of new policy initiatives promoting technology entrepreneurship were also released at the same time in order to firm up coordination between scientific infrastructure and industrial capacity. In 1997, an interagency team comprising representatives from the NSTB, the Economic Development Board, and the Singapore Productivity and Standards Board was formed to conduct an extensive discussion on strategies for innovation in consultation with various industrial departments. Subsequently, a National Innovation Framework for Action (NIFA) was drafted the following year to identify critical success factors for innovation to flourish, and to advise the government accordingly. The eight critical success factors include education and training, government policies, government support, information, infrastructure, technology, the market, and human resources.

In the first two S&T National Plans, the government started to realize that it should work more efficiently with private companies in exploiting technological innovation by facilitating them to develop their innovation capacities. In this regard, a number of financial assistances and tax incentive programs were therefore designed to promote innovation, especially among SMEs. For example, it extends the pioneer or postpioneer status for SMEs who undertake approved R&D activities with a concessionary tax rate, provides more liberalized double deductions for R&D expenses, permits an investment allowance for all capital expenditures incurred for approved R&D activities, and allows for a tax-exempted R&D reserves for companies. Major financial schemes that aim at promoting technology commercialization include the Research Incentive Scheme for Companies, the Research and Development Assistance Scheme, and the Patent Application Fund.[1]

The Third S&T National Plan (2001–2005) marked another phase of R&D in Singapore as it emphasized the crucial role of research institutions and universities in undertaking research in several strategic areas with medium- to long-run relevance. Half of the S$7 billion budget was channeled into technology development and R&D experiments, while 30 percent was used to encourage corporate labs to set up research centers in Singapore. The remainder has been pumped into broad-based manpower development, which includes fellowship training programs and postgraduate scholarships. In addition, the fourth S&T National Plan from 2006 to 2010 was intended to strengthen the support to SMEs, promote technology transfer and intellectual property management, and create incentives that could attract international talent to Singapore.

In Singapore, the private sector is the main driver of R&D activities, as it is the biggest spender of R&D monies and the largest employer of R&D manpower. Nevertheless, the government remains the most influential strategic planner. Since the 2000s, Singapore has put more effort into building the hardware and software of Singapore's national innovation system, as well as reorganizing the governance of R&D activities to strive for higher efficiency. For hardware research infrastructure, in 2000 the government announced a devolvement fund of S$15 billion to establish a new science park targeting biosciences and information technology as new growth engines of Singapore's economy. This so-called One-North Project was modeled after Silicon Valley to create a multifaceted high-tech research community. With a focus on knowledge-intensive activities in critical growth sectors, it would provide an intellectually stimulating and creative physical environment for entrepreneurs and researchers to congregate and exchange ideas. Focusing on the full range of production activities, it includes not only research institutes and business offices, but also residential properties, shopping, public parks, and other facilities.

Like many other science parks around the world, the new science parks are located adjacent to several universities: the National University of Singapore, the Institute of Technical Education, Singapore Polytechnic, and the National University Hospital. Developed by JTC at a cost of S$500 million, the first phase of Biopolis, a custom-built biomedical R&D hub at One-North, comprises a seven-building complex and five biomedical sciences subresearch institutes, which are home to 2,000 scientists. A total of four phases were finished by 2010. Another milestone in One-North development, the Fusionopolis, is an R&D center for electronics and information technology launched in 2003. Fusionopolis's research teams will be formed by scientists from multiple disciplines, including materials science and engineering, data storage, microelectronics, manufacturing technology, high-performance computing, and information and communications. Companies in Fusionopolis could colocate and engage in R&D collaboration with the Science and Engineering Research Council, making Fusionopolis an icon for public-private joint R&D in the physical sciences and engineering. The efforts being put together by the Singapore government have paid off since the global ranking of the city-state in the area of innovation has improved in recent years.

For strengthening in software, Singapore has long been very keen to nurture local talent and attract foreign talent. Like its counterparts in South Korea, Taiwan, and Hong Kong, Singapore's universities are keen to nurture S&T students. Apart from the Singapore Management University, which is more specialized in business administration, the National University of Singapore had about half of its students enrolled in S&T disciplines. The ratio was even higher for the Nanyang Technological University where more than 60 percent of students studied S&T subjects.[2]

To attract talents, one of Singapore's main strategies is to offer strong incentives to talents engaging in S&T studies and R&D activities. Many scholarships are conducted by A*STAR alone, but some are collaborative initiatives with universities. For instance, in 2007, A*STAR collaborated with NTU and NUS to launch the Singapore International Graduate Award (SINGA) program to attract international students to come to Singapore to pursue PhD studies in S&T.[3] In particular, SINGA aims to target potential students from nontraditional source countries, such as Eastern Europe, Russia, and the Middle East, in order to diversify and expand the talent pool for Singapore

(Nanyang Technological University 2008, 34). In fact, Singapore's search for S&T talent begins at a very young age. For example, the A*GA's Youth Science Program, which is hosted by A*STAR and is in closer partnership with the Ministry of Education and the Singapore Science Centre, aims to target students in primary schools, secondary schools, and junior colleges. A number of exhibitions, seminars, and S&T competitions are organized throughout the year to heighten recognition and arouse the interests of students in science and innovation.[4]

In fact, besides individual talents, the dynamism of SMEs can also be regarded as an important part of the fabric of a successful national innovation system. To encourage younger entrepreneurs and their business start-ups to innovate, the Standards, Productivity and Innovation Board (SPRING Singapore) has offered a number of Innovation and Entrepreneurship Supporting Schemes to start-up entrepreneurs, angel investors, as well as schools and students (see table 6.1). As monetary incentives are important to induce companies and entrepreneurs to innovate, apart from providing seed funding, the government also created an innovation incentive in the tax system. In 2010, the Singapore government announced in the annual budget the creation of the Productivity and Innovation Credit (PIC) to offer tax benefits to companies engaging in six kinds of innovation-related activities—acquisition or leasing of PIC automation equipment; training of employees; acquisition of intellectual property rights; registration of patents, trademarks, designs, and plant varieties; research and development activities; and investment in approved design projects. In particular, companies would receive up to a 400 percent tax deduction and other benefits from investments in employee training.[5] Apart from financial support, the government also offered support to help companies build up their own networks. For instance, in 2002, the Economic Development Board created the "Hub of Technopreneurs" (HOTSpots), a business network that links together technopreneur development centers and technology start-ups and companies in Singapore, which hopes to make the innovation market more dynamic and interactive (Singapore Economic Development Board 2003, 92).

With regard to R&D governance, in Singapore, R&D and industrial policies were organized and led mainly by two governmental agencies—the Ministry of Trade and Industry (MTI) and the Ministry of Education (MOE). MTI is responsible for driving mission-oriented R&D by coordinating efforts of its key agencies, the Economic Development Board (EDB); the Agency for Science, Technology and Research (A*STAR); and the Standards, Productivity and Innovation Board (SPRING Singapore); MOE is accountable for supervising academic S&T research. In order to better coordinate R&D activities nationwide, in 2006 the government set up the National Research Foundation to provide secretariat support to the Research, Innovation and Enterprise Council (RIEC), which is chaired by the prime minister, to develop a national

Table 6.1 SPRING Singapore's Innovation and Entrepreneurship Supporting Schemes

Schemes	Supporting Measures
For Start-up	
Biomedical Sciences Accelerator (BSA)	As part of the Research, Innovation and Enterprise (RIE) 2015 Plan, the government has approved the establishment of sector specific accelerators (SSA) to identify, invest, and grow start-ups in strategic but nascent sectors, starting with the biomedical science sector. Nascent sectors are characterized by few local enterprises, a limited pool of domain experts, and an absence of early-stage investors. While these sectors received significant R&D funds, there are insufficient enterprises to commercialize the intellectual property resulting from the R&D; hence the economic benefits are not realized. The SSA approach was deemed an effective way to address the identified issues. S$40 million has been set aside to pilot the SSA initiative via the Biomedical Science Accelerator (BSA) with an initial focus on the medical technology (MedTech) subsector. Two BSA operators have been appointed. SPRING SEEDS Capital (SSC), the manager of the BSA program, will co-invest in the start-ups identified by the BSA operators on a 1:1 basis. The two BSA operators are Clearbridge BSA Pte. Ltd. and Singapore Medtech Accelerator Pte. Ltd.
Business Angel Scheme (BAS)	In encouraging experienced angel investing, SPRING SEEDS Capital works closely with preapproved private business angel investors to co-invest and nurture growth-oriented, innovative start-ups. Similar to the Start-up Enterprise Development Scheme (SEEDS), this is an equity-based co-financing option for Singapore-based early-stage companies.
SPRING Start-up Enterprise Development Scheme (SPRING SEEDS)	This is an equity-based co-financing option for Singapore-based start-ups with innovative products and/or processes with intellectual content and strong growth potential across international markets.
Technology Enterprise Commercialization Scheme (TECS)	The purpose is to catalyze the formation and growth of such start-ups based on strong technological Intellectual property and a scalable business model. The TECS is a competitive grant in which proposals are ranked based on the evaluation of both technical and commercial merits by a team of reviewers, and the best are funded.
Work Pass for Foreign Entrepreneur (EntrePass)	The EntrePass is for non-Singaporean entrepreneurs who are ready to start and operate a business in Singapore.

Continued

Table 6.1 Continued

Schemes	Supporting Measures
For Start-up Partners	
Angel Investors Tax Deduction Scheme (AITD)	The Angel Investors Tax Deduction Scheme is a tax incentive that aims to stimulate business angel investments in Singapore-based start-ups and encourage more angel investors to add value to these start-ups. The scheme applies to an approved angel investor who commits a minimum of S$100,000 of qualifying investment in a qualifying start-up. An approved angel can enjoy a tax deduction, equal to 50 percent of his investment amount, at the end of a two-year holding period. The tax deduction will be subject to a cap of S$250,000 in each year of assessment (YA) and will be offset against total taxable income.
Incubator Development Programme (IDP)	The $30 million Incubator Development Programme (IDP) provides incubators and venture accelerators with a grant to enhance capability development programs for innovative start-ups. IDP provides up to 70 percent grant support to incubators and venture accelerators in areas such as programs to nurture start-ups, mentoring start-ups, and operating expenses.
Young Entrepreneurs Scheme for Schools (YES! Schools)	YES! Schools provides schools with grants of up to S$100,000 to put in place a comprehensive structured entrepreneurship learning program for their students.

Source: SPRING Singapore, Entrepreneurship, http://www.spring.gov.sg/Entrepreneurship/FS/Pages/work-pass-for-foreign-entrepreneurs.aspx.

R&D plan, coordinate research activities of different government agencies, and manage R&D funding allocation.[6] The NRF has adopted both a top-down and a bottom-up approach to boost R&D activities. In the top-down approach, since its inception the NRF has identified several strategic research programs which are essential to Singapore's economic development and meeting national challenges. Those programs include biomedical sciences, environment and water technologies, interactive and digital media, and marine and offshore research. Different from the top-down approach where the government plays the dominant role, the bottom-up approach aims to offer money incentives, provide infrastructure, and launch supporting programs to engage with other R&D stakeholders.

The setting up of the Competitive Research Program (CRP) Funding Scheme provides opportunities for public and private organizations to bid for financial support. In terms of infrastructure, the Campus for Research Excellence and Technological Enterprise (CREATE) was established. CREATE is a research and innovation campus located at the National University of Singapore, which houses research centers set up by top foreign universities and corporate labs, technology incubators, and start-up companies. In addition, the NRF also set up five Research Centers of Excellence at university campuses. The five centers, namely the Centre for Quantum Technologies (CQT), Cancer Science Institute Singapore (CSI), the Earth Observatory of Singapore (EOS), the Mechano-Biology Institute (MBI), and the Singapore Centre on Environmental Life Sciences Engineering (SCELSE), are expected to achieve international recognition within a decade. In terms of supporting programs, the NRF set up the National Framework for Innovation and Enterprise (NFIE), under which a whole series of initiatives were launched to establish support for academic entrepreneurship in universities, create enterprise support structures, enhance technology transfer, and support innovation policy studies.[7]

In addition to the direct funding of research and innovation activities, the Singapore government also supports these activities through its tax system. The government introduced its Productivity and Innovation Credit (PIC) in its 2010 budget and enhanced the credit in its 2011 and 2012 budgets, providing tax benefits for investments by businesses in a broad range of activities along the innovation value chain. The six activities that qualify for PIC benefits are the

- acquisition or leasing of specific automation equipment;
- training of employees;
- acquisition of intellectual property rights;
- registration of patents, trademarks, designs, and plant varieties;
- research and development activities; and
- investment in approved design projects.

From 2011 to 2015, all businesses can enjoy deductions/allowances at 400 percent up to S$400,000 of their expenditures per year on each of the six qualifying activities. For research and development, eligible expenditures include costs incurred on staff and consumables for qualifying activities carried out in Singapore. This includes expenditures on research contracted to universities, and for research performed in Singapore the balance of qualifying expenditures exceeding the cap receives a deduction of 150 percent.[8] The tax exemption measures adopted by the Singapore government would definitely encourage more enterprises to invest in research and development to promote innovation and entrepreneurship in the city-state.

Higher Education Development

Singapore has the smallest number of universities among the Four Little Dragons. Originally with only two universities until the 1990s, Singapore has been committed to expanding the higher education sector since the 2000s, first with the establishment of a new university and then second with the plan of bringing in more foreign universities. As a small city-state with a small endowment of natural resources, Singapore faces immense pressure in tackling challenges posed by globalization and the knowledge economy. Since the 1990s, it has developed its higher education as a globally tradable export service, with the ambition to forge itself as a regional hub of education which could also contribute to its economic growth. Accordingly, the Ministry of Education not only created the third national university, Singapore Management University (SMU) in 2000 with a new and innovative governance and funding styles, but also corporatized the two existing public universities, the National University of Singapore (NUS) and the Nanyang Technology University (NTU), as not-for-profit companies in 2005 to make their governance more autonomous. Incorporation of public universities makes them more self-conscious and accountable for their operation, and thus enhances competition among these three universities, not only on educational quality but also on recruitment of local and international students and faculties.

In regard to bringing in foreign HEIs, in 2002 the government launched the Global Schoolhouse program to develop Singapore as a higher education hub in Asia. The goals of the program are twofold: first, to attract leading higher education institutions in the world to establish branch campuses in Singapore, and second, through bringing in leading universities to Singapore, the Global Schoolhouse program aims to attract more foreign students. In 2002, there were less than 50,000 foreigners studying full time in Singapore. In 2005, the number had increased to about 70,000, and it was expected that there would be 150,000 foreign students by 2015 (Singapore Economic Development Board 2006, 83).

Since the inception of the program, a number of leading world-class universities have set up branch campuses or joint teaching or research programs in Singapore, such as Stanford University, Massachusetts Institute of Technology, Johns Hopkins University, the University of Pennsylvania's Wharton School, the University of Chicago's Graduate School of Business, Georgia Institute of Technology, INSEAD, the Technical University of Eindhoven, the Technical University of Munich, Shanghai Jiao Tong University, and New York University's Tisch School of the Arts. However, not all institutions are successful in their moves to Singapore. For instance, in 2004, the University of New South Wales was invited by the Singapore Economic Development Board to set up the first comprehensive private university in Singapore to offer bachelor to PhD programs in a wide range of disciplines. It was expected that the campus would attract 15,000 students, 70 percent of whom would be foreign students (Singapore Economic Development Board 2004, 40). The campus officially opened in January 2007 but was shortly closed in June due to unsatisfactory student admissions numbers. The university's original target was to enroll 300 students in the first semester, but it could only admit 148 students, 100 of whom were Singaporeans. The university estimated that this situation would lead to a potential financial shortfall of S$15 million per year and therefore decided to close down the S$22 million Singapore campus immediately (Forss 2007).[9] Another failing case was the University of Warwick, which turned down the Singapore government's invitation to build a Singapore campus in fear of lack of academic freedom and financial risk (Burke 2005).[10]

But these failures did not stop Singapore from continuing the strategy of building a global schoolhouse. In recent years, the Singapore Ministry of Education has partnered with foreign universities to set up new institutions, such as the Singapore Institute of Technology (in 2009), the Singapore University of Technology and Design (in 2009), and the Yale-NUS Liberal Arts College (expected in 2013), to meet the rising higher education demands.[11] At the same time, the government keeps investing in public higher education. In 2011, Prime Minister Lee Hsien Loong said in the National Day Rally, the annual national address to the Singaporean people, that for Singapore's economy to get more mature, the university sector had to be expanded.[12] Then the Singapore government set up the Committee on University Expansion Pathways beyond 2015 (CUEP) to investigate ways to raise the publicly funded cohort participation rate (CPR) of 26 percent to 30 percent by 2015. In fact, since the turn of the twenty-first century, Singapore has already recognized the need to expand, diversify, and internationalize the university sector.

Recent R&D Performances of Top Universities in Singapore

Singapore's higher education sector has continued to perform in terms of applying and acquiring patents and generating S&T revenue from licensing and commercialization over the past decade. The fact is that the three universities—the National University of Singapore, Nanyang Technological University, and the Singapore Management University—have done much to advance R&D and entrepreneurial activities.

National University of Singapore

The National University of Singapore (NUS) is the oldest and most well-established public university in Singapore, which leads in teaching and research but also aims to become an entrepreneurial university. A university-level cluster called the NUS Enterprise (ETP) was formed to achieve this goal.[13] There are seven pillars of NUS ETP, which are NUS Overseas Colleges, NUS Industry Liaison Office, the NUS Entrepreneurship Centre, NUS Extension (which provides continuing education to adults), NUS Press, NUS Technology Holdings, and a partnering venture capital fund. Particularly related to innovation promotion, entrepreneurship cultivation, and research commercialization within NUS are the NUS Overseas Colleges, NUS Industry Liaison Office, NUS Entrepreneurship Centre, and NUS Technology Holdings.

NUS Overseas Colleges offer a full-year internship program to undergraduates and a short program to both undergraduates and graduate students. The two programs provide internship opportunities in overseas universities and companies and venture capital firms in countries such as the United States, China, India, Sweden, and Israel. In addition, the Innovative Local Enterprise Achievement Development (iLEAD) program is offered to undergraduates who are interested in local start-up companies.[14] The NUS Industry Liaison Office was set up in 1992 to forge research ties among the university, industry, government, and other research institutions, and to manage technology licensing and the creation of spin-off companies.[15] Recently, it created the online "Research to Market (R2M) Platform" to foster a more accessible exchange among different stakeholders.[16] And the NUS Technology Holdings Pte. Ltd. aims to help new technology companies to commercialize university research.[17]

The NUS Entrepreneurship Centre (NEC) has a longer history in NUS. It was established in 1988 in a different organizational form as the Centre for Management of Innovation and Technopreneurship.[18] NEC is responsible for entrepreneurship and innovation research; experiential education (mainly offering technopreneurship courses to the NUS community, including students, staff, and CEOs of NUS start-ups); and entrepreneurship development (mainly organizing events, such as business plan competitions, entrepreneurship summits, and venturing forums). In addition, NEC also hosts the NUS Enterprise Incubator (NEI) to provide services (e.g., training workshops, venture capital matching, business networking); infrastructure support (e.g., physical facilities); and seeding funding to NUS start-ups.

According to the February 2013 Research Highlight of the Month, the Department of Bioengineering at the National University of Singapore demonstrated greater Photodynamic Therapy (PDT) efficacy with the dual photosensitizer approach compared to single ones as revealed by enhanced singlet oxygen generation and reduced viability in PDT-treated cells. In vivo studies also showed tumor growth inhibition in PDT-treated mice by direct injection of UCNs into melanoma tumors or intravenously injecting tumor-targeting-agent conjugated UCNs into tumor-bearing mice. Believed to be the first demonstration of the photosensitizer loaded UCN as an in vivo targeted PDT agent, this may serve as a platform for future noninvasive deep cancer therapy.[19]

Nanyang Technological University

While NUS is a comprehensive university, another public university, Nanyang Technological University (NTU), which was established in 1991, is a specialized S&T research university. In NTU, there are three key innovation and entrepreneurship-related units. In 2000, NTU set up the Nanyang Innovation and Enterprise Office to conduct commercialization of NTU research and intellectual property.[20] In 2001, NTU collaborated with Singapore's Economic Development Board to set up the Nanyang Technopreneurship Center.[21] NTU Ventures Pte. Ltd., the commercial arm of NTU, was also established to facilitate NTU staff and students on matters of incubation and setting up start-up companies.[22] In 2008, NTU Ventures Pte. Ltd. launched an incubation scheme to support and encourage the establishment of NTU start-up and spin-off companies.

NTU has had notable R&D achievements in the past decade or so. In 1995, NTU had 11 patents filed and 5 patents granted. In 2009, 119 patents were filed and 36 were granted. From 1995 to 2009, 44 spin-off companies were created (Nanyang Technological University 2009b, 82). From 2006 to 2009, the total research revenue of NTU increased from S$107.0 million to S$171.4 million. In particular the share of research revenue from industries and other R&D projects have increased from 3.2 percent to 13.0 percent (Nanyang Technological University 2009a, 68). For instance, in 2007, NTU received a S$9 million investment from Advanced RFIC Pte. Ltd. in a collaborative R&D project in radio frequency integrated circuit (RFIC) technology. The investment was used for the construction of a new laboratory and for scholarships for 30 postgraduate students.

In recent years, NTU has conducted a number of collaborative arrangements in teaching and research with different industry partners within and beyond Singapore (such as the Bosch Group, Rolls Royce, European Aeronautic Defence and Space Company, Regency Steel Asia Pte. Ltd., and the United States Air Force Academy) (NTU Annual Report 2008, 36). Also, in partnering with the Confederation of Indian Industry, an Indian business body, the NTU Business School tailor-made executive programs for the corporate sector of India (Nanyang Technological University 2007). In addition, NTU's collaborations with local public institutions also reveal the important role of universities in serving the country's development agenda. For instance, in 2009, NTU collaborated with the Infocomm Development Authority to set up a new talent program to nurture info-communications professionals. Students from the School of Computer Engineering participated in the industrial attachments, mentorships, and academic projects offered by the program (Nanyang Technological University 2009a, 39).

NTU has also put efforts into fostering entrepreneurial education. In 2002, the Masters of Science in Technopreneurship and Innovation Program was launched. According to NTU's estimates, for the 2008 cohort, 51 percent of them joined SMEs after graduation, and 27 percent started their own businesses. Also, recently a new track in innovation and technopreneurship was introduced in the applied physics program (Nanyang Technological University 2008, 38). In 2009, NTU launched a "PhD Entrepreneur-in-Training" (PET) program to cultivate postdoctoral students with a market sense. The students would receive training in market feasibility studies and are supported and more importantly funded to develop business plans to commercialize their research into technological products (NTU Annual Report 2010, 23). To promote entrepreneurial education, NTU is active in joining hands with foreign partners. For example, in 2008, NTU became a Kauffman campus in forging a partnership with the Ewing Marion Kauffman Foundation in the United States, which is a foundation devoted to entrepreneurship education (Nanyang Technological University 2009a, 10). The Kauffman Global Scholars Program, co-organized by the Kauffman foundation and NTU, offers exchange opportunities to S&T students in NTU and those in America.

According to the most recent research report (2010/11) of Nanyang Technological University, the university president, Professor Bertil Anderson, received the prestigious Wilhelm Exner Medal in November 2010; Assistant Professor Tan Nguan Soon won the TI Food and Nutrition Publication Prize in 2010; Assistant Professor Brendan Orner and his research team made significant findings about the protein architecture of ferritin; Dr. Adrian Yeo won the Watermark Award in 2010; Business School student Christopher Ngoi won the inaugural Global Climate Solution Award; and the eco-car invented by the university broke the green milestone in fuel efficiency. Moreover, Nanyang Technological University (NTU) and the National Healthcare Group (NHG) collaborated to set up the NTU-NHG Innovation Seed Grant, and 10 medical innovation projects were supported by a fund of $500,000. Nanyang Technological University and Geneva-based International Air Transport Association (IATA) collaborated to develop training programs to upgrade human capital for the global aviation industry.[23]

Singapore Management University

The younger Singapore Management University (SMU) also developed similar agencies to promote technology transfer and to foster entrepreneurship education and culture within the campus. In 2005, SMU established the UOB-SMU Entrepreneurship Alliance (USEA) Centre with the United Overseas Bank Ltd. (UOB). As of 2010, it has collaborated with about 200 SMEs to promote entrepreneurial management and offer enterprise consulting (Singapore Management University 2010, 21).

In 2009, SMU established the Institute of Innovation and Entrepreneurship (IIE) with a so-called SMU Plus Strategy to reach out to the entrepreneurial community beyond the SMU campus by organizing university-industry collaborative activities through the IP Management Office, joint R&D programs, and networks with SMEs, large enterprises, business mentors, serial entrepreneurs, and angel investors. The services of incubation and seed fund-raising are also offered to start-ups.[24] In addition, there are promotional and training programs for SMU stakeholders interested in innovation and entrepreneurial activities. Under the SMU Plus Strategy, IIE also claims to pioneer the concept of "entrepreneurship," which encourages entrepreneurs-in-residence to co-found businesses with students.

In terms of curriculum, SMU intends to imbue students with entrepreneurship education. An entrepreneurship major was introduced in the Lee Kong Chian School of Business, and a technopreneurship track under the advanced business technology major was added in the School of Information Systems (Singapore Management University 2009). A SAS Enterprise Intelligence Laboratory was set up in 2008. The university attaches importance to innovation and entrepreneurship. It hosts 14 competencies plus real-world test beds related to innovation and entrepreneurship, and there are also an Institute of Innovation and Entrepreneurship and a UOB-SMU Entrepreneurship Alliance Centre in the university.[25] In 2012, SMU launched a new postgraduate degree program, the master of innovation, under the Lee Kong Chian School of Business, which not only targets fresh bachelor degree graduates but also, more importantly, working professionals in private industry.

Our above discussion clearly suggests that universities in Singapore have responded positively to working with enterprise, especially when they see the benefits and mutual advantages that strong linkages being built between the university sector and the business/industry could offer. After engaging in innovation promotion over the last two decades, Singapore has obtained promising results in terms of patents and revenue generation by participating in knowledge transfer activities. By 2012, Singapore was home to over 100 global biomedical science companies, including many leading multinational corporations. This led to a proposal that the Science Council should be replaced by a National Science and Technology Board (NSTB). As a result, the NSTB began operation in January 1991 and fell under the auspices of the Ministry for Trade and Industry. The board prepared Singapore's first five-year National Technology Plan, with a budget of S$2 billion, to set the direction for the development of science and technology in Singapore. The plan emphasized the need for research that would contribute to national competitiveness, that government must work in close collaboration with industry, and that government's research institutes must support and complement industry's efforts in working toward a common end. These themes are apparent in all subsequent plans. In January 2002, the NSTB became the Agency for Science, Technology and Research (A*STAR) and was given the primary mission of raising the level of science and technology in Singapore so as to develop and attract higher-value knowledge-based industries. The most recent five-year plan invests S$16.1 billion from 2011 to 2015 (a 20 percent increase over the amount invested from 2006 to 2010) and has six main thrusts:

1. Continued support for basic research,
2. A continued focus on talent attraction and development,
3. More emphasis on competitive funding,

4. The fostering of increased private-public sector collaboration,
5. A stronger focus on economic outcomes, and
6. Strengthened support for commercialization activities.

Discussion and Conclusion

Facing the growing challenges of globalization, the Singapore government has tried to further diversify its higher education system by promoting vocational and technical education. Realizing the important role of vocational and technical education in nation building, the overall development strategy is to closely integrate vocational and technical education in Singapore with the market, adjusting vocational training courses according to the changing industrial structure, and developing and managing vocational and technical education programs in response to the needs of industry and the call for technological advancement. Surveys show that graduate employment rates of vocational and technical education are getting close to full employment, while employers are satisfied with the performance of the majority of these graduates. More importantly, international research also reports that the vocational and technical education programs offered by Singapore command very high standards internationally.

With a strong urge to further enhance the city-state's leading role in innovation and technology, the Singapore government has not only adopted the measures discussed above to promote technological advancement and innovation promotion but has also invested more in vocational and technical education by further differentiating the roles of different higher education institutions. Paying more attention to learning from successful international career and technical education, the Singapore government is very keen to establish/promote vocational and technical education. For example, the government attempts to model after the German "grammar+career" two-track system of education by adopting an "education factory" philosophy. Following this pathway, the Singapore government hopes that the "education factory" philosophy will bring the actual factory environment into the teaching and learning environment by creating a more work-related environment to enhance experiential learning for students. As if students were learning in various departments of a large enterprise, complete effective theoretical knowledge education and practical skills training would be integrated for helping students to apply theories into practice. More importantly, students would have the opportunity to join hands with their teachers to participate in the pilot scheme offered by the manufacturer or product developer. From design, testing, and assembly to finished products, teachers and students could work together for enhancing the professional standard.

Managing vocational and technical education in line with the "education factory" conceptualization, Singapore's universities and enterprises have established a closer relationship through this training mode. In the near future, we expect that Singapore's vocational and technical education will be more closely linked with hundreds of large and medium university-business-industry partnerships. Currently, Singapore's universities cooperate closely with over 1,000 enterprises inside and outside of Singapore, especially with internationally renowned enterprises and large companies, forming an operation mechanism of production, learning, and research.

There are many factors that account for this success. One of the most important is that the government attaches great importance to the development of human resources in technical and vocational education. Teachers of vocational and technical education must have at least five years of working experience in enterprise and go to enterprises to receive training on a regular basis. Teachers are also encouraged to study overseas.[26]

With strong government support and clear strategic directions guided by the government, the industry-business-university relationship will inevitably be bridged and strengthened. Most interesting of all, the present chapter has clearly demonstrated the important and strategic role that the government can play in promoting industry-business-university cooperation in stadium-sized enterprises, creating special platforms for student learning and practices. The proactive role of the state in transforming the university sector and promoting entrepreneurship in Singapore definitely sets a model for other countries/societies to draw lessons for policy transfer.

Chapter 7

Promoting Entrepreneurship and Innovation:
Enhancing Research and Reforming University Curriculum in China

Introduction

Consisting of 28 provinces and three special administrative regions that present considerable diversity in resource endowment as well as policy preferences, China can be seen as a large national innovation system (NIS) with the integration of numerous regional innovation systems (RISs). While NIS is important in the context of China's highly centralized authoritarian regime which set the basic parameters and guidelines for regional diversification, it might be profitable to also take the RIS seriously, since it comprises distinguishable private and public actors in the market interacting to create local arrangements and promote indigenous innovations (Hu and Mathews 2005). This chapter sets out against the context in which the Chinese government has called for advancement of technology and promotion of innovation and entrepreneurialism in higher education with a strong conviction to transform the country from a "world factory" which primarily depends on manufacturing to drive economic growth to a culturally strong, technologically advanced and innovative country, and examines the major strategies adopted by the Chinese government to achieve these goals. The first part of the chapter provides the historical and policy context for promoting entrepreneurship and innovation in China. The second part focuses on how research has been enhanced through various state-driven initiatives to transform Chinese universities into world-class universities with strong research capacity. The last part of the chapter discusses how university curriculum is being transformed to promote entrepreneurial education in China.

Historical and Policy Context for Promotion of Entrepreneurship and Innovation

Soon after the establishment of the People's Republic of China in 1949, the Chinese government adopted the Soviet Union's model of science and technology development that aims to build an NIS composed of both comprehensive and specialized universities and a pervasive network of public research institutes under the governance of a central agency (1950s–1970s) (Segal 2003). According to this design, public research institutes were given the duty of scientific research, while universities were designated with the pedagogical function of S&T with limited involvement in R&D. One of the typical examples concerned is the China Academy of Science (CAS). Founded in 1949 in Beijing, it has expanded steadily across the country by establishing directly controlled institutes and supportive organizations, and has become the nation's highest academic institution of natural science and high technology.[1]

Since the recovery from the Cultural Revolution (1966–1976) and the launch of economic reforms in the late 1970s, the Chinese NIS has been undergoing dramatic reforms through a process of decentralizing the central government's power. In line with the orientation of building a strong internal market in the early stage of economic reforms, the government pressured foreign-invested enterprises to conduct technologically advanced research in China, meanwhile encouraging domestic enterprises to improve their research capacity through active absorption of the imported technology (Hu and Mathews 2008). As a latecomer to the international S&T market, China has enjoyed the advantage of cheap costs at S&T imitations and quickly utilized them to boost economic growth. Yet similar to most East Asian Tiger economies – Taiwan, South Korea, Singapore, and Malaysia – which adopted the same approach earlier, diminishing benefits from S&T imitation would eventually force China to focus on self-innovation.

The central government thus began to encourage the establishment of horizontal, market-based ties between research institutes/universities and enterprises in various forms (Mok and Kan 2013). Recognizing the sluggish circulation of innovation in the industrial sector due to the lack of in-house R&D capacity in most industrial enterprises, steps have been taken to strengthen entrepreneurship within the NIS. To begin with, malfunctioning public research institutes were eliminated through mergers with the existing industrial or university-affiliated enterprises. Secondly, essential technological and infrastructural supports were given to enable enterprises to gradually establish their own in-house R&D facilities. Strategies applied to industrial enterprises, particularly those after the National Technology and Innovation Conference in 1999, have boosted R&D performance and patent acquisition in the university sector. The performance of industrial enterprises in the nation's R&D has increased from less than 40 percent to over 65 percent in ten years from the mid-1990s to the mid-2000s.

Moreover, by encouraging research institutes to engage in launching commercial spin-offs based on applicable research outputs, spin-off enterprises have increased rapidly in number and contribute considerably to the funding of research institutes. Meanwhile, in order to frame a nationally unified intellectual patent system, the Chinese Patent Office was set up in 1980, and the patent law and copyright law was enacted in 1985 and 1990 respectively. In 1999, the State Council gave approval to the Several Provisions on Promoting the Transformation of Scientific and Technological Achievements, introduced a generous rewarding mechanism for commercially useful discoveries, and allowed research personnel to enjoy greater mobility between their research and industrial careers.

In parallel with its effort to catalyze collaboration between industries and universities/research institutes (URIs), the government collectively held a series of national-scale research programs at the beginning of the 1980s.[2] The largest S&T program in China in the twentieth century was the Key Technologies R&D Program launched in 1982. Given the orientation toward national economic construction, the main purpose of this program was to solve key and comprehensive problems encountered during the Chinese social and economic reform era. After almost three decades since its first launch, this program has covered a wide range of S&T fields, such as agriculture, electronic information, energy resources, and transportation, and has attracted tens of thousands of personnel from over 1,000 research institutes nationwide. In March 1986, after reviewing a thorough study conducted by several hundreds of Chinese scientists from the S&T sector, Chinese leader Deng Xiaoping approved and initiated another program named the National Hi-Tech R&D Program, or the 836 Program, toward high-end technological exploration, such as biotech, space flight, information, and lasers, with a total of 20 themes. Unlike the Key Technologies R&D Program, state intervention in the operation of this program is considerably less, except for the sake of macromanagement or the provision of necessary legal and administrative services.

Two years later, the Chinese Ministry of Science and Technology initiated a nationwide innovation program, the Torch Program, to further develop its high-tech capability in the fields of new materials, biotechnology, electronic information, integrative mechanical-electrical technology, and advanced energy-saving technology. This program indeed plays the most important role in bringing into full play the potential and strength of China's S&T capacity. It reduces the burden of excessive regulation on S&T development and provides physical support for infrastructure to attract foreign high-tech companies and private investors, as well as promotes commercialization, industrialization, and internationalization of the national S&T market. By the end of 2008, 54 national S&T industrial parks have been built in close proximity to URIs. These zones have experienced rapid growth, but there are critics that much of this growth is in product assembly that does not meet the Western standard of high technology. Nevertheless, the balance of China's national import and export of high-tech products began to reverse since 2004, reaching a surplus of US$342,000 million in 2006.

In 2006, the State Council promulgated the Medium- and Long-Term National Plan for S&T Development 2006–2020.[3] Among the strategies introduced are the promotion of S&T development in selected key fields and the enhancement of indigenous innovation capacity. Considering enterprises as the major players in technological innovation, fiscal and tax policies were reviewed to create a favorable climate for entrepreneurial innovation. Moreover, integration among universities, research institutes, and enterprises was also encouraged. A total of 11 fields, 68 topics, 16 special programs, 27 frontier technologies, 18 basic science questions, and 4 research plans are identified, forming the country's research priority over the next 15 years.

Finally, over the last decade, a steady growing trend in terms of both gross expenditure on R&D and patenting activities has emerged. Through doubling the percentage of R&D expenditure from 1.23 percent in 2004 to 2.5 percent in 2020 and increasing innovative patents for the next 15 years, the objective is to make China an innovation-oriented country by 2020 and a global leader in S&T by the mid-twenty-first century.

Strategies for Enhancing Research and Development

In the post-Mao period starting from the late 1970s, the Chinese government began to put concerted efforts into advancing its research and technology. In recent years, the Chinese government is particularly keen to transform the country into a culturally strong and technologically advanced nation to cope with the growing challenges resulting from the knowledge-based economy. Different special funding schemes have been adopted since the 1990s to drive universities to perform, with additional funding attached to those universities with excellent performance benchmarked with world-class standards. The following section highlights a few major initiatives that the Chinese government has adopted in the last few decades to enhance university research capacity and technological advancement.

Strategies for Enhancing Universities' Global Competitiveness

University restructuring was part of the plan to increase China's competitiveness in the global marketplace. Up to the mid-1990s, top Chinese universities were not good enough by international standards. To improve China's higher education and train high-level professional manpower, the Chinese government initiated Project 211 in 1995. The idea was to achieve remarkable progress in teaching, research, and administration in about 100 higher education institutions and in certain key disciplinary areas in the twenty-first century. During the ninth Five-Year Plan period (1996–2000), a total of 18.6 billion yuan (RMB) was invested in 99 universities, with 2.8 billion yuan from the central government. During the tenth Five-Year Plan period (2001–2005), another 18.8 billion yuan was spent on 107 universities, with the central government contributing 6 billion yuan. In the eleventh Five-Year Plan period (2006–2010), the project's third phase, the central government planned to spend 10 billion yuan. The total investment was not large. In fact, the total government expenditure on regular higher education institutions reached 196.3 billion yuan and 428.6 billion yuan in the 1996–2000 and 2001–2005 periods, respectively.

Project 211 accounted for 9.5 percent of total government expenditure on higher education in the 1996–2000 period, but fell to 4.4 percent in the 2001–2005 period. While its financial significance has been declining, becoming a Project 211 university matters a great deal for the status of a university in China. Although Project 211 universities make up only 6 percent of China's regular higher education institutions, they take on the responsibility of training four-fifths of doctoral students, two-thirds of graduate students, half of students abroad, and one-third of undergraduates. They account for 85 percent of the country's key subjects, 96 percent of national key laboratories, and 70 percent of scientific research funding.

Project 211 was soon overshadowed by another initiative known as Project 985. Speaking at the one-hundredth anniversary of Peking University on 4 May 1998, then President Jiang Zemin stressed that "China must have a number of world-class universities." Project 985 was launched thereafter. Immediately, building up world-class universities became a national policy. The MOE proposed increasing the share of educational expenditures in the central budget by 1 percent every year for three successive years. At first, Peking University and Tsinghua University were handpicked by the central government. Each received 1.8 billion yuan from MOE within three years from 1999. From July to November 1999, another seven universities joined the project. Unlike the first two, they belong to the category of "joint development," thus receiving funding from both central government and local governments. The list was further expanded in 2001 and afterward to include 30 other universities.

Because they entered the list later than the first nine, these 30 universities were considered relatively lower in status. In recognition of this difference, the first nine Project 985 universities formed the C9 League in 2003 and met annually to ritualize their exclusive membership.

Project 985 and Project 211 provided a new method of certifying the status of a university. On their websites, none of the Project 985 universities or Project 211 universities can afford not to declare their newly gained status, as they are largely judged by their listing in these projects. While there were elements of meritocracy in the listing of the universities, the universities' relationship with the state was the most important determinant. "Vice-ministerial" universities and centrally administered universities had a much higher chance of being listed than other universities. For Project 985, all 31 vice-ministerial universities made the list. This means that out of nearly 2,000 universities and colleges without a vice-ministerial rank, only eight could become a Project 985 university. Without exception, the eight universities that made the list are all centrally administered universities (see tables 7.1 and 7.2).[4]

For Project 211 all 31 vice-ministerial universities are on the list. In fact, all the 39 Project 985 universities are also Project 211 universities, suggesting

Table 7.1 Funding for China's First Nine Project 985 Universities

University	Funding (billion RMB)	Source of Funding
Peking University	1.8	MOE
Tsinghua University	1.8	MOE
University of Science and Technology of China	0.3 + 0.3 + 0.3	MOE + Chinese Academy of Science + Anhui
Nanjing University	0.6 + 0.6	MOE + Jiangsu
Fudan University	0.6 + 0.6	MOE + Shanghai
Shanghai Jiaotong University	0.6 + 0.6	MOE + Shanghai
Zhejiang University	0.7 + 0.7	MOE + Zhejiang
Xi'an Jiaotong University	0.6 + 0.3	MOE + Shaanxi
Harbin Institute of Technology	0.3 + 0.3 + 0.4	MOE + Commission for Science, Technology and Industry for National Defence + Heilongjiang

Source: Zhao, L. T., and J. J. Zhu, "China's Higher Education Reform: What Has Not Been Changed?," http://www.eai.nus.edu.sg/Vol2No4_ZhaoLitao&ZhuJinjing.pdf.

Table 7.2 China's Vice-Ministerial Universities and Project 985 Universities

University	Vice-Ministerial Rank	Funded by Project 985
1. Peking University	Yes	Yes
2. Tsinghua University	Yes	Yes
3. Renmin University of China	Yes	Yes
4. Beijing Institute of Technology	Yes	Yes
5. Beihang University	Yes	Yes
6. Beijing Normal University	Yes	Yes
7. Chinese Agricultural University	Yes	Yes
8. University of Science and Technology of China	Yes	Yes
9. Fudan University	Yes	Yes
10. Shanghai Jiaotong University	Yes	Yes
11. Xi'An Jiaotong University	Yes	Yes
12. Harbin Institute of Technology	Yes	Yes
13. Zhejiang University	Yes	Yes
14. Nankai University	Yes	Yes
15. Tianjin University	Yes	Yes
16. Nanjing University	Yes	Yes
17. Wuhan University	Yes	Yes
18. Sichuan University	Yes	Yes
19. Sun Yat-sen University		Yes
20. Jilin University	Yes	Yes
21. Xiamen University	Yes	Yes
22. Dalian University of Technology	Yes	Yes
23. Shandong University	Yes	Yes
24. Tongji University	Yes	Yes
25. Huazhong University of Science and Technology	Yes	Yes
26. Southeast University	Yes	Yes
27. Central South University	Yes	Yes

Continued

Table 7.2   Continued

University	Vice-Ministerial Rank	Funded by Project 985
28. National University of Defence Technology	Yes	Yes
29. Chongqing University	Yes	Yes
30. Lanzhou University	Yes	Yes
31. Northwest A&F University	Yes	Yes
32. Ocean University of China	No	Yes
33. Hunan University	No	Yes
34. University of Electronic Science and Technology	No	Yes
35. South China University of Technology	No	Yes
36. Northeastern University	No	Yes
37. Northwestern Polytechnic University	No	Yes
38. Minzu University of China	No	Yes
39. East China Normal University	No	Yes

Source: Zhao, L. T, and J. J. Zhu, "China's Higher Education Reform: What Has Not Been Changed?," http://www.eai.nus.edu.sg/Vol2No4_ZhaoLitao&ZhuJinjing.pdf.

that Project 985 is more selective and of a higher status than Project 211. Out of the 111 centrally administered universities, 71 were funded by Project 211 in the first phase, while only 20 local universities could benefit from the project. A new tiered system has thus emerged with C9 League members at the top, followed by 30 other Project 985 universities. Below them are dozens of Project 211 universities. Further down the hierarchy are centrally administered universities that failed to make it onto the two lists. At the bottom are local and *minban* higher education institutions. Though the structure may look somewhat different from before, the underlying stratification mechanism remains the same. Project 211 and Project 985 served to reinforce the importance of administrative ranks of Chinese universities and consolidate the state as a status conferrer vis-à-vis the university.[5]

After the 211 and 985 projects, the C9 League was established in 2009. The aim of the C9 is to allow universities to communicate with each other in order to foster better students by sharing their resources, including campuses, teachers, and so on. More importantly, they have committed themselves to world-class excellence. In the first phase, nine universities were selected and allocated funding for an initial period of three years: Fudan University, Harbin Institute of Technology, Nanjing University, Peking University, Shanghai Jiao Tong University, Tsinghua University, the University of Science and Technology of China, Xi'an Jiao Tong University, and Zhejiang University. Peking University and Tsinghua University are in Beijing, the capital and a municipality of China. Fudan University and Shanghai Jiao Tong University are in Shanghai, a municipality in East China. Nanjing University is in Nanjing of Jiangsu Province. The University of Science and Technology of China is in Hefei of Anhui Province. Zhejiang University is in Hangzhou of Zhejiang Province. These five universities are in the greater Yangtze River Delta region. The other two universities are in Western China and Northeast China respectively. Xi'an Jiao Tong University is in Xi'an of Shaanxi Province, and the Harbin Institute of Technology is in Harbin of Heilongjiang Province.

On October 10, 2009, these nine universities made up the C9 League. The league was self-organized, and they had made a much anticipated decision to formalize an elite group that is pitched as China's equivalent of the Ivy League. (The Ivy League, which includes some notable US institutions, however, is thus named because it constitutes a real athletic league, in which the institutions compete in a variety of athletic fields.) As a matter of fact, the nine universities account for 3 percent of the country's researchers but receive 10 percent of national research expenditures. They produce 20 percent of the journal articles published and 30 percent of total citations. The establishment of the C9 League has been welcomed by Chinese public opinion. Its central idea of building world-class universities has been well supported by both government and society. However, although there are few criticisms of C9, there are still some concerns, such as how to share the benefits of the C9 with other universities in China.[6]

Advancing Technology and Research Development: National High-Tech R&D Program (863)

The 863 Program was approved by Deng Xiaoping. Implemented during three successive Five-Year Plans, the program has boosted China's overall high-tech development, R&D capacity, socioeconomic development, and national security. In April 2001, the Chinese State Council approved continued implementation of the program in the tenth Five-Year Plan. As one part of the national S&T program trilogy in the tenth Five-Year Plan, the 863 Program continues to play an important role.

Objectives of this program during the tenth Five-Year Plan period are to boost innovation capacity in the high-tech sectors, particularly in strategic high-tech fields, in order to gain a foothold in the world arena; to strive to achieve breakthroughs in key technical fields that concern the national economic lifeline and national security; and to achieve "leapfrog" development in key high-tech fields in which China enjoys relative advantages or should take strategic positions in order to provide high-tech support to fulfill strategic objectives in the implementation of the third step of its modernization process.

During the tenth Five-Year Plan period, the 863 Program will continue to aim at the forefront of world technology development, intensify innovation efforts, and realize strategic transitions from pacing front-runners to focusing on "leapfrog" development. Through efforts made over the five years, the program will greatly enhance China's high-tech innovation capacity in selected fields and improve the international competitiveness of major industries. It will master a number of technologies with industrial potential and proprietary IPR (International Patent Registration). It will nurture a number of high-tech industrial growth sources which will optimize and upgrade China's industrial structure as a way of fostering both the individual and the overall strength of high-tech industries. It will also develop innovative and enterprising talents for high-tech R&D and industrialization. Major tasks of the program include the following:

- Develop key technologies for the construction of China's information infrastructure.
- Develop key biological, agricultural, and pharmaceutical technologies to improve the welfare of the Chinese people.
- Master key new materials and advanced manufacturing technologies to boost industrial competitiveness.
- Achieve breakthroughs in key technologies for environmental protection, resources, and energy development to serve the sustainable development of Chinese society.[7]

Key Technologies R&D Program

The Key Technologies R&D Program is the first national S&T program in China. It aims to address major S&T issues in national economic construction and social development. Initiated in 1982 and implemented through four Five-Year Plans, the program has made remarkable contributions to the technical renovation and upgrading of traditional industries and the formation of new industries. It has also boosted the sustainable development of Chinese society and enhanced national S&T strength and innovation capacity.

As one part of the national S&T program trilogy in the tenth Five-Year Plan, the program maintains its goal of serving national economic construction. It is geared toward major demands of economic construction and sustainable social development. It focuses on promoting technical upgrading and restructuring of industries, and tackling major technical issues concerning public welfare. It works to provide technical support to industrial restructuring, the sustainable development of society, and the enhancement of living standards by achieving breakthroughs in key technologies, introducing technical innovations, and applying high and new technologies.

The major goal of the program is to address pressing major S&T issues in national economic and social development. The program concentrates on the R&D of key and common technologies that drive the technical upgrading and restructuring of industries that promote sustainable social development. The program provides advanced and applicable new technologies, materials, techniques, and equipment to industrial and agricultural production, while facilitating the application and industrialization of high-tech achievements to enhance the international competitiveness of key industries and human welfare. It also aims to cultivate an elite group involved in key technology R&D and to establish a number of internationally recognized technical innovation bases.

By organizing and supporting a number of major projects, priority projects, and guidance projects while implementing relevant measures, the program is expected to accomplish the following six major tasks during the tenth Five-Year Plan period:

1. An initial effort is to promote in-depth agroproduct processing by developing a number of key technologies and products for sustainable agricultural development. By doing this, the expectation is to upgrade technical levels in agricultural preproduction, production, and postproduction; optimize the agricultural structure; improve the quality and efficiency of agricultural development; and enhance the competitiveness of agricultural products.
2. With the manufacturing industry as a gateway to new innovations, redouble efforts to develop common key technologies for basic and pillar industries. Also, speed up the application of IT and other high technologies in traditional industries. Strengthen engineering research in application technologies; develop technologies and equipment for clean energy, intelligent traffic systems, and textile posttreatment; enhance the added value of products, and boost the technical level and domestic content of a complete set of equipment.
3. With informatization processes in the financial sector as a priority, accelerate the development of IT and other high technologies, along with related industrial development, to render technical support to the informatization of the national economy.
4. With environmental protection and rational utilization of resources as priorities, develop key technologies in urban environmental pollution

control, push forward the rational utilization of water resources, develop and demonstrate technologies for the improvement of regional ecology and environment, intensify technical research in the exploration and development of oil and gas fields and strategic solid mineral resources, establish technical supporting systems for disaster prevention and mitigation, and promote sustainable social development.
5. With the modernization of traditional Chinese medicine (TCM) as a gateway to innovation, develop key technologies in the TCM industry to secure its world-leading position.
6. With promotion of the social cause as a goal, intensify research on major public welfare technologies and develop advanced and applicable technologies and products to further enhance the living standards of the Chinese people. Intensify research on technical standards and measurements to facilitate the establishment of China's technical standardization system.[8]

National Basic Research Program of China (973 Program)

Based on the existing basic research programs conducted by the National Natural Science Foundation and early-stage basic research key projects, the 973 Program organizes and implements key projects to meet national strategic needs. The strategic objective of the program is to mobilize China's scientific talents in conducting innovative research on major scientific issues in agriculture, energy, information, resources and environment, population and health, materials, and related areas. This is in accordance with the objectives and tasks of China's economic, social, and S&T development goals leading up to 2010 and the mid-twenty-first century. The program will build up a solid S&T foundation for the sustainable socioeconomic development of the Chinese nation. Through the implementation of the program, a contingent of scientific talents will be trained and a number of high-level national research bases will be established to upgrade the primary innovative capacity of the nation.

During the tenth Five-Year Plan period, the 973 Program adopts a people-oriented approach to perform its three major tasks:

1. Strengthen and support research on a number of major scientific issues concerning national socoieconomic development. In line with national strategic demands, the program continues to strengthen major basic research in agriculture, energy, information, resources and environment, population and health, materials, and other areas. It promotes research and innovation in order to seek breakthroughs in major frontier

fields of far-reaching and strategic importance, such a life science, nanotechnology, information technology, earth sciences, and so forth. It also reinforces comprehensive cross-disciplinary research and innovative integration to develop new ideas, concepts, inventions, and theories so as to lay a solid foundation for the "leapfrog" advancement of social productivity.
2. Consolidate a highly qualified contingent for basic research and cultivate a number of personnel with innovative capabilities. Establish and adhere to the strategic principle – "people-oriented" to vigorously practice a talent strategy. Work toward stabilizing key personnel while nurturing reserve forces by providing more support to research communities led by young and middle-aged scientists. Adopt effective measures to create a people-oriented environment that will cultivate generations of talent by using the project as the cord, the base as the backbone, and human resources as the core. Introduce high-caliber personnel from overseas, promote international exchanges and cooperation, and encourage and support a number of established scientists with organizational skills and international influence to play a role in the global arena, thereby raising China's international S&T status.
3. Improve and perfect program management to create a sound environment for primary innovation. Establish and improve a scientific assessment and management system to serve innovation and overcome the folly of pursuing short-term, quick results. Encourage scientists to courageously explore new research fields and guide them in conducting innovative researches in line with national demands and the scientific frontiers.[9]

Enhancing Knowledge Transfer and Promoting University-Enterprise Cooperation

During the mid-1980s in China, science and technology development was not conducted by enterprise but largely by universities and research institutions. In this particular period, universities were not simply educational institutions but were put in the crucial position of functioning as research institutions. At that time in China, there was no particular means to transfer technology held by universities to enterprises for translating them into products sellable in the market. It is against this context that experts within the university created their own enterprises. Representative of the university-run enterprises created during that period were companies like Peking University Founder, Tsinghua Tongfang, and Neusoft.

Realizing the importance of university-enterprise and university-industry cooperation, the Chinese government has begun to introduce a preferential tax policy to encourage the establishment of high-tech enterprises, which made it possible for researchers in the university sector to start venturing into the business world without losing their university jobs since the 1990s. Through these measures, the entrepreneurial desires of university researchers were aroused, and a milieu that was supportive of business start-ups was formed. Since then, university-run high-tech enterprises have expanded rapidly. High Tech Universities took on the risk of directly entering the market and supplemented a portion of the industrial creation.[10]

At the dawn of the twenty-first century, university-run enterprises faced a major transition. "University-run" enterprises underwent a structural transformation to become "university-owned" enterprises. Along with the development of university-run enterprises, various problems emerged between universities and enterprises in relation to property rights and the management authority of enterprises. At the time university-run enterprises were established, the universities assumed the risks and held unlimited responsibility for management. However, with the increase in university-run enterprises, the large amount of business risk undertaken by university-run enterprises that had been directly managed by universities became a heated topic concerning the future state of relationships between university-run enterprises and universities. Soon after, due to administrative guidance from the government, university-run enterprises, beginning with Peking University and Tsinghua University, underwent a structural reformation beginning in 2002.

In 2006, a reform began of university-run enterprises throughout China based on the sequence of events of university-run enterprise reformation at Peking University and Tsinghua University. The management structural changes in university-run enterprises were primarily conducted in three aspects:

1. Establish a holding company, commission that same company to manage the assets of the university, and manage the enterprise under its auspices. Furthermore, the university does not directly manage outside investments but must go through the holding company for everything.
2. Regarding the use of university names, existing university-run enterprises adjusted their naming, and in principle, use of university names was prohibited.
3. From a human resources perspective, concurrent posting at the enterprise with a teaching position at the university was prohibited in principle.

The establishment of a university holding company required permission from a government agency, specifically the Ministry of Education, and the holding company assumed the position as the enterprise managing the national

Table 7.3 A Comparison of University-Run Enterprises before and after Structural Reform

	Before Structural Reform (University-run enterprises)	After Structural Reform (University-owned enterprises)
Liability of the university	Unlimited liability	Limited liability
Operations division	Government division within the university	Holding company
Relationship between university and enterprise	Directly managed by the university Personal connection Administrative connection	Solely an indirect financial connection through the holding company
Business risk	Unlimited liability for the university	Limited liability for the University

Source: Jin, A., 2013, "Entrepreneurial Universities and Industrial Creation in China," http://hermes-ir.lib.hit-u.ac.jp/rs/bitstream/10086/25503/1/070hjbsWP_166.pdf.

assets held by the university. Following this guidance, holding companies were established in the form of limited liability companies within universities. In essence, holding companies fulfilled the role of a firewall allowing the universities to avoid the business risks associated with the university-run enterprises. Furthermore, this presented the opportunity for structural reform of university-run enterprises at each university and thus began the introduction of the enterprise structure of today (see table 7.3).

By 2009, 157 of the 484 universities nationwide had already established holding companies. Total sales of the 157 holding companies reached 115.13 billion yuan, accounting for 81.5 percent of the 141.23 billion yuan in total sales of university-run enterprises.[11]

Moreover, the implementation of intellectual property policies and guidance, such as the "Twelfth Five-Year Plan (2011–2015) on National Intellectual Property Development" and the "Twelfth Five-Year Plan on Patents" have increased the confidence of foreign-invested companies to conduct R&D in China. The reform of the tax system is another key factor that encourages multinational companies to improve products and processes, enhance productivity, and set up R&D centers in China, and the Chinese government has maintained its fiscal support for R&D.

In addition, the reform of value-added tax offers potential tax benefits to enterprises carrying out R&D activities. Many services that were previously subject to business tax are now subject to value-added tax. As a result, the tax burden of many foreign-invested enterprises may fall considerably. For example, R&D activities such as technical consulting and technology licensing that were previously subject to business tax are now subject to value-added tax, but the key difference is that foreign-invested enterprises can now offset their value-added tax payable. This ultimately means more money in the hands of the taxpayer.

Encouraging and fostering R&D activities is a national policy of the Chinese government and is a key content of the twelfth Five-Year Plan. Such R&D incentives include the following:

- A 50 percent R&D "Super Deduction" in addition to the actual expense deduction for R&D spending. If a company spends RMB 10 million on eligible R&D, it will receive a net benefit of RMB 1.25 million.
- A preferential corporate income tax rate of 15 percent (the standard rate is 25 percent) for companies recognized as a High New Technology Enterprise.
- A preferential corporate income tax rate of 15 percent for companies recognized as an Advanced Technology Service Enterprise, with qualified incomes exempt from business tax.
- Exemption from import customs duty and value-added tax on qualified R&D equipment imported by R&D centers.

R&D activities potentially eligible for Chinese government's incentives in various industry sectors could include the following:

- new techniques or methodologies to extract minerals from complex ore bodies;
- improvements to water use and irrigation technologies;
- development of innovative functionality and improved approaches to solving software problems;
- application of engineering principles previously developed in the aerospace industry in, for example, the automotive industry;
- computer-aided engineering and simulation software developed as part of a larger R&D project in any industry;
- development of new processes and technologies to minimize adverse environmental impacts across all industries;
- development of new compounds with improved therapeutic properties;
- development of nondestructive testing techniques to analyze material fatigue with pharmaceutical products; and
- application of off-the-shelf software products in new and previously unproven ways.[12]

The online news site *Computerworld* on 24 December 2012 predicted that the

> USA may lose its global R&D leadership in 2023. Based on current trends, China is on track to overtake USA in spending on R&D in about 10 years, as federal R&D spending either declines or remains flat. USA today maintains a large lead in R&D spending over China, with federal and private sector investment expected to reach $424 billion in 2013, a 1.2 percent increase. By contrast, China's overall R&D spending is $220 billion in 2013, an increase of 11.6 percent over 2012. Although the United States still has a significant lead and advantages in R&D over all other countries, other countries continue to grow their R&D capabilities, how long can the USA maintain that advantage?

In fact, foreign debts, a high unemployment rate, social welfare relief, and enormous military expenditures aggravate the United States' burden. The White House believes that China may overtake the United States in R&D spending: "China's investment as a percentage of its GDP shows continuing, deliberate growth that, if it continues, should surpass the roughly flat United States investment within a decade."[13]

The magazine *Asian Scientist* on 25 February 2013 reported that China's R&D spending increased 17.9 percent year on year to RMB 1.02 trillion in 2012; R&D expenditure represented 1.97 percent of the GDP in 2012, up from the 1.84 percent and 1.75 percent in 2011 and 2010 respectively; China's annual R&D spending had grown on average by more than 20 percent for six straight years since 2006; a total of 217,105 invention patents to domestic and overseas applicants were approved in 2012, up 26.1 percent from 2011. Plans were announced in 2011 to increase the annual enrollment of postdoctoral researchers at key universities and research institutes to 17,000 in 2015 as part of a five-year blueprint for scientific development in the country.[14]

China Daily on 2 March 2013 reported that China spent a record RMB 1 trillion on R&D in 2012, of which 74 percent came from enterprises; China's research personnel reached 3.2 million in 2012, the highest in the world; and the value of technical contracts inked in 2012 in China exceeded RMB 600 billion while the aggregate output value of high-tech industries topped RMB 10 trillion. Moreover, calling 2012 a landmark year for China's science and technology development, a special team had been assembled by the State Council to lead reform of the country's scientific and technological system to strengthen top-level design in this regard. Since the ministry introduced online evaluation and administrative approval of research projects, domestic researchers are estimated to have saved RMB 70 million in total on traveling expenses and 60,000 work days annually. Wan Gang, the vice chairman of the National Committee of the Chinese People's Political Consultative Conference said,

> To build China into an innovative country, I think we must confidently stick to the path of self-dependent innovation with Chinese characteristics, and at the

same time, broaden our horizons to learn from foreign countries and share our experiences with others. The key task for his ministry is to facilitate original innovation, promote rational deployment and sharing of scientific know-how and equipment, step up training of young researchers and skilled personnel, and to improve the environment for research and development. Research on basic science, frontier technologies and commonly needed spheres will receive more support from central government public finances. Meanwhile, efforts will be made to improve the innovation capability of small and medium-sized and micro enterprises.[15]

Transforming Curriculum for Promoting Entrepreneurship Education

The changing socioeconomic transformation needs a variety of personalities, imaginations, talents, and skills to deal with the new challenges. Entrepreneurship is increasingly regarded as a key competence and the engine fueling innovation, employment generation, and economic growth. According to Matlay (2001), it is becoming fashionable to view entrepreneurship and entrepreneurship education as the panacea for stagnating economic activity in both developed and developing countries. Although the theory of entrepreneurship education was initiated by Professor Myles Mace of Harvard Business School and Professor David Birch of the Massachusetts Institute of Technology (MIT) more than half a century ago, as an international practice and trend, entrepreneurship education has mainly been promoted by some important international organizations in recent years.

With a strong conviction for establishing a laboratory of ideas and a catalyst for international cooperation, the United Nations Educational, Scientific and Cultural Organization (UNESCO) is a very active advocator of entrepreneurship education. In the *World Declaration on Higher Education for the Twenty-First Century: Vision and Action* adopted in the World Conference on Higher Education (WCHE) in 1998, UNESCO admonished its member states, "Developing entrepreneurial skills and initiative should become major concerns of higher education, in order to facilitate employability of graduates who will increasingly be called upon to be not only job seekers but also and above all to become job creators" (UNESCO 1998). Since then, UNESCO reiterated in the communiqué of the 2009 World Conference on Higher Education that "the training offered by HEIs should respond to and anticipate societal needs. This includes promoting research for the development and ensuring the provision of technical and vocational training, entrepreneurship education and programmes for lifelong learning" (UNESCO 2009). The International Labor Organization (ILO), another important international organization, also recommended that its members consider pursuing development of entrepreneurial attitudes through the system and programs of education, entrepreneurship, and training linked to job needs and the attainment of economic growth and development (International Labor Organization 1998). The World Economic Forum (WEF), an independent international organization committed to economic and industrial issues, began to be concerned with entrepreneurship education as well. In a report titled on *Educating the Next Wave of Entrepreneurs*, the WEF highlighted entrepreneurship and education as two such extraordinary opportunities that need to be leveraged and interconnected if we are to develop the human capital required for building the societies of the future (World Economic Forum [WEF] 2009).

Launching Entrepreneurship Education

In 2002, a pilot program on entrepreneurship education was launched in nine universities under the supervision of the MOE, which marked a new stage of development in entrepreneurship education in China. Since then, both governments and HEIs have made consistent efforts to explore various strategies to benchmark their programs with international practices and experiences. After the pilot program was launched, China's universities have begun teaching basic courses on entrepreneurship to encourage undergraduate students to start businesses and become self-employed after graduation in order to make students more competitive in the knowledge-based economy. According to the draft teaching plan "Entrepreneurship Foundations" released by the Ministry of Education, the courses required no less than two credit units and 32 hours.

Instead of starting businesses after college, most Chinese graduates look for employment opportunities. According to the statistics of the Ministry of Education in China, there were 6.6 million college graduates nationwide in 2011. However, only 1.6 percent of them decided to start businesses, according the 2012 Chinese College Graduates Employment Annual Report. The MyCOS Institute, a consulting company, released the report in June. "Becoming an entrepreneur in China, especially for new graduates, is a tough decision," said Wang Hao, a 25-year-old Tsinghua University alumnus who runs his own business. After graduating from Tsinghua in 2010, Wang went to the United States to pursue a master's degree in mechanical engineering. "I thought about finding a job or internship in the USA in 2011, just before my graduation, but I decided instead to follow my dream to come back to China to start my own business," Wang said. He and two friends from school now run HHT Tech Co., a medical appliance design business. Wang started his first business in high school. He edited his biology notes and study strategies and made a book. "The test guidebook actually had great sales," he said. While skeptical about the concept of entrepreneurship courses, Wang believes that a basic introduction to entrepreneurship in Chinese universities is necessary. "Students lack a basic understanding of entrepreneurship, which has been considered unstable, risky, and very difficult. But it is not. Starting a business is like a regular job, a job you really enjoy," Wang said.

Tsinghua University, a hotbed of Chinese entrepreneurship and leadership, provides a fertile learning environment to its students. Deng Yongqiang, general manager of Qidihoude Co., a technical and media incubator of Tsinghua's new ideas, said that Tsinghua has been working on cultivating students' entrepreneurship ability and awareness for years. "Although we don't have a detailed plan with the Ministry of Education, we are already working to provide reliable entrepreneurship education to students. It will be big progress to have required entrepreneurship courses at colleges," he said. The regulation also emphasizes pragmatic exercises and encourages schools to create practical opportunities for students, such as internships. Wang, the Tsinghua graduate, also agrees with the idea that practical work is necessary in one's education in entrepreneurship. "We do have many lectures and activities to teach how to start a business, such as writing business plans or researching the business environment. However, in the United States, students are encouraged to do business instead of research. There is a big gap between writing plans and implementing them," he said.

Another essential goal of entrepreneurship education is to increase the students' awareness of entrepreneurship. "There was a fear in my parents' generation that starting up a business meant being at risk and unsafe. They asked me to consider thoroughly before I decided to start a business. But my original thought of a start-up is pretty simple. I just want to stay with my major. I just don't want to lose something I love, and also want to have time and money to have fun and enjoy life. Then I started a business, it is just a job I am really into," said Wang.

Duan Huaqia, a professor of executive management at Anhui University, said that entrepreneurship education in college is acceptable to a point: "It is not necessarily good for it to become a required course. Instead, the course should be based on innovative education, and focus on training, to create an entrepreneurial atmosphere and awareness." He also said that it is hard to find a job, but even harder to start a business. Given the lack of appropriate teaching materials and practical exercises, colleges need to prepare more for entrepreneurship courses.[16]

In fact, entrepreneurship education for college students initially originated in the United States in the 1940s. Now it has been greatly accepted and popularized by many countries. But different from American entrepreneurship education where colleges create demand, entrepreneurship education in China has mainly been advocated by the central government in the past decade because of higher pressure on university graduates seeking employment. The practice of entrepreneurship education has been gradually introduced to China from the 1990s. Entrepreneurship education has drawn unprecedented attention from institutions of higher learning after the launch of "The Challenge Cup," a business plan competition by Tsinghua University in 1997, supported by the National Students' Federation, Central Communist Youth League, and the Ministry of Education. At the same time, the Ministry of Education designated nine Chinese universities as entrepreneurial education pilot colleges in 2002. From then on, many universities in China have carried out various forms of entrepreneurship education activities.[17]

University-Industry Partnership Promoting Experiential Learning

In order to foster a good environment for university-industry cooperation, the Chinese government has offered multidimensional support in the form of funds, sites, experience, and practice to college students who are willing to set up their own businesses. Considering that work experience is an important component and facilitating factor to build up entrepreneurial capacities, the China-UK Graduate Work Experience Programme, a joint initiative launched by the Chinese Ministry of Education and the British Department of Education and Skills (DfES) in 2006, aimed at strengthening university and business links between the two countries. According to the agreement, the program provides 12 to 50 weeks of work experience with UK employers for up to 200 of the most promising final-year and postgraduate students in China. From 2006 to 2010, seven intakes of over 1,000 Chinese students each have been placed with employers in the UK, including Accenture, Standard Chartered Bank, EC Harris, JPMorgan, Tesco, and Somerset County Council.

Financial support is indispensable for the new start-ups to get their ideas off the ground. Therefore, in view of this, more and more local governments began to set up entrepreneurship foundations, also called angel foundations, for college graduates. The Shanghai Technology Entrepreneurship Foundation for Graduates (STEFG) was the first nonprofit public fund for entrepreneurial activities by graduates in China. It was initiated by the Shanghai Municipal Education Commission (SMEC) and the Science and Technology Commission of Shanghai Municipality (STCSM) and invested by the Shanghai municipal government in 2006 (Science and Technology Commission of Shanghai Municipality [STCSM] 2005). From 2006 to 2010, the Shanghai government invested a total of CNY500 million in this foundation. STEFG works mainly through two subschemes. One is the Eyas Scheme to provide seed funding of no more than CNY100,000 to projects that could achieve a balance of profit and loss with a small investment. The other is the Eagle Scheme to provide venture funding of no more than CNY300,000 to projects with high-tech quality or market prospects.[18] By June of 2012, STEFG has received 2,336 applications and funded 514 projects. (Shanghai

Technology Entrepreneurship Foundation for Graduates [STEFG] 2012). Statistic shows that the survival rates for funded enterprises within three years reach 30 percent, and the revenue of 10 percent funded enterprises exceeds CNY10 million (Zhang 2011). Similar cases are the Zhejiang Foundation for Youth Entrepreneurship and Employment (ZFYEE) founded by the Zhejiang provincial government together with 11 private enterprises in 2007 with a total fund of CNY110 million and the Shandong Entrepreneurship Foundation for Graduates (SEFG) founded by the Shandong provincial government and China Unicom Shandong in 2009 with funding of CNY35 million.

In China, under the background of innovation and entrepreneurship, University Science Park has been given a new mission, that is, to promote the development of entrepreneurship education in HEIs and foster high-level innovative and entrepreneurial talents. Since 15 pilot university national science parks (UNSP) were approved by the MOE and the Ministry of Science and Technology (MOST) in December 1999, 86 UNSPs have been established in 24 provinces along with 134 HEIs (MOE 2011; MOST 2011). The UNSP created a unique mode of cultivating entrepreneurial talent through its strong atmosphere of entrepreneurship, the close interaction between university and enterprise, and the plentiful opportunities of practice and internships for the students. Taking Zhejiang University National Science Park (ZUNSP) as an example, student entrepreneurs not only can be supported by rent a subsidy for a 50-square-meter office for two years and a CNY20,000 to CNY200,000 entrepreneurship fund, but can also be provided various services including a weekly entrepreneurship salon and entrepreneurial training and instructions (ZUNSP 2012). By far, 41 UNSPs have been identified as the practice base of technology entrepreneurship for college students. It can be expected that the total number of UNSPs will reach 100 in 2015. Based on these UNSPs, the Chinese government planned to develop 3,000 hi-tech enterprises set up by university students, transfer 10,000 scientific and technological achievements, and cultivate 100,000 innovative and entrepreneurial talents in the coming five years (MOE 2011; MOST 2011).

Co-curricular Activities Enhancing Entrepreneurship Education

Another approach to enhancing entrepreneurship among university students is to engage them in extracurricular or co-curricular activities ranging from training programs and business plan competition to entrepreneurship clubs. This can play an indispensable role of fostering a campus culture of entrepreneurship and expanding students' involvement. As for training programs, Know about Business (KAB), Generate Your Business (GYB), Start and Improve Your Business (SIYB), and Expand Your Business (EYB), developed by the

International Labor Organization (ILO), constitute a well-integrated training system in entrepreneurship. Among them, KAB is a more popular training program to promote youths' entrepreneurial consciousness and capacities carried out widely in over 30 countries throughout the world. In order to learn from this successful international experience and explore a path fit for China's practice, the All China Youth Federation (ACYF) and the Central Committee of the Communist Young League (CCYL), in collaboration with the ILO, introduced the KAB Program in HEIs in 2005. Since then, the four systems of the KAB program, including curriculum construction, teacher training, quality control, and exchange and promotion, have been increasingly developed. KAB courses are provided as a public optional course in Chinese HEIs. Students can get academic credits by choosing and completing the program. As a supplement, students can also attend some extracurricular activities such as a KAB club, summer camp, or classroom. The KAB program obtained very rapid development in China. As of February 2011, the training course "KAB Entrepreneurship Education" was provided in 600 HEIs, a KAB club was established in 100 HEIs, and 2,931 teachers and 200,000 students in 850 HEIs have been involved in related KAB activities (Know about Business [KAB] (China) Promotion Office 2012).

Since its initiation by American universities in the 1980s, the Business Plan Competition (BPC) is available over the world. It has gained more and more attention and has been brought to China as well. In 1998, the first pilot BPC in China was organized by Tsinghua University. It then spread rapidly into a national event held every two years supported by MOE, the China Association of Science and Technology (CAST), and ACYF. Since 1999, seven "Challenge Cup" national BPCs have been hosted at different universities.[19] The competition systems of three levels (institutional, provincial, and national competition) and three rounds (preliminary, semifinal, and final competition) have also been well established and developed. This event has aroused great enthusiasm for innovation and entrepreneurship in college students. With the support of government and enterprise, many business plans were adopted and applied in practical operations, which promoted the further combination of technology, capital, and markets. The practice demonstrates that BPCs are an effective approach to improving entrepreneurial consciousness and competence for college students.

Promotion of Entrepreneurialism in China: Challenges and Issues

The present chapter examines how China has engaged in transforming the country by promoting entrepreneurship and innovation in higher education in order to strengthen national competitiveness in the global competitive environment.

Analyzing the recent initiatives employed by China in promoting an entrepreneurial spirit and practice in higher education, we have noted that increasing interconnections of the global economy and society pose common problems for higher educational systems around the world. Among those, how to increase the creativity and employability of graduates and the social relevance of higher education in an era of massification of higher education is undoubtedly the crucial one. This is the reason why entrepreneurship has become synonymous with and a catchword for students, HEIs, and even national success (OECD 1998). And in an intensifying globalizing setting, the increase in worldwide social relations links distant localities in such a way that local happenings are shaped by events occurring many miles away (Held 1991, 9).

Not surprisingly, the challenges generated from the strong need for promoting innovation, together with the exposure to new international ideas and experiences, have inevitably fostered the development of entrepreneurship education in Chinese higher education systems. Our present case studies have vividly reflected what was indicated by Mok and Lee (2003, 15), that governments around the globe, particularly in East Asia, have tried to make use of the globalization discourse to address local political agendas. However, instead of simply a process of globalization, the formulation of national policies is the result of complicated and dynamic processes of "globalization" (Mok 2003, 126). The above discussion has clearly suggested that the Chinese government could creatively adopt different strategies and measures when making responses appropriate to the challenge and pressure of the globalizing trend of entrepreneurship in higher education. However, a close scrutiny of what has been implemented in Chinese higher education in terms of entrepreneurship education has not touched upon the core academic structure, which is the most essential part when promoting creativity and innovation in learning.

As Mok and Chan argued elsewhere (Mok and Chan 2012), the Chinese government is at a crossroads in its development of higher education. On the one hand, the growing prominence of transnational higher education (TNHE) has posed potential problems related to quality assurance and management of the increased number of these program. On the other hand, an international review of higher education governance conducted by the OECD has suggested that the Chinese higher education system is overregulated and centralized, but not well planned. According to the OECD review, there is a growing role for the nonpublic sector, including the private/*minban* higher education institutions. But the review recommends "inculcating civilizing values among students, which emphasize rational enquiry, tolerance and respect, the pursuit of truth and respect for human rights within a sense of global citizenship" (Gallagher et al. 2009, 50). In short, the OECD review identifies one major weakness of the Chinese higher education system, which is the lack of "critical democratic thinking." In view of the national strategy to transform the country from a strong economic power relying heavily on manufacturing to a world force with strong brainpower, the Chinese government has no choice but to review the conventional higher education governance system, which has been characterized as "the university president's leadership under the guidance of the CCP." Nonetheless, without a fundamental change in the relationship between the Party and academic administration, academics in Mainland China have found it problematic to push further reforms, since academic decisions have long suffered from "interference" by administrative and political matters under the unique co-leadership of universities by the Party and academic community (Mok 2009). In order to emancipate human minds and inculcate a spirit of innovation and creativity among university academics and students, the Chinese government has to rethink how the higher education system is to be governed by exploring the possibility of a structural reform that will not only touch upon the administrative structure, but will also touch upon the Party's role in steering academic development. In 2010, former president Hu Jintao and Primier Wen Jiaobo openly declared the importance of deepening political reforms in order to drive Chinese economic development to a new level during the celebration of the thirtieth anniversary of the Shenzhen Economic Zone, one of the zones for testing new ideas of reforms on the mainland (Mingpao, 7 September 2010). Central to their message is the need to create a proper platform to nurture future generations with creative minds and innovative skills. Without structural reforms in the higher education system, it would be difficult to achieve the goal of enabling the country to scale new heights as a world power with a great civilization, strong human capital, and soft power.

Discussion and Conclusion

This chapter has attempted to review major policies and measures adopted by the Chinese government in particular and universities in general to promote entrepreneurship and innovation. Recognizing that the country has confronted significant challenges during the transition from a manufacturing-based economy to the knowledge-based economy, the Chinese government has made serious efforts to promote innovation and entrepreneurialism in higher education through the engagement of faculty members and students to work closely between the university sector and industry. The success in the promotion of innovation and entrepreneurship in higher education is not only related to how curriculum is designed but also to the academic structure and university management. Without serious reviews and critical reflections upon its current university governance structure with strong political influences from the Communist Party in university governance, it would be difficult to make significant changes in Chinese higher education.

Although China has successfully achieved a global outlook adapted to local conditions, further development of entrepreneurship education in higher education is still restricted by some problems. For instance, the government dominates and actively promotes entrepreneurship education with the clear intention of employment generation, enterprises lack dynamics and have limited interests in involving the support of government, and most HEIs are isolated from the business world and passively carry out such cooperation. As the way forward in the future, China could follow the action recommended by WEF (2009) to build an entrepreneurial ecosystem in which multiple stakeholders including government, HEIs, and enterprises can interact with each other and work together.

As for the government, legislation should be adopted and funding mechanisms should be create to support relations between private enterprises and HEIs in developing action learning programs, leading to new entrepreneurial skills. In the meanwhile, networks and programs should be developed to bring together different HEIs and enterprises in a common strategy in sharing information, good practices, and experiences. Different departments of the government could set up a coordinated program to underpin the above legislation and add a financial budget to it. With a long-term plan, enterprises should actively get involved in related activities on entrepreneurship within HEIs, in providing backup infrastructure (venture capital, incubators, and bodies) that can improve entrepreneurial skills, as well as to take an active role in organizing business plan competitions and in providing support for getting winning ideas off the ground. They should also facilitate successful entrepreneurs and business practitioners to dedicate time and effort to teaching, out of a sense of contribution to society and as part of their social responsibility.

HEIs have a critical role as intellectual hubs in the entrepreneurial ecosystem. HEIs should establish a framework to support and help their academic entities to develop and expand their entrepreneurship mission and activities, with a vision beyond utilitarianism to focus more on student personal development for lifelong learning. It is better for HEIs to identify key skills and integrate entrepreneurship across different subjects and courses, notably within scientific and technical studies, and they should encourage teaching staff mobility between HEIs and the business world. At the same time, a background in academia and recent experience in business, such as in consulting for or initiating entrepreneurial initiatives, will be very helpful for teaching staff.

In conclusion, the present chapter has shown how the Chinese government has made attempts to identify good or best practices overseas to reform its higher education delivery. However, the promotion of innovation and entrepreneurialism in higher education will be doomed to failure without a careful contextualization of best practices adopted elsewhere within the particular context of Mainland China. It is against this context that we must be critical about policy learning and policy transfer. Without contextualizing good practices to solve local problems, we are bound to witness policy copying instead of effective policy learning. This chapter has clearly demonstrated the importance of sensitization to the policy context when new and good practices are introduced to Chinese universities. Perhaps the Chinese government really needs to consider structural reforms in its higher education sector in order to unleash the energy and dynamism necessary for embracing the changes being called for in the enhancement of innovation and entrepreneurship in China.

Brief Conclusion to Section Two

As a brief conclusion not only for the present chapter but also for chapters in this section, the "visible hands" of the government in the promotion of R&D and entrepreneurship are easily seen in East Asia, especially in the inception and early phase of development. The important role of the state in the strategic development of the national innovation system can also be witnessed after the 1997/98 Asian financial crisis and the 2008/09 global financial crisis, when the financial and R&D capacity of firms and industries have been rendered problematic in an unstable global economic environment. Therefore, we have seen that the governments of the Four Little Dragons have stepped up during the crisis to expand investments in R&D activities. Overall, in the national innovation system of the Four Little Dragons, the governments perform a very important, if not an entirely dominant, role by acting as the initiator and promoter at the outset, a facilitator and collaborator in between, and the regulator in the end.

Among the Four Little Dragons, Hong Kong is the only exception because its government has been restrained from playing a strong steering role until the past decade when it has started to realize the need for catching up with other technologically advanced countries in order to diversify the economy and fuel future economic growth. Previously, R&D activities were largely conducted by private companies and universities. Comparatively, Taiwan, South Korea, and Singapore have a closer and more interactive cooperation among the government, industry, and academia. Despite this, these economies are different in their innovation systems, especially with regard to the nature of the industry involved in R&D activities. While Singapore enthusiastically welcomes foreign investment and companies, Taiwan and South Korea are more focused on nurturing local corporations, as they regard local industries to be their national strengths, which need to be protected and supported. Therefore, while Singapore is described as a "technoglobalist" country, South Korea as well as Taiwan can be categorized as "technonationalist" countries (Keller and Samuels 2002).

In regard to university reform, under the trend of the emergence of entrepreneurial universities since the 1990s, many universities in East Asia have in one way or another simultaneously undergone significant restructurings along the line of marketization, corporatization, privatization, and commercialization in order to be more flexible and managerial in responding to market needs. Such restructurings are not only propelled by the national call for economic development and the industrial need for product development, but also by the universities' own ambition to excel in governance in order to attain world-class status.

Part II

Internationalization and Transnationalization of Higher Education and Student Learning

Chapter 8

The Call for Internationalization:
Questing for Regional Education Hub Status and Transnationalizing Higher Education in Malaysia, Singapore, and Hong Kong

Introduction

The rise of transnational higher education in the Asia-Pacific region has undeniably reflected the growing pace of globalization and the subsequent pressures imposed by it. Malaysia, Singapore, and Hong Kong, among others, are three notable cases in which states have explicitly declared their intentions to make their country/territory a regional education hub, and hence we have witnessed rapid development of transnational higher education in these Asian societies in recent years. Malaysia, Singapore, and Hong Kong are the top three source countries for the UK's transnational higher education provision[1]; apparently the pressing need for transformation into a knowledge-based economy has exceeded the capacity of many states to promptly expand their public institutions to offer sufficient opportunities for higher education to their population. The proliferation of higher education providers, coupled with the global trends of marketization and privatization of higher education, have subsequently created a much diversified ecology of higher education; this development has also fundamentally blurred the line between public and private.

"Transnational education" is being applied here as a term to denote education "in which the learners are located in a country different from the one where the awarding institution is based" (UNESCO/Council of Europe 2001). It could therefore include both collaborative and noncollaborative transnational arrangements, such as franchising, twinning (dual degree), and joint degree programs in the former, and branch campuses in the latter. Obviously, cross-border education has become a major component of the transformations taking place within the higher education private sector environment, as well as a central element of how quality is recognized within higher education (East-West Centre 2010).

This chapter critically examines the policy origins of the quest for regional education hubs taking place in Malaysia, Singapore, and Hong Kong. More specifically, this chapter compares and contrasts the policies, strategies, and practices adopted by these Asian societies. This chapter also critically evaluates the recent developments of regional education hub projects, with particular reference to changing university governance and regulatory regimes responsible for monitoring transnational education in Malaysia, Singapore, and Hong Kong.

The Rise of Transnational Education: Policy Contexts and Recent Developments

Malaysia

Malaysia's ambition to become a regional education hub was first sketchily noted in the grand development blueprint of *Wawasan 2020* (Vision 2020) initiated by the Mahathir administration in 1991.[2] According to Vision 2020, the government is keen to meet the policy target of having 40 percent of youth aged 19 to 24 admitted into tertiary education. By 2020, it hopes that 60 percent of high school students will be admitted into public universities, with the rest going to private colleges and universities. The publication of the *National Higher Education Strategic Plan 2020* and the *National Higher Education Action Plan, 2007–2010* (both launched in August 2007) are the most recent responses to the changing socioeconomic and sociopolitical circumstances in Malaysia. Given that the global higher educational environment has significantly changed, the National Higher Education Strategic Plan 2020 outlines seven major reform objectives, as follows: widening access and enhancing quality; improving the quality of teaching and learning; enhancing research and innovation; strengthening institutions of higher education; intensifying internationalization; enculturation of lifelong learning; and finally, reinforcing the MOHE's delivery system.

In December 2008, the Malaysian government again revealed its seriousness in pursuing that ambitious goal by amending the Universities and University Colleges Act significantly in order to further improve governance and reduce bureaucracy.[3] Among other things, it has introduced more prominent professionals into the composition of public university boards of directors. Also, selection committees would be set up by the MOHE for the appointment of every vice chancellor of the public universities, and the vice chancellors would have the authority to extend the services of academics beyond retirement age on a contractual basis. Nevertheless, as pointed out by a specific World Bank report, the current governance regime of Malaysian public higher education is still restrictive, particularly in respect to three critical decision-making capacities, namely the Malaysian universities' ability to select their students on their own terms, the freedom to offer competitive remuneration packages to attract the most talented faculty internationally, and the authority to appoint a highly qualified and capable university leader (World Bank 2007, 35–36).

In terms of transnational higher education in Malaysia, the *Report by the Committee to Study, Review and Make Recommendations Concerning the Development and Direction of Higher Education in Malaysia (Halatuju Report)* was published in July 2005, containing 138 recommendations. Though it was controversial (Wan Abdul Manan 2008), central to this report is the need for local higher education institutions to engage in self-promoting activities in the outside world. In addition, the report also recommends that the government invest more in international student and staff exchange programs, which would promote more collaboration between local and transnational education institutions. Based on inputs from the cabinet, another report named the *Transformation of Higher Education Document* was issued in July 2007 to combine the relevant elements in the Ninth Malaysia Plan and recommendations from the *Halatuju Report*. Subsequently, the latest publication for this long-term plan, the *National Higher Education Strategic Plan*, was put together in August 2007. According to the plan, the Malaysia government is trying to attract 100,000 students from overseas by 2010.

As mentioned earlier, distance learning arrangements, notably twinning programs, have long been prosperous in Malaysia ever since the mid-1980s. Yet the establishment of international branch campuses could only become possible after the construction of a new legal framework in 1996.[4] Since then, various forms of transnational higher education have swiftly emerged in Malaysia, especially in the Klang Valley where Kuala Lumpur is a major component. The development of international branch campuses here is particularly impressive. In Malaysia, branch campuses of foreign universities can only be established by an invitation from the Ministry of Education or the Ministry of Higher Education (after 2004). The invited foreign universities, however, need to establish themselves as Malaysian companies, with majority Malaysian ownership, to operate their campuses. For instance, the University of Nottingham has run its programs in its Malaysia campus since 2000, with a new campus recently set up at Semenyih, Negeri Sembilan, for the 2005/06 academic years. The other three international branch campuses in Malaysia, to date, are all Australian universities, namely the Monash University (Petaling Jaya campus 1998), Curtin University (Miri campus 1999), and the Swinburne University of Technology (Kuching campus 2000). According to the Observatory on Borderless Higher Education (2002), Monash University cooperates with the Sunway Group—a pioneer of twinning arrangements in the field of education as early as the late 1980s—and the latter provides funding for its Malaysia campus. Similarly, the local partner of Swinburne University of Technology in Malaysia is the Sarawak state government, which cooperates indirectly with the university through its Yayasan Sarawak (Sarawak Foundation) and Sarawak Higher Education Foundation.

Malaysia's increasing cooperation with foreign universities has coincided with the increased regulation regarding transnational provisions (McBurnie and Ziguras 2001). After establishing the partnership with local corporations, foreign university campuses in Malaysia have done well. For instance, Monash University was the first to build its overseas branch campus in Malaysia. With its five faculties including medicine and health sciences, engineering, information technology, business, and arts and sciences, the Monash University–Malaysia now offers various undergraduate and graduate programs to almost 4,000 students. Its purpose-built campus was opened in 2007, which provides a high-tech home for the university. The Nottingham Malaysia campus has also successfully recruited more than 2,700 international students from more than 50 countries. According to the Malaysian Qualifications Agency, as of 21 April 2009, there are altogether four branch campuses (having one set up by the UK university and three by Australia) running 84 programs in the country (interview conducted in Malaysia, April 2009). Official statistics also indicate that the private sector has played an increasingly important role in enhancing access to higher education in Malaysia. In 2004, 32 percent of students were enrolled in private higher education institutions in Malaysia. Furthermore, 27,731 international students were studying in Malaysian private higher education institutions in 2004. I was also informed during my recent visit to the Malaysian Qualifications Agency that 19 UK universities are now running 110 twinning programs accredited in the list of the Malaysian Qualifications Register (MQR), while 18 Australian universities are offering 71 programs of this kind in the country. Institutions from other countries like New Zealand, the United States, Egypt, and Jordan are also offering twinning programs in Malaysia (interview conducted in Malaysia, April 2009).

And finally, the government has also initiated a general regulatory framework for quality assurance of higher education. In fact, the private education sector was initially the only focus of this regulatory framework. Lembaga Akreditasi Negara (National Accreditation Board) was established under the Lembaga Akreditasi Negara Act of 1996 as a statutory body to accredit certificate, diploma, and degree programs provided by the private institutions of higher learning. Yet later in April 2002, the Ministry of Education also set up its own Quality Assurance Division to coordinate and manage the quality assurance system in public institutions of higher learning. With the rise of transnational education programs and the rapid expansion of private higher education, the government eventually decided to streamline these existing regulatory frameworks in 2003, and thereafter adopted the unified Malaysian Qualifications Framework (MQF) in 2004, governed by the newly established Malaysian Qualifications Agency (MQA) in 2007 to accredit qualifications awarded by all institutions of higher education.

Malaysia's successful transnational higher education initiative received the attention of guests and participants of the recent International Education Summit held in Washington in May 2012. Professor Siti Hamisah said, "We are now the champion in transnational higher education among emerging countries and they welcome Malaysian colleges to open up branch campuses in their countries." The Malaysian government has begun to engage in active promotion and marketing to make Malaysia an excellent hub for higher education in Asia, and has been actively involved in rebranding and upgrading local higher education institutions to meet international standards in order to attract more overseas students. Working hard for around a decade, Malaysia has obtained some achievements. Currently, out of a total of 1.1 million students in higher education, about 10 percent (100,000) are foreign nationals from Indonesia, China, India, Africa, and the Middle East studying mainly technology-related subjects, which will eventually help with their nation building. According to official estimates, each foreign student normally spends about RM 30,000 per year for tuition, room, and board. A female student from the Middle East may spend more if she comes with her family members, thus creating a multiplier effect in terms of tourism and medical tourism, estimated at RM 3 billion a year. The ministry estimates the foreign student population to grow to 150,000 by 2015 and to 200,000 by 2020.[5]

Hong Kong

Compared to other Asian societies, the University Grant Committee, a public organization responsible for developing higher education development in the city-state of Hong Kong, believes that the strong competitive edge of Hong Kong over its regional competitors in this regard was first and foremost "its strong links with Mainland China," followed by other elements such as its geographical location and cosmopolitan outlook and its internationalized and vibrant higher education sector, which are also frequently claimed by Singapore in its bid for the Global Schoolhouse aspiration.[6] To the government of the HKSAR, it seems that as far as transnational higher education is concerned, it was initially regarded by the government as some sort of supplementary means to meet the domestic demands under the tide of expansion of higher education (Chan and Lo 2007) rather than as a tool for another, more aggressive strategy. With limited resources due to its low-tax policy and particularly after the Asian financial crisis, the Hong Kong government has had to rely more on nonstate financial sources as well as service providers (including overseas academic institutions) to cater to the further development of its higher education.

Another feature worth mentioning is the fact that institutional collaborations between Hong Kong and Mainland China seized much attention from policy makers throughout the first decade of post-handover Hong Kong, which resulted in a population of nonlocal tertiary students, consisting mainly of Mainland Chinese.[7] It was only in 2007 that Donald Tsang, then chief executive of Hong Kong, explicitly stated his intention to expand the population of international students by "increasing the admission quotas for non-local students to local tertiary institutions, relaxing employment restrictions on non-local students, as well as providing scholarships" (Tsang 2007, 40). And in June 2009, based on recommendations made by the Task Force on Economic Challenges set up after the distressing impact of the global financial tsunami, the government declared its resolution to develop six economic areas where Hong Kong still enjoys clear advantages, with educational services being one of them.[8]

Different from Malaysia, transnational education in Hong Kong is mainly provided in the form of joint programs, distance learning, and twinning programs. In the context of financial constraints, all the local publicly funded higher education institutions have to develop more self-financing programs or joint programs with their overseas partners in order to recover costs and generate incomes (Yang 2006; Chan 2008).[9] For instance, continuing education units as well as community colleges have been established in turn by these institutions, and the full-time self-financing local programs that they offer have steadily increased from 41 in 2001/02 to 347 in 2008/09, with academic qualifications ranging from higher diplomas (128) and associate's degrees (161) to bachelor's degrees (58).[10] As for nonlocal higher education and professional courses, the expansion of their numbers is even more impressive. Recognizing the fact that Hong Kong can offer very good market conditions for transnational higher education, especially with its geographical proximity to Mainland China, overseas institutions have become increasingly proactive in setting up their academic programs in Hong Kong during the last few years to attract mainland students (Yang 2006). However, on the other hand, top universities from Mainland China have also begun to offer programs in Hong Kong and to expand their market share (currently occupying 5 percent of those registered courses and 7 percent of exempted courses), which unequivocally reflects the closer ties between both sides, particularly after they struck a memorandum on mutual recognition of academic degrees in higher education in 2004. For example, Tsinghua University and Peking University, in collaboration with the HKU SPACE[11] and Hong Kong Shue Yan University, offer academic programs ranging from professional certificates to master's degrees in law, economy, literature, and architecture respectively. Likewise, universities in Hong Kong have also started to export their education programs to the mainland.

Yet despite the exuberance for nonlocal courses, the Hong Kong government has, by far, set out only a code of practice for these courses (HKCAAVQ 2007), which is considered moderately liberal.[12] Foreign universities can easily enter or quit Hong Kong's market. Currently, all courses conducted in Hong Kong leading to the award of nonlocal higher academic qualifications (i.e., associate's degree, degree, postgraduate, or other postsecondary qualifications) or professional qualifications must be properly registered or be exempted from registration. Any overseas institution is required to obtain accreditation or other formal permission from the Education Bureau (EDB)[13] prior to its operation. However, this category is diverse, ranging from compulsory registration to formal assessment of academic criteria. The EDB will normally seek the independent expert advice of the Hong Kong Council for Accreditation of Academic and Vocational Qualifications (HKCAAVQ)[14] as to whether a course can meet the criteria for registration or be exempted from registration. Yet again, the relevant requirements are considered to be straightforward and nonburdensome.

Hong Kong has gained considerable success in transnational higher education. According to Education Bureau statistics in 2012, a total of 105 institutions from the UK, Australia, United States, Mainland China, Canada, and other countries exported 659 exempted programs (exempted from registration, offered in collaboration with a local university or government-funded education institution) to Hong Kong, while a total of 136 institutions exported 429 registered programs (properly registered under the registration criteria of Cap. 493: "Non-local Higher & Professional Education Regulation Ordinance") to Hong Kong. For exempted programs, 351 are master's or postgraduate, 228 are bachelors, 65 are subdegree, 12 are doctoral, and 3 are other academic levels. For registered programs, 185 are bachelors, 139 are master's or postgraduate, 66 are subdegree, 22 are doctoral degrees, and 17 are other academic levels. Business and administration, science and technology, arts and social science, education and language, and general education are the most popular subjects. Some overseas universities have established offices or campuses in Hong Kong, for example, the University of Middlesex, the University of Ulster, the University of Warwick, and the University of Oxford from the United Kingdom; the University of British Columbia and the University of Waterloo from Canada; the University of New South Wales from Australia; the Savannah College of Arts and Design from the United States; and Jinan University from China. In return, Hong Kong's diversified higher education system, internationally recognized curricula, provision of scholarships, English as a medium of instruction, and unique blend of Chinese and Western cultures attracts foreign students to come to Hong Kong.[15]

However, with the new government led by the new chief executive, the Honorable C. Y. Leung, the drive for making education a new pillar of industry (i.e., education services) is no longer regarded as the top priority without a consensus shared among Hong Kong citizens. In this regard, whether the HKSAR government will continue to push for the regional education hub is subject to further analysis, especially as we have to wait to see whether the new government will engage in the education hub project in the future.

Singapore

As a city-state with meager natural resources, the Singapore government has always taken the quality of its human resources very seriously. Being aware of the importance of a more inclusive, energetic, and creative higher education, it has initiated various comprehensive reviews of its higher education system since the late 1980s. Two major policy directions have been set in this regard: first, the expansion of postgraduate education and research at the universities, and second, the enhancement of undergraduate curricula with a stronger emphasis given to students' creativity and thinking skills.

Yet as far as the quest for a regional hub of education is concerned, policies of quality enhancement and corporatization of public universities alone may be far from sufficient. The provision of more opportunities for higher education, both in terms of the number and variety, has to be delivered to domestic Singaporeans as well as to foreign learners from the region. The mid-1980s school-leaver boom saw the beginnings of transnational higher education in Singapore, and as Richard Garrett pointed out, this school-leaving cohort (20- to 24-year age group) will rise again and reach its peak around 2010 (Garrett 2005, 9). However, by 2003, Singapore's public universities and polytechnics could only enroll around 40,000 and 56,000 students respectively; while on the other hand, 119,000 students were enrolled by around 170 private tertiary providers, 140 of which offered programs in collaboration with foreign institutions and enrolled 75 percent of the total student population in this section (Garrett 2005, 9–10). The importance of a transnational education provision in Singapore has therefore become obvious.

Meanwhile, in order to tap into the lucrative education market more aggressively, the Singapore government had launched its Global Schoolhouse initiative in 2002. In fact, ever since 1998, the government, through efforts taken by its Economic Development Board (EDB) instead of its Ministry of Education,[16] has strategically invited "world-class" and "reputable" universities from abroad to set up their Asian campuses in the city-state. As a result, Singapore is today home to 16 leading foreign tertiary institutions and 44 pre-tertiary schools offering international curricula.[17] The prestigious INSEAD (Institut Européen d'Administration des Affaires, its Singapore branch campus established in 2000), the University of Chicago Booth School of Business (2000), the S. P. Jain Center of Management (2006),[18] New York University's Tisch School of the Arts (2007), and the DigiPen Institute of Technology

(2008) are among the list of these foreign tertiary institutions, ranging impressively from business, management arts, media, and hospitality to information technology, biomedical sciences, and engineering.

In 2003, a further and more integrated step was taken by the government to promote Singapore as a premier education hub. "Singapore Education," a multigovernment agency initiative, is led by the EDB and supported by the Tourism Board, SPRING Singapore, International Enterprise Singapore, and the Ministry of Education. According to the official website of Singapore Education,[19] EDB is responsible for attracting "internationally renowned educational institutions to set up campuses in Singapore," whereas the Tourism Board is tasked with overseas promotion and marketing of Singapore Education,[20] and the International Enterprise Singapore is in charge of helping quality local education institutions (e.g., Anglo-Chinese School [International] and Raffles Education) to develop their businesses and set up campuses overseas. And last but not least, SPRING Singapore is given the role of administering quality accreditation for private education institutions in the city-state.

Another significant strategy adopted by the government in promoting transnational higher education is the joint-degree program arranged between the local universities and their overseas partners. Local Singapore universities are actively collaborating with peer universities across the world in a diversified spectrum of academic programs, bringing together affluent resources in such fields. Students are granted with the freedom to study at both campuses and receive supervision and teaching from faculties at both universities. A representative example is the Singapore-MIT Alliance (SMA), an innovative engineering education and research enterprise jointly founded by the National University of Singapore, the Nanyang Technological University, and the Massachusetts Institute of Technology (MIT) in 1998. This alliance has so far developed five graduate degree programs and has created a distance learning environment at the forefront of current technology.

And finally, as part of its policy to support transnational higher education, the Singapore government also offers a comprehensive package of financial aid to international students through several public channels (Cheng, Ng, Cheung, et al. 2009). The tuition fees for them are only 10 percent above the local rate, and they can apply for whatever financial assistance schemes are open to local students, including scholarships provided by the "Singapore Scholarship" and tuition grants conditional on the agreement of working for a Singapore-registered company for at least three years upon graduation. Moreover, there are numerous bursaries provided by individual tertiary institutions, and student loans are also available at favorable interest rates. Interviewing senior administrators of selected transnational education institutions like James Cook University Australia and the ESSEC IRENE Business School (Institute for Research on Education) from Paris, the author learned that both institutions have received financial subsidies and other forms of assistance like providing them with good amenities or identifying very good sites for campus buildings. Seeing the potential of developing their campuses in Singapore as a solid platform reaching out to Asian students, these overseas institutions are attracted with preferential treatment given by the Singapore government to venture onto Asian soil (filed interviews conducted in Singapore, August 2010). Recent immigration policies that aim to attract talented and skilled individuals to live and work in Singapore, in addition, have also facilitated the development of its transnational education industry. In short, the most recent achievements of transnational higher education in Singapore are as follows:

- According to World Cities Culture Report 2012, there were 91,500 international students studying in Singapore.[21]
- According to World Education News & Reviews 2013, Singapore is the top country for offshore higher education.[22]
- By 2013, there are 34 international schools in Singapore, including local schools which offer a foreign education system.[23]

Raffles Education Corp, the largest private education group in Asia, established its international headquarters in Singapore in 1990. It has grown its portfolio from one college in Singapore to 33 colleges in 30 cities across 13 countries in Asia-Pacific.[24]

Although Singapore has such achievements, it has to be noted that the number of international students in Singapore has dropped significantly after seeing a steady climb over several years. Figures obtained by *The Straits Times* (October 2012) suggest that as of July, there were only 84,000 international students enrolled in private and government-run schools and institutions, including the polytechnics and universities, while there were 100,000 international students in 2008. Student recruiters attribute the drop largely to two factors: the government putting a cap on the number of foreign students being admitted into public schools and institutions, and stricter regulations for private schools that have led to half of them shutting down. They also note that fewer foreigners are applying to study at government-run schools and institutions in Singapore because of a hefty hike in fees for foreigners. The three universities, five polytechnics, and the Institute of Technical Education raised tuition fees in 2012, with the heftiest hikes levied on foreigners. Foreign students at polytechnics pay US$7,500 a year, 28 percent more than the fees in 2011. Some ten years ago, the government set a target of hosting 150,000 international students by 2015 as part of its plan to grow Singapore as a top education hub, but recently, the local Singaporean government has become xenophobic. The Education Ministry announced that the number of foreign students in universities would fall from the current 18 percent to 15 percent by 2015, even as more places are created for Singaporeans. Education Unlimited Singapore, an agency that matches foreign students to schools, says that many foreign students are now considering other destinations such as Australia and Malaysia.[25]

Changing State and Market Relations: A Comparison

Malaysia: Market-Accelerationist State with an Undecided Regulatory Regime of Simultaneous Centralization and Decentralization

In terms of governance and regulatory reforms on transnational higher education, the integrative framework constructed by the Malaysian government for quality assurance is arguably more comprehensive than that in Hong Kong. As mentioned, the Lembaga Akreditasi Negara (LAN, or National Accreditation Board) was established in 1996 with the limited function of accrediting only programs offered by private institutions of higher learning. Under this regulatory structure, these institutions were obliged to apply for approval from the minister of education (instead of the ministry itself) to conduct a program based on the recommendation of LAN. Various guidelines on the criteria and standards of programs at different levels or in different modes were to be met, and LAN was even authorized to conduct site audit visits to ascertain the compliance of these institutions to minimum standards or, where required, accreditation. Moreover, LAN had also built a database concerning these private institutions, which included the evaluation of their staff qualifications and facilities, as well as their student-teacher ratio.

The Malaysian Qualifications Framework (MQF), a unified quality assurance structure that covers both private and public higher education institutions, was adopted in 2004, and the framework has become even more centrally controlled since the founding of the Malaysian Qualifications Agency (MQA, or Agensi Kelayakan Malaysia) on 1 November 2007. The MQA is a merger of LAN and the Quality Assurance Division of the Ministry of Higher Education, which is now responsible for the implementation of MQF. Nevertheless, the MQA is still a subordinate agency placed directly under the Ministry of Higher Education. In terms of accreditation, a new feature worth noting is that under the MQA Act of 2007, there is now a possibility of the conferment of "self-accrediting status" to mature higher education institutions that already have well-established internal quality assurance mechanisms. However, to be so conferred, the institution concerned needs to undergo an institutional audit, and if successful, all qualifications it offers will then be automatically registered in the Malaysian Qualifications Register

(MQR).²⁶ Thus a complete process of the MQA quality assurance is as follows: program accreditation → institutional audit → self-accreditation.²⁷

The MQA claims that these processes are further supported by continuous monitoring in order to consistently ensure the quality of programs offered by institutions of higher education. Moreover, the Ministry in Malaysia has a list of accredited overseas universities or, in some cases, a list of accredited programs of certain universities. In other words, not only is the state involved in the assessment of all the domestic public and private tertiary programs in Malaysia (transnational programs included), but overseas programs as well. Yet this seemingly impeccable framework obviously entails a powerful, significant, and centralized bureaucracy to act as its administrative support, and a powerful bureaucracy may adversely imply more hassles than benefits. Moreover, in terms of execution, the lackluster track record of the concerned Ministry of Education/Higher Education during the past few decades may also worry some observers regarding the effectiveness of the framework.²⁸

The strong tendency of state intervention can also be found in other aspects of the governance of transnational higher education in Malaysia. While a series of decentralized policies, including the drastic liberalization of the private higher education sector and corporatization of public universities, has been pushed forward since the mid-1990s, the Malaysian government has also paradoxically strengthened its governance—though in some cases indirectly—of higher education, particularly in those public institutions. For instance, Abdul Razak Ahmad (2008) remarked recently that the Malaysian higher education system is still very much dominated by the state to the point that it has virtually become part of the government bureaucracy. The establishment of the Ministry of Higher Education in 2004 clearly reveals the state's intention to retain its centralized control in this respect.²⁹ The ministry, however, "introduced new and superfluous bureaucratic procedures onto a system which has already been noted for its inefficiency" (Abdul Razak 2008, 9).

This paradoxical or rather undecided regulatory regime of simultaneous centralization and decentralization of higher education could again be epitomized by the recent conferment of the privileged position of "APEX university" to Universiti Sains Malaysia (USM) and the subsequent developments. The Malaysian government designated four public universities in 2006 as "research universities" based on their satisfactory track records in research.³⁰ Among them, USM was further selected in 2008 to participate in the government's Accelerated Program for Excellence (APEX), which made it the first and only APEX university in Malaysia. Upon selection, this university is then supposed to be adequately endowed and empowered so as to achieve world-class status and be included as one of the top 100 in global university rankings by 2013, and a member of the top 50 by 2020. However, as Morshidi and Abdul Razak (2009) worryingly point out, the government has yet to show its political will in offering a bold and liberal new legal and regulatory framework that is "radically" different from the current framework practicing under the Universities and University Colleges Act since 1996 (Morshidi and Abdul Razak 2009, 4, 9). Admittedly, as far as private and transnational higher education providers are concerned, it is, to date, still evident that the state's regulatory approach is comparatively liberal. However, the insistence of the Malaysian government in keeping its role for the promotion of "national interest" is equally evident, thus resulting in a reservation of its regulatory powers through existing legal frameworks even toward the sector of private and transnational higher education (Morshidi 2009b). Being asked to comment on the swing between centralization and decentralization in higher education governance during a regional conference on comparative education and development in Taiwan held in September 2009, Morshidi clearly argued that the Malaysian government adopts "selective decentralization," which is clearly reflected by a "policy yo-yo" in education policy and management (Morshidi 2009a, 19).

Hong Kong: Market-Facilitating State with Comparatively More Liberal Regulation

As noted, the Hong Kong government initially tended to see transnational higher education as simply a supplement to local universities. It was therefore a sector allowed to generate its own revenue and operate under a free market mechanism, with hardly any public resources committed to, or proactive regulation imposed on, its development. While the government has become increasingly committed to the progress of transnational higher education since 2007, particularly since the Task Force on Economic Challenges pinpointed "educational services" as one of the key industries for Hong Kong's future development in 2009, closer scrutiny reveals that it still refrains from any direct intervention or regulation on either the content or quality of courses offered by foreign educational institutions.

The reliance on a market mechanism implies a regulatory regime of transnational higher education that focuses primarily on providing sufficient market information for consumers to choose, as well as on defending their interests through quality assurance of the "products." Nevertheless, ever since the restructuring of the Hong Kong Council for Academic Accreditation (HKCAA), and thereafter the establishment of a more inclusive accreditation authority (HKCAAVQ) on 1 October 2007, a similar quality assurance mechanism has been constructed as in Malaysia. Though in comparison HKCAAVQ is still not as inclusive or versatile as its Malaysian counterpart MQA, a more rigorous—at least formally—qualifications framework (QF)[31] and an associated qualifications register (QR)[32] are now in place and administered by the HKCAAVQ. This brand new structure is made possible through the provision of the Accreditation of Academic and Vocational Qualifications Ordinance (Chapter 592), which became fully operational only as of 5 May 2008. One of the functional differences between HKCAAVQ and MQA is that the former only assesses academic and vocational programs conducted by non-self-accrediting institutions, whereas the exempted list of self-accrediting institutions is indeed a significant one that includes all eight UGC-funded institutions[33] and the Open University of Hong Kong.[34]

Under this newly constructed qualifications framework, a four-stage quality assurance process is implemented, as delineated by the HKCAAVQ: stage 1) initial evaluation; stage 2) program validation, revalidation; stage 3), program area accreditation; stage 4) periodic review.[35]

This new quality assurance framework, as rigorous as it may seem, is still a fairly moderate approach as far as nonlocal higher and professional education courses are concerned. These courses are regulated by the Nonlocal Higher and Professional Education (Regulation) Ordinance (Chapter 493) through a system of registration, yet the registration criteria set for nonlocal higher academic qualifications, for instance, are rather lenient, consisting of only two points:

1. The awarding institution should be a nonlocal institution recognized in the home country.
2. Effective measures should be in place to ensure that the standard of the course is maintained at a level comparable with a course conducted in the home country leading to the same qualification. And it should as such be recognized by that institution, the academic community in that country, and the relevant accreditation authority in that country (if any).[36]

Moreover, nonlocal courses conducted in collaboration with all the eight UGC-funded institutions and several other local institutions[37] are exempt from registration. Likewise, in respect to the standing of these courses in local society, the Hong Kong government has taken an approach that "it is a matter of discretion for individual employers to recognize any qualification to which this course may lead."[38] Thus as McBurnie and Ziguras (2001) rightly observed, this government is adopting a far more liberal approach in dealing with transnational education. Unlike Malaysia, Hong Kong simply performs the role of "market facilitator" instead of "market generator" (McBurnie and Ziguras 2001, 102).

The rationale behind this civil society regulatory regime is closely related to the tradition of the "free market economy" that it has long committed to. Hence the objective of the ordinance, as claimed by the official website of the Education Bureau, is "to protect Hong Kong consumers by guarding against the marketing of substandard non-local higher and professional education courses conducted in Hong Kong."[39] Further elaboration of this neoliberal approach came from Nigel French, then secretary general of the Hong Kong University Grants Committee, when he suggested in 1999 that a key function of the regulatory regime was to provide Hong Kong consumers with detailed information from providers regarding their offerings. Once this information was made publicly available, the government would leave individual consumers to decide, providing that their choices were informed ones (French 1999).

Unlike Malaysia, even when the government of the HKSAR has announced its policy intent to establish the city-state as a regional hub of education, the government has never come up with concrete plans or specific strategies but rather relies upon the market (private sector) to respond to the quest for the regional education center project. Strongly believing in the market, the HKSAR government is rather reluctant to get involved in creating a "governed education market" to compete with its regional competitors.

Singapore: A Highly Proactive and Systematic Regulator

It is quite obvious that the Singapore government resorts to a fairly systematic, controlled, and measured approach toward the promotion and regulation of its transnational higher education. With the grandiose objective "to make Singapore a Global Schoolhouse providing educational programs of all types and at all levels from pre-school to post-graduate institutions, and that attracts an interesting mix of students from all over the world" in mind, the government not only maintains its guidance over the developmental path of public universities through certain forms of "decentralized centralism" (Tan and Ng 2007), but also handpicks prestigious foreign universities for its list of invitation to be allowed to set up their overseas campuses in Singapore. In fact, under the current framework of GATS, the government is supposed to relinquish some of its ability in picking and choosing new universities, as GATS is against restrictions on market entry. Thus a clearer and more transparent framework may need to be worked out in order to treat foreign universities "no less favorably" than it treats the local universities in the city-state (Ziguras 2003).

The government is also actively involved in the regulatory affairs of its transnational higher education. As Ziguras pointed out, online courses and other forms of distance education that do not have a local presence in Singapore could be exempted from approval. However, foreign programs offered by a local partner institution must obtain permission from the Ministry of Education, and both the awarding university and its local partner must provide detailed information to convince the ministry that they are capable of delivering their programs up to the equivalent standard at which these could be offered in the home institutions (Ziguras 2003, 100). Moreover, in order to make clear the division of labor and responsibilities between the local partners and overseas degree-awarding institutions, the ministry allows the local agents/partners to offer only administrative support instead of engaging in any teaching and learning activities. Yet despite this regulation, it is still difficult to know whether in reality local partners are entirely forbidden to engage in any teaching and learning activities. As Ziguras suggests, local tutors employed by the overseas institutions have been engaging in teaching tutorials and even lectures on some occasions.

Such observations seem to suggest that no lucid guideline is available for regulating external programs so far, and closer scrutiny further reveals that there is no central authority in Singapore that assesses or grants recognition for degrees obtained from overseas universities, and the Ministry of Education does not have a list of accredited overseas universities. This decentralized approach is based on the rationale that the employers should be the ones deciding whether a degree holder has the qualities desired for the job and the qualifications most relevant to his needs. Professional overseas degrees, such as those in engineering, medicine, law, and accountancy, should therefore rely on inspection and accreditation by the respective local professional bodies. As for the courses offered by overseas universities in Singapore through their local agents, the ministry opines that the institutions concerned and their agents are responsible for all aspects of the programs.

Nevertheless, the proactive role played by the state in the formation of Singapore's transnational higher education could plainly be seen from its highly selective process of inviting overseas partners to set up branch campuses, as well as its strategic master plan to guide and orchestrate various sectors in the city-state toward its goal of promoting Singapore as a major exporter of higher education in the region. The government does intervene in the market by deciding who the partners are and what programs can be launched to fulfill its nation-building agenda. In terms of resources, the government may offer attractive financial incentives (including land) to woo top foreign universities, yet in return, the latter are also expected to live up to its expectations (Chan and Ng 2008). A recent example in this vein is the closure of the Division of Biomedical Sciences of John Hopkins University in Singapore in July 2006. It was ordered by the government-affiliated Agency for Science, Technology and Research (A*Star) on the grounds that the division failed to achieve several key performance indicators, including the recruitment of doctorate degree students and also internationally reputable scholars into its Singapore campus (Lee and Gopinathan 2008, 579–580). In light of the conceptual framework set out for this study, the rise of transnational higher education in Singapore has shown a rather successful operation of the state-corporatist regulatory regime, in which the state has make use of various procompetition instruments to accelerate market forces toward its desired developmental model.

Discussion and Conclusion

After comparing and contrasting the role of the state in the promotion of regional education hubs between Malaysia, Singapore, and Hong Kong, this study discovers that although the economic dimension of higher education expansion has been well recognized by these Asian states, we should also note the importance of the political dimension in the quest for regional hub status. The present study has found that the varied role of the state, in Hong Kong as opposed to Malaysia, is actively promoting regional education hubs as a solution to unequal access within the nation, while the Global Schoolhouse project taking place in Singapore is not necessarily for domestic needs but for asserting Singapore's global and regional leadership in higher education. In addition, the varied role of the state is clearly demonstrated in the quality assurance of the growing prominence of transnational higher education, especially when Malaysia has adopted a more centralized approach to assure quality while Hong Kong has relied on the providers to uphold the quality of their program delivery. Most importantly, the quest for regional education hubs in Malaysia, Singapore, and Hong Kong is not only for the purpose of economic benefit but also for asserting "soft power" and "political influence" in the region.

Chapter 9

Transnationalization of Higher Education in China: Development Trends, Salient Features, and Challenges for University Governance

Introduction

In the last decade or so, we have witnessed the rise of transnational higher education in Asia. The rise of transnational higher education in Malaysia, Singapore, and Hong Kong in general and the quest for regional hub status in particular has clearly suggested that these Asian governments are particularly keen to expand the education market not only for income generation but also for "soft power" assertion to enhance their national competitiveness in the global marketplace (Mok and Ong 2012). Similarly, the expansion of transnational higher education in China is not only related to the state's strategy of making use of overseas programs and academic institutions to help transform and internationalize the higher education system in Mainland China (Mok and Chan 2012) but also as part of its strategy to transform the country from a strong economic power to a country with strong cultural and soft power influences. Let us now discuss the policy background for the rise of transnational higher education in China, especially examining how transnational higher education has become more prominent after China has become a member of the World Trade Organization (WTO). The major objectives of this chapter are to examine the policy background of the rise of transnational higher education in China, with particular reference to examining the central features of these programs and major reasons accounting for the emergence of transnational higher education. In addition, this chapter also discusses how major universities in Mainland China have tried to engage in international cooperation with leading overseas partners to promote international student exchanges and other forms of research and academic cooperation, examining the challenges for university governance when higher education is increasingly transnationalized and internationalized in China.

China Joining the WTO and Transnationalizing Higher Education

Since the 1990s, there has been a series of major legislation governing transnational education in China. The most important national legislation is the Education Act of the People's Republic of China issued in 1995, encouraging exchange or cooperative education with foreign partners (Huang 2005). Based upon this act, two other documents concerning transnational education were promulgated and implemented, namely the Interim Provisions for Chinese-Foreign Cooperation in Running Schools issued by the State Education Commission (SEC, renamed as the Ministry of Education in 1998) in 1995 and the Regulations of the People's Republic of China on Chinese-Foreign Cooperation in Running Schools. According to the first legal document, transnational education was introduced with a Chinese name of Zhongwai Hezuo Banxue, which means that overseas higher education institutions can only provide academic programs in collaboration with local institutions in China, instead of providing academic programs solely by themselves.

In addition, the 1995 document also restricts the levels and forms of academic programs by stipulating that "Chinese and foreign parties may run educational institutions of various forms at varying levels, excluding China's compulsory education and those forms of education and training under special provisions by the state" (State Education Commission [SEC] 1995, Chapter 1, Article 4). Most important of all, the document also makes it explicit that the running of academic programs by overseas institutions should not be profit making. According to the 1995 document,

> Chinese-foreign cooperation in education shall abide by Chinese law and decrees, implement China's guideline for education, conform to China's need for educational development and requirement for the training of talents and ensure teaching quality, and shall not seek profits as the objective and/or damage the state and public interests. (SEC 1995, Chapter 1, Article 5)

Apparently, the notion of "profit making" in transnational education in China is very different from the experiences of other overseas institutions in Australia, the United States, and the United Kingdom, since most of these institutions set up their offshore academic programs in order to generate additional income for their home institutions. Before China joined the WTO and gave its consent to GATS, the government adopted transnational education as a policy tool to help create additional higher education learning opportunities for local high school graduates, instead of viewing it as a commercial enterprise. In 1997, the Academic Degrees Committee of the State Council (ADCSC) issued another document entitled "Notice on Strengthening the Management of Degree-granting in Chinese-Foreign Cooperation in Running Schools," as an important supplement to the 1995 document, which further emphasized that all Chinese-foreign cooperation in the running of schools should be governed by the legal framework of China. Nonetheless, the Chinese administration experienced difficulties in implementing the newly enacted laws when confronted with the increase of these overseas programs.

After joining the WTO, the Chinese government revised its legislation to allow overseas institutions to offer programs in the mainland in line with WTO regulations. In September 2003, the State Council started implementing the Regulations of the People's Republic of China on Chinese-Foreign Cooperation in Running Schools, thus providing further details concerning the nature, policy, principles, application processes, leadership, organization, teaching, financial management, supervision, legal liability, and other aspects of the collaboration. Unlike the 1995 document that attaches importance to vocational education, the 2003 document encourages a broader range of transnational higher education. Specifically, the 2003 document encourages local universities to cooperate with renowned overseas higher education institutions in launching new academic programs in order to improve the quality of teaching and learning, as well as to introduce excellent overseas educational resources to local institutions (State Council 2003, Chapter 1, Article 3). More importantly, the 2003 legal document removes the restriction on overseas institutions of higher learning making profits for running courses in China. According to Huang (2006b), the fundamental changes in the 2003 document showed that transnational education has gone through "a transfer from the previous informal, incidental and laissez-faire phase to a more structured, systematic and well-regulated phase after 1995" (Huang 2006b, 25). It should also be noted that, unlike the policies of other states which are practicing the ideas of neoliberalism to enable the evolution of an "education market," China has created a "governed market" or "state-guided market," characterized by heavy regulation, as part of a transitional economy (Lin et al. 2005; Mok 2006c).

The State Council, based on the above-mentioned WTO commitments, thus finally promulgated the Regulations of the People's Republic of China on Chinese-Foreign Cooperation in Running Schools (hereafter the "2003 CFCRS Regulations") on 1 March 2003 to further regulate the activities concerned and to assert the legal rights of the stakeholders involved (Wang 2005, 188–189; Zhang 2005, 130).[1] This is undoubtedly the most significant CFCRS regulation by far, and the Ministry of Education subsequently released a set of corresponding measures in June 2004 to deal with more specific issues in relating to the implementation of CFCRS. The 2003 CFCRS regulations not only reveal the state's blessing in developing CFCRS, but more importantly, it does not forbid foreign institutions from making profits through such activities.

The motivations for developing TNHE in China have varied over time, focusing variously on the concerns of the consumers, of the state, and of individuals, while the concerns of institutions of higher education are situated somewhere in the middle (Zheng 2009, 36). In the 1980s, right after the initiation of economic reform and its open-door policy, higher education was regarded as a priority by the state for realizing the "four modernizations" of industry, agriculture, national defense, and science and technology, in the face of a desperate need for qualified professionals and new technologies. Students and scholars were sent by the state for overseas studies as a direct, immediate, and major effort to tackle this problem. The burgeoning TNHE programs within the national education system during this period were unregulated and informal and scattered throughout the coastal provinces like Shandong and Jiangsu and big cities like Shanghai and Beijing.

However, by the 1990s, several factors had advanced the development of TNHE in a dramatic way. On the one hand, there was the pressing need to boost the enrollment rate in Chinese tertiary education in order to sustain the nation's soaring economic growth and meet the challenges posed by globalization. TNHE programs, in this regard, could be very helpful both in terms of the internationalization of Chinese universities' curricula and their quest for world-class status. On the other hand, concerns over the "brain drain" of human capital and the outflow of financial capital spent on overseas education also prompted the government to rethink its monopolistic approach to governance of education, resulting in a more cautious yet encouraging attitude toward transnational higher education (Wang and Liu 2010).

Recently, the State Council published the National Strategic Plan for Educational Development ("The Plan") in July 2010. One of the major goals of the Plan is to further internationalize the higher education sector in the mainland through collaboration with leading universities overseas or within the region. The Chinese government is very keen to invest more in education in order to develop strong human capital, and welcomes collaboration with overseas higher education institutions through joint programs, high-level professional and research training programs, and international research projects as a means to advance the knowledge base and to develop state-of-the-art technology for the country (State Council 2010).

Phases of Transnational Higher Education Development

It is within this wider socioeconomic context that transnational higher education in China has evolved from an informal, incidental, and rather laissez-faire activity into a more systematic and regulated one, after the issue of the Notice on Cooperation with Foreign Institutions and Individuals in Running Schools in China in 1993, and the promulgation of the Provisional Stipulation on Chinese-Foreign Cooperation in Running Schools (CFCRS) by the then State Education Commission[2] on 26 January 1995. The Provisional Stipulation on CFCRS was particularly significant in the sense that it symbolized the formal inclusion of CFCRS activities under the management of state bureaucracy. The necessity of initiating CFCRS in China, its coverage, its application procedure, and the defining authority over its program appraisal and approval, the managerial framework for its institutions, and the awarding mechanism of its degrees/diplomas have all been clearly specified in this stipulation.[3]

On 11 December 2001, transnational higher education was again given a momentous promotion in China when the country finally gained access to the WTO. China has consequently promised to open up its education sector for commercial activities in the five subitems of primary, secondary, higher, and adult education, as well as "other educational services,"[4] thus giving a green light to transnational higher education under the legal framework of the international agreement. Foreign partners are now allowed to secure a majority ownership of CFCRS institutions concerned, yet they remain prohibited from establishing and running an institution solely on their own. Also, the privilege of enjoying 'national treatment' may not be granted to them as an entitlement during this process.

The development of transnational higher education in China thus far could therefore be broadly divided into three main phases in accordance with the shift of national policies (Wang 2005, 189–190), namely:

1. The first stage of laissez-faire exploration, i.e., before the promulgation of the Provisional Stipulation on CFCRS in January 1995.
2. The second stage of progressive standardization initiated by the state, i.e., from 1995 to the promulgation of CFCRS regulations in March 2003.
3. The third stage of progressive legalization and regulation advanced by the state, i.e., from March 2003 onward after the promulgation of the CFCRS regulations up to the present.

Major Features of Transnational Higher Education Programs in China

CFCRS programs in China today vary considerably in terms of their quality, source of students, curriculum, and degree or certificate conferred, as well as in transnational arrangements. Despite a certain degree of liberalization to allow both *minban* or private and transnational education to develop, the predominant pattern remains state planned, which is a tradition originating from the Soviet style of education system entrenched under Mao Zedong from the 1950s to the 1970s. As far as the CFCRS programs are concerned, the source of students is the first characteristic of state planning. Broadly speaking, students recruited for CFCRS programs are either state-planned students or non-state-planned students. The former refers to students who pass the National Entrance Examination to universities and can therefore secure a place in a certain university according to the national quota; the latter refers to those who are not offered a place through this mechanism—they may be fee-paying or simply mature students.

In terms of the degree(s) awarded, the CFCRS programs confer either a single degree or a double/dual degree. A single degree refers to a foreign degree from the partner HEI involved in the collaboration, while a double or dual degree comprises a degree award from both the local HEI and the foreign partner HEI. Zheng (2009) suggested that there was indeed a correlation between the type of students recruited and the type of degree awarded: state-planned students are always awarded a double degree, whereas non-state-planned students are always awarded merely a single degree. This is due to the fact that state-planned students are guaranteed a Chinese HEI's degree provided they can fulfill all the academic requirements set by the university. In contrast, non-state-planned students are not automatically entitled to a Chinese HEI's degree because they are not part of the national quota for higher education, and so they are allowed to receive only the degree awarded by the foreign HEI (Zheng 2009, 40). Indeed, these subtle differences have impacted in diverse ways how the Chinese HEIs offer CFCRS programs to students.

If we combine the nature of the curriculum offered with the type of degree or certificate awarded, a total of five categories of CFCRS programs may be identified:

1. **Joint curriculum and foreign degree:** The program is offered collaboratively by both the local Chinese HEI and the foreign HEI, but only the foreign HEI confers a degree.
2. **Joint curriculum and double degree:** The program is offered collaboratively by both partners, and a double degree is conferred jointly by both institutions.
3. **Joint curriculum and foreign degree + Chinese certificate:** The program is offered collaboratively by the local Chinese HEI and the foreign HEI, and a foreign degree plus a Chinese certificate is conferred.
4. **Foreign curriculum and foreign degree:** The program is offered exclusively by the foreign HEI, and it confers its own degree.
5. **Foreign curriculum and Chinese degree + foreign certificate:** The program is offered exclusively by the foreign HEI, but a Chinese degree plus a foreign certificate is conferred (see figure 9.1).

However, in terms of the transnational arrangement of CFCRS programs at the undergraduate level, closer scrutiny reveals that, at present, twinning is the prevailing model. Among the numerous twinning programs, it seems that 2+2

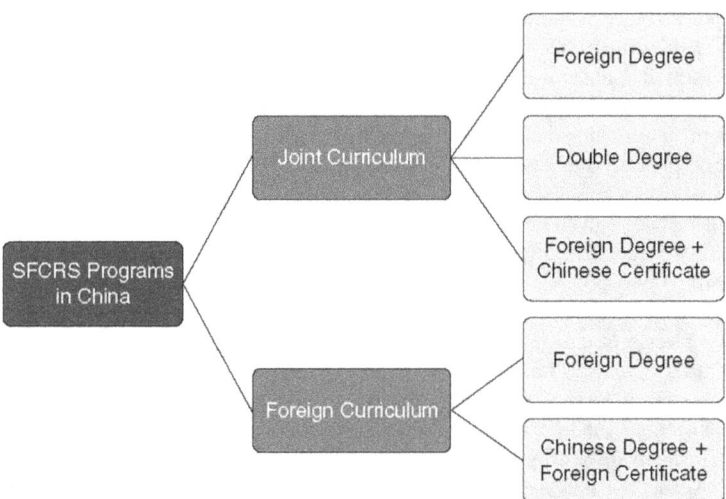

Figure 9.1 Typology of CFCRS Programs in China (Based on Curriculum Offered and Degree/Certificate Awarded)
Note: CFCRS institutions could have one more option than CFCRS programs in terms of the degree/certificate awarded. If they succeeded in acquiring approval from the State Degree Office, they could then confer their own degree on students. Such institutions include the China Europe International Business School collaboration between Shanghai Jiaotong University and the European Foundation for Management Development and the Cheung Kong Graduate School of Business (founded by the Hong Kong tycoon Li Ka Shing).
Source: Author.

and 3+1 are currently the most popular kinds of arrangement. The popularity of these twinning programs is due, first and foremost, to their financial affordability compared to programs abroad. In fact, these programs not only charge less than the equivalent overseas programs, but they are in general also more affordable than programs offered by the CFCRS institutions in China. For instance, the tuition fee charged by the University of Nottingham in the UK for its international undergraduate students in arts, law, and social sciences is a whopping £10,880 (around RMB 113,000) for the 2010 intake,[5] while in comparison the University of Nottingham-Ningbo, a CFCRS institution in China, charges domestic students a mere RMB 60,000 (around £6,500) for all its undergraduate programs over the same period of time.[6] Exactly the same amount of money (RMB 60,000) is also required by the Xi'an Jiaotong–Liverpool University, another CFCRS institution in China, for all its undergraduate programs in 2010.[7] However, the 3+1 twinning programs offered collaboratively by the Qingdao University in Shandong and the Holmes Colleges Australia (international business, business English, marketing, accountancy) charge only RMB 16,000 per annum for the first three years of study in China (2008/09 academic year).[8] And finally, unsurprisingly, the local undergraduate programs offered by the public Chinese universities are the cheapest, with their tuition fees usually only around a few thousand RMB per annum.

The second advantage that contributes to the popularity of twinning programs in China is their transitional role in enabling Chinese students to continue their studies abroad. First, they could facilitate the Chinese students' overseas visa applications for the second phase of their studies, an important consideration given that US visa applications, for instance, are problematic, as Chinese students individually sometimes encounter difficulties and rejection by the American embassy. They could also assist Chinese students in overcoming the language barrier by introducing a teaching and learning environment in a foreign language prior to their studies abroad. Last but not least, their popularity may also have something to do with a common perception among Chinese students and their parents that a genuine overseas experience matters, and a degree incorporating an overseas component is more valuable than one that was awarded after an entirely domestic 4+0 program.

Again, the prevalence of twinning programs as a recent development in transnational higher education in China is reminiscent of the past scenario in Malaysia. This is, indeed, a logical and sensible development given their similar socioeconomic contexts, as well as the pressing educational demands in today's China and Malaysia during the 1980s and 1990s (Mok 2008). During a training program for senior university administrators organized by the MOE in Beijing in September 2010, Professor Zhang Li, director of the National Research Centre for Educational Development of the MOE, stated that the Chinese government has taken a positive approach in encouraging and facilitating foreign universities to set up their branch campuses or programs on the mainland. When asked about the most acceptable model of TNHE, Professor Zhang pointed to the University of Nottingham at Ningbo campus. Recognizing that Nottingham University embarked upon a highly innovative project in offering nonprofit TNHE for Chinese students, the Chinese government would like to see more collaborations and projects of this kind flourish. However, despite the Chinese government's policy of welcoming such initiatives, the growing popularity of TNHE poses various challenges for higher education governance.

Beyond Transnational Higher Education: Promotion of International Student Exchanges

Following the publication of the Medium and Long-Term Development of Education (also known as the Education Blueprint) in 2010 by the Ministry of Education, more international cooperation between local universities and overseas institutions has been supported by the Chinese government. The following identifies some major universities and discusses some of their transnational higher education programs or international cooperative projects between mainland universities and overseas partners.

Peking University

The International Cultural Festival is held in October every year, and it has become a grand event at Peking University which comprises a large-scale exhibition showing the university's multiethnic global vision to welcome international students from different parts of the world. During the festival, representatives from various embassies, university heads, and student representatives from home and abroad are invited to participate in the grand opening ceremony. This festival indeed provides a good platform for local students to mingle with international students to share different cultures and traditions.

Students' International Communication Association (SICA)

Since its establishment in 1997, SICA was closely involved in the international exchange of Peking University, including the reception and interviews of distinguished guests to Peking University, such as heads of foreign states, ambassadors, university presidents, social and commercial celebrities, and so forth. In the last decade, SICA has developed into a friendly interface for student exchange by organizing various international forums and festivals inviting participation from Chinese and international students both from home and abroad. For instance, some events include the JING Forum with the University of Tokyo, the Beida-Harvard Exchange Camp, and the Peking Globalist with Yale University.[9]

Shanghai Jiao Tong University

Shanghai Jiao Tong University offers a summer semester exchange program from 1 July 2013 to 28 July 2013; foreign students will come to Shanghai Jiao Tong University to have a transnational learning experience together with the host students. During the exchange period, students can take courses with credits, including Western Judicial System and Cultures, An Introduction to Heritage Sciences: World Art Histories and Heritage in the 21st Century—a Global Challenge, International Law and Global Orders, Introduction to the European Culture, Contemporary Sino-Foreign Diplomacy, Eurasian Cultural Festivals Discussion, Model of Industrial and Entrepreneurial, Chinese and Western Architectural Culture, Japanese Floral Art, and Economic

Globalization and the Rise of China.[10] Through such an international summer school, local students in the mainland can mix with overseas students, while foreign students can learn from the host students about the most recent developments in China.

Tsinghua University

Like Peking University and Shanghai Jiao Tong University, Tsinghua University continues strengthening cooperation with prestigious universities, research institutions, and enterprises around the world, and sends students overseas for degree programs, joint education, student exchanges, joint research, short-term exchanges, summer internships, and international conferences. A total of over 4,000 students were sent overseas in 2012 to Yale, Harvard, MIT, Stanford, Cambridge, Oxford, and other world-class universities. These international exchange programs have received favorable comments from faculty and students and obtained strong support from the university's offices, schools, and departments. Furthermore, a series of featured programs, such as the distinguished freshmen overseas study program, the summer research program, and summer courses, have been developed, in addition to further developing the student exchange programs.[11]

Nanjing University

Similarly, Nanjing University has established academic exchange relations with over 200 institutions in the world. It sends teachers abroad, employs international teachers, receives international visitors and lecturers, hosts international academic conferences, operates joint education programs, and conducts international research collaboration.

The Johns Hopkins University–Nanjing University Center for Chinese and American Studies

Established in 1986, the Hopkins-Nanjing Center for Chinese and American Studies is an educational joint venture between NJU and the Johns Hopkins University in the United States. Chinese students study the United States and the international system in English with American professors, while international students focus on contemporary China and are taught by Chinese professors in Mandarin. Additionally, with collaborative research projects, joint seminars, and cross-registration opportunities, the center fosters a rich cross-cultural learning experience. Each year, it has approximately 100 students in the certificate program and 40 in the MA program (half Chinese and half international).

Sino-German Institute for Legal Studies

Established in 1989, the Sino-German Institute for Legal Studies is a successful joint venture between NJU and the University of Göttingen, with a vision for promoting dialogue between German and Chinese legal studies circles. Its teaching and research work shows both width and depth. During the past 18 years, the institute has made significant contributions to studies of law in China and Germany and thus enjoys a good reputation in two countries. One focus of the cooperation is on the training of graduate students, who will one day play important roles in the legal field of their own countries.

Sino-Dutch International Business Center of Nanjing University

With distinguished faculty from both China and Europe, the SDIBC's primary objective is to foster professionals in business management who can adapt to the increasingly globalized economy and engage in international economic and technological cooperation and competition.

The Center of Chinese and Japanese Studies

The Center of Chinese and Japanese Studies (CCJS) in NJU, which promotes communication between the two countries in academic study and culture, was established in 2002. It has successfully held three sessions of the International Academic Symposium of Hiromatu Wataru and Marxist Philosophy not only in Nanjing but also in Tokyo. In 2005, Studies of Cultural and Representation, which was highly praised by students and scholars, was opened in NJU. In addition, the Japanese Language Knowledge Contest in East China has been organized by NJU three times has received commendation from the sponsors and the media in Japan. The CCJS library has a collection of over 10,000 volumes, and dozens of works, including originals and translated works, have been published under the patronage of this institution.

Nanjing University EMBA Program with Cornell University

The NJU-Cornell EMBA program addresses the needs of middle and high-level management for professional and career development. It focuses on cultivating elite management professionals with innovativeness, decisiveness, and more importantly a global vision.

Sino-Canadian College

Sino-Canadian College was established in 2005 cooperatively by NJU and the University of Waterloo (UW) in Canada. It offers joint academic programs, currently at the undergraduate level, based on a 2 +2 model. That is, students are enrolled by NJU, and their initial two years of study are undertaken at NJU;

upon meeting UW's academic requirements, students are eligible to transfer to UW for their final two years of study. Students who successfully complete the requirements of the joint program receive degrees from both universities.

The Hwaying Education and Culture Foundation

The Hwaying Education and Culture Foundation was established in 1988 with a donation of US$7.43 million by Mr. Yu Chi Chung and Mrs. Yu, alumni of NJU and Southeast University. The foundation aims at cultivating professionals in economics, science, and technology; promoting international academic exchanges; and improving the quality of education. Its specific programs include supporting outstanding young faculty for overseas studies or attending international conferences, inviting top-level scholars to NJU to teach or lecture, and awarding graduates who choose teaching as their professions.

Institute for International Studies, Nanjing University

The Institute of International Students, founded in 1955, has received more than 18,000 international students from over 70 countries. Its present enrollment is around 1,700. Its website provides information about academic programs, application and admissions, tuition, HSK, and so forth.[12] All these different forms of programs have clearly suggested how keen Nanjing University has been in promoting international academic exchanges and cooperation.

Xi'an Jiaotong University

Like other major universities in China, Xi'an Jiaotong University also set up the International Cooperation and Exchange Office to promote more cooperation between the university and overseas partners. More specifically, this office is charged with the tasks to:

1. Establish and maintain the contact and cooperation of Xi'an Jiaotong University with foreign universities, educational institutions, and the relevant units.
2. Receive visiting scholars from all around the world and be responsible for long-term and short-term administration of foreign experts' works in the campus.
3. Be in charge of the Ministry of Education and the management of international cooperation and exchange projects, the application of specific funds, the audit work, the contact of various types of cooperative education programs, and all kinds of management and coordination.
4. Be in charge of signing agreements and developing and managing any cooperation and exchange programs.
5. Grant honorary titles to international celebrities and scholars.

6. Report and manage international meetings.
7. Be in charge of staff's long- and short-term procedures abroad, as well as study abroad at their own expense, to visit relatives or travel abroad.
8. Recruit and nurture Hong Kong, Macau, and Taiwan students; be responsible for the day-to-day management and foreign affairs of Hong Kong, Macao, and Taiwan students.[13]

Institute of International Education

Xi'an Jiaotong University started to recruit Russian and Mongolian students in 1959, and started to recruit Vietnam students in 1965. During the period of the Cultural Revolution, the university stopped the recruitment of foreign students. Starting from 1980, the university began recruiting foreign students again and established a scholarship fund for them. The Institute of International Education was found in 2006, in charge of recruiting, managing, and nurturing foreign students. Now the university has foreign students who come from five continents, including over 51 countries, for example Pakistan, Nepal, South Korea, Japan, USA, France, and Belgium.[14] The trend of "Chinese Fever" attracts foreign students to come to China to learn Chinese language and culture. Xi'an is an ancient capital of the Qing dynasty, where the tomb of Qin Shi Huang and the terra-cotta warriors and horses are situated, making Xi'an Jiaotong University a very attractive place for study.

Wuhan University

Wuhan University has developed cooperative and exchange associations with over 350 universities and research institutions in more than 40 countries and regions, and signed long-term cooperative agreements with 200 of them. Each year it welcomes over 3,000 overseas visitors for academic visits and exchange, hosts 30 international and cross-strait conferences, and invites over 100 long-term foreign experts and 500 short-term foreign experts for teaching and lectures. Each year more than 1,000 faculty members travel overseas for academic conferences and exchange. Wuhan University has opened a number of international joint education classes and built more than ten international joint labs and research centers. Now Wuhan University is endeavoring to shape itself into a world-class comprehensive research university domestically and internationally.[15] Major partners of Wuhan University include institutions from the United States such as the University of Illinois at Urbana-Champaign, Ohio State University, the University Board for Christian Higher Education in Asia, Case Western Reserve University, the University of North Carolina at Greensboro, the University of Massachusetts Medical School, Northwestern Polytechnic University, Trimble Navigation Limited, Coe College, the University of Tennessee–Knoxville, the

Table 9.1 Wuhan University's International Joint Programs

Program Name	Participant Schools and Departments of Wuhan University	Partner	Start-up Year
Sino-French Joint Class for Dual Bachelor's Degree in Economics and Arts	Economics and Management School	Université de La Rochelle and Université d'Auvergne, Clermont Ferrand 1	1993
Sino-German Joint Class for Dual Bachelor's Degree in Science and Engineering	Schools and departments in science and technology	University of Stuttgart	2001
Sino-French Joint Class in Medicine (seven-year program)	Faculty of Medicine	Université Henri Poincaré, Nancy 1	2001
Sino-French Joint Class for Dual Bachelor's Degree in Law and Arts	School of Law	Université d'Auvergne, Clermont Ferrand 1; Université Paris-Sud 11; Université Lille 2 Droit et Santé	2002
Sino-French Joint Program in Mathematics	School of Mathematics and Statistics	Université des Sciences et Technologies de Lille 1	2004
Sino-Irish Collaborative Program in Software Engineering	International School of Software	Dublin City University	2005
Sino-German Joint Master's Program in Printing and Packaging	Department of Printing and Packaging	University of Wuppertal	2005
Sino-French Joint Class in MBA	Economics and Management School	Rouen Business School	2005

Sino-French Joint Class in Finance	Economics and Management School	Rouen Business School	2005
Sino-German Joint Class for Bachelor's Degree in Law	School of Law	Philipps-Universität Marburg and Saarland University, etc.	2006
Sino-French Joint Program in Power and Mechanical Engineering	School of Power and Mechanical Engineering	Université Henri Poincaré, Nancy 1	2006
Sino-French Joint Program in Chemistry	College of Chemistry and Molecular Sciences	Université Paris-Sud 11	2006
Sino-French Joint Program in Sciences and Engineering	School of Physics and Technology	Université Claude Bernard Lyon 1	2006
Sino-French Joint Program in Resources and Environmental Sciences	School of Resources and Environmental Sciences	Université des Sciences et Technologies de Lille 1	2006
Sino-Singaporean Joint Program in Electrical Engineering	School of Electrical Engineering	Nanyang Technological University	2006
Sino-German "1+1" Dual Master's Degree Program in Geodesy and Geomatics	School of Geodesy and Geomatics	University of Stuttgart	2007
Sino-American "1+2+1" Joint Bachelor's Degree Program	International School of Software	James Madison University	2007
Sino-American "1+1" Joint Master's Degree Program	International School of Software	University of Wisconsin-La Crosse	2007

Continued

Table 9.1 Continued

Program Name	Participant Schools and Departments of Wuhan University	Partner	Start-up Year
Sino-British Dual Bachelor's Degree Program	College of Foreign Languages and Literature	University of Aberdeen	2007
Sino-Australian "2+2" Dual Degree Program	School of Geodesy and Geomatics	University of New South Wales	2009
Sino-Canadian "2+2" Dual Degree Program	School of Resources and Environmental Sciences and School of Remote Sensing and Information Engineering	University of Waterloo	2009
Sino-British "3+1+1" Joint Program	School of Civil Engineering and other schools and departments in sciences and engineering	University of Dundee	2009
Sino-German Joint Bachelor's Degree Program in Printing and Packaging	Department of Printing and Packaging	University of Wuppertal	2010
Sino-French Joint Degree Program in Nuclear Energy	School of Power and Mechanical Engineering	Université Paris-Sud 11, etc.	2010
Sino-American "2+2" Joint Bachelor's Degree Program	International School of Software	Eastern Michigan University	2010

Source: Wuhan University, http://en.whu.edu.cn/info.php?rid=597.

University of Wisconsin–La Crosse, the University of Arizona, Project HOPE—Health Opportunity for People Everywhere, the University of Chicago Medical Center, the University of California, the University of Pittsburgh, Seton Hall University, La Roche College, the University of Hawaii System, the University of Scranton, George Mason University, the American Society for Quality, the University of Michigan, Drexel University, the University of Miami, the University of North Carolina at Charlotte, the University of Chicago, and Texas A&M University. Other partners come from Canada, the UK, France, and many other countries, which clearly shows how popular international academic exchanges are at Wuhan University. Table 9.1 shows the diversity of cooperation in terms of academic programs with a transnational nature. This diversity of partnering institutions provides strong evidence in support of the claim that China is particularly keen to push the "Going Global" agenda as specified in the recent Education Blueprint 2020.

Transnationalization of Higher Education: Major Challenges for Higher Education Governance

Regulated in Form, Irregularities in Practices

One major challenge related to the growing prominence of TNHE in China is the irregularities in CFCRS activities today found not only in matters of program approval, but also in the actual operations and practices of listed (approved) institutions and programs. As transnational higher education in China has entered a stage of speedy expansion after the promulgation of the 2003 CFCRS regulations, the key weakness of the ministry's regulatory framework—stronger emphasis on the required procedures of appraisal and approval for the CFCRS institutions and programs, yet less attention paid to the operational management of CFCRS and its quality assurance—has become even more glaring over the past few years. Moreover, the great variety in today's CFCRS arrangements, sources of students, types of diploma or degree conferred, as well as the highly ambiguous public versus private differentiation during this transitional period have all added to the difficulties of state governance of transnational higher education.

Discrepancies between the regulated and formal form of operation and the actual practices of certain CFCRS institutions and programs could first be detected in their related web pages. For instance, in the case of Sias International University, information presented on its official Chinese website and its English website is rather different, particularly in terms of the nature of the institution itself and its leadership. Sias is, first of all, a "university" rather than a CFCRS institution (as indicated in the approved list of the MOE) in its English website.

Moreover, it boasts that it is "the first solely American-owned University in Central China," even though the website does mention its affiliation with Zhengzhou University.[16] In contrast, the Chinese website clearly mentions in the first place that Sias is a CFCRS institution with investment by the American Sias Group and affiliated with Zhengzhou University as its "second-tier college," with help from the Fort Hays State University of Kansas.[17] Not surprisingly, this corresponding Chinese webpage makes no mention about the "sole ownership" of Americans of this university or this "international college," as that would obviously be against the policy. The tricky part in this story is that the founder and chairman of Sias International University, Shawn Chen, who is also president of the Sias Group, is a Chinese American educated both in China and the United States. With regard to leadership of the University, Shawn Chen is the only person mentioned under the subtitle of "Administrative Staff" on Sias's English website,[18] whereas the corresponding Chinese website lists Shawn Chen together with the university's Party (CCP) secretary and deputy secretary, and the director and deputy director as members of its top administration.[19] An interesting contrast could also be found in the case of the Missouri State University branch campus in Dalian, or the LNU-MSU College of International Business, Liaoning Normal University. Again, discrepancies could be detected between its English and Chinese websites, with the former highlighting the "international" aspect of the branch campus[20] and the direct link of its programs with the mother university, while the latter begins with an ambiguous yet "politically correct" statement of introduction, emphasizing the equal partnership between Liaoning Normal University and Missouri State University, as well as stressing the importance of nurturing national—rather than international—business talents through this Chinese-foreign cooperation.[21] Moreover, as in the first case of Sias International University, the Chinese website of the LNU-MSU College of International Business highlights its Joint Management Committee, which includes representatives from both institutions, while this piece of information is simply ignored by its English website.

Our recent field visit to Harbin again shows how local governments in particular and universities in general have tactically adopted different measures in making use of the collaborative framework to expand nonstate university places to cater to the pressing educational needs of local residents. For instance, we learned from the interview with the president of Harbin University of Science and Technology that the Harbin government had allowed local universities to co-launch programs with overseas partners, but many of these programs are taught primarily by local faculty members, and students graduating from such programs only obtain local degrees rather than foreign diplomas. When asked about the rationale behind such a development, we learned that these arrangements are to protect those *minban* colleges from being forced to close down because of a new policy stipulated by the Ministry of Education in Beijing for quality assurance in the context of the proliferation of programs run by *minban* colleges. The popularity of loosely defined joint programs in the Harbin area clearly indicates how local government has attempted to implement policies issued by the center to adapt to the unique local policy context (field interview with President Li Da Yong, November 2010, Harbin, China). Cases like these seem to suggest that, as far as CFCRS institutions are concerned, even though all of them have been approved and listed by the ministry, they may increasingly act as autonomous entities largely governed by the foreign HEIs, with less and less control from their "local partners." These foreign HEIs, having gradually realized the interpretive nuances and loopholes within the existing legal framework of CFCRS, have become wiser in reaching a consensus with local public HEIs for a cooperation of minimum interference, particularly in the running of their teaching programs, yet formally keeping the affiliation with these local public HEIs simply to fulfill official requirements. Members from their local partners would still be included in the governing body or management team of the institutions; however, they are in general only responsible for the administration and student management of the institutions.

With regard to the Party organizations within CFCRS institutions (committees of the CCP and the Communist Youth Leagues), which are indeed a crucial mechanism of control and surveillance that could be exerted by the state or Party, signs also indicate that the foreign HEIs have learned how to diminish the influences of these Party organs through institutional renovations. The United International College (UIC) in Zhuhai, Guangdong,[22] for example, does not impose the leadership of CCP upon its president and the management team, but instead resorts to a British–Hong Kong style "Council" as the supreme governing body, with no CCP representative.[23] This is a governance framework copied directly from the UIC's "foreign" co-founder—Hong Kong Baptist University—rather than following the mainland model of the UIC's local co-founder, Beijing Normal University.

The ascendancy of foreign partners in the governance of CFCRS institutions is likewise conspicuous in the case of the recently founded Xi'an Jiaotong–Liverpool University (2006), and even more so in the case of the University of Nottingham-Ningbo. Again, even though the latter is legally simply another "CFCRS institution" co-founded by the University of Nottingham and Zhejiang Wanli Education Group in 2004,[24] the university in fact operates as a branch campus of the University of Nottingham in almost every aspect of its governance.

In short, it seems that the phenomenon of "regulated in form, irregularities in practice" is prevalent today among CFCRS institutions and programs. This is, above all, due to the intention of the foreign HEIs to circumvent unwanted restrictions imposed by the legal framework of CFCRS. However, occasionally, the provincial governments and the local HEIs may also tend to facilitate such irregularities based on various considerations. Intriguingly, this phenomenon of blatant irregularities could also be found among the private HEIs in Malaysia during the 1980s and 1990s when the government liberalized and marketized the higher education sector, and subsequently allowed the introduction of TNHE programs.

Regulatory Reform and Quality Assurance

The irregular practices among the CFCRS discussed above have raised concerns about quality assurance in the MOE. Zheng (2009) pointed out that even though approval from the MOE is a requirement for any CFCRS institution or program, not all CFCRS programs currently run by Chinese HEIs (public and private HEIs inclusive) are registered with the ministry. Her research findings from a series of interviews with a total of 124 Chinese university staff show that nearly all the single-degree programs are not registered with the MOE.[25] In contrast, in the case of the double-degree programs, those from prestigious public universities are registered, whereas those from less prestigious public universities are not.[26] It is also notable that quite a substantial number of CFCRS programs offered by "international colleges" are single-degree programs and have not been registered with the MOE (Zheng 2009, 40).

The causes behind this phenomenon, according to Zheng's respondents, were, first of all, the intention to circumvent cumbersome restrictions imposed by the MOE. The procedures of program application and approval could be very time consuming, and the requirements may also be too strict. The MOE encourages local public universities to cooperate with the top HEIs worldwide in subject areas that are needed but less developed in China. However, up to now, the MOE is still not ready to unleash the full power of the market-oriented dynamism of the Chinese HEIs. Nonetheless, the reality is that many less prestigious Chinese HEIs today—for instance, provincial universities which are totally excluded from the lists of both the 211 Project and the 985 Project—have become very market oriented by offering single-degree programs for non-state-planned students (Zheng 2009, 40–41).

It seems that, for those prestigious Chinese universities which enroll state-planned students for their CFCRS programs, the incentives concerned are generally about expanding their national and international influence, as well as facilitating their reforms on curriculum development and research. In view of this perspective, CFCRS activities are therefore an element of their grand strategy to internationalize their universities so as to achieve world-class status. On the contrary, financial benefit is clearly the main thrust behind the endeavors undertaken by less prestigious HEIs in developing CFCRS programs, and they are therefore willing to cater particularly to those students who are excluded from the national quota of higher education. Thus, even though transnational collaboration may sometimes be unprofitable and administratively inconvenient in the Chinese context, there is now in general an enthusiasm in developing CFCRS programs among both the prestigious and the less prestigious public HEIs. Though it is still difficult to get a clear picture of the proportion of formal CFCRS programs (i.e., those that have been approved and listed by the MOE) versus informal CFCRS programs, owing to the lack of relevant statistics, it is believed that the latter are now flourishing on a remarkable scale, as shown in the field interviews in Zheng's (2009) study.

Openly recognizing the growing popularity of TNHE, the Chinese government is very concerned about the overall academic standard of these programs. In a recent professional training program for senior university administrators in Beijing, the speakers from the MOE, including the deputy minister of the MOE and the director of the National Research Centre for Educational Development of the MOE, repeatedly emphasized the importance of quality assurance of academic matters, especially as some of the TNHE programs have been found to be problematic in their delivery and quality assurance (Mok 2009). In order to properly manage these TNHE programs, the MOE needs to establish a regulatory system appropriate for managing these activities.

Most important of all, the rapid expansion of transnational higher education has rendered the conventional form of state-market-university relations inappropriate. The irregularities in university governance discussed earlier clearly show how local governments have tried to interpret and reinterpret national policies differently to devise measures to protect local interests. The dilemma that the Beijing government is confronting also reveals a huge gap between the highly advanced development in the economy and the far slower changes taking place in the political aspect. As structural Marxists suggest, the fundamental changes to the economic base require complementary transformations in the superstructure, that is, the political and legal system, culture, and so on. The rapid expansion of transnational higher education requires a more flexible regulatory framework in governance, but the existing university governance arrangements have failed to respond appropriately to the ever-changing environment. Hence, the tensions between governments at various levels and the universities running transnational education are clearly visible. It is therefore not surprising to witness vacillations between compliance and defiance in local governments' responses to policy directives issued by the central government. The vacillations and tensions revealed in the transformations in higher education suggest that the superstructure (i.e., the governance structure) is not compatible with the changes taking place in the economic base (i.e., the proliferation of higher education). In order to maintain national competitiveness through transforming the higher education sector, the Chinese regime needs to initiate structural reform in higher education.

Discussion and Conclusion

The above discussion suggests that China's higher education has gone through significant transformations not only in reforming its management and governance styles but also in diversifying the learning experiences of students and the modes of delivery in higher education. A better understanding of the rise of transnational higher education in general and the call for internationalizing higher education in particular could be obtained by contextual analysis of how and why transnational higher education is encouraged by the Chinese government. According to the twelfth Five-Year Plan of the People's Republic of China, one of the major national goals is to transform the country from purely an economic power to a power with strong cultural and soft power influences globally. Similarly, the Medium and Long-Term Development Strategy (Education 2020, in short) published by the Ministry of Education in 2010 further reinforces the importance of diversifying modes of higher education delivery by inviting overseas higher education institutions (including those from Hong Kong, Macau, and Taiwan) to cooperate with institutions on the mainland for offering a more diversified learning experience to promote students' innovation and creativity.

Depending on universities based in Mainland China to transform their structures and systems for enhancing student learning experiences would take a long time to achieve the national goal; in particular the transformation from "within" would definitely encounter structural barriers that would delay the reform processes. For this reason, the Chinese government has made serious attempts to engage local education institutions to work with overseas partners in order to inject new energy and ideas to make changes to higher education in China. Well aware of the importance of transforming the Chinese economy from heavily reliant upon manufacturing to engaging in knowledge-based production activities, the call for transnationalizing and internationalizing higher education has a significant historic mission for the country, not only in education but also for nation building and the assertion of soft power in the global world (Mok and Yu 2012).

This chapter has reviewed major policies governing the transnationalization of higher education in China, critically examining different phases and unique features of transnational higher education, as well as discussing how students who have enrolled in transnational higher education programs reflect upon their learning experiences. This chapter has also highlighted the social and political significance of the rise of transnational higher education in China, moving beyond education to politics and international relations. With the growing popularity of cooperation between local institutions in Mainland China with overseas campuses and partners, one major issue related to education is to monitor quality assurance issues as transnational higher education is mushrooming in China. Moving beyond transnational programs, major universities on the mainland have engaged in various forms of international research cooperation, student and staff exchanges, and a diversity of academic programs to enhance student learning experiences. The following chapter will focus on how students evaluate their learning experiences after participating either in transnational higher education programs or international exchange activities.

Chapter 10

Transnationalization and Student Learning Experiences

Introduction

In addition to policy reviews discussed in the previous chapters regarding how transnationalization of higher education has developed in Hong Kong, Singapore, Malaysia, and China, the present chapter reports fieldwork being conducted by the author in these Asian societies to examine how and why students have chosen to enroll in transnational higher education. More specifically, this chapter also discusses findings generated from the fieldwork when asking students who have enrolled in transnational higher education programs to reflect on their learning experiences from 2010 to 2012. The chapter will compare and contrast student learning experiences in these Asian societies not only based upon the fieldwork materials but also extended to examine how international exchange students comment on their learning experiences as additional perspectives in understanding transnational higher education and its impacts on student learning.

Research Methods of the Study

The findings reported and discussed in this section are generated from a public policy research project funded by the Research Grant Council in Hong Kong. The case report on Singapore and Malaysia is part of a larger research project examining the rise of transnational higher education in Hong Kong, Singapore, Malaysia, and Mainland China. We adopted both quantitative and qualitative methods for data collection. With a particular focus on examining student evaluation of their learning experiences after studying in transnational higher education programs, online surveys were conducted in these Asian societies, followed by a series of focus group discussions. In 2010 to 2011, the author and his team conducted focus group discussions on transnational higher education in Singapore and Malaysia, engaging students from a number of HEIs throughout these Asian societies. These focus group discussions, in most cases, were held on the campuses of the HEIs concerned, and each took around an hour to be completed. Some of the students being interviewed were those who showed interest in talking to us when filling out the online surveys.

Regarding the sampling method, we adopted a snowball sampling method in identifying our respondents by getting the program leaders of selected transnational higher education programs to refer students to us. Meanwhile, we also got the consent from the institutions during our field visits to talk to students whom we met on campus. The questions asked were rather similar to those that we asked in our survey, yet they were usually followed up with an in-depth discussion, with the aim of exploring more firsthand information from students concerning their actual learning experiences. Since we have only limited space in this chapter, we focused on just some of the key findings of the focus group discussions conducted in these Asian societies. Table 10.1 presents

Table 10.1 Schedules of Focus Group Discussions with Students Enrolled in TNHE Programs

Date and Time	Remarks on Participants	Venue
Hong Kong		
22 June 2010 3:00–4:30 p.m.	One part-time undergraduate and one full-time doctoral student from the School of Continuing Education, Hong Kong Baptist University (HKBU-SCE).	Room B5-425, Academic Building, City University of Hong Kong, Tat Chee Avenue, Kowloon.
10 July 2010 3:00–4:30 p.m.	Four part-time undergraduates from the School of Continuing Education, Hong Kong Baptist University (HKBU-SCE).	Room B5-121, Academic Building, City University of Hong Kong, Tat Chee Avenue, Kowloon.
Trip to Singapore		
3 August 2010 5:45–6:30 p.m.	Three full-time master's students and one staff from the ESSEC Business School (Singapore campus).	ESSEC's campus, 100 Victoria Street, National Library Building #13–02.
4 August 2010 4:00–4:30 p.m.	Two full-time undergraduates from the Informatics Academy.	Informatics campus, 12 Science Centre Road.

Continued

Table 10.1 Continued

Date and Time	Remarks on Participants	Venue
5 August 2010 11:00 a.m.–12:30 p.m.	Two full-time undergraduates and four full-time master's students from James Cook University (JCU) Singapore.	JCU Singapore's campus, Room C03–04 (Block C), 600 Upper Thomson Road.

Trip to Malaysia

10 August 2010 3:25–4:30 p.m.	Five full-time undergraduates from Nilai University College (NUC).	NUC's campus, discussion room, NUC Library, 1, Persiaran Kolej BBN, Putra Nilai, Nilai, Negeri Sembilan.
12 August 2010 3:45–4:30 p.m.	Eight full-time undergraduates from the International Medical University (IMU).	IMU's campus, No. 126, Jalan Jalil Perkasa 19, Bukit Jalil, Kuala Lumpur.
13 August 2010 3:00–4:00 p.m.	Nine full-time undergraduates from the New Era College (NEC).	NEC's campus, Lot 5, Seksyen 10, Jalan Bukit, Kajang, Selangor.

Trip to Harbin, Heilongjiang Province, China

16 November 2010 10:00–10:50 a.m.	Five full-time undergraduates from the Harbin University of Science and Technology (HUST).	HUST's campus, 52 Xuefu Road, Harbin City, Heilongjiang.
17 November 2010 2:00–3:00 p.m.	Seven full-time undergraduates and one full-time master's student from the Harbin Normal University (HRBNU).	HRBNU's campus (松北主校區): 1 Shida South Road, Harbin City, Heilongjiang.

Trip to Suzhou, Jiangsu Province, and Shanghai, China

15 December 2010 3:20–4:20 p.m.	Seven full-time undergraduates from the Sino-German College of Applied Sciences, Tongji University (CDHAW-Tongji).	CDHAW-Tongji's campus (嘉定校區), Room 255, Cao'an Highway, Jiading District, Shanghai.
16 December 2010 10:40–11:40 a.m.	Eight full-time undergraduates from the Sino-British College, University of Shanghai for Science and Technology (SBC-USST).	SBC-USST's campus, Room 203, Admin. Building, 1195 Fuxing Road Middle, Shanghai.

Continued

Table 10.1 Continued

Date and Time	Remarks on Participants	Venue
16 December 2010 3:00pm–4:00 p.m.	Eight full-time undergraduates from the University of Michigan–Shanghai Jiao Tong University Joint Institute (UM-SJTU Joint Institute).	UM-SJTU Joint Institute's campus, 800 Dong Chuan Road, Shanghai.
17 December 2010 11:15–12:15 a.m.	Three full-time undergraduates and three staff members from Shanghai Normal University (SHNU).	SHNU's campus (徐匯校區): 100 Guilin Road, Shanghai.
17 December 2010 2:00–3:20 p.m.	Five full-time master's students, one master's graduate, one full-time doctoral student, and two staff members from the East China Normal University (ECNU).	ECNU's campus (中山北路校區), 3663 Zhongshan North Road, Shanghai.

Trip to Zhengzhou and Luoyang, Henan Province, China

6 January 2011 10:30–11:30 a.m.	Eight full-time undergraduates from the College of International Education, Zhongyuan University of Technology (ZUT).	ZUT's main campus, 1 Huaihe Road, Xinzheng Shuanghu Economic Development Zone, Zhengzhou City, Henan.

Trip to Ningbo, Zhejiang Province, China

27 January 2011 4:30–5:30p.m.	Five full-time undergraduates from the University of Nottingham-Ningbo (UNN).	UNN's campus, Administration Building, 199 Taikang East Road, Ningbo City, Zhejiang.
27 January 2011 5:45–6:45 p.m.	Five bachelor graduates (Year 2008 and Year 2009) from the University of Nottingham-Ningbo (UNN).	UNN's campus, Aroma Coffee Shop.

Trip to Zhuhai, Guangdong Province, China

9 March 2011 3:00–6:00 p.m.	Seven full-time undergraduates from the Beijing Normal University–Hong Kong Baptist University United International College (UIC).	UIC's campus, Reboot Cafe, 28 Jinfeng Road, Tangjiawan, Zhuhai City, Guangdong.

Source: Author.

the details of interview schedules with students of a total of 17 higher education institutions running transnational higher education programs.

Students involved were mostly undergraduates. Among them, some had in fact experienced their overseas studies under the various TNHE arrangements, particularly under the 2+1+1 twinning arrangement in which students still have to return to the local HEIs after completing their one-year studies abroad. Participants engaged in our discussion organized in the Harbin Normal University on 17 November 2010, for example, all belonged to this category. As TNHE programs in the postgraduate level have become increasingly popular over the past few years, we have tried to engage postgraduate students in the discussions as well. Thus occasionally the groups in discussion might consist of both undergraduate and postgraduate students. Notably, in the case of East China Normal University where the discussion was held on 17 December 2010, all student participants were at that time engaged in postgraduate studies.

In terms of the number of participants, in most cases it fell in the range of five to eight persons, with a mixture of participants who came from diverse fields of study. This is again a deliberate arrangement in order to cover the diversity of TNHE programs today as much as possible. For instance, our focus group discussion organized in the Sino-British College, University of Shanghai for Science and Technology,[1] on 16 December 2010 was attended by a total of eight undergraduates. Among them, three students majored in electrical engineering, two in mechanical engineering, two in events management, and the remaining one in accounting and finance. It is also worth noting that as we have assured all the discussants that their personal data would be treated strictly confidentially in order to achieve a free and candid discussion, detailed background information about the discussants will not be revealed here.

In terms of the geographical coverage, admittedly fewer focus group discussions were conducted in Hong Kong, Singapore, and Malaysia as compared to Mainland China (see table 10.2. However, this uneven endeavor may well be a legitimate one given the larger population of students in Mainland China in absolute terms. As regards the case of Mainland China specifically, our five trips to Mainland China taken from November 2010 to March 2011 had tried to cover most of the geographical regions with emerging or substantial TNHE development in recent years. Consequently, we approached students from HEIs located in Heilongjiang, Jiangsu, Henan, Zhejiang, and Guangdong provinces and Shanghai City.

Nevertheless, as far as the research methodology is concerned, we were definitely constrained by a critical yet insurmountable limitation: apart from the two occasions of discussion conducted in our base of Hong Kong as well as the other three occasions in Singapore, Malaysia, and Mainland China respectively where we could invite participants on our own initiative,[2] we had to rely on the HEIs concerned for the arrangement. Thus, though requests regarding

Table 10.2 Summary: Focus Group Discussions by Region

Region	Focus Group Discussions Held	Total Number of Participants
Hong Kong	2	6
Singapore	3	12
Malaysia	3	22
Mainland China	11	75
Harbin, Heilongjiang Province	2	13
Suzhou, Jiangsu Province, and Shanghai	5	38
Zhengzhou and Luoyang, Henan Province	1	8
Ningbo, Zhejiang Province	2	10
Zhuhai, Guangdong Province	1	7
Total	19	115

Source: Author.

the diversity and number of participants were made by us in advance, they might not necessarily have been accommodated. And on top of that, participants invited through this channel may tend to bear a more positive attitude toward the related TNHE programs and be less critical against it. In other words, opinions expressed by these discussants might not be well represented among their fellow students. In this regard, the results of our survey conducted between April 2010 and March 2011, which was based on the very same concern, would be drawn as a supplementary reference for analysis. Hopefully it could somewhat reduce the bias caused by this specific research limitation.

Major Findings: Students' Learning Experiences

Singapore

The author and his research team conducted a few focus group discussions in Singapore, engaging with students both from branch campuses of the overseas HEIs (the ESSEC Business School of France and the James Cook University of Australia) and from the local private HEIs. These are the two main vehicles of TNHE programs in Singapore. Based upon our field interviews, we made the following observations related to student evaluations of their learning experiences.

- TNHE in Singapore differs significantly from TNHE in Hong Kong in the sense that it is very much global/regional oriented and manifestly profit seeking. In many cases, the various branch campuses set up by prestigious overseas HEIs in Singapore cater to foreign students rather

than the locals, particularly students from the surrounding ASEAN countries, China and India.
- TNHE programs offered by the local private HEIs aim for both foreign and local students, but unlike the prestigious overseas HEIs, which were in fact invited to Singapore by the government itself (the Economic Development Board [EDB] in particular), they usually receive much less attention and assistance from the authorities. It is only recently that the government has tried to exert more regulation upon them in order to assure the quality of their programs, and at the same time incorporated them as part of the national effort to become an excellent hub of education. It is thus understandable that in terms of TNHE programs, the contexts in the branch campuses of overseas HEIs and in the local private HEIs may be quite different.
- In general, interviewees whom we met in Singapore were by and large satisfied with the quality of their enrolled TNHE programs. Interviewees from the ESSEC business schools had shown a common satisfaction with many aspects of their TNHE programs, including the highly flexible transnational arrangement of the school designed to maximize the international experiences of its students,[3] the quality of the program, as well as their opportunities for internships in reputable corporations. When asked to comment on the quality of teaching, the three full-time master's students from the ESSEC Business School in Singapore observed, "It has been excellent. The teachers coming from Paris are very good." As for the language classes, "We also go to local language schools for learning Chinese, and the classes are very good." On courses concerning Asian societies, "each professor is an expert in his subject, so it is very interesting. They share a lot of their research experiences with us" (field interview, 3 August 2010).
- The thing that was cherished most by the discussants from ESSEC is the "Asian experience or Asian perspective" which they deemed would greatly facilitate their future career in the business world. In this respect, Singapore is regarded as an ideal destination both commercially and culturally. ESSEC does admit Asian students, but these Asian students would prefer to stay in Paris rather than Singapore for European exposure; while on the other way round, ESSEC students from Europe and the Middle East long for Asian exposure. Consequently, most students in its little Singapore campus (this "campus" is in fact a mere floor within the National Library Building) are non-Asians. However, the current situation may change when ESSEC commences its bachelor's degree programs in 2012.
- Interviewees from the James Cook University (JCU) Singapore have shown a similar satisfaction about the quality of TNHE programs in general, but some did have grievances about the infrastructure of the campus, which is a suburb premise renovated from the campus of a secondary school. Unlike the ESSEC Business School, the student population of JCU Singapore comprises largely Asians, both locals and non-locals. A common message conveyed by the discussants (two full-time

undergraduates and four full-time master's students who came from Myanmar, Vietnam, Taiwan, Mainland China, India, and England respectively) was that the excellent reputation of Singapore as a superior locality for study really mattered in their decision to choose here rather than other places for their undergraduate studies.
- A probe into this rationale given particularly by Asian discussants from JCU Singapore revealed four elements which they suggested have made Singapore so attractive. It is first of all the relevance of English as the teaching medium. Second is the multiethnic and multicultural setting of Singapore, which is "truly Asia." Third is the opportunity to stay and work in Singapore after one's graduation.[4] And last but not least is the rather unexpected emphasis given by most Asian discussants on "Singapore as a safe city" for study and living. One respondent, a full-time student from India, made it explicitly clear to us the advantage of enrolling in TNHE in Singapore:

> Another reason I came to Singapore is that it is a very safe country. At first I planned to do the master's degree in Australia, but then I found the "Indian problem" [anti-Indian movement] in Australia and finally decided to come to Singapore. After learning about the anti-Indian crisis, my parents insisted that I should go to Singapore. But still I prefer Australia. (field interview, 5 August 2010)

His remark that Singapore is a safer place has also been echoed by two full-time undergraduates who came from Myanmar and Vietnam respectively. Feeling safe studying in Singapore is also confirmed by our online survey. In addition to safety, the multicultural environment also appeals to students choosing Singapore as their destination for studying overseas. The remarks expressed by a Taiwanese discussant are worth quoting here:

> The reason I chose James Cook University is that it offers a one-year master's program, while I need to spend two years in Taiwan. The second reason is the language environment. In James Cook, all the lectures are taught in English. And since the students are from different countries, we can use English quite often. But there is one problem. The majority of students here are Chinese and Indians, while the rest are from Malaysia, Vietnam, Burma [Myanmar], and others. . . . For those who can speak Mandarin, they tend to speak Mandarin in the campus. . . . The third reason I came to Singapore rather than Canada or the US is that there is a multicultural and multireligion environment in Singapore, which is very unique. I consider Singapore as a hub between East and West. The Asian economy is booming. . . . I can know students coming from the whole of Asia, and I get good connections. It will be very good for students who plan to enter the world of international business. So Singapore is a very unique place, especially the expenses are lower than that in Canada, the US, and Australia. (field interview, 5 August 2010)

The focus group discussion in JCU Singapore, however, did reveal that given the short history of JCU in Singapore (first enrollment was in 2003 with 50 students), there was room for improvement in terms of its teaching and learning. Again, similar to our case studies in Hong Kong, discussants pointed out that albeit the lecturers were good and knowledgeable in their respective field of studies, the performance of the tutors—some of them were merely part-time staff—was not as satisfactory. Moreover, even among the lecturers, some of them were part-time staff recruited locally instead of coming from the main campus in Australia.

Impressively, the two undergraduate discussants from the Informatics Academy, a local private HEI, have also highlighted the attractiveness of Singapore as a safe destination for study and living. Moreover, the overall message conveyed by them was that they have strong confidence in Singapore as an excellent hub of education, and this sort of highly positive perception existed even long before they stepped into Singapore. In short, the reputation of its education system really matters. The discussant from India has in fact shifted his study from a Malaysian private HEI to Informatics Academy after being disappointed by the overall provision of TNHE in Malaysia;[5] and the discussant from Sri Lanka unequivocally claimed that "Singapore is the best place in Asia when you consider education." Singapore's education, in the eyes of his countrymen, was not only excellent in the region, but "strict" enough disciplinarily (4 August 2010).

- As in the case of other discussions in Singapore, the two discussants from Informatics Academy also praised the helpfulness of their lecturers and were satisfied with the academy's administrative management. For instance, although on-campus accommodation was not provided by the academy, assistance was readily offered by its staff. The only reservations expressed by them—again in similarity with others in Singapore—were firstly concerning the campus facilities (canteen services in particular), and secondly the lack of industrial affiliations of their TNHE programs.

Putting the above observations together, Singapore stands out as a popular choice for overseas students as their destination for learning because of its multicultural environment, the secure and safe society, the high quality of education, and reasonable program fees. Our interviewees studying in the TNHE programs in Singapore were generally happy with their stay in Singapore. Part of the reason for their satisfaction was also related to how the Singapore government has done in promoting the city-state globally, particularly positioning Singapore as the meeting point of West and East and emphasizing the quality education services that the city-state can offer. The empirical evidence from our field interviews clearly suggested that the promises made by the Singapore government do come.

Malaysia

The three focus group discussions that we held in Malaysia engaged students from Nilai University College, International Medical University, and New Era College. These are all local private HEIs, but New Era College differs from the others in terms of its teaching media: Mandarin is being applied as a primary medium of instruction, together with English. Unlike the case in Singapore, local private HEIs have long been the prime vehicle of TNHE programs in Malaysia ever since their debut in the 1980s. Major observations are generated from the interviews as below.

- Grievances and criticisms could be heard in the focus group discussions held at both Nilai University College (10 August 2010) and International Medical University (12 August 2010). The general impression that one could get from these two occasions was that most students regarded the quality of their TNHE programs as something substandard/unsatisfactory compared to equivalent programs abroad. Nevertheless, given the limitations that they faced at the moment, particularly the financial constraint and the less conspicuous qualifications of the students themselves, most would also agree that their current options might not be that bad anyway. In short, reluctantly, the programs concerned might still be an "acceptable" or even "the best possible" alternative.
- Discussants from Nilai University College (NUC) comprised five full-time undergraduates who are Malaysians, Vietnamese, and Maldivians respectively, and the programs that they enrolled in were 3+0 twinning programs which entailed a full period of study in Malaysia. One of the common complaints raised by them was about their lecturers. The discussants claimed that most of their lecturers were locals (Malaysians), and even though a few of them were foreigners, they haven't met any lecturers from the overseas partner of their TNHE programs yet. They tended to suggest that these lecturers were less competent in teaching compared to their overseas counterparts. For instance, some mentioned that they usually offer insufficient explanation during their lectures, and hence students ended up cramming for examinations. However, in this regard, some discussants did suggest that it was also prevalent among local students—or broadly speaking, among Asian students—in clinging to this "cramming" style of study, a mentality which tends to shun classroom participation and discussion but simply follows the instruction of lecturers (field interview, 10 August 2010).
- Other pedagogical issues raised by NUC discussants included the handling of examinations by the lecturers. Allegedly, lecturers of the various TNHE programs offered by the local private HEIs—that is, not merely confined to lecturers from NUC—tend to "tip off" students before examinations. At NUC, they tend to inform students of the "focus areas" before examinations, and the programs' assessments are usually based wholly on written examinations. Students would accordingly focus on these areas for preparation and nothing more. Some respondents shared the following with us during the interviews:

"Most students do not actually learn what is required in the syllabus," claimed a discussant, but are obsessed with passing examinations and earning their degrees. Discussants with previous experience or with friends in other local private HEIs also stated that in some extreme cases, "the lecturers will give you the same questions before exam," thus allowing students to enjoy "a very relaxed kind of study. To the lecturers, the incentive of doing so was simple: as long as more students could secure good scores, fewer complaints would be raised, and the management of institutions concerned would likewise be happy with it" (field interview, 10 August 2010).

- The lack of effective mechanisms for quality assurance of these TNHE programs could also be supported by the claim from students that NUC did not take their feedback (either through course evaluation questionnaires or lodging complaints) seriously enough, though the president of NUC, Professor Emeritus Tengku Dato' Shamsul Bahrin, has claimed otherwise. In our interview with Professor Emeritus Bahrin on 10 August 2010, he highlighted the significance of course evaluations in NUC's appraisal of its lecturers. He said, "The results of course evaluation from students would make up 50 percent of the appraisal, thus affecting significantly the wage adjustment and promotion of lecturers concerned."
- Apart from the quality of teaching and program assessment, discussants at NUC also expressed many grievances regarding campus facilities as well as about the administrative supports offered by TNHE programs concerned. According to these students, NUC's Internet system is disappointingly inefficient and slow, student services are insufficient, and most significantly, there is a lack of academic resources. The last issue was twofold: (1) a lack of books and other resources in the library, and (2) inadequate provision of electronic databases for research, and crucially the inaccessibility of online library systems and databases of the overseas HEI which collaboratively offers such programs.[6] The discussants not only felt that they were being discriminated against, but that they were receiving poor "value for their money" after paying a considerable sum in tuition fees.
- In retrospect, nonlocal discussants expressed their disappointment and "disenchantment"—though with different degrees—prompted by the gap between expectations and reality prior to and after their arrival in Malaysia/NUC. The Vietnamese discussant noted that the reputation of the overseas HEI was much more relevant than that of NUC in his decision to take this TNHE program, and another equally important consideration was the relatively reasonable fees charged by NUC. The Maldivian discussant, however, emphasized that he would no longer recommend any student to study at NUC, and he urged the Malaysian government to strengthen the regulation on its industry of higher education while pursuing its ambition of becoming a regional hub of education.[7] Instead

of focusing merely on quantitative indicators, he suggested that Malaysia should pay more attention to improving the quality of its TNHE.
- Nevertheless, this Maldivian student did admit that Malaysia could still be an advantaged competitor in the Asian market of higher education, as "Malaysia is homelike to every nationality" in terms of its weather and other elements of hospitality. He claimed that this was particularly true to Muslim students from South Asia (i.e., Pakistan, Bangladesh, India, Sri Lanka, Maldives), since the multicultural Malaysian society, with its dominant population of Malay Muslims, was much more comfortable to them than places like China, Taiwan, or even Singapore; "at least there is no difficulty here for us to have halal foods."[8] The three Malaysian discussants also mentioned that according to their observations, most African students seemed to enjoy their studies and felt cozy enough to stay in Malaysia. In fact, I was impressed by the degree of internationalization of NUC's student population while wandering its campus on 10 August 2010.
- The TNHE strategy adopted by the International Medical University (IMU) is rather different from NUC's. Based on a credit transfer agreement with IMU's "partner medical schools" in Australia, New Zealand, Ireland, Canada, the United States, and the UK, IMU undergraduates would have to complete their "Phase 1" studies (2.5 years) in Malaysia before they could be matched to a partner medical school abroad for another 2.5 to 3 years of studies (Phase 2).[9] Such an arrangement of "advance standing" implies that the local medical programs offered by IMU (Phase 1) could have nothing to do with the Phase 2 programs offered by overseas HEIs.
- IMU students could of course choose to wrap up their entire medical studies locally and end up with a degree from IMU. However, predictably, all of the eight full-time undergraduates engaged in the discussion at IMU categorically indicated that they would seek the transfer to overseas HEIs. In fact, IMU could better be regarded as an "agent institution" that facilitates locals as well as international students for medical higher education abroad rather than functioning as a local medical university by itself. Students who went through this transfer process would finally earn the sole degree of the overseas HEI but not the IMU one. Nevertheless, according to the discussants, roughly a half of IMU medical students might still have to finish their programs locally primarily for two reasons: (1) financial limitations, and (2) their academic results were not good enough to meet the requirements set by the partner medical schools, thus disqualified them from the matching process.
- Some respondents shared that they chose IMU because "this is the only (medical) university which offer this kind of transfer arrangement." Moreover, "it is easier to get into IMU than to other universities." When asked whether it would affect their choices if they were offered a place by the local public medical schools, for instance by the

prestigious Department of Medicine at the University of Malaya, the answers were varied. Only a few of them preferred to take medical programs in the public universities if given the opportunity; most were in fact longing for a "decent" foreign medical degree as well as opportunities abroad and therefore preferred IMU, even though IMU's tuition fee was comparatively much more expensive, and the provision of its "Phase 1" programs may also be less satisfactory. Notably, most of the "partner medical schools" of IMU are prestigious overseas HEIs, which include the University of New South Wales in Australia, the University of Auckland in New Zealand, and the University of Edinburgh, the University of Glasgow, and the University of Manchester in the UK. Thus as one discussant put it, "I will choose IMU, because it allows me to get through decent universities. By 'decent' I mean universities from countries like Australia. . . . I know the knowledge is all the same all over the world, but some universities can just make you look better. I just want to be honest." A Belgian discussant also bluntly observed that he did not actually care about the public or private nature of the HEI concerned; "as long as I can finally get the degree from my desired Australian university, that's fine" (12 August 2010).

Similarly, a local student replied, "if I consider working in Malaysia, then it doesn't really matter whether the degree is from a local or foreign university. But if I want to work in other countries after graduation, for example in Singapore, then I may have to get a degree from an overseas university" (field interview, 12 August 2010).

- Complaints raised by discussants at IMU were rather similar to those discussed at NUC, which revolved around the quality of lecturers as well as campus facilities, but with a considerably milder tone. As regards lecturers, the international student from Belgium was much more critical than others, who claimed that there were very few good lecturers at IMU, and good lecturers would probably leave after a few years. It is however worth noting that according to the discussants, about 80 percent of the IMU lecturers were foreigners, who were recruited primarily from India, Sri Lanka, Myanmar, and Vietnam. It in fact shows that the management team of IMU is highly flexible and ingenious in approaching resources to establish the first private medical university in Malaysia given all the domestic limitations, which is also a feature shared by many other local private HEIs.
- However, understandably, without the government's funding, IMU is also facing a similar problem of insufficient facilities as the other local private HEIs. Some discussants raised the issue of inaccessibility to cadavers for medical studies, and some kept complaining about the uncomfortable reality that more than 2,000 students would now have to compete

for every facility in the small IMU campus (computers, library resources, sports facilities, and even parking lots). The IMU campus is no more than a new block of building equipped with advanced facilities, but IMU enrolls around 200 medical students per semester, and there are two intakes per year. The Belgian discussant again sarcastically described IMU as "a big factory" and money minded, and others commented that sometimes a lecturer might have to pathetically face a class of up to 200 students. Yet this is obviously a dilemma commonly shared by private TNHE providers in Malaysia. The Belgian discussant was also not happy about the management style of IMU, which he described as authoritative. To him, it seemed that the management team could not tolerate any criticism, he saw the management style as, "These are the rules, you just follow them, or you may leave." However, as a local discussant pointed out in this regard, "the education system in Malaysia is generally like that. So if you want to compare this to the public universities, I am sure it will be even more so there" (field interview, 12 August 2010).

- A comment that deserves particular attention was that twinning programs might be a better arrangement than credit transfers. It was a point raised by a local discussant, and according to her observation, the only twinning program offered by the IMU, the pharmacy program, was operated well enough, since "the structure of the program was all coming from the other side." The superiority between these two models in this specific case is indeed arguable, but the tangible involvement of foreign partners in teaching and learning may be crucial to the quality assurance of TNHE programs in most cases.

Generally speaking, insufficient resources offered by the HEIs was a poignant criticism that most of the discussants enrolled in TNHE programs in Malaysia have in one way or another raised against their HEIs. A strong sense of dissatisfaction concerning the quality as well as the implementation of these programs could also be easily detected among the discussants. Our preliminary explanation for this general phenomenon, based on personal observations made through the series of fieldwork conducted since June 2010, is first of all about the different socioeconomic contexts that the discussants in Singapore and Malaysia have faced respectively. The general satisfaction expressed by discussants in Singapore may primarily be attributed to more efficient regulation/supervision by the authorities upon TNHE programs, as well as better coordination between the local HEIs and their overseas partners. Moreover, HEIs concerned in Singapore are generally paying more attention to their own institutional reputations, thus resulting in a cautious selection of their overseas partners and better coordination for TNHE programs. On the other hand, a different sense of "consumer rights" and "value for money" among students of the two societies, coupled with the existence of a more responsive complaint mechanism, has also helped to influence the quality of TNHE programs in general.

Moreover, the general dissatisfaction shown by discussants in Malaysia may first and foremost be attributed to the fast expansion yet less effective and efficient mechanism of quality assurance in its sector of TNHE. The Malaysian Qualifications Agency (MQA) may be able to exert better regulation on public HEIs, but when it comes to private HEIs—the prime vehicle of TNHE programs in Malaysia—the various complaints from discussants seem to suggest insufficient supervision. Moreover, the Malaysian higher education market is disadvantaged further by the fact that it has yet to carry a brand image as prestigious as its Singapore counterpart, resulting in difficulty seeking prestigious foreign partners as well as in recruiting outstanding overseas students. Apart from quality assurance, the less accommodating state policies in supporting overseas students has also become a hot topic among the discussants in Malaysia, particularly the issue of being unable to apply for a working permit right after graduation. It is nevertheless notable that from the diverse nationalities of participants engaged in the three focus group discussions we held in Malaysia in August 2010, namely the Malaysians, Vietnamese, Maldivian, Chinese, Bangladeshi, Indonesian, and Belgian, Malaysia has indeed shown a substantial degree of success in recruiting students from most parts of Asia.

Hong Kong

The two focus group discussions that we held in Hong Kong engaged only students from the School of Continuing Education, Hong Kong Baptist University (HKBU-SCE). The views expressed in the discussions may therefore be less representative. The author would refer to results and comments collected from the corresponding survey as a supplement.

- As mentioned, discussants were by and large satisfied with the quality of their enrolled TNHE programs.
- TNHE in Hong Kong, as reflected in the discussions, is still very much a product of local concern rather than globally or regionally oriented. It caters mainly to local students, particularly (1) those who need a top-up degree program after wrapping up their associate's degree programs in Hong Kong and (2) mature students who seek to upgrade their professional qualifications after a certain period of working. A significant number of students enrolled in TNHE programs in Hong Kong are therefore part-time students, and the programs suit them well as a practical option both financially (less expensive than the equivalent programs abroad) and in terms of their career management (no need to halt their current career for overseas studies).
- Since these TNHE programs cater primarily to local students, TNHE has yet to become a significant ingredient in the industry of higher education in Hong Kong. The industry of higher education has in fact been

identified as one of the six key sectors to be promoted by the HKSAR government since the second half of 2009.
- Consequently, less attention has been paid by the authorities to the development of TNHE. It seems that the quality of most TNHE programs could still be maintained due to the fact that they are predominantly offered by self-financed branches of the public HEIs, which have already equipped themselves with an established mechanism of quality assurance, and more importantly, the leeway to select from among their fairly prestigious overseas partners.
- In fact, in the case of Hong Kong, overseas collaborators may have much more to do in assuring the quality of programs than their local partners. As reflected in the answers to questions 2 and 3 in our survey and from the discussions, most (66.7 percent for "agree" and 7 percent for "strongly agree" among the Hong Kong respondents) in fact agree that "the quality of the program has been ensured particularly through the effective supervision of the original institution."[10] As revealed by the discussants, local institutions are rarely involved in the teaching of programs concerned; instead they act more as the providers of local infrastructure as well as the administrative coordinators of programs. There are indeed local tutors, but in most cases, these tutors are employed and attached to the overseas HEIs instead of acting as a staff member of the local HEIs.
- This may cause trouble for students—particularly postgraduate students— who are looking for a frequent contact with or face-to-face supervision from their overseas teachers.[11] Some discussants had also indicated that the local tutors are in general less devoted to teaching and less competent in English than their overseas counterparts.
- The common grievances that we could find from both the group discussions and survey exercise in Hong Kong are about the supportive resources offered by the programs, for example, campus facilities and library services. However, these complaints are generally mild in nature.
- Most discussants admitted that the TNHE programs that they were attending were not their first choice. It might be the best possible/realistic option that they could pursue given all the limitations that they faced, but if they did have the leeway to choose, they would either opt for local programs offered by the public HEIs, which they think are more useful to their careers in Hong Kong,[12] or they might simply head abroad for study in overseas HEIs.
- Impressively, in terms of the role of government in regulating and supervising TNHE programs, most Hong Kong discussants expressed an almost identical view as that of the HKSAR government, namely the neoliberal ideology of "small government" and free market regulation. Government intervention is deemed totally unnecessary, and most of them are happy with the existing mechanism of quality assurance, with the strong conviction that market forces would eventually wash out those unqualified or unsatisfactory TNHE program providers.[13]

China

A total of 11 focus group discussions were held in Mainland China which had engaged 75 participants from various geographical regions. This series of discussions, conducted between November 2010 and March 2011, was not only notable for its comprehensive coverage, but for the great variety of cases in terms of TNHE arrangements as well.

Although students from as many as ten HEIs in Harbin, Suzhou, Shanghai, Zhengzhou, Ningbo, and Zhuhai were involved in this series of discussions, based on the nature of their TNHE programs, we could in effect categorized these HEIs into three groups, in which the discussions tended to reflect similar issues or concerns. These broad categories are as follows:

1. Institutions of the Chinese-Foreign Cooperation in Running Schools (hereafter CFCRS Institutions).[14] HEIs concerned are
    a. Sino-German College of Applied Sciences, Tongji University (CDHAW-Tongji)
    b. Sino-British College, University of Shanghai for Science and Technology (SBC-USST)
    c. University of Michigan–Shanghai Jiao Tong University Joint Institute (UM-SJTU Joint Institute)
    d. University of Nottingham-Ningbo (UNN)
    e. Beijing Normal University–Hong Kong Baptist University United International College (UIC)
2. CFCRS programs offered by the prestigious HEI, the East China Normal University (ECNU).
3. CFCRS programs offered by the less prestigious HEIs. HEIs concerned are:
    a. Harbin University of Science and Technology (HUST)
    b. Harbin Normal University (HRBNU)
    c. Shanghai Normal University (SHNU)
    d. College of International Education, Zhongyuan University of Technology (ZUT)

Positive Learning Experiences

- Intriguingly, albeit concerns and issues of discussion varied in each category, the most conspicuous common ground of this series of discussions in Mainland China was the high degree of satisfaction generally expressed by the students. It seemed that most of them—though with grievances—commonly bore a considerably positive attitude toward TNHE. Such a positive sentiment among students of CFCRS programs/institutions is also reaffirmed by the results of our survey taken between April 2010 and March 2011.

- Generally speaking, discussants in Mainland China tended to suggest that they have benefited from the CFCRS programs/institutions in two major aspects, namely:
    1. The accessibility to quality educational resources as well as superior pedagogical approaches from abroad with affordable costs.
    2. The transitional role that CFCRS programs/institutions could play in facilitating students to continue their studies abroad eventually.
- For the first point, almost all of the Mainland Chinese discussants commented in one way or another that the pedagogical approaches adopted by foreign (mostly Western) lecturers were indeed "very different" from those by local lecturers, and they really appreciated that. This usually referred to a friendly and egalitarian teaching style among foreign lecturers, which was a sheer contrast to the authoritative and patriarchal teaching style of local lecturers.[15] Moreover, according to them, staff from the overseas HEIs were in general pedagogically superior to the locals in the sense that they could explain difficult concepts in a vivid way with good examples; inspire students during classroom discussions; and, in the case of foreign language teachers, maintain a good interaction with students even beyond the classroom.[16] Apart from pedagogical issues, discussants from the two "branch campuses" of overseas HEIs in China, namely the University of Nottingham-Ningbo and the Beijing Normal University–Hong Kong Baptist University United International College,[17] were also deeply impressed by the different philosophies of management adopted by their HEIs compared to local HEIs, which they thought contributed to a significantly freer and transparent milieu of campus life that facilitated academic debates as well as the creativity of students[18] (27 January 2011 and 9 March 2011).

Major Concerns of Students

- It is nevertheless worth noting that students enrolled in the CFCRS programs, particularly in the CFCRS programs offered by less prestigious HEIs, had less exposure to foreign teaching staff than those enrolled in the CFCRS institutions, as most of the CFCRS programs were struggled to meet the mere one-third requirement set by the authorities for teaching hours conducted by staff from the overseas partners. Discussants did complain about the transient nature of their foreign lecturers for professional subjects, who usually spend a mere two weeks to one month in China, as the programs simply could not afford the expenses needed for longer stays. It therefore implies an intensive process of teaching and learning during that very short period of time. CFCRS programs in China however are usually split into Phase 1 and Phase 2, which is two years of study each, and foreign language teachers responsible for the foundation courses of Phase 1 would station in China in most cases.

"Branch campuses" of the overseas HEIs, on the contrary, tend to have more foreign lecturers (though not necessarily foreign staff from the overseas HEIs) who station in China, and discussants from these "branch campuses" realized the implications of this pedagogical privilege dearly. In fact, some of them even claimed that foreign lecturers have opened up both their eyes and minds (27 January 2011 and 9 March 2011).

- As most CFCRS programs/institutions were established only over the last decade and have been continuously confronted by lots of uncertainty in their operations, occasionally discussants did have something to grumble about concerning foreign lecturers. For instance, a full-time undergraduate from the University of Michigan–Shanghai Jiao Tong University Joint Institute (UM-SJTU Joint Institute) pointed out that lecturers, in particular foreign lecturers, came and went frequently in her institute, so much so that the very same course might be conducted by different lecturers every year. It could therefore affect the quality of teaching due to hasty preparation of new lecturers as well as their disconnection from previous teaching experiences.
- In regard to the second point of facilitating students to continue their studies abroad, Discussants from both the CFCRS programs and institutions agreed overwhelmingly that these TNHE arrangements could offer them a well-fitted transitional period to prepare for overseas studies ahead. In fact, this is particularly the case for Mainland Chinese undergraduates, and most discussants suggested that apart from financially benefiting from these TNHE arrangements where they could spend less for the same overseas qualifications, their fractional or entire study period in China (2+2, 3+1, 2+1+1, or 4+0)[19] could also equip them with much-needed foreign language competency as well as a boost to their confidence in facing challenges abroad. And last but not least, they could facilitate students' overseas visa applications for their Phase 2 studies, particularly concerning US visa applications in which Chinese students may sometimes encounter troubles and be rejected by the American embassy.[20]
- As far as CFCRS programs were concerned, it was very clear that most discussants prefer to opt for the TNHE arrangements of 2+2, 3+1, or 2+1+1 rather than 4+0, since a common perception among the Mainland Chinese discussants was that a genuine overseas experience matters, and a degree associated with such a genuine overseas experience was more valuable than one awarded through the entirely domestic 4+0 program. However, understandably, only a fraction of the discussants could in effect opt for their Phase 2 studies abroad either due to personal financial constraints or a less qualified academic record, and intriguingly in several cases, also due to the fact that their parents preferred to keep them in China since they were the only child in their families. Yet discussants from the two "branch campuses" of overseas HEIs had a different

story to tell. Most of them, obviously from well-off families, adamantly expressed their intentions to continue their studies abroad without any hesitation or consideration of the exorbitant expenses involved. It seems that these "branch campuses" of overseas HEIs have become exclusive institutions for the wealthy in China,[21] totally fending off students from lower classes and therefore limiting their educational contributions to contemporary Chinese society.
- Most discussants however were aware that Mainland Chinese society in general did not have a positive perception toward CFCRS programs and institutions. Although they all acknowledged that irregularities and malpractices in management were prevalent among CFCRS programs/institutions, discussants tended to refute allegations as far as their programs were concerned, and also expressed their chagrin at the "misperception" of others against them. For instance, a discussant from the Sino-German College of Applied Sciences, Tongji University (CDHAW-Tongji),[22] lamented that "in fact we have to learn harder and to face more challenges in CDHAW than in other 'ordinary' colleges. Yet people may still bear the misperception that we are enrolling in CDHAW simply because we have failed to meet the recruitment criteria of 'ordinary' colleges. This is not true, and we are really annoyed by that" (15 December 2010).

Diverse Learning Experiences

- Undeniably, however, sources of students recruited by CFCRS programs/institutions affiliated with prestigious HEIs could be very different from those affiliated with less prestigious HEIs in the Mainland Chinese context. Obviously, discussants from the latter were having less grievances about the "misperception" of others, and were more grateful for the extra opportunities offered through TNHE arrangements. It implies a "second chance" for them to seize a valuable degree—either an overseas one or a local one—after failing to perform well enough in the National Higher Education Entrance Examination. Those who eventually wish to study abroad could utilize their Phase 1 studies in China as a mere preparatory period to improve their foreign language competency. In fact, a few discussants admitted that they might head for other "nonpartner" foreign university after spending one or two years in a specific CFCRS program/institution. Their wealthy parents might already have an alternative arrangement for their studies abroad, and some have also admitted that they preferred to work and stay permanently in foreign countries after wrapping up their studies abroad.[23] In short, TNHE was one of the ways that could facilitate their exodus out of China.
- The motivation of prestigious public HEIs in establishing CFCRS programs/institutions with overseas HEIs is rather different from that of

the less prestigious public and *minban* HEIs. The former seem to have more concern about their own agenda of internationalization and of learning something from others for self-improvement than the potential profits generated by CFCRS programs/institutions. Thus, as commented on by a master's graduate from the East China Normal University, students enrolled in the university's CFCRS postgraduate programs have to endure intensive learning pressure throughout this process, since "we have to satisfy program requirements set by both of the institutions," which happened to be prestigious HEIs in China and France respectively (17 December 2010). Likewise, prestigious overseas HEIs may not aim primarily for earnings in their collaboration with Chinese public HEIs. As Professor Sun Wei put it,[24] they "tend to look for good students rather than profits. And the reason why they do not care much about profits is exactly because they are prestigious HEIs" (interview with Professor Sun Wei, 6 January 2011). In this connection, Professor Zhang Shensheng[25] had also offered an almost identical observation in our interview with him on 16 December 2010.

- Above all, these prestigious overseas HEIs aim to recruit qualified Chinese students with great potential in research, and if possible try to further their collaborations with the academic staff of the Chinese partner HEIs to advance their research interests in contemporary China. Discussants from the CFCRS programs/institutions concerned—for example CFCRS programs offered by the East China Normal University, or the UM-SJTU Joint Institute which is affiliated with Shanghai Jiao Tong University—seemed to be aware of this privilege of status. Moreover, among those who had already spent a period of time in prestigious overseas HEIs, a high degree of contentment could be detected with regard to their learning experiences.
- A unique yet interesting issue was raised specifically by discussants from the two "branch campuses" of overseas HEIs, namely the University of Nottingham-Ningbo (UNN) and the United International College (UIC). A full-time undergraduate from UNN groused about the suspicious "double standard" adopted by the university's main and branch campuses in student assessment. "I am not sure whether the marking criteria are exactly the same as that of the main campus, because our average marks are often lower than that of the students who exchanged to the main campus" (27 January 2011). Similarly, several full-time undergraduates from UIC also complained that it was unfair for the main campus (i.e., Hong Kong Baptist University, HKBU) to impose its strict GPA policy indiscriminately on the Zhuhai branch campus, in which the allocation of "grade A" is sternly confined to only 10 percent of the students. In their view, it was indeed a reflection of the HKBU's "lack of understanding of the actual situation in UIC" (field interview, 9

March 2011). The crux of the issue is that discussants from these "branch campuses" might bear the feeling that even though they have performed as excellently as—or even better than—their counterparts in the main campus, they were "discriminated" against by the institution in deliberately watering down their assessment results.

Limitations of Transnational Education Programs

- The insufficient facilities, resources, and administrative support offered by CFCRS programs/institutions remain a very common issue among discussants, particularly in the case of CFCRS programs offered by less prestigious HEIs. There were also grievances from discussants who enrolled in CFCRS institutions about "discrimination" imposed by the local partner HEIs in using the campus facilities. Harsh criticism could likewise be heard among discussants from the "branch campuses" of overseas HEIs in this regard. For instance, discussants from UIC commented that "contrasted with the quality of teaching, the administrative efficiency of UIC needs to be improved way forward;"; "the administrative staff are much inferior to the academic staff"; "unsatisfactory student services"; as well as "collections in the library are both limited and outdated" (field interview, 9 March 2011).
- The use of foreign languages as a medium of instruction was not as prevalent as what most CFCRS programs/institutions claimed to be. This was particularly the case for CFCRS programs offered by the less prestigious HEIs. Discussants enrolled in these programs tend to have substantial problems with foreign languages being used as a medium of instruction. On the one hand, they were not "first batch" students who had excelled in the National College Entrance Examination (*gaokao*); on the other hand, Chinese HEIs with less prestigious status were generally much weaker in their academic provisions, and thus less capable of facilitating this process of language transition. Frustrations with language barriers were therefore commonly experienced by discussants. In fact, the issue of language barriers was not only raised by students in the discussions but echoed by senior administrators in certain interviews as well. For instance, Professor Sun Wei, director of the Department of Educational Cooperation and Exchange of the Zhongyuan University of Technology (ZUT),[26] admitted that one of the great challenges ZUT was facing in advancing CFCRS programs remained the unsatisfactory English competency of its students. As revealed, the foreign partner of its CFCRS programs—the prestigious University of Manchester—was "surprised" to learn about this cruel reality during the earliest stage of their collaboration.[27] According to Professor Sun, albeit the UK university did not bear a high expectation of the English competency of ZUT students in the first instance, they were still very much disappointed. "They keep

reminding us about this weakness of students throughout the collaboration, and have tried hard to improve it together with us" (interview with Professor Sun Wei, 6 January 2011).

- The creative approach adopted by the College of International Education, ZUT, in dealing with the language barrier faced by its students may worth mentioning. For professional courses which involved foreign lecturers throughout students' last two years of study, each foreign lecturer would have to collaborate with a local lecturer in every aspect of the course. It thus refers to a process that covers course designing, teaching, assignment, as well as the final assessment of students.[28] Student discussants from the ZUT claimed that they had indeed benefited from this pedagogical adaptation, while from the perspective of senior administrators, local lecturers could both help the students and also learn something for themselves from their foreign partners. This refers not only to pedagogical skills but English language as well, since they are also commonly haunted by the difficulties of teaching in English.

A Comparison of Student Learning Experiences in Asia

As far as the experiences of TNHE students are concerned, we suppose we may also adopt the typological framework set out above to compare and contrast the development of TNHE in Hong Kong, Singapore, Malaysia, and Mainland China. Accordingly, we may then try to explore the possible correlations between these elements (i.e., global or local concern; public or private funding) and the common learning experiences of TNHE students. The central issue that really matters, however, remains the role that the state intends to play, as well as the corresponding TNHE policies that each has taken subsequently.

TNHE in Hong Kong today is rather insignificant even though the government has vowed to nurture a successful and lucrative industry of education. TNHE in Hong Kong is still very much locally oriented, and its main vehicle is the self-financed branches of public HEIs rather than the feeble private HEIs. UGC (University Grants Committee)-funded programs offered by the resourceful and dominant public HEIs have in general marginalized the TNHE programs, and have degraded them to a lackluster status of primarily catering to "less qualified" or mature students. In short, the possibilities of TNHE in Hong Kong are far from being fully explored. Accordingly, the population of TNHE students in Hong Kong is rather small and receives little attention from society. Local Hong Kong HEIs usually collaborate passively with their foreign partners in TNHE programs, and the general satisfaction of

Hong Kong discussants could be attributed more to the latter rather than the former. However, inevitably, the lack of facilities and resources has become a common grievance among the Hong Kong discussants due to this marginalized status of TNHE programs in Hong Kong, coupled with the authority's refusal to "intervene" as far as possible.

Several similarities could be found in the development of TNHE between Mainland China and Hong Kong. CFCRS programs/institutions in Mainland China are by and large conducted by or affiliated to public HEIs in a self-financed manner, and are likewise catering primarily to local students. The role of *minban* HEIs in CFCRS is almost negligible. However, TNHE development in Mainland China is far more diversified, booming and chaotic compared to Hong Kong's, and could in fact be regarded as the most diversified and chaotic case among the four territories. It is "chaotic" not only in the sense that it lacks a set of common and basic rules that regulate TNHE (or CFCRS in the Mainland Chinese context) development, but short of a truly effective mechanism in regulating HEIs throughout the whole of China as well. There are of course rules and regulations promulgated by the central and local governments from time to time, but the effective enforcement of these rules as well as the related coordination between the central and local governments is a different story. Nevertheless, the lower starting point of TNHE programs in Mainland China in terms of its socioeconomic development level, coupled with a powerful educational demand among the locals, has resulted in a by and large highly positive judgment on CFCRS programs/institutions among the discussants.[29] Grievances are many, but discussants may unconsciously tone them down due to their gratefulness to the opportunities offered by TNHE arrangements and an optimistic conviction that things have changed in a better direction. Also, both the central and local governments, albeit less coordinated in many cases, are aggressive enough in advancing the development and experiments of CFCRS.

In comparison, unlike Hong Kong and Mainland China, TNHE in Singapore is driven by the state yet conducted primarily by private HEIs, that is, branch campuses of overseas HEIs and local private HEIs, and it caters to foreign students rather than locals. In other words, TNHE in Singapore is more business oriented than simply playing a supplementary role in meeting the domestic demand for higher education. From what we could learn from the discussants, it seems that by far Singapore's strategy of inviting prestigious overseas HEIs to come and of closely supervising the quality of the programs is rather successful, yet the performance of TNHE programs offered by its local private HEIs remains to be seen. As a plus, the "brand name effect" should also be highlighted from our discussions with TNHE students in Singapore. Both the branch campuses of overseas HEIs and the local private HEIs enjoy a common privilege of bearing a reputable brand name as part of the Singapore education system, which, according to most discussants, is not only good in its academic quality, but implies a safe and disciplined study environment as well. This brand-name effect thus enables a virtuous cycle in the development of TNHE in Singapore. Nevertheless, Singapore could not be spared the criticism of insufficient campus infrastructure given its very limited land resources as a city-state. It remains an issue constantly raised by international students who study TNHE programs in Singapore, as they have all paid a substantial tuition fee for the programs.

The main vehicle for TNHE in Malaysia is its local private HEIs, and to some degree also branch campuses of the overseas HEIs. Unlike the case of Singapore, they cater equally for the locals as well as foreign students. TNHE in Malaysia is both a business for bagging foreign currencies and a meaningful supplement to domestic higher education resources, which are always inadequate. Compared to Singapore, the Malaysian government is now struggling to enable a virtuous cycle for its educational brand name, and has indeed enjoyed a certain success so far. It is worth mentioning that the local private HEIs, though disadvantaged by the less reputable brand name as part of the Malaysian education system, have generally had a long history in developing TNHE programs, and they are therefore experienced enough in making swift adjustments to meet new challenges. As revealed by the discussants, it seems that the Malaysian private HEIs are by and large still competitive and, to a substantial degree, have consolidated their share of the Asian higher education market for "second-tier students." Today Malaysia attracts overseas students not only from ASEAN, China, and South Asia, but from Sub-Saharan Africa and the Middle East as well, thus creating an impressive diversity in its international student population. However, a complaint, if not an accusation, that we could commonly hear from the discussants in Malaysia was that private HEIs were generally in the pursuance of "quantity over quality," in which some have accused them of becoming too money minded. Thus, it seems subjectively that discussants in Malaysia have had the least satisfying learning experiences as far as TNHE programs are concerned (see table 10.3).

At first glance, it seems invalid for us to categorize TNHE along the line of funding mechanism, since the dominant funding mechanism of TNHE in all four territories is private funding. However, "private funding in public HEIs" and "private funding in private HEIs" may still make a difference. In the first scenario, TNHE programs/institutions conducted by or affiliated with certain public HEIs could still very much benefit from "public resources" in terms of the reputation of a public HEI, its well-established managerial framework or institution, its international networking, its campus facilities (though with limited access in most cases), its functioning mechanism of quality assurance, and even its academic staff. This is particularly the case for TNHE in Mainland China, since the line between public and private resources is still very blurry. And in practice, this "appropriation" of public resources to self-financed TNHE programs seems helpful in providing a better learning environment for students, and thus the achievement of a high degree of satisfaction among the discussants. In contrast, many local private HEIs in Malaysia are

Table 10.3 TNHE in Hong Kong, Mainland China, Singapore, and Malaysia: A Comparison

Territory	Hong Kong	Mainland China	Singapore	Malaysia
Orientation on Student Recruitment	Locally oriented	Locally oriented	Globally oriented	Locally and regionally oriented
Main Vehicle for TNHE	Self-financed branches of public HEIs	CFCRS programs/institutions conducted by or affiliated with public HEIs	Branch campuses of overseas HEIs and local private HEIs	Local private HEIs and branch campuses of overseas HEIs
Dominant Funding Mechanism for TNHE	Private funding (public HEIs)	Private funding (public HEIs)	Private funding (private HEIs)	Private funding (private HEIs)
Main Driver For TNHE	Market	Market (before 2003) State (after 2003)	State	Market (before mid-1990s) State (after mid-1990s)
Realistic Effectiveness of the Mechanism of Quality Assurance in General	Fair	Weak but improving	Strong	Fair

Source: by Author.

disadvantaged by the total lack of public resources in this respect. The local private HEIs in Singapore are also facing a similar problem, yet for those branch campuses of the prestigious overseas HEIs, this is much less a problem since they stand on a solid foundation of both the reputation and resources of their mother institutions.

Another correlation that we could vaguely draw from this series of focus group discussions is that territories with more inward-looking TNHE development (i.e., locally oriented in terms of student recruitment) tend to see fewer grievances among their TNHE student populations, as these local students might more or less be grateful for the extra opportunities given under the various TNHE arrangements.

Yet in the case of Malaysia, international students tend to act more like a "picky customer" after paying such a considerable tuition fee and yet feel disenchanted by the gap between their imagination and the day-to-day reality in Malaysian campuses. In fact, international students enrolled in TNHE programs offered by minor private HEIs in Singapore were likewise making lots of complaints by 2008, as reflected in media reports and informal discussions in online forums. These have subsequently prompted the state to enact the Private Education Act in September 2009, later also followed by the establishment of the Council for Private Education on 1 December 2009 as a statutory board tasked with quality assurance of the private education industry in Singapore.[30]

Our focus group discussions with TNHE students situated in the four territories did show that in general, international students were much more critical than their local counterparts when it came to the provision of TNHE providers, as well as to the larger issue of their overall learning experiences. Thus an outward-looking TNHE development (i.e., globally or regionally oriented in terms of student recruitment) entails a stronger regulation/intervention from the state, or else it risks uncertainty in quality assurance. Obviously, it bears a greater burden in avoiding a discredit to its education system than those that are more locally oriented.

In fact, apart from quality assurance, an outward-looking TNHE development entails more supportive functions from the state. For instance, an issue which was also raised by foreign discussants and survey respondents in Malaysia was about their working prospect in Malaysia right after their graduation. Restrictions imposed by the Malaysian government in this respect are "notorious" compared to Singapore's aggressive policy of human capital, yet the Malaysian industry of TNHE could do nothing about it except lobbying for a change in state policy.[31] In contrast, among the foreign discussants in Singapore, some did admit that they were attracted by the prospect of staying and working in Singapore right after their graduation. We may therefore tentatively conclude after going through this long series of focus group discussions from June 2010 to March 2011 in Hong Kong, Singapore, Malaysia, and Mainland China, that as far as TNHE is concerned, the role of the state remains significantly relevant in assuring a satisfactory and beneficial study environment for students, regardless of their nationality.

Discussion and Conclusion: What International Exchange Students Say

In addition to the fieldwork data reported above, a recent study conducted by David Cheng at the City University of Hong Kong examining how inbound and outbound exchange students in Hong Kong evaluate their learning experiences could provide additional perspectives for assessing student learning experiences when universities are becoming more serious about internationalization.

Cheng (2013) found that there are five items at the top of both inbound and outbound students' list of expectations:

1. becoming independent,
2. traveling and seeing the world,
3. having a better understanding of different cultures,
4. making friends from different backgrounds, and
5. understanding more about the host countries.

According to Cheng (2013), "Both inbound and outbound students seem to have gained what they set out to achieve. For Hong Kong students, being independent is a much stronger reason for exchange, while inbound students give a higher priority to gaining better understanding of different cultures."[32]

According to the same study, most Hong Kong parents are high-handed, overbearing, dictatorial, and peremptory, and they do not trust their children because they think their children will learn bad habits easily during puberty. This is Hong Kong's tradition. Therefore, parents push their children to get good performances in school and force them to learn many musical instruments. In some extreme cases, parents don't let their children (especially girls) go out with friends even when they are in high school, or more extremely they still monitor their children even when they are at university. This may be the reason that Hong Kong students want to become independent.

Cheng (2013) found out that "in terms of student development, both inbound and outbound students experienced improvement in the areas of cultural awareness, interpersonal skills and communication skills. Compared with the inbound, Hong Kong students were more positive about their experience in development skills in problem-solving and critical thinking, and being proactive and innovative, and they reported gains in knowledge in their fields of study and in motivation to learn."[33]

Moreover, Cheng (2013) also found that inbound students reported a higher level of satisfaction with university academic resources than those outbound. While both groups reported a positive experience in communicating with instructors and participating in academic activities in host institutions, Hong Kong students found the learning environments in host institutions more stressful.[34]

Furthermore, regarding social experience, Cheng found that Hong Kong students reported a higher level of integration into the local community. Both groups felt that they had adapted to the host institution well and had a sense of community with others around them, and they also perceived being stereotyped by others because of their cultural backgrounds.[35] In addition, Cheng asked Hong Kong students to identify issues related to exchange programs, discovering that they have significantly higher levels of academic and financial problems.[36]

Conclusion

This chapter critically examines how students enrolling in transnational higher education in Hong Kong, Singapore, Malaysia, and China have evaluated their learning experiences. In addition, we have also reviewed how inbound and outbound exchange students based in Hong Kong reflect their learning experiences. Putting all these observations and findings together, we believe going global and internationalization has become increasingly popular in shaping higher education in Asia. Such an expansion of transnational higher education would not only affect the education sector but also bring about economic, social, cultural, and political results in societies flourishing with overseas campuses and academic programs. Therefore, we should not underestimate the policy implications when experiencing the rapid expansion of transnational higher education.

Chapter 11

Changing Regulatory Regimes and Governance in East Asia

Introduction

The emergence of transnational higher education in Malaysia, Singapore, and Hong Kong has been commonly prompted by the irresistible trend of globalization, and fueled by the inclusion of higher education as an industry under the GATS (General Agreement on Trade in Services) framework (Knight 2002). However, due to the diverse politico-economic contexts of these societies, it is promoted and developed under different considerations by each state; hence a variety of governance and regulatory systems are put in place between the state and transnational higher education providers. This chapter attempts to critically reflect upon the changing regulatory regimes and governance in East Asia, especially when higher education provision is increasingly proliferated.

Varieties of Regulatory Regimes in Governing Transnational Education

The following examination of transnational education in Malaysia, Singapore, and Hong Kong will draw on the theoretical framework adopted from Mok (2008b) for analyzing the changing governance and regulatory framework of transnational education in these Asian economies (see table 11.1).

Table 11.1 shows the varieties of regulatory regimes from the perspectives of state regulation on the one hand, and from market regulation on the other. A broad categorization of four types of states, namely the market-accelerationist state, the interventionist state, the market-facilitating state, and the

Table 11.1 Varieties of Regulatory Regimes

	Market Regulation (planned)	Market Regulation (unplanned)
State Regulation (centralized)	Authoritarian liberalism Market-accelerationist state State-corporatist regulatory regime	State socialism Interventionist state Command-and-control regulatory regime
State Regulation (decentralized)	Economic liberalism Market-facilitating state Civil society regulatory regime	Market socialism Market-coordinating state (Coordinated) market regulatory regime

Source: Developed and modified from Levi-Faur (1998) by the author.

market-coordinating state, can then be discerned in accordance with the context of strong or weak state and civil regulations. In the Asia-Pacific region, developmental states, while prevalent throughout the 1970s and 1980s, have to undergo a series of decentralization and deregulation today in making themselves more competitive and entrepreneurial to face the growing challenges of globalization. Yet a closer scrutiny of the states' capacity, as shown in cases of their governance of transnational higher education, may reveal certain new possibilities that could actually sustain the pivotal role of the state.

Overall, the fundamental impetus behind the prosperity of transnational higher education in these two cases may well be economic. Though domestic demands for higher education (as in the case of Malaysia where non-Malays are discriminated against in their accessibility to public universities) could initially be the catalyst for the state to introduce or allow the advancement of transnational higher education, it finally boils down to "the competitive rush for international students and their money" (Chan and Ng 2008, 291). In this sense, regardless of the nuance between the grand strategies/initiatives of the so-called Global Schoolhouse or Regional Hub of Education, higher education as an exportable product of services should be kept under strict supervision of quality control to achieve sustainability and competitiveness in such a booming yet fiercely competed market. Thus as McBurnie and Ziguras (2001) point out, Southeast Asia is now something like a laboratory in the development and regulation of transnational education. The region combines high demand and keen competition among service providers, and the regulatory regimes in host countries range from relatively laissez-faire to strongly interventionist. Let us first examine the policy contexts for the growing prominence of transnational education and then discuss the most recent developments of transnational education in these Asian economies.

Between the State and the Market: Searching for New Governance in Asia

Analyzing the recent developments of transnational higher education and the growing privateness in higher education in these three Asian societies in the light of the theoretical framework outlined above, we can easily realize that they are experiencing fundamental changes in their governance and regulatory models, shifting to an interactionist focus (government with society), with a growing realization of government-society interdependence, as Kooiman (1993) has suggested. With heightened expectations from their citizens for better and higher education, it is obvious that depending upon the provision of the states alone is no longer sufficient, particularly when most Asian states have experienced economic setbacks after the Asian financial crisis in 1996/97. Public universities in these societies thus began to diversify their funding sources from nonstate actors or sectors since the 1990s, and the market, the community, and the civil society at large have subsequently been revitalized by governments in Malaysia, Hong Kong, and Singapore to engage in higher education financing and provision. Analyzing these cases in the light of the theoretical framework set out at the beginning of the chapter (table 11.1), the rise of transnational higher education, coupled with the growing importance of privateness in higher education, has suggested more or less a shift from the conventional centralized model of governance and regulation of these Asian states. Nevertheless, while they no longer monopolize the provision, financing, and regulation of higher education, a further review and comparison among these three cases demonstrates that paradoxically, the states' capacity may not necessarily fade away, and there are varieties of regulatory regimes which indeed epitomize the dialectical conflicts between market efficiency and state capacity.

While governments in Malaysia and Singapore have played far more of a "market generator" role, not only in setting out strategic directions but also proactively orchestrating developments in transnational higher education to meet their national agenda, the Hong Kong government is, conversely, far more committed to free market economic principles, thus performing the role of "market facilitator." The Malaysian government stepped into a similar path of development to boost its transnational higher education, yet the lack of strategic and philosophical consistency in its planning has created the paradox of a regulatory regime of simultaneous centralization and decentralization (Mok 2010). Similarly, the Singapore government has taken a very proactive and selective approach by inviting leading universities from overseas to set up their branch campuses or joint programs in Singapore. Playing the role as a "market-accelerationist state" as Mok (2008c) argued, Singapore has now become a very credible regional education hub in Asia with a critical mass of international students and famous transnational higher education operating in the city-state. Overall, the highly selective approach adopted by the government in directing developments of transnational higher education clearly shows that Malaysia and Singapore are not altogether market-embracing states. Rather, they are market-accelerationist states that operate on the logic of the market but intervene in order to remove inefficiencies found there. This new form of market-accelerationist state demonstrates that the developmental states in East Asia have not entirely given way to neoliberal globalization. The Malaysian and Singapore governments now pursue "regulation-for-competition" rather than "regulation-of-competition," aiming to enhance the state's competitiveness through regulation in order to achieve its goals of economic nationalism (e.g., Malaysia's master plan of Vision 2020 and Singapore's Global Schoolhouse project).

In comparison, the governance and regulatory approach taken by the Hong Kong government toward transnational higher education is the more liberal one; several significant changes, as mentioned earlier, can be identified over the last few years. These recent reforms all point to the direction of stronger state regulation, as well as a more proactive role played by the state. For instance, apart from the very new efforts of constructing a more inclusive qualifications framework, the government has also become more aggressive in providing financial incentives to lure international students with talent and expertise,[1] while at the same time relaxing immigration policies to facilitate their stay in Hong Kong. It has also planned to raise the international student rate in Hong Kong beyond the current 10 percent threshold, and actively promotes business-related programs, which are most popular among Asian students.

It is thus intriguing for us to see that as far as the governance and regulatory regimes of transnational higher education are concerned, both the market-accelerationist state (Malaysia and Singapore) and the market-facilitating state (Hong Kong), after roughly two decades of experiencing and adjusting to the rapid development of transnational higher education in their societies, have gradually approached a similar direction of reform: Malaysia may have to reduce its strong inclination toward state intervention in order to maintain the vitality and efficiency of the sector of transnational higher education, while Singapore has tried to steer from a distance to create a market with a critical mass of transnational higher education institutions attracting overseas students to study in Singapore to realize its national goal for regional hub status. On the other hand, the Hong Kong government may be forced to wield its state capacity more proactively in industrializing the same sector, so as to make it more conducive to the territory's economy. After all, it is not easy either in theory or practice to strike a balance between a market economy and a strong regulatory state. More importantly, the variations regarding the regulatory regimes of these Asian transnational higher education systems are closely related and the governments of Hong Kong, Singapore, and Malaysia have not decided which are the best and most effective governance/regulatory methods in monitoring the rapid growth of transnational education programs. Such differences are clearly revealed by the ways these systems differ in terms of information provision/accreditation, program delivery, and social issues such as equity/equality stemming from the rise of transnational education in these Asian societies.

Organizational Hybridization, Network Governance, and State Capacity

The increase in transnational education programs in Malaysia, Hong Kong, and Singapore has inevitably challenged the conventional university governance model used to make the ministry of education as the core agent governing and directing education service delivery. In view of the growing transnationalization of education, Ball argues that such a development would lead "to new terrain of governance, complex and sometimes convoluted, which involves problems of coordination (and accountability and transparency), especially when dealing with multi-national businesses, but which can bring to the state benefits in terms of flexibilities, and forms of flexibilization and substitution which are not normally possible in administrative systems" (Ball 2009, 10). Our above discussion has clearly shown how proliferated the education providers have become. By inviting or allowing overseas or local "educational entrepreneurs" to start their operations by offering a wide range of education programs in these Asian states, the complexity resulted from the hybridization of organizations and evolving heterarchies in educational management has inevitably rendered the traditional form of higher education governance inappropriate. Hence, we have witnessed the call for "reinvention" of the state (Mok 2007a) and the changing relationships of the trends outlined above to changes in the delivery of educational services and concomitantly in the values and ecologies of educational organizations (Ball 2009). As Ball has rightly highlighted, "heterarchies, national and transnational are made up of a variety of types of relationships, and concomitant blurring and hybridities" (Ball 2009, 10; different partners engaged in running the rapidly expanding transnational education would also involve diverse interests especially when the state has to deal with multinational business. The growing hybridization of organizations as a result of the rise of transnational education may force the nation-state to become more flexible in higher education governance.

In order to resolve the problems of coordination against the context of heterarchies and hybridization of organizations, new forms of governance would evolve to enable different actors to participate in managing/governing these newly but rapidly developing organizations. According to Ball (2009), the new kinds of "willing" subjects are keen to participate not only in the decision-making process but also in management/governance of the transnational education enterprises. Such a development will lead to the search for "network governance," that is, for "webs of stable and ongoing relationships which mobilize dispersed resources towards the solution of policy problems" (Pal 1997). Although the emergence of this new governance model by means of "network governance" does not completely overturn conventional policy instruments, it does create considerable pressure for making the policy-making process more "parallel to and across state institutions and their jurisdictional boundaries,"

(Skelcher et al. 2004, 3), and "in the process parts of *the state and some of its activities are privatized*" (Ball 2009, italics in original).

Having realized the changing governance due to the growing complexity in organizations and heterarchies in managing transnational education, however, we should not discard the importance of the state throughout the processes of transnational education development. Despite the variations from nation to nation internationally, the state is normally vigorous within these governance processes. Following Fukayama, Mok (2007) draws a distinction between the scope and capacity of a state in governance. Our above analysis has suggested that the reach of the state may decline with the rise of the "tangled web" of policy networks, especially when transnational education has to rely more on "self-administered" policy communities through a "regulated self-regulatory" regime (Mok 2008c). Nonetheless, the "core executive" retains a substantial authoritative and coordinating presence over policy (Marinetto 2003) and in some respects and certainly in education has achieved an enhancement of "capacity to project its influence and secure its governmental partners or stakeholders" (Jessop 2002, 199). As we discussed earlier, both Singapore and Malaysia are performing the role of the market-accelerationist state; this form of state is so intriguing because it intervenes in markets in order to accelerate market forces. Thus, it is not altogether a market-embracing model of the state. Instead, the market-accelerationist state operates according to the logic of the market but intervenes in markets in order to remove inefficiencies (Mok 2005a). The selective adaptation to globalization in Singapore and Malaysia has clearly suggested how politically skillful and tactical these Asian states are in tackling their global challenges. Their responses could be interpreted as a form of "defensive modernization," as many nation-states are reluctant to be entirely converted by major global/contemporary trends with strong justifications for preserving local cultures and traditions (Mok 2012b).

Discussion and Conclusion: Contested Local-Global Relations and Changing Governance

Chapters 8 to 11 in this volume have discussed the growing proliferation of providers in higher education and student learning, especially when transnational higher education has become increasingly popular in Singapore, Malaysia, Hong Kong, and Mainland China. The quest for becoming a regional hub of education has inevitably diversified educational programs in these Asian societies, and this development has also changed the relationship between the state and the market in educational provision and financing. In addressing the increasing complexity of the organization and delivery of transnational education, comparative education researchers and analysts have to critically examine the changes taking place in the governance and management of transnational higher education, with particular reference to analyzing the regulatory regimes governing and assuring the academic quality of the newly emerging transitional education programs. After a close look at the changing governance and regulatory regimes of transnational higher education in Hong Kong, Singapore, and Malaysia, we have found the complexity of heterarchies and hybrid organizations when global education is rapidly expanding. With the proliferation of higher education providers, coupled with the mobility of students and the diversification of educational services, the conventional public-private distinction is rendered inappropriate. The above comparative study has clearly demonstrated the growing complexity of transnational education, especially when modern states have to deal with multiple players/providers of educational services in the context of market multilateralism, as Susan Robertson has suggested (Robertson 2010).

Having highlighted how these Asian states tactically respond to globalization challenges by selective adaptation, we must be aware that the network of complex relationships also has "a life of its own"; thus we should also take the unique sociopolitical and socioeconomic contexts in which such network governance is formulated into serious consideration. More importantly, we should be aware of the tensions and interactions between global and local forces as "these processes are located within a global architecture of political relations that not only involves national governments, but also IGOs, transnational corporations and NGOs. Policies are developed, enacted and evaluated in various global networks from where their authority is now partly derived" (Lingard and Rizvi 2009, 338). Transnationalization involves the "input" and "export" of policy ideas, models, practices, and sensibilities through political and advocacy networks (Keck and Sikkink 1998) and even commercial networks as discussed above. It is therefore not surprising that the discourses and practices of governance move through and are embedded within transnational policy networks of various kinds (Ball 2009).[9] A huge diversity of models and patterns in terms of partnerships and collaborations should have driven national governments to become more flexible and responsive to the hybridities and heterarchies in transnational education management/organizational structures.

It is thus intriguing for us to see that as far as the governance and regulatory regimes of transnational higher education are concerned, both of the market-accelerationist states (Singapore and Malaysia), after roughly two decades of experiencing and adjusting to the rapid development of transnational higher education in their societies, have gradually approached a similar direction of reform: Singapore and Malaysia may have to reduce their strong flavor of state intervention in order to maintain the vitality and efficiency of their sectors of transnational higher education. Unlike Singapore and Malaysia, Hong Kong still tries to maintain a "small government, big market" approach by playing the role of "market-facilitating state" when promoting transnational higher education. Against the increasingly competitive environment, how far Hong

Kong can maintain this approach to enhance its regional competitiveness is subject to question. In response to the growing pressures and challenges from other Asian cities, the new government led by Chief Executive C. Y. Leung has made some attempts to strengthen the steering role of the government when developing new economic components like the regional hub of education, but the civil service in the city-state has not entirely followed this particular call for a more visible hand of the government in the market. The dilemmas that Hong Kong is currently facing have clearly demonstrated the complexity of changing government-market-civil society relations, especially when education providers are highly diversified (Leung 2012).

No matter how government-market-civil society relations are changing, we should not underestimate the capacity of these Asian states in steering the transnationalization of education, although they have encountered growing pressures to become more flexible in governing transnational education. After all, it is not easy both in theory and practice to strike a balance between a market economy and a strong regulatory state. More importantly, we must be aware of the unique political economy of these Asian states, especially when the government has long played a central role in directing the nation-building project (i.e., the quest for a regional hub of education is one of such projects). Equally important, there is no simple local-global dualism that can be evoked here rather than a set of "connections" which cut across scales and territories. Therefore, we should be sensitive about particular policy contexts, histories, and traditions and the forms of governance embedded when conceptualizing changing governance and regulatory regimes as education is increasingly transnationalized.[2]

Part III

University Performance, Changing University Governance and Policy Implications for East Asia

Chapter 12

Questing for Entrepreneurial Universities in East Asia: Impacts on Academics and University Governance

Introduction

Higher education plays important roles in fostering innovation in various ways. First and foremost, higher education is a key to the "competence building" of an economy that wants to excel in innovation, by cultivating a capable workforce equipped with essential skills and knowledge—this is the so-called human capital. While infrastructures like research institutes, factories, and machines are hardware and physical capital, human capital is a nontangible capital, the software component of national technological capability. Only with the help of universities to nurture local talent or attract foreign talent in the first place are research institutes and private firms able to hire them to conduct indigenous research. Second, higher education institutions can contribute to innovation by conducting entrepreneurial activities in the form of research, knowledge transfer, technology licensing, and commercial spin-offs. These entrepreneurial activities are either conducted by universities alone, or in cooperation with the industry sector.

Our previous chapters have critically examined how universities and governments in selected East Asia societies have responded to the growing challenges of globalization by promoting innovation and research development, driving new initiatives in knowledge transfer and engaging in internationalization and transnationalization of higher education. After adopting these measures, have universities in these East Asian societies enhanced their global competitiveness? This chapter focuses on assessing how universities in

East Asia have performed through the international benchmarking exercises such as university league tables and other major forms of international competitiveness studies. In addition, this chapter also critically reflects upon how the quest for entrepreneurial universities has affected the academic community and university governance in East Asia.

How Do Asian Universities Rank in Global University League Tables?

Many famous universities in East Asia have good reputations. For example, according to the *Times Higher Education* University Ranking–International rank of 2012/13, the University of Tokyo was ranked number 27, the National University of Singapore was ranked number 29, the University of Hong Kong was ranked number 35, and the Pohang University of Science and Technology was ranked number 50. Universities in Japan and the Four Little Dragons performed very well in Asia, always dominating the top ten (see tables 12.1 and 12.2).

According to the Shanghai Jiao Tong University's Academic Ranking of World Universities 2012, an international benchmarking that puts more emphasis on the research performance (especially in science and technology) of universities than other rankings, the region of Asia/Pacific lagged behind Europe and the Americas. The top 19 universities were all from the United States and the UK. Only one university from Japan was in the top 20.[1]

How Do Students in East Asia Perform Internationally?

With regard to student performances, East Asian students have long been the "champions" of international standard tests in mathematics and the sciences, as well as in literacy. International standard tests like the Third International Mathematics and Science Study (TIMSS) and the OECD's Program for International Student Assessment (PISA) have ranked students of Taiwan, Hong Kong, South Korea, and Singapore top among their international and Asian counterparts. In the 2011 TIMSS, Taiwan, South Korea, Singapore, and Hong Kong were the top four countries in eighth grade students' achievement in mathematics. East Asian students also performed well in the OECD's Program for International Student Assessment in mathematics, sciences, and reading.[2]

Table 12.1 *Times Higher Education* University Rankings, 2011/12–2012/13

School	Economy	Regional Rank		International Rank	
		2012/13	2011/12	2012/13	2011/12
University of Tokyo	Japan	1	1	27	30
University of Hong Kong	Hong Kong	3	2	35	34
National University of Singapore	Singapore	2	3	29	40
Peking University	China	4	4	46	49
Kyoto University	Japan	7	5	54	52
Pohang University of Science and Technology	South Korea	5	6	50	53
Hong Kong University of Science and Technology	Hong Kong	9	7	65	62
Tsinghua University	China	6	8	52	71
Korean Advanced Institute of Science and Technology	South Korea	10	9	68	94
Tokyo Institute of Technology	Japan	13	10	128	108
Seoul National University	South Korea	8	14	59	124
Chinese University of Hong Kong	Hong Kong	12	15	124	151
National Taiwan University	Taiwan	14	16	134	154
Nanyang Technological University	Singapore	11	18	86	169
City University of Hong Kong	Hong Kong	19	20	182	193
National Tsing Hua University	Taiwan	31	23	226–250	201–225
Korea University	South Korea	30	26	226–250	226–250
National Chiao Tung University	Taiwan	32	27	251–275	226–250

Source: Times Higher Education University Rankings, http://www.timeshighereducation.co.uk/world-university-rankings/2012–13/world-ranking/region/asia.

Table 12.2 Asia University Rankings 2013 Top 100, *Times Higher Education* World University Rankings

Rank	Institution	Location
1	University of Tokyo	Japan
2	National University of Singapore	Singapore
3	University of Hong Kong	Hong Kong
4	Peking University	China
5	Pohang University of Science and Technology	South Korea
6	Tsinghua University	China
7	Kyoto University	Japan
8	Seoul National University	South Korea
9	Hong Kong University of Science and Technology	Hong Kong
10	Korea Advanced Institute of Science and Technology	South Korea
11	Nanyang Technological University	Singapore
12	Chinese University of Hong Kong	Hong Kong
13	Tokyo Institute of Technology	Japan
14	National Taiwan University	Taiwan
15	Tohoku University	Japan
16	Hebrew University of Jerusalem	Israel
17	Osaka University	Japan
18	Tel Aviv University	Israel
19	City University of Hong Kong	Hong Kong
20	Yonsei University	South Korea
21	Technion Israel Institute of Technology	Israel
22	Middle East Technical University	Turkey
23	Sungkyunkwan University	South Korea
24	Fudan University	China
25	University of Science and Technology of China	China
26	Nagoya University	Japan
27	National Tsing Hua University	Taiwan
28	Bilkent University	Turkey
29	Korea University	South Korea
30	Indian Institute of Technology, Kharaqpur	India
31	Koc University	Turkey
32	National Chiao Tung University	Taiwan
33	Hong Kong Polytechnic University	Hong Kong
34	Indian Institute of Technology, Bombay	India

Continued

Table 12.2 Continued

Rank	Institution	Location
35	Nanjing University	China
36	Tokyo Metropolitan University	Japan
37	Boqazici University	Turkey
38	Istanbul Technical University	Turkey
39	Tokyo Medical and Dental University	Japan
40	Shanghai Jiao Tong University	China
41	Renmin University of China	China
42	Sharif University of Technology	Iran
43	University of Tsukuba	Japan
44	Hokkaido University	Japan
45	Zhejiang University	China
46	National Sun Yat-sen University	Taiwan
47	National Cheng Kung University	Taiwan
48	Kyushu University	Japan
49	King Abdulaziz University	Saudi Arabia
50	Hong Kong Baptist University	Hong Kong
51	Sun Yat-sen University	China
52	National Taiwan University of Science and Technology	Taiwan
53	Keio University	Japan
54	National Central University	Taiwan
55	King Mongkut's University of Technology, Thonburi	Thailand
56	Indian Institute of Technology, Roorkee	India
57	Waseda University	Japan
58	Wuhan University	China
59	Wuhan University of Technology	China
60	Juntendo University	Japan
61	Mahidol University	Thailand
62	King Fahd University of Petroleum and Minerals	Saudi Arabia
63	Tehran University of Medical Sciences	Iran
64	Kyung Hee University	South Korea
65	Bar-Ilan University	Israel
66	Harbin Institute of Technology	China
67	Hiroshima University	Japan
68	National Taiwan Normal University	Taiwan

Continued

Table 12.2 Continued

Rank	Institution	Location
69	China Medical University	Taiwan
70	Osaka City University	Japan
71	Yuan Ze University	Taiwan
72	Chung Yuan Christian University	Taiwan
73	Kobe University	Japan
74	Hanyang University	South Korea
75	Chiba University	Japan
76	National Taiwan Ocean University	Taiwan
77	King Saud University	Saudi Arabia
78	Sogang University	South Korea
79	Pusan National University	South Korea
80	Dalian University of Technology	China
81	Tokyo University of Agriculture and Technology	Japan
82	Chulalongkorn University	Thailand
83	National Chung Cheng University	Taiwan
84	Kyungpook National University	South Korea
85	Okayama University	Japan
86	United Arab Emirates University	United Arab Emirates
87	Universiti Kebangsaan Malaysia	Malaysia
88	American University of Beirut	Lebanon
89	National Yang-Ming University	Taiwan
90	Xi'an Jiaotong University	China
91	Inha University	South Korea
92	Konkuk University	South Korea
93	National Chung Hsing University	Taiwan
94	Chung-Ang University	South Korea
95	Isfahan University of Technology	Iran
96	Kanazawa University	Japan
97	Yokohama National University	Japan
98	Feng Chia University	Taiwan
99	Huazhong University of Science and Technology	China
100	National Taipei University of Technology	Taiwan

Source: http://www.timeshighereducation.co.uk/world-university-rankings/2012–13/regional-ranking/region/asia.

In the arena of higher education, East Asian students have a liking for S&T disciplines, as they account for a large proportion of the science and engineering student population around the world. In 2008, 11.7 percent of the world's students earned their first university degree in the natural sciences. By country, students who earned their first degree in the natural sciences accounted for 11.2 percent of American students, 6.3 percent of Japanese students, 13.2 percent of Chinese students, 13.0 percent of Taiwanese students, 12.0 percent of South Korean students, and 11.7 percent of Singaporean students. In the field of engineering, East Asian students also dominated in numbers: 33.9 percent of Singaporean students, 31.2 percent of Chinese students, 24.5 percent of South Korean students, 24.2 percent of Taiwanese students, and 17.1 percent of Japanese students earned their first university degree in engineering.[3]

In comparison, in the field of social sciences and other non-S&E fields, there were higher proportions of students from the United States and EU, and hence fewer East Asian students. In fact, over the last decade, the number of S&E students in East Asia has been soaring. For instance, in China, the number of students earning their first university degree in the natural sciences has increased from 68,400 in 2000 to 297,300 in 2008. In the same period of time, the number of students earning their first university degree in engineering has also jumped from 213,000 in 2000 to 704,600 in 2008.[4]

All in all, the above discussion suggests that universities and students in East Asia have compared comfortably well to key international performance indicators, while universities in East Asia have shown improvements as indicated by various international university ranking exercises. However, the call for internationalization and the quest for world-class universities in East Asia have inevitably intensified competition among universities and students in the region, resulting in some unintended consequences. The following section identifies a few major impacts generated from the intensification of competition among universities in East Asia because of the increasing energy and attention university management has given to international benchmarking and university ranking exercises.

Impact on Academics and University Governance: Critical Reflections

Growing Inequalities in Higher Education

With a strong intention to position their university systems favorably in different global university ranking exercises, our earlier discussion in previous chapters has already highlighted how universities in Asia have made attempts to concentrate their funding on selective institutions in order to boost them to become research-intensive and globally competitive institutions. Not surprisingly, we have heard complaints from academics in Asia about the widening gap between well-established and newly set-up universities. It is becoming increasingly prevalent that government funding is linked with the performance and ranking of individual universities, while higher education institutions are under pressures to move beyond the first and the second missions (i.e., teaching and research) to the third mission (serving economic and social development through engagement in various kinds of entrepreneurial activity) (Mok 2005c).

Preferential treatment and funding based on selectivity is clearly found in South Korea. Terri Kim has offered a critical analysis of how universities in South Korea are incorporated, identifying the key issues that universities in South Korea are confronting. But one point that deserves attention here is that unlike other Asian university systems which have experienced reductions in state funding (except Singapore), the South Korean government has increased its financial support to the university sector in order to boost a few universities in South Korea to climb up the world university ranking league tables. For example, Kansei University, aspiring to move up the global university league table, has issued a new personnel policy to recruit faculty from overseas to teach instead of appointing local Korean scholars. This new staffing policy has raised deep concerns in South Korea (Kim 2006). Similar experiences can be easily found in other Asian societies such as the "211 Project" in Mainland China, the "Flagship Project" in Japan, the "Brain 21 Project" in South Korea, the "Academic Excellence Project" in Taiwan, and "Areas of Excellence" in Hong Kong.

Critically reflecting on the world of globalized higher education, Altbach (2004) openly notes that globalization has reinforced existing inequalities and erected new barriers in many ways. Economists Joseph Stiglitz (2002) and Dani Rodrik (1997, 1999), among others, have argued that globalization has damaged the interests of developing countries in many aspects, as the powerful university systems in developed economies such as the United States and the UK have always dominated the production and distribution of knowledge. The growing popularity of the quest for world-class universities has further widened the gap between developed and developing economies. Although some Asian universities have successfully climbed up the ladder in the global university league tables, "the major international academic centers—namely the leading research-oriented universities in the North, especially those that use one of the key world languages (particularly English)—occupy the top tier. . . . Even within countries at the center of the world academic system in the early 21st century—the United States, Britain, Germany, France, and to some extent Australia and Canada—there are many peripheral institutions" (Altbach 2004, 5).

It is clear then that globalization has intensified the problems of disparity between universities in well-established and less developed economies. Therefore, universities in less developed economies would encounter difficulties in performing well in global university league tables, not to mention those academic institutions at the periphery with insufficient resources to transform into world-renowned universities. Our above discussion regarding how Asian governments have attempted to enhance their institutions to become world-class and research-led universities has clearly suggested the deepening of inequalities and disparities in higher education not only within the national system but regionally and globally as well. Welch, for instance, points out the dilemmas that many higher education institutions in Southeast Asia have confronted in the midst of the quest for world-class university status. Without sufficient funds, higher education institutions in Indonesia, Malaysia, the Philippines, Thailand, and Vietnam have real difficulties in competing with other well-established universities concentrated in the West and the other wealthier parts of East Asia. Hence, the university systems of these Asian countries are disadvantaged because they fail to assert their academic standing in the global university ranking exercises, patents granted, and papers and citations (Welch 2007). Thus, it is not surprising to see some of the debates about globalization centering around the problems of social integration and social justice (Held 2004), while the acceleration of globalization has indeed retarded social development and deepened divisions between the North and the South (Welch and Mok 2003). Michael Polanyi even regards the freedom of neoliberalism as a poisoned chalice, liberating us from everything, "even from obligations towards truth and justice" (Polanyi 1975, 14).

Undervaluing Teaching with Much Emphasis on Research

In our earlier discussion, we described how university governance has been impacted by the educational reforms taking place in Asia in which ideas and practices along the lines of new managerial-oriented doctrines are being adopted. Responding to the growing impact of globalization, all the Asian states have reviewed their education systems and launched reforms to pursue the commercialization of technology as a source of economic growth (Wong, Ho, and Singh 2011). Correspondingly, the demand for research and knowledge, as well as investments in R&D, has steadily increased in Asian universities. However, the quantity and quality of research staff have not kept up with this demand in Asian universities at this initial phase. The result is that Asian universities are expected to experience an increase in academic staff and enhancement of research productivity (Meek and Suwanwela 2006). Since teachers place more emphasis on research work, they are usually inclined to focus on research and neglect teaching.

Two additional reasons account for the growing tension between teaching and research in these Asian universities. First, the quest for university ranking has inevitably changed the academic lifestyle in Asia. As mentioned earlier, an increasing number of Asian universities are eagerly engaging in world-class university competition, especially trying to deploy resources for improving their international university ranking. The criteria or yardsticks for university performance in general and research assessment in particular are unquestionably determined by Anglo-Saxon traditions and practices, with much emphasis on research (Mok 2007b). When comparing the ranking index systems among *U.S. News & World Report*, the *Times Higher Education Supplement*, and Shanghai Jiao Tong University respectively, that of Shanghai Jiao Tong University puts more weight on research, in which HiCi, Publication in Natural and Science and Citations occupy 60 percent, while this proportion in the US system is 20 percent (Hou 2008). It is against such a context that overemphasis on research achievements has triggered a publishing boom of internationally refereed papers among Asian universities. From 1990 to 2003, Asia's share of the world's total S&E articles rose from 11.5 percent to 19.0 percent, while the EU share and the US share declined slightly to 30.0 percent until 2003 (National Science Foundation 2007). Among the total outputs of Asia from 1990 to 2003, the shares of China and Taiwan were more than doubled, reaching 22 percent and 7 percent respectively in 2003, and South Korea's share went up dramatically from 2 percent to 11 percent. Thus, it is not surprising that there is intense pressure for research and publication; a phenomenon of "publish or perish" has emerged, which has significantly affected the performance of universities and job evaluations of academics. It is against this context that teaching and learning have received relatively less attention in universities.

Secondly, state funding policies and mechanisms also shape the way universities are governed and managed. In keeping with the creation of research universities, many Asian countries have prioritized this long-standing aim through more targeted funding for research. Many Asian universities nowadays introduce internal and external competition for enhancing research productivity. In order to obtain additional funding, individual departments or groups of departments/programs jointly apply for funds. It is against this context that universities have to identify their own strengths by developing centers of excellence for research through pulling expertise together for bidding on external and internal funds. The idea of establishing centers of excellence is great since it can result in bringing a critical mass of academic faculties together for research collaboration. However, the same process has also resulted in polarization of funding support, with the centers being identified as excellent receiving more funding support while the rest receive less. What makes the research disparity situation worse is when universities have attached more weight to the hard sciences and medicine but less to humanities and the social sciences. For example, China approved a national Natural Science Foundation of China in 1986 and built research universities as part of its 985 Project. Similar programs were created elsewhere in Asia: the 1999 Brain Korea 21 (BK 21) program in South Korea, the 2002 Center of Excellence program in Japan (Yonezawa 2007), and the National Higher Education Strategic Plan beyond 2020 and the National Higher Education Action Plan 2007–2010 in Malaysia (Ahmad, Farley, and Naidoo 2012). Although these research enhancement strategies adopted by these Asian countries have been very successful in jump-starting the research productivity of scholars at the targeted universities, such strategies have inevitably led to internal inequalities between disciplines being identified as key strategic areas of development and those without such a privilege. Worse still, many universities in Asia nowadays put far more emphasis on research, but teaching and learning are ignored, particularly when a significant proportion of full professors and associate professors do not teach any undergraduate courses (Yu 2006).

In addition, as more universities join the quest for a better position in global university leagues, they have also changed their pay structure to attract, retain, and promote faculty members with a high quality of international publications. In recent years, we have seen many Asian universities create different kinds of schemes to reward highfliers and great performance in research. There is nothing wrong with rewarding and recognizing good performance in research. However, such incentive and reward systems create tension between research and teaching because institutions prize research performance over teaching and learning. It is this incentive structure with more emphasis on research that has undervalued teaching. Moreover, higher education is no longer elite education anymore as there are increasing demands to equip students with the industrial skills to adapt to economic development within a short cycle. As a consequence, Asian universities reform themselves by changing the curriculum to become more industry friendly and work based in orientation, while sometimes it may undervalue disciplines which are not found immediately "useful" or "sensitive" to the emerging labor market or economic development needs. Hence, it is not surprising that quite a number of studies related to the academic profession in Asia have revealed many academics serving in the fields of humanities and social sciences complaining about their academic status being undervalued, while academic freedom in the university is shaken because the university administration is under tremendous pressure to run the university as a corporation that should be sensitive to market needs (Currie, Peterson, and Mok 2005).

Rectifying the imbalanced tension between research and teaching, some countries have taken initiatives in seeking to boost teaching quality. In China, the Ministry of Education issued a directive in 2003 stating that full professors were required to teach undergraduate courses. This proposal was adopted as a major indicator for the national evaluation of Chinese universities (Yu 2006).

The Ministry of Education in Taiwan launched the Teaching Excellence Project in 2004, with granted subsidies ranging from NT$15 million to NT$85 million to bring the teaching evaluation back to the academic profession. Meanwhile, the Taiwan government is keen to articulate teacher quality, curriculum design, teaching resources, and student performance into the national evaluation system (MOE of Taiwan 2011a). Similarly, the University Grants Committee in Hong Kong has started teaching and learning quality reviews and quality assurance audits since the mid-1990s to assure student learning experiences in publicly funded universities in Hong Kong (Mok 2012a). The strategies being implemented by different Asian university systems to ensure student learning are good, but how far such measures really "protect" teaching in the context of increasing pressure for global university ranking with strong links to research performance rather than teaching and learning is still in doubt. Putting these observations together, the lifestyle of academics in Asia is inevitably affected by the growing tide of weighting research heavier than teaching and learning. For survival and career promotion, it is not surprising to see academics in Asian universities putting more energy and attention in research instead of teaching and learning in.

Entrepreneurial Universities and University Governance

Under "academic capitalism" (Slaughter and Leslie 1997; Slaughter and Rhoades 2004) or "knowledge capitalism" (Olssen and Peters 2005), it is now very commonplace to speak of higher education in industry and commercial terms, such as "the knowledge factory" (Aronowitz 2000), "capitalization of knowledge" (Viale and Etzkowitz 2010), "the entrepreneurial university" (Clark 1998, 2004), "corporate-linked university" (Newson 1998), "the corporate campus" (Turk 2000), and "the campus inc." (White and Hauck 2000). In the model of the entrepreneurial university, the government, industry, and academia are brought closer to each other, and each of them has to transform its own traditional role in the interactive process. As Leydesdorff and Etzkowitz (2001, 1) delineate,

> A transformation in the functions of university, industry, and government is taking place as each institution can assume the role of the other. Under certain circumstances, the university can take the role of industry, helping to form new firms in incubator facilities. Government can take the role of industry, helping to support these new developments through funding programs and changes in the regulatory environment. Industry can take the role of the university in developing training and research, often at the same high level as universities.

However, the above-described blurring of the traditional role boundary of government, industry, and university has triggered much worry and controversy. To some who see higher education as a fuel to innovation and economic growth, the recent trend of academic entrepreneurship is worth celebrating. However, to those who hold more to the belief that teaching and pure academic research should be the foundations of universities, the aggressive "intrusion" of commercial elements in higher education is a threat to the ideal of higher education. Outcries such as "the corporate takeover of higher education" (Giroux 2005, 19) or "selling out higher education" (Giroux 2003, 180) can be increasingly heard from these critics.

In her celebrated book *University Inc.: The Corporate Corruption of Higher Education*, Jennifer Washburn documented how the rise of academic capitalism in the United States has undermined the public character of higher education. She identified the single greatest threat to the future of American higher education as "the intrusion of a market ideology into the heart of academic life" (Washburn 2005, 10). As she argued, "the problem is not university-industry relationships per se; it is the elimination of any clear boundary lines separating academia from commerce" (Washburn 2005, 10). In other words, the issue at stake is the increasing confusion in higher education between whether it is conceived as a public good or a private good. Such blurring of this boundary will bring with it many conflicts unheard of before the strong tide of academic entrepreneurship, such as the fight for intellectual property rights between the research staff and the university, the conflict of interest of academics involved in university-industry partnerships, the challenge of business culture to the integrity of research, a biased redefinition of science that it is increasingly seen as valuable only if it is useful and profitable to industry and economically beneficial to society (Evans and Packham 2003).

In a similar vein, reflecting upon the US experience since the 1970s, Gumport argues that the transformation of higher education from a social institution to an industry has given rise to a new kind of academic management, academic consumerism, and academic stratification. Under a new kind of academic management, universities have been run like an enterprise underpinned by managerial logic. The relationship between universities and other stakeholders (e.g., taxpayers, employers, research funders, and students) has increasingly involved economic interests. To maximize profits and satisfy consumer demand, academic subjects have been stratified, with some being regarded as having more economic value (use value and exchange value) than others, which are determined by market forces. As a result, the historical and moral legitimacy of higher education was challenged (Gumport 2000).

Besides the repositioning of universities' visions and missions, university staffs also have to adjust their roles in the university bureaucracy. The following paragraph by Slaughter and Leslie (1997, 9) succinctly describes the changing status of university faculty staff under "academic capitalism":

[Academic capitalism is] the reality of the nascent environment of public research universities, an environment full of contradictions, in which faculty and professional staff extend their human capital stocks increasingly in competitive situations. In these situations, university employees are employed simultaneously by the public sector and are increasingly autonomous from it. They are academics who act as capitalists from within the public sector; they are state-subsidized entrepreneurs.

Kenway and colleagues (2004, 334) also describe that, in engaging in joint R&D activities with the industry sector, the university staff are no longer the traditional scientists who mainly engage in pure or applied research, but have increasingly become "techno-scientists," who "presumes a much narrower subjectivity that combines scientific rationality with an instrumental and opportunistic sensibility."

Neoliberalism and Academic Freedom

The introduction of more market-oriented and neoliberalist principles and measures to reform the university governance was originally intended to empower universities to manage their business with more flexibility and autonomy. But comparative and international experiences of university governance reforms have suggested that the adoption of decentralization, marketization, and corporatization strategies have not really liberated universities or empowered academics. Instead, academics and university administrators have only found themselves confronted with intensified pressures to prove their performance through the implementation of quality assurance/international benchmarking/performance assessment. Hence, it is not surprising that the implementation of decentralization in university governance has resulted in re-regulation and recentralization through various kinds of accountability measures and performance checks. A strong tide of "centralized decentralization" has significantly affected the way contemporary universities are governed. It is against this context that a growing number of academics have begun to complain about academic freedom being threatened as a result of the decentralization and corporatization of universities.

Our discussion in this book has indicated how different Asian societies have interpreted the notion of "world-class" university and in what way their higher education systems have responded to the growing impacts of world university rankings. Other recent research has also reported a few major measures being adopted by universities in Asian societies to restructure and transform university governance through the processes of "incorporation" and "corporatization." Jun Oba's recent work provides a clear policy background for enlightening us about why and how Japanese universities have gone through the process of incorporation. Unsatisfied with the "centralized" governance model in university governance, the Japanese government has amended its university law to turn all state universities into independent legal entities, and they are supposedly given more financial and management autonomy in order to make the systems more responsive to rapid changes. Recent fieldwork conducted in Japan has revealed that although state universities have "incorporated," frontline academics have not really experienced genuine changes, while university senior management has enjoyed relative flexibility in financial matters (fieldwork in Japan, January 2006). Oba's article has pointed out the reality and prospects of the incorporation project in Japan, indicating the difficulties involved in changing Japan's highly state-regulated university sector. Although the Japanese government has a strong intention to transform university governance in line with corporatization strategies, academics interviewed during various field visits to Japan have repeatedly indicated that the proposed changes have encountered tremendous resistance (fieldwork in Japan by Mok, January 2006).

Similar to Japan, universities in Hong Kong and Singapore have been experiencing restructuring exercises. In the case of Hong Kong, the East Asian financial crisis had significantly affected the finance of the university sector by 2004. Facing severe government budget cuts, the university sector in Hong Kong had to venture into different kinds of income generation activities by launching more self-funded programs and turning their research into commercial products (Lee 2005b). In addition, universities in Hong Kong have been under great pressure to perform well internationally by asserting their world-class status through international publications (Mok 2005c). Besides this, Jan Currie and Carole Peterson have reviewed the "Robert Chung Affair" and the "Amendment of Basic Law," as well as discussing how the university sector in Hong Kong has experienced significant restructuring and governance change. More specifically, they have highlighted the way academic freedom is affected under the pressures of higher education restructuring (Peterson and Currie 2007). Like Hong Kong, Singapore's higher education system has gone through significant transformations, particularly when the government attempted to introduce internal competition into the university sector in order to enhance the efficiency and competitiveness of the system. Michael Lee and Saravanan Gopinathan examine critically what has been achieved and what the problems are resulting from the university restructuring in Singapore. One of the major challenges that universities in Singapore are facing is the dilemma between "accountability" and "autonomy." Lee and Gopinathan again show how decentralization has gone hand in hand with recentralization, resulting in more control of the state on university governance in the context of quality assurance and international benchmarking (Lee and Gopinathan 2007).

Running universities and assessing academics' performance as businesslike organizations, especially in neoliberal states, has revealed an observable tendency to emphasize both agency and consumer forms at the expense of professional and democratic forms, particularly when countries are involved in large-scale shifts from traditional Keynesian welfare state regimes to more market-oriented and consumer-driven systems (Peters 2005). One major criticism of such paradigm shifts is "that the agency/consumer couplet instrumentalizes, individualizes, standardizes, marketizes and externalizes accountability relationships at the expense of democratic values such as participation, self-regulation, collegiality, and collective deliberation that are said to enhance and thicken the relationships involved" (Peters 2005, 106). All of this has negatively affected traditional concepts of academic freedom.

Critically scrutinizing the quest for world-class universities, we can easily find that a "Common World Education Culture" (CWEC) approach has emerged, seeing globalization as an emerging movement toward cultural homogeneity, as a cultural endpoint, a telos leaning toward the neoliberal institutional view celebrating the influence of major supranational organizations such as UNESCO, the World Bank, and the IMF. Central to the CWEC approach is the spread of western values, characterized by hyperliberalism, governance without government, and commodification. For the sake of survival in this highly competitive global marketplace, many states have reinvented themselves by reducing these core activities/businesses, making new arrangements for involving or revitalizing other nonstate sectors in public management and social policy delivery (Dale 2000; Mok 2005a). All these transformations have clearly demonstrated how vulnerable the developing countries could become when their economic, social, cultural, and political developments are increasingly determined by supranational organizations.

Discussion and Conclusion

This chapter has critically examined how universities and students in East Asia have performed in an increasingly competitive world. Our discussion has clearly suggested that both students and universities in East Asia have performed well, as clearly reflected by various forms of international benchmarking and university ranking exercises. The calls for internationalization and the quest for entrepreneurial universities have clearly transformed the universities in the region to make them more innovative and proactive in response to changes generated domestically and internationally. However, this chapter has also highlighted a few major unintended consequences when universities are transformed along the lines of marketization and privatization. More seriously, the quest for world-class status and running universities increasingly like businesses have definitely undermined the collegial approach in university governance, while academic freedom may be negatively affected as our previous discussions have shown in this volume.

Conclusion

Our discussions in the previous chapters have clearly highlighted how universities in East Asia have made serious attempts to become more entrepreneurial in coping with the growing challenges of globalization. Through engaging in deep cooperation with industry and business, those universities working comfortably well would support the drive for diversifying funding sources through corporatization and markertization of universities. Meanwhile, many governments in East Asia have been driving the university sector to further support social and economic developments by setting up university-run enterprises or joint ventures with business or industry to turn the research findings into commercializable products. Adopting an active and even proactive approach in the quest for entrepreneurialism would make universities focus more on research and related activities for global ranking and diversification of funding sources to support further university development. Such moves are not necessarily wrong, but we have witnessed a number of universities in East Asia going through successful transformations resulting from the adoption of the reform measures outlined above.

However, when most of the attention is given to commercialization of research products, diversification of funding, and competition for global ranking, all these drives would inevitably divert faculty members' attention from teaching and learning. Worse still, when performance assessment of faculty members is increasingly determined by readily quantifiable research and commercializable outputs, academics will tend to focus on research outputs instead of teaching and learning. Even worse, what really makes the East Asian universities vulnerable is when the performance evaluations of universities are significantly affected by international standards and practices with strong influences from the Anglo-Saxon paradigm and neoliberalism commonly shared among western societies as guiding principles for university management and governance. The following discussion highlights a few major policy implications for East Asian universities in general and governments in particular and encourages critical reflection when adopting or even copying models and practices from the West.

Respecting Asian Traditions and Reinventing Asian Scholarships

As discussed above, there is nothing wrong with making universities more entrepreneurial and questing for world-class status. However, what has been occurring among East Asian university circles continues to undermine the development of local cultures and traditions, particularly when East Asian universities place their emphasis on seeking world-class status through participation in different forms of international benchmarking. What is the consequence of this drive for restructuring for world-class status, something that can only be achieved by, as Altbach (2004) points out, a very small number of institutions within each country? As well as a few winners, there are inevitably going to be a lot of losers. In the UK, there have been department closures in difference disciplines (particularly but not exclusively in the laboratory-based disciplines) at various universities as a consequence of low research assessment exercise (RAE) grades or the struggle for funds to maintain them. In the Netherlands, the professional higher education institutions have struggled to keep pace with the reforms of higher education institutions. In countries like Germany, it seems inevitable that students in publicly funded institutions will lose their right to free tuition, as they already have in many countries. We have also noted the wholesale extent of restructuring and reform particularly in the UK, Germany, and the Netherlands as well as in other EU countries. In Europe as a whole, we have observed that the European Commission has been discussing ways in which European universities can compete worldwide collectively as well as individually, so as to raise the overall profile. In East Asia, several countries have engaged in wholesale restructuring of their higher education systems in the search for world-class positioning and have engaged in a series of internal benchmarking exercises in order to strengthen their global positioning (Mok, Deem, and Lucas 2008).

Concentration of research funding (as a means of ensuring "world-class status" for the few) has implications for the development of national higher education systems in many ways. The national role of universities may be ignored in favour of the international role (as in East Asia where publication in English-language journals has taken precedence over publication in other languages). There may develop a related quest for an international academic labor market. Kwiek has noted the problems faced by Central European universities in funding the enlarged mass public higher education systems (Kwiek 2004). A report for Universities UK on "Funding Research Diversity" included a comparison of regional differences across England, Wales, Scotland, and Northern Ireland.[1]

Using research assessment exercise grades, citation indexes, publication rates, and rates of staffing, the report was able to demonstrate disparities across these various regions in England and also Scotland, Wales, and Northern

Ireland and to investigate how further concentration of research resources might affect levels of research achievement. The report found overwhelmingly that the three regions in the southeast of England, including London, had the highest density of departments rated 5/5* in the RAE. If further concentration of research resources from the RAE continues, then universities in these areas will be set to gain more funding whereas places such as Wales and the East Midlands would be set to lose dramatically, and places in the West Midlands and the northeast would suffer less harsh losses (http://bookshop.universitiesuk.ac.uk/downloads/funding_tech.pdf). The substantial losses of some regions would result, they argue, in "reduced regional research capacity (that) will have knock-on effects for regional economic performance and the capacity for technology innovation" (Adams and Smith 2004, 12). The negative consequences of further concentration of research resources cannot be overstated in this regard (Adams and Smith 2004).

Such a situation is also likely to be the case for other countries too. So while the governments of many East Asian countries may believe that only their quest for world-class status matters, some of the institutions may beg to differ. At the same time, it is often difficult or impossible for institutions in any one country to opt out of the quest altogether, as "at some stage and for some important purpose, every institution is going to rely on the strength and reputation of the system as a whole" (Watson 2006, 15). For each country involved in the restructuring of its higher education systems, there is also an issue about where such ideas come from and how well they work in different contexts. One major danger of primarily following the model or yardstick dominated by Anglo-American values and practices is that universities in East Asia may one day lose the beauty and heritage deeply embedded in their traditions and cultures, which would definitely undermine the future development of research and scholarship in Asia and eventually undervalue the potential that future generations of scholars based in Asia have to contribute to the international academic and research community through presenting their works with Asian characteristics.

Policy Learning Rather than Policy Copying

Evidence presented in this book indicates how educational restructuring and university reforms taking place in Asia have been significantly influenced by western managerial-oriented doctrines and neoliberalist ideologies and practices. Responding to the growing impact of globalization, all of the East Asian states considered here have reviewed their education systems and launched reforms along the lines of marketization, privatization, and corporatization with the intention of improving their governance and management (for details, see Mok 2006d and 2010). In addition, international benchmarking and intensifying competition for ranking in the "global university league" has inevitably influenced the way that Asian universities are governed. We should not simply understand "internationalization" in Asia as merely following American or Anglo-Saxon standards and practices. Although the academic communities in Europe and the United States have been regarded as more "advanced" than their Asian counterparts, higher education institutions in general and academics in particular must critically reflect on the extent to which the so-called good practices identified from the West can really integrate well with nonwestern education systems.

Despite the fact that many of the Asian societies discussed here were "decolonized" after the Second World War, many of them have not really "decolonized" in practice, since most of them have been influenced strongly by Anglo-Saxon standards and ideologies. A number of Asian countries have just followed the academic practices of the Anglo-Saxon paradigm. The introduction of English as the medium of instruction; the adoption of curricula from Australia, the UK, and the United States, and sending students to study overseas and establishing international exchanges, coupled with the quest for world-class universities as defined predominately by the Anglo-Saxon world, has not only created a new "dependency culture" but also reinforced an American-dominated hegemony, particularly in relation to league tables, citation indexes, and the kind of research that counts as high status. Asian societies seem to have treated internationalization as westernization and modernization, or Americanization, since the nineteenth century (Mok 2006d).

Analyzing such internationalization experiences in the light of Kazuhiro Ebuchi's (1997) framework, "internationalization" could be interpreted as an intransitive verb or a transitive verb. The concept of "internationalization" as a transitive verb in English "is a historical concept, which emerged from a nation with 'hegemony' in the international order, while that of 'internationalization as an intransitive verb' is one from a 'smaller nation' which was forced to follow a 'larger nation'" (Ebuchi 1997, 10). Thus not only European but also Asian states should be aware of the differences between policy learning and policy copying. If we copy policy practices without proper adaptation and careful contextualization, we might easily encounter problems, including in Asia a process of recolonization, resulting in reproducing learning experiences which do not fit the specific cultural and political environments in the East. Therefore, we need to critically examine the following questions when attempting to internationalize universities: Can the standards and practices commonly available in the West be coherently adapted to Asian traditions and cultures? Would the adoption of such western practices be distorted, especially without proper contextual analysis? Most important of all, would there be only one "international standard" as defined solely by or even dominated by the Anglo-Saxon paradigm? Who should be involved in defining the international benchmarks? Without proper contextualization, the adoption of such "global trendy strategies" or "global reform measures" may prove to be counterproductive in terms of public sector reforms (Fukayama 2005).

In this book, we have examined some of the reasons why the quest for world-class status of universities (Mok 2005c) is so alluring to governments and universities in both Europe and Asia. We have looked at the developing discipline of world rankings of research and other performance indicators and some of the problems involved in such rankings. If research in universities is to be reduced to a form of game playing (Lucas 2006), and if all teaching is to be organized in similar ways, what happens to system and institutional diversity? Does it become simply a consolation prize for those who have no chance of achieving world-class status? We examined recent attempts at reform and restructuring of higher education in the context of increased global competition for research success, students, and academic labor in both Europe and East Asia. We drew attention to some of the less desirable consequences of the search for world-leading research and teaching for those systems and institutions that are not successful. We also noted the tendency for developments to be copied slavishly in many countries, without necessarily paying attention to the local contextual factors that may affect implementation (Deem 2001). Globalization processes are very complex, often contradictory, and do not lend themselves easily to oversimplification. The quest for world-class status in higher education is clearly not going to disappear, but we should not underestimate the social and political costs of higher education's engagement in globalized policy copying.

Internationalization or Recolonialization of Higher Education

Nowadays, most literature on internationalization and regionalization of higher education attributes the trend to the impact of economic globalization starting from the 1970s and 1980s. However, Adam Nelson from the University of Wisconsin provides a different historical perspective on the regional collaboration of higher education in America and East Asia. Nelson's analysis traces the history of collaboration between the United States and Asia back to the 1950s and 1960s. The push for regionalization and internationalization of higher education was part of America's "global development" and Cold War "grand strategy." At the same time, in the other part of the globe, universities in Asia were equally keen on forging university partnerships, also for political and development purposes. In recounting an academic conference held in Hong Kong in 1966 about the regionalization of Asian universities, Nelson (2013) notes that the core debate among the academics at that conference focused on how university partnership could help tackle regional challenges in Asia (e.g., the promotion of science and technology for national development) and help reposition Asian universities for new forms of global engagement in the context of the Cold War. In contrast, today the discussions about internationalization and regionalization of higher education tend to revolve around economic competition and enhancement. Nelson's work (2013) reminds us of the importance of the political dimension. As he writes, "university collaborations, then as now, were deeply enmeshed (or entangled) in geopolitics, and one must not overlook this part of the story. It may be the most important part of all."

In addition to Adam Nelson's historical and political remarks, academics and policy makers in Asia should be aware of the potential danger of "recolonialization" or another form of "cultural imperialism" when Asian universities are trying very hard to follow the success story of western universities. As Altbach (2010) argues, "Singapore and Hong Kong have accomplished considerable success simply by building Western universities in Asia, by hiring large numbers of nonlocal academic staff, using English, and copying Western norms of academic organization and management." Mohrman (2008) further argues that the emerging "global model of a university" is increasingly modeled on the research-intensive universities embodied by the West's elite universities. International benchmarking through ranking or performance comparison would inevitably reinforce the "standardization" of university performance in line with the "Western university model." This in turn could potentially undermine local cultures, indigenous values, and traditions (Mok 2007b). Similarly, neoinstitutionalism believes that isomorphism or homogenization are "a constraining process that forces one unit in a population to resemble other units that face the same set of environmental conditions" (DiMaggio and Powell 1983, 149). The three distinct mechanisms, coercive isomorphism, mimetic processes, and normative pressures, in the processes of imitation of the "western model" would inevitably force universities in Asia to conform to the so-called universal standard dominated by the Anglo-Saxon paradigm.

Concluding Remarks

The chapters incorporated in this volume present different perspectives on how Asian universities have transformed in coping with the growing impact of globalization. Critical analysis and reflections discussed in above chapters again alert us the social, political, and cultural implications of the quest for world-class university status. When questing to enhance this world-class status, we must remember that the Asian global cities/world cities are experiencing significant social and economic transformations. As Castells (2000, 429) argues, the global informational economy is "ushering in a new urban form, the informational city," which "is not a form but a process, a process characterized by the structural domination of the space of flows." More concretely, he suggests that key "global" cities are increasingly prominent in this informational economy, concentrating key industrial sectors into a small number of large metropolitan agglomerations. While Asian governments have put serious efforts into transforming their higher education systems to support the informational city or to enhance their national competitiveness in the knowledge-based economy, we should also note that the same processes of transformation would widen the gap between different "knowledge classes." The quest for "world-class" university status would definitely intensify inequality and disparity; such a development also requires our attention and action appropriate for establishing a society which could bring people to live in harmony (Mok and Green 2013).

The completion and publication of this book have very much depended upon the kind support of the following publishers for granting permission for the author to adopt and adapt some materials based upon previous work with major revisions and updated data for the present volume, and I acknowledge the original sources of these papers.

"The Quest for World-Class Status: Globalization and Higher Education in East Asia." In *Higher Education and Equality of Opportunities*, ed. F. Lazin, M. Evans, and N Jayaram. Lanham, MD: Rowan & Littlefield, 2010 [co-authored with John Hawkins].

"Contested Concepts, Similar Practices: The Quest for the Global University." *Higher Education Policy* 21 (2008): 429–438.

"The Quest for Regional Hub of Education: Growing Heterarchies, Organizational Hybridization and New Governance in Singapore and Malaysia." *Journal of Education Policy* 26, no. 1 (2011): 61–81.

"The Rise of Transnational Higher Education in Asia: Student Mobility and Learning Experiences in Singapore and Malaysia." *Higher Education Policy* 25, no. 2 (June 2012): 225–241.

"Transforming Higher Education in Whose Image? Exploring the Concept of the 'World-Class' University in Europe and Asia." *Higher Education Policy* 21 (January 2008): 83–97 [co-authored with Rosemary Deem and Lisa Lucas].

Notes

INTRODUCTION

1. Some parts of the book are based upon revised versions of the author's previous publications but already been updated and adapted to the present volume.

1   GLOBALIZATION AND HIGHER EDUCATION

1. Tshepo Gwatiwa, 2013, "Trends of higher education in the Asia Pacific," UNESCO Bangkok, http://www.unescobkk.org/education/higher-and-distance-education/news/article/trends-of-higher-education-in-the-asia-pacific.
2. Times Higher Education World University Ranking 2012–2013, http://www.timeshighereducation.co.uk/world-university-rankings/2012–13/world-ranking/region/asia.
3. Times Higher Education World University Ranking 2012–2013, http://www.timeshighereducation.co.uk/world-university-rankings/2012–13/subject-ranking/subject/engineering-and-IT.
4. Times Higher Education World University Ranking 2012–2013, http://www.timeshighereducation.co.uk/world-university-rankings/2012–13/subject-ranking/subject/life-sciences.
5. Shanghai Jiao Tong University's Academic Ranking of World Universities, http://www.shanghairanking.com/ARWU-Statistics-2012.html; Shanghai Jiao Tong University's Academic Ranking of World Universities, http://www.shanghairanking.com/ARWU-Statistics-2012.html.

2   POLICY CONTEXT FOR THE QUEST FOR INNOVATION AND ENTREPRENEURIAL UNIVERSITIES IN EAST ASIA

1. World Bank (2012, 8).
2. The World Bank, World Development Indicators 2012, http://data.worldbank.org/sites/default/files/wdi-2012-ebook.pdf; UNESCO Science Report 2010, http://unesdoc.unesco.org/images/0018/001899/189958e.pdf; UNESCO Science Report 2010, http://unesdoc.unesco.org/images/0018/001899/189958e.pdf.

3 Diversifying the Economic Pillars and Enhancing Innovation and Research Development

1. Census and Statistics Department, 2011, *Hong Kong Monthly Digest of Statistics: Hong Kong's External Trade in High Technology Products and Technology Balance of Payments*, 2000, 2005 and 2010, http://www.censtatd.gov.hk/hkstat/sub/sp120.jsp?productCode=FA100045; Hong Kong Innovation Activities Statistics 2011, http://www.statistics.gov.hk/pub/B11100102011AN11B0100.pdf.
2. Hong Kong Business Angel Network, http://www.hkban.org.
3. The Chinese University of Hong Kong, City University of Hong Kong, Hong Kong Baptist University, the Hong Kong Polytechnic University, the Hong Kong University of Science and Technology, and the University of Hong Kong.
4. Hong Kong Automotive Parts and Accessory Systems R&D Centre, Hong Kong R&D Centre for Logistics and Supply Chain Management Enabling Technologies, Hong Kong Research Institute of Textiles and Apparel, Nano and Advanced Materials Institute, and Hong Kong Applied Science and Technology Research Institute.
5. The 13 technology focus areas include:
    (1) advanced manufacturing technologies;
    (2) automotive parts and accessory systems;
    (3) Chinese medicine;
    (4) communications technologies;
    (5) consumer electronics;
    (6) digital entertainment;
    (7) display technologies;
    (8) integrated circuit design;
    (9) logistics/supply chain management enabling technologies;
    (10) medical diagnostics and devices;
    (11) nanotechnology and advanced materials;
    (12) opto-electronics; and
    (13) textile and clothing.
6. Innovation and Technology Commission, HKSAR government, http://www.itc.gov.hk/en/rdcentre/rdcentre.htm.
7. Innovation and Technology Commission, HKSAR government, http://www.itc.gov.hk/en/rdcentre/rdcentre.htm.
8. Key Statistics on UGC-funded Institutions, 2012, http://cdcf.ugc.edu.hk/cdcf/searchStatisticReport.do; University Grants Committee, HKSAR, http://cdcf.ugc.edu.hk/cdcf/searchStatisticReport.do.
9. Research Grants Council, Hong Kong PhD Fellowship Scheme, awardees for admission to PhD programs in the 2011/12 academic year, http://www.ugc.edu.hk/eng/ugc/publication/press/2011/pr30032011_annex.pdf; Hong Kong statistics of awardees for admission to PhD programs in the 2010/11 academic year, http://www.ugc.edu.hk/eng/ugc/publication/press/2010/pr30032010_annex.pdf.
10. University Grants Committee, Hong Kong, http://www.ugc.edu.hk/eng/ugc/activity/kt/kt.htm.

11. University Grants Committee, http://www.ugc.edu.hk/eng/ugc/activity/kt/kt.htm.
12. Technology Transfer Center, Hong Kong University of Science and Technology, http://www.ttc.ust.hk/en/home.asp.
13. Ibid.
14. Entrepreneurship Center, Hong Kong University of Science and Technology, http://www.ec.ust.hk/index.html.
15. HKUST R&D Corporation Ltd., http://www.rdc.ust.hk/eng/index.html.
16. Hong Kong University Grants Committee Annual Report 2011–2012, p. 77, http://www.ugc.edu.hk/eng/ugc/publication/report/figure2011/pdf/UGCAnnualReport.pdf.
17. Hong Kong University Grants Committee Annual Report 2011–2012, p. 78, http://www.ugc.edu.hk/eng/ugc/publication/report/figure2011/pdf/UGCAnnualReport.pdf.

4 Promotion of Innovation and Knowledge Transfer

1. Ministry of Education, South Korea, National R&D Program, http://english.mest.go.kr/web/1715/site/contents/en/en_0217.jsp.
2. Korea Research Foundation website, http://www.krf.or.kr/KHPapp/eng/mainc.jsp.
3. http://eng.smba.go.kr/pub/kore/kore020301.jsp#top01.
4. http://eng.smba.go.kr/pub/kore/kore020201.jsp.
5. http://eng.smba.go.kr/pub/curr/curr050101.jsp.
6. "Becoming an S&T Power Nation through the 577 Initiative, Science and Technology Basic Plan of the Lee Myung Bak Administration," Ministry of Education, Science and Technology, Korea Institute of S&T Evaluation and Planning.
7. http://bizkorea365.blogspot.hk/2013/02/park-geun-hye-government-launched.html#!/2013/02/park-geun-hye-government-launched.html.
8. MEST website, http://english.mest.go.kr/enMain.do
9. Ministry of Education, Science and Technology (MEST), South Korea, http://english.mest.go.kr/web/1734/site/contents/en/en_0228.jsp.
10. Hye-Jung Lee, 2009, Higher Education in Korea, Seoul National University, Korea, http://www.eastwestcenter.org/fileadmin/resources/education/ed20 20_docs/Korea.pdf.
11. MEST website, http://english.mest.go.kr/enMain.do.
12. MEST website.
13. Korea Research Foundation, http://www.krf.or.kr/KHPapp/eng/board/notice_v.jsp?flag=02&no=342&p=1.
14. Ministry of Education, Taiwan, http://epaper.edu.tw/windows.aspx?windows_sn=2686.
15. Ministry of Employment and Labor, South Korea, http://www.kdi.re.kr/kdi_eng/highlights/govern_view.jsp?no=6462&page=5&rowcnt=50.
16. Baidu, China, http://baike.baidu.com/view/6467424.htm?fromTaglist.
17. Ministry of Commerce of the People's Republic of China, http://www.mofcom.gov.cn/aarticle/i/jyjl/m/201209/20120908343559.html.

5 AFTER MASSIFICATION OF HIGHER EDUCATION

1. NSC website, http://web1.nsc.gov.tw/ct.aspx?xItem=9205&CtNode=995&mp=7.
2. M. J. Lin and S. Hsiao, "Revenues of Science Parks up 5.2% in 2012," http://focustaiwan.tw/ShowNews/WebNews_Detail.aspx?Type=a ALL&ID=201302200039.
3. Yun Qing Liau, 2012, "Taiwan R&D Spending Hit 3.02 Percent of GDP," http://www.zdnet.com/taiwan-r-and-d-spend-hit-3-02-percent-of-gdp-7000008948.
4. National Science Council, 2011, Indicators of Science and Technology 2011.
5. SMEA, Ministry of Economic Affairs, ROC.
6. Small and Medium Enterprise Administration, Ministry of Economic Affairs, ROC, http://www.moeasmea.gov.tw/ct.asp?xItem=6011&ctNode=469&mp=2.
7. Song and Tai (2007, 324); "Program for Promoting Teaching Excellence of Universities" and "Top University Project," http://www.edu.tw/FileUpload/1052-14816%5CDocuments/%E9%AB%98%E6%95%99%E7%B0%A1%E4%BB%8B2012-2013(%E6%B2%92%E6%9C%89%E8%A3%81%E5%88%87%E7%B7%9A).pdf.
8. Department of Manpower Planning Council for Economic Planning and Development, Executive Yuan (2011) Manpower Indicators.
9. National Science Council, Taiwan, http://web1.nsc.gov.tw/ct.aspx?xItem=9214&ctNode=995&mp=7.
10. National Science Council, 2011, Indicators of Science and Technology 2011.
11. National Science Council, Taiwan, http://web1.nsc.gov.tw/lp.aspx?ctNode=433&CtUnit=525&BaseDSD=5&mp=1.
12. SME Administration, Ministry of Economic Affairs, ROC, 2013, http://www.moeasmea.gov.tw/ct.asp?xItem=5959&ctNode=469&mp=2.
13. National Chiao Tung University, Taiwan, http://www.tlo.nctu.edu.tw/NCTUTLO/english/english.aspx.
14. National Chiao Tung University, Taiwan, http://iic.nctu.edu.tw.
15. National Chiao Tung University, Taiwan, http://nctuiic.meworks.cc/page1.aspx?no=111004.
16. National Chiao Tung University, Taiwan, http://diamondprj.nctu.edu.tw.
17. http://diamondprj.nctu.edu.tw/DiamondPlan/modules/catalog_1/custom_NavigationLink/view.php?l_id=6.
18. National Chiao Tung University, http://www.nctu.edu.tw/english/middle_article.php?id=31.
19. Research & Development Office, National Tsing Hua University, Taiwan, http://my.nthu.edu.tw/~rd/revised/index_c.html.
20. Operations Center for Industry Collaboration, National Tsing Hua University, Taiwan, http://ocic.nthu.edu.tw/ocic.
21. Operations Center for Industry Collaboration, National Tsing Hua University, Taiwan, http://ocic.nthu.edu.tw/ocic/en_Content01.aspx?c=emenu0123.

22. Innovation Incubation Center, National Taiwan University, Taiwan, http://www.ntuiic.com/eng/intro.htm.
23. National Taiwan University web page. http://www.ib.ntu.edu.tw.
24. Yu Fen Chen and Lai Ming Chuan, 2007, "The Entrepreneurial Curricula in Taiwan," *Journal of Entrepreneurship Research* 2(3): 117–147, http://www.erj.org.tw/search/JournalFile/v02n03/V02N3-6.pdf.

6 Asserting Its Global Influence

1. A*STAR, Agency for Science, Technology and Research, Singapore, http://www.a-star.edu.sg/tabid/915/default.aspx.
2. National University of Singapore Annual Report (2007/08–2011/12); National Technological University Annual Report (2007/08–2009/10); Singapore Management University Annual Report (2007/08–2009/10).
3. Singapore International Graduate Award, https://www.singa.a-star.edu.sg/index.php.
4. A*STAR Agency for Science, Technology and Research, Singapore, http://www.a-star.edu.sg/AwardsScholarships/ScholarshipsAttachments/tabid/424/Default.aspx.
5. Inland Revenue Authority of Singapore, https://efile.iras.gov.sg/irasHome/PIcredit.aspx#About_Productivity_and_Innovation_Credit.
6. National Research Foundation, Singapore Government, http://www.nrf.gov.sg/nrf/default.aspx.
7. For more details about the different initiatives, refer to National Research Foundation, Singapore government, http://www.nrf.gov.sg/nrf/otherProgrammes.aspx?id=1206.
8. The Group of Eight, 2012, "The University-Innovation Nexus in Singapore," http://www.go8.edu.au/__documents/go8-policy-analysis/2012/go8backgrounder28_singapore.pdf.
9. Channel NewsAsia, http://www.channelnewsasia.com/stories/singaporelocalnews/view/277897/1/.html.
10. *Sydney Morning Herald*, http://www.smh.com.au/news/national/university-plays-down-fears-about-singapore-offshoot/2005/10/25/1130239521814.html.
11. Ministry of Education, Singapore, http://www.moe.gov.sg/feedback/2011/committee-on-university-education-pathways-beyond-2015/singapore-university-landscape.
12. Ministry of Education, Singapore, http://www.moe.gov.sg/feedback/2011/committee-on-university-education-pathways-beyond-2015.
13. National University of Singapore, http://www.nus.edu.sg/enterprise.
14. National University of Singapore, http://www.overseas.nus.edu.sg.
15. National University of Singapore, http://www.nus.edu.sg/ilo.
16. National University of Singapore, http://R2M.nus.edu.sg.
17. National University of Singapore, http://www.nus.edu.sg/enterprise/nth.

18. National University of Singapore, http://www.nusentrepreneurshipcentre.sg.
19. N. M. Idris et al., 2012, "In Vivo Photodynamic Therapy Using Upconversion Nanoparticles as Remote-Controlled Nanotransducers," http://www.nus.edu.sg/dpr/files/research_highlights/2013_02Feb_In_vivo_photodynamic_therapy_using_upconversion_nanoparticles_as_remote-controlled_nanotransducers.pdf.
20. Nanyang Technological University, Singapore, http://www.ntu.edu.sg/nieo/Pages/default.aspx.
21. Nanyang Technological University, Singapore, http://www.ntc.ntu.edu.sg/Pages/Home.aspx.
22. NTU Ventures, Singapore, http://www.ntuventures.com.
23. Nanyang Technological University, Singapore, "Research Report 2010/11," http://research.ntu.edu.sg/News/Documents/Research%20Report/NTU%20Research%20Report%202010–11.pdf.
24. Singapore Management University, Singapore, http://www.smu.edu.sg/institutes/IIE/About%20IIE/iie_landing_page.asp.
25. Singapore Management University, Singapore, http://smu.edu.sg/topics/innovation-and-entrepreneurship.
26. SINA Corporation, http://blog.sina.com.cn/s/blog_68661afa0100udhi.html.

7 Promoting Entrepreneurship and Innovation

1. CAS, China 2009, http://home.sinica.edu.tw/en/about/history_and_mission.html.
2. Ministry of Science and Technology, China, 2009, http://www.most.gov.cn/eng/programmes1/index.htm.
3. MST, China, 2009, http://www.most.gov.cn/eng/pressroom/200507/t20050706_22978.htm.
4. L. T. Zhao and J. J. Zhu, "China's Higher Education Reform: What Has Not Been Changed?," http://www.eai.nus.edu.sg/Vol2No4_ZhaoLitao&ZhuJinjing.pdf.
5. Ibid.
6. Wikipedia, "C9 League," http://en.wikipedia.org/wiki/C9_League.
7. The Sci-Tech Academy of Zhejiang University, "National High-Tech R&D Program (863 Program)," http://rd.zju.edu.cn/en/index.php?c=main&a=detail&id=91.
8. The Sci-Tech Academy of Zhejiang University, "Key Technologies R&D Program," http://rd.zju.edu.cn/en/index.php?c=main&a=detail&id=92.
9. The Sci-Tech Academy of Zhejiang University, "National Basic Research Program of China (973 Program)," http://rd.zju.edu.cn/en/index.php?c=main&a=detail&id=93.
10. Hua Jin, 2013, "Entrepreneurial Universities and Industrial Creation in China," http://hermes-ir.lib.hit-u.ac.jp/rs/bitstream/10086/25503/1/070hjbsWP_166.pdf.

11. Hua Jin, 2013, "Entrepreneurial Universities and Industrial Creation in China," http://hermes-ir.lib.hit-u.ac.jp/rs/bitstream/10086/25503/1/070hjbs WP_166.pdf.
12. Cheng Liang Zhang, "Legal and Policy Changes in China Have Greatly Changed What Is at Stake," http://chinaipsummit.com/2012/press_1123/30.html.
13. *China Daily*, http://chinadailymail.com/2012/12/25/china-set-to-surpass-us-in-rd-spending-in-10-years.
14. Asian Scientist Publishing Pte. Ltd., 2013, "Chinese 2012 R&D Spending Reached One Trillion Yuan," http://www.asianscientist.com/topnews/chinese-scientific-expenditure-1-trillion-2012.
15. *China Daily*, 2013, "China's Annual R&D Spending at New High," http://www.chinadaily.com.cn/bizchina/2013-03/02/content_16269593.htm.
16. What's on Xiamen, 2012, "Chinese Universities Ordered to Teach Courses on Entrepreneurship," http://www.whatsonxiamen.com/education/4691.html
17. M. C. Qian and C. A. Lai, 2012, "Entrepreneurship Education: A Chinese University Case Study," *International Journal of Business Strategy* 12(4). http://www.freepatentsonline.com/article/International-Journal-Business-Strategy/312014388.html.
18. STEFG, 2012, "The Introduction of Angel Fund," http://fund.stefg.org/about.html.
19. The Organizing Committee of the National "Challenge Cup" Business Plan Competition, *An Overview of Successive National "Challenge Cup" Business Plan Competitions*, http://www w.tiaozhanbei.net/review2.

8 THE CALL FOR INTERNATIONALIZATION

1. HE Global, UK, "An Introduction to Transnational Education," http://heglobal.international.ac.uk/tne.aspx.
2. Wawasan 2020 as an ambitious national goal of development was introduced by the then prime minister of Malaysia, Mahathir Mohamad, during the tabling of the Sixth Malaysia Plan in 1991. The vision proposes the achievement of a self-sufficient, industrialized, and well-developed Malaysia by the year of 2020. In terms of the economy, it has set the target of eightfold stronger by 2020 than the economy in the early 1990s http://en.wikipedia.org/wiki/Wawasan_2020 (accessed 2 October 2013).
3. The amendment has come into effect from 1 February 2009.
4. Before 1996, private higher education institutions in Malaysia had no degree-awarding power. Even right after the enactment of the Private Higher Education Act 1996, the undergraduate degree program could only be offered by private institutions with their degree-awarding foreign partners, with students being required to transfer between Malaysia and another country to complete their studies (Quality Assurance Agency for Higher Education 1999). It was only since 1998 that the Ministry of Education allowed private institutions to deliver degree programs through the so-called 3+0 arrangement with their foreign partners.

5. Star Publications (M) Bhd., 2012, "Economic Impact of Higher Education," http://thestar.com.my/education/story.asp?file=/2012/5/13/education/11262383.
6. Since the issue of the *Higher Education Review 2002*, the Closer Economic Partnership Arrangement (CEPA) between Hong Kong and Mainland China was signed on 29 June 2003 and brought into force. Hong Kong political leaders, thereafter, have worked in the policy direction of broadening and deepening its collaboration with Mainland China – particularly with the Pearl River Delta – across all fronts, including education.
7. For instance, there were 7,293 nonlocal students enrolled in UGC-funded institutions in the academic year 2007/08, while 2,811 others attended various programs at different higher education institutions on a self-financed basis. For the former, only 542 of them (7 percent) were students who came from countries other than Mainland China, while for the later, only 619 of them (22 percent) were non-Mainland Chinese (Cheng, Ng, Cheung, et al. 2009, 41, 45).
8. These six areas are educational services, medical services, testing and certification, environmental industry, innovation and technology, and finally cultural and creative industries (Task Force on Economic Challenges, Hong Kong 2009).
9. The budget cuts on government funding in higher education from 1999 to 2004, in particular, had driven the higher education sector in Hong Kong to look to the market for additional funding.
10. Statistics provided by the Information Portal for Accredited Self-Financing Post-secondary Program (IPASS), HKSAR, http://www.ipass.gov.hk/eng/stat_pg_index.aspx (accessed 1 September 2009).
11. HKU SPACE refers to the School of Professional and Continuing Education, University of Hong Kong.
12. For instance, in its preamble, the code of practice clearly states that it has "no mandatory effect and institutions should be able to put in place policies and guidelines to reflect their own mission and philosophy" (HKCAAVQ 2007, p. 1).
13. EDB was previously the Education and Manpower Bureau (EMB). Its manpower portfolio was transferred to the new Labor and Welfare Bureau in July 2007, thus streamlined to become the Education Bureau.
14. HKCAAVQ is a rather new statutory body established under the HKCAAVQ Ordinance (Chapter 1150) which came into effect on 1 October 2007. It was previously the Hong Kong Council for Academic Accreditation (HKCAA). The new HKCAAVQ is appointed by the secretary for education as the accreditation authority and qualifications register (QR) authority under the current qualifications framework (QF).
15. C. M. Young, 2012, "Development of Continuing Education and Transnational Education in Hong Kong," pp. 15–23, Seminar on QF and Progression Pathway, 27 September 2012, http://www.hkqf.gov.hk/img/evt/evt20120927/02_2012%2009%2027%20Develop%20of%20CE%20%26%20Trans%20Edu%20in%20HK.pdf.

16. The Economic Development Board of Singapore is a statutory body overseen by the Ministry of Trade and Industry. Its involvement in the Global Schoolhouse initiative is a clear indication that the Singapore government has redefined higher education as industry and business.
17. Data from the official website of the Global Schoolhouse initiative, http://www.edb.gov.sg/edb/sg/en_uk/index/industry_sectors/education/global_schoolhouse.html.
18. The transnational programs offered by the S. P. Jain Center of Management in Singapore are particularly worth mentioning. The center offers a truly global MBA program conducted jointly from both of its campuses in Dubai (2004) and Singapore. Students choosing finance or IT streams would first complete their core curriculum in Dubai and then transfer to Singapore campus for their specialized curriculum, while those from the streams of marketing, global logistics, and human resources management would do the reverse. In addition to studying in Dubai and Singapore, students enrolling in either category would also be given the option to study core curriculum in Toronto. This one-year, three-cities program thus exposes students to varied business cultures, multinational companies, cross-national networking, and international market challenges.
19. Council for Private Education, Singapore, http://www.singaporeedu.gov.sg/htm/abo/abo01.htm.
20. This task is entrusted to its Education Services Division.
21. Pressrun.net, 11 August 2012, "International Students in Singapore, London and Other Cities," http://www.pressrun.net/weblog/2012/08/international-students-in-singapore-london-and-other-cities.html.
22. Nick Clark, 2012, "Understanding Transnational Education, Its Growth and Implications," World Education News & Reviews, http://www.wes.org/ewenr/12aug/practical.htm.
23. Wikipedia, "List of International schools in Singapore," http://en.wikipedia.org/wiki/List_of_international_schools_in_Singapore.
24. Raffles Education Corp, http://www.raffles-education-corporation.com/index.html.
25. Sandra Davie, 2012, "Foreign Student Numbers Drop Sharply after Climbing Steadily," AsiaOneNews, http://www.asiaone.com/News/Latest%2BNews/Edvantage/Story/A1Story20121009-376559.html.
26. Information from the section regarding the "quality assurance system," official website of the MQA, Ministry of Higher Education Malaysia, http://www.mqa.gov.my.
27. The section on the "quality assurance system," official website of the MQA, Ministry of Higher Education Malaysia, http://www.mqa.gov.my.
28. Several historical cases may be drawn on to show the relative ineffectiveness of project execution of the ministry when compared with its Singapore counterpart. For instance, the policy of switching the teaching medium of science and mathematics subjects in Malaysian primary and secondary schools from Malay/Mandarin/Tamil to English since 2003 has recently been declared a failure, and consequently was phased out and completely discarded. In terms

of quality assurance, another noteworthy example is that prior to 2004, all lecturers in public tertiary institutions were required to have certain postgraduate qualifications. However, allegedly due to the shortage of lecturers, this prerequisite was removed in October 2004 by the Ministry of Higher Education to allow applications from industry professionals even though they did not possess any postgraduate qualifications.

29. For instance, though as previously mentioned the Ministry of Higher Education has introduced the mechanism of a search committee for the appointment of senior leaders of public universities in 2005, it is the minister himself/herself who takes consideration of the committee's recommendations and makes the final decision. However, the fact that after more than a half century of nationhood Malaysia has yet to see any non-Malay appointed as the vice chancellor of any public university indicates that this is still a highly biased selection process based primarily on domestic ethnic-political considerations rather than on the principle of meritocracy, and that the ministry still holds final control. In fact, even the senior appointment of non-Malays as deputy vice chancellors is rare, and it was not until 2007 that the ministry decided to create another position of deputy vice chancellor to accommodate non-Malay candidates (Abdul Razak 2008, 14).

30. These are Universiti Sains Malaysia (Science University of Malaysia), Universiti Malaya (University of Malaya), Universiti Kebangsaan Malaysia (National University of Malaysia), and Universiti Putra Malaysia (Putra University of Malaysia).

31. The qualifications framework is a cross-sectoral hierarchy of qualifications (seven levels in total) covering both academic and vocational qualifications required by various industries.

32. The qualifications register is a centralized online database of qualifications and learning programs as well as their providers/operators.

33. The eight UGC-funded institutions are the City University of Hong Kong, Hong Kong Baptist University, Lingnan University, the Chinese University of Hong Kong, the Hong Kong Institute of Education, the Hong Kong Polytechnic University, the Hong Kong University of Science and Technology, and the University of Hong Kong. Among them, the Hong Kong Institute of Education's self-accrediting status is applicable to its teacher education programs only.

34. Information from the section on the "quality assurance mechanism," official website of the Qualifications Framework, Education Bureau, HKSAR, http://www.hkqf.gov.hk/guie/QA_mech.asp. It is also worth noting that since all these UGC-funded institutions are today increasingly involved in the provision of self-financing subdegree programs, they have formed a Joint Quality Review Committee (JQRC) to oversee the quality of such programs and to assess them for classification onto the QR. (Information retrieved from the same section.)

35. Operators who have completed at least two cycles of program revalidation in relevant program area(s) can be considered for program area accreditation (PAA). With PAA status, the operators concerned can develop and offer new

programs within a defined scope of the program area and at specified QF level(s). Also, the qualifications of these programs can be included on the QR without being subject to external quality assurance by the HKCAAVQ within the PAA validity period. Reconstructed from HKCAAVQ (2008, 2).

36. Information from the Q&A section regarding "non-local higher and professional courses," official website of the Education Bureau, HKSAR, http://www.edb.gov.hk/index.aspx?langno=1&nodeid=1251.
37. These institutions are Hong Kong Shue Yan University, the Hong Kong Academy for Performing Arts, and the Open University of Hong Kong.
38. This is the statement that all advertisements of registered or exempted courses, by regulation, should contain.
39. Q&A section regarding "non-local higher and professional courses," official website of the Education Bureau, HKSAR, http://www.edb.gov.hk/index.aspx?langno=1&nodeid=1251.

9 Transnationalization of Higher Education in China

1. The enforcement of the regulations, however, only started from September 2003 onward.
2. The Chinese Ministry of Education was called the "State Education Commission" from 1985 to 1998. The author wants to thank the Research Grant Council of the Government of the HKSAR for offering funding support to the project [HKIEd 7005-PPR-6].
3. Regarding the management of CFCRS degrees, the Academic Degrees Committee of the State Council subsequently issued the Notice on Improving the Management of Degree-Awarding in Activities of CFCRS on 22 January 1996 so as to legalize and systemize the format of degrees awarded by CFCRS institutions and programs.
4. Nevertheless, compulsory education (local primary and junior secondary education) and special subitems regarding military education, police education, and political education, as well as party schools' education, are excluded from the list since no corresponding commitment was made by the Chinese government.
5. University of Nottingham, http://www.nottingham.ac.uk/ugstudy/introduction/finance/international-students.php.
6. University of Nottingham, http://www.nottingham.edu.cn/content.php? d=112.
7. Xi'an Jiaotongtong-Liverpool University, http://www.xjtlu.edu.cn/cn. It is however worth noting that both the University of Nottingham-Ningbo and the Xi'an Jiaotong–Liverpool University charge their international students with foreign passports 1/3 more than the domestic Chinese students. Thus the tuition fee for international students of 2010 intake is RMB 80,000 per academic year for all undergraduate programs.
8. CFCE.CN, http://www.cfce.cn/web/Recruit/Bachelor/200806/533.html.
9. Peking University, China, http://english.pku.edu.cn/CampusLife.

10. Shanghai Jiaotong University, China, "Summer Semester Exchange Program," http://um2.umac.mo/apps/com/bulletin.nsf/nrsview/2057C973AA4D1084 48257B0300097DE9.
11. Tsinghua University, China. "Student Exchange," http://www.tsinghua.edu.cn/publish/then/5999/index.html.
12. Nanjing University, China. "International Cooperation," http://www.nju.edu.cn/html/eng/InternationalfhCooperation.
13. Xi'an Jiaotong University, China, http://www.xjtu.edu.cn/hzjl/442.html.
14. Xi'an Jiaotong University, China, http://www.xjtu.edu.cn/hzjl/444.html.
15. Wuhan University, China, "Overview of International Cooperation," http://en.whu.edu.cn/info.php?rid=572.
16. http://www.sias.edu.cn/en/introduction.php?article_id=53 (accessed 4 July 2010).
17. http://www.sias.edu.cn/article_class.php?classID=1&article_id=118 (accessed 4 July 2010).
18. http://www.sias.edu.cn/en/article_class.php?classID=4&classname=&article_id=192 (accessed 4 July 2010).
19. http://www.sias.edu.cn/article_class.php?classID=1&classname=&article_id=114&article_title=学院领导 (accessed 4 July 2010).
20. For instance, it emphasizes that the "Missouri State University-Branch Campus in Dalian has a diverse student body," and that it is a "truly international school and we encourage students from all over the world to join us." http://chinacampus.missouristate.edu/about.htm (accessed 5 July 2010).
21. http://smsu.lnnu.edu.cn/xueyuan.htm (accessed 5 July 2010).
22. This is a CFCRS institution established in 2005 through collaboration between the Beijing Normal University and Hong Kong Baptist University.
23. United International College, http://uic.edu.hk/en/index.php?option=com_content&task=view&id=62&Itemid=192.
24. The university is formally "the first Chinese-foreign University in China" with approval from the Chinese Ministry of Education.
25. It was in fact Zheng Lin's PhD research which wrapped up in 2008. These 124 interviewees were from various types of universities in China in different regions. Also, they were composed of university staff with different duties, namely academic staff, senior administrative officials, and staff from international offices (Zheng 2009, 39).
26. In terms of the quantity of degrees conferred, CFCRS programs in China could be broadly differentiated into two categories (Zheng 2009, 40), namely:.
    1. A "single-degree program" where only one degree is awarded at the end of the program. In most cases, it refers to a foreign degree from the partner HEI involved in the collaboration.
    2. A "double/dual-degree program" where two degrees are awarded at the end of the program, one from the local HEI, the other from the foreign partner HEI.

10 Transnationalization and Student Learning Experiences

1. The Sino-British College of the University of Shanghai for Science and Technology is by itself a highly complicated product of TNHE collaborations in China. Under the legal framework of Chinese-Foreign Cooperation in Running Schools (CFCRS) in Mainland China, foreign partners that collaborate with the University of Shanghai for Science and Technology in this case are a total of nine British universities. The universities are the University of Bradford, the University of Huddersfield, the University of Leeds, Leeds Metropolitan University, Liverpool John Moores University, Manchester Metropolitan University, the University of Salford, the University of Sheffield, and Sheffield Hallam University.
2. Such an occasion in Singapore was the one held at Informatics Academy, whereas in Malaysia it was the one held at Nilai University College, and in Mainland China at the University of Nottingham-Ningbo. In the latter occasion, we refer to our discussion with the university's bachelor graduates (years 2008 and 2009).
3. Students from the ESSEC Business School are requested to have a six months of international exposure, going to anywhere but France. No additional tuition fee would be charged for that. Also, the six-month international exposure could be in the form of exchange, internship, or, in this case, a stay at the ESSEC's Singapore campus. Exactly where a student chooses to go, and when and how to go, is his/her own responsibility. And finally, they could stay in more than one country during this six-month period.
4. An MBA student from Guangzhou, China, unequivocally stated, "I want to find a job here" and that "it is easier to get a job in Singapore than in the Western countries." Nevertheless, he also indicated that "after I get some working experiences here, I can then go back to China to do businesses" (field interview, 5 August 2010).
5. The main consideration for choosing that Malaysian private HEI in the first place, according to the discussant, was the more affordable expenses of study and living in Malaysia compared to the UK. However, "the facilities in the campus are fairly good, yet the whole environment outside the campus is not. The place is not even safe."
6. Some discussants complained that they have to rely on the help of friends in other private HEIs in gaining access to other more resourceful databases for their assignments and professional research. (field interview, 10 August 2010).
7. As far as the government's regulation is concerned, the discussant suggested that it should supervise the management of HEIs rather than meddling in the affairs of programs. Also, he insisted that the authorities should ensure the accuracy of information provided by Malaysian HEIs to prospective students abroad in order to avoid disillusion caused by dishonest statements. And finally, it should establish a mechanism to collect and study feedback from students (10 August 2010).

8. According to him, the Maldivian student population in Malaysia was just around 20 to 30 five or six years ago, but it has reached nearly 2,000 at the moment. Instead of heading to their previously preferred destination of India and Sri Lanka, the Maldivian students would now opt for Malaysia and Singapore (10 August 2010).
9. Partner Medical School (PMS) Enrollment, official website of the International Medical University, http://www.imu.edu.my/partner-medical.html.
10. The term "original institution" has different meanings in different contexts in the survey. For a "distance-learning program," it refers to the host institution; for a "joint/twinning program," it refers to the overseas institution that collaborates with its local partner in offering such program; and for a "program offered directly by the branch campus of an overseas institution," it refers to the main/central campus of the institution concerned.
11. For instance, a full-time doctoral students in Hong Kong (22 June 2010) complained that "all teachers are from the University X. They fly to Hong Kong and stay for a week to teach. It is difficult for me to seek help in Hong Kong while all the teachers are in Australia." Having said that, he was still very much satisfied with the quality of the program.
12. It is worth noting that not all the TNHE programs currently offered in the Hong Kong education market are recognized by the government. Advertisements concerned would usually bear a short sentence at the bottom of the columns, reminding the potential students themselves to check out whether that specific program has secured recognition by the Hong Kong government or not.
13. For instance, a mature part-time undergraduate commented that as far as quality assurance is concerned, it is rather useless to distribute questionnaires for students' feedbacks at the end of each course. "Things that really matter for the improvement of the quality of lecturers are market forces."
14. This acronym of CFCRS may alternatively be used as an equivalent to "transnational education" in the following discussion. It is notable that CFCRS as a concept for TNHE development in China has become increasingly tricky over the last few years, which implies a great variety of collaborations from equal partnerships to extremely unbalanced cases.
15. For instance, many discussants from CFCRS institutions remarked that they were particularly impressed by the respectful gesture of overseas lecturers in treating them as peers rather than as students. A discussant from the University of Nottingham-Ningbo also forthrightly noted, 'I like this sort of education system.... Another important point is that in our university, lecturers usually request us to find answers by ourselves. In contrast, students in most Chinese universities would simply learn the contents "taught" by their lecturers" (27 January 2011).
16. Foreign language teachers tend to stay at the Chinese HEIs for a much longer period than those who teach professional subjects under the various CFCRS arrangements, as students concerned would have to take English courses for the first two years of their studies.

17. According to the current legal framework of CFCRS, these institutions are by no means "branch campuses" of overseas HEIs. For instance, the University of Nottingham-Ningbo (UNN) is legally run by the University of Nottingham UK, together with its Chinese partner – Zhejiang Wanli University. However, in reality, Zhejiang Wanli University, as the local partner, only provides logistical support to the operation of UNN, yet leaves its administrative and academic management to the University of Nottingham UK. UNN is therefore a branch campus of the University of Nottingham UK in effect.
18. We were particularly impressed by the outspoken articulation and critical mind-set shown by the five bachelor graduates of the University of Nottingham-Ningbo (UNN) while conducting a group discussion with them on 27 January 2011. As the first and second batch of graduates of the UNN (years 2008 and 2009), they admitted that they might not perform well enough in the National Higher Education Entrance Examination (gaokao) before entering UNN, yet UNN has transformed them significantly, particularly in honing their skills of critical thinking and in boosting their self-confidence.

Equally intriguing were remarks made by discussants from the United International College (UIC) on 9 March 2011. UIC is a CFCRS institution collaboratively established by the Hong Kong Baptist University and Beijing Normal University in Zhuhai, Guangdong Province. In fact, UIC's campus is located just beside the Zhuhai Campus of Beijing Normal University, which implies that students from these institutions are actually living together in a larger community. However, according to discussants from UIC, the milieus in these two campuses were "rather different," with the population at UIC being "generally gentler, more considerate to others, and daring to express their different opinions," even though Beijing Normal University did recruit students with higher scores on the gaokao in the first place.
19. The TNHE arrangement of 2+1+1 refers to the design of spending the initial two years in China, then another year in the collaborative overseas HEIs, and finally returning to China for the very last year of the program. As for the 4+0 arrangement in China, students could indeed finish their entire studies domestically, yet they could merely earn the degree of the local HEI upon graduation. The only exception is programs offered by "branch campuses" of overseas HEIs in China.
20. This is indeed an important selling point, that Chinese HEIs that offer such programs tend to highlight it in their related web pages.
21. For instance, the University of Nottingham-Ningbo charged its domestic Chinese students a sum of RMB 60,000 for tuition fees for its 2010 intake. In comparison, tuition fees charged by the local public HEIs are recently merely around RMB 5,000.
22. CDHAW-Tongji is a CFCRS institution co-founded by Tongji University and a consortium of German universities of applied sciences in 2004. Initially, the consortium had included only 11 German universities. However, it has expanded to cover 26 universities by mid-2011.

23. For instance, during the focus group discussion held in Sino-British College, University of Shanghai for Science and Technology (SBC-USST), on 16 December 2010, most of the discussants (full-time undergraduates) expressed their eagerness to work and stay abroad, by and large with strong support from their parents.
24. Professor Sun Wei was then the director of the Department of Educational Cooperation and Exchange, Zhongyuan University of Technology.
25. Professor Zhang Shensheng was then the deputy dean of the University of Michigan–Shanghai Jiao Tong University Joint Institute.
26. The Zhongyuan University of Technology (ZUT) is currently not a prestigious HEI in China, or more specifically, not even one of the best HEIs in Henan Province where it is located. Having said this, ZUT is a rising technology-based HEI which keeps making great efforts in advancing its cooperation with overseas HEIs in various forms over the last decade. Moreover, it is sturdy enough in the field of textile engineering.
27. In terms of CFCRS programs, by far the university has four undergraduate and three vocational CFCRS programs. The four undergraduate programs concerned are on textile engineering, marketing, accounting, and arts and design. Apart from the one on arts and design, these are all CFCRS programs in collaboration with the University of Manchester, UK.
28. For instance, in terms of assessment, students would have to deal with two papers in each examination: one prepared by the foreign lecturer in English, and the other by his/her local counterpart in Chinese. These papers are equally important in the assessment of students (both 50 percent). The rationale behind this innovative arrangement was the attempt to reduce as much as possible a bias of judgment caused by an English language barrier.
29. This by and large highly positive judgment on CFCRS programs/institutions was in accordance with the result of our survey which examined the same theme. For instance, among the 75 respondents who enrolled in CFCRS programs/institutions, 74 of them (98.7 percent) either strongly agreed (31, 41.3 percent) or agreed (43, 57.3 percent) that "overall, the transnational arrangement of the program has benefited my study."
30. The Council for Private Education is a statutory board empowered with the legislative power to regulate Singapore's private education sector as well as to facilitate efforts in uplifting its standards. The introduction of a quality certification scheme called "EduTrust" since 2008 is also part of the government's endeavors to improve its regulation on quality assurance.
31. For example, a Pakistani survey respondent from Nilai University College, Malaysia, complained that "there is a high level of discrimination in Malaysia. For the international students, there is no any opportunity [sic] to go for higher education unless you are so rich and have so much money to spend in their country like what I am doing in NUC. Furthermore, there is no job offer for international students, no scholarships. Then how can we go further?'
32. X. Cheng, 2013, "Assessing Student Exchange Programmes: Putting Students at the Centre of Internationalization Efforts," in Going Global: Identifying

Trends and Drivers of International Education, ed. M. Stiasny and T. Gore (pp. 183–192). UK: Emerald Group.
33. Ibid.
34. Ibid.
35. Ibid.
36. Ibid.

11 Changing Regulatory Regimes and Governance in East Asia

1. The most recent example is the launch of the Hong Kong PhD Fellowship Scheme by the Research Grants Council (RGC) in 2009. The fellowship will provide a monthly stipend of HK$20,000, as well as a conference and research-related travel allowance of HK$10,000 per year for a maximum period of three years. A total of 135 PhD fellowships will be awarded for the 2010/11 academic year.
2. The present chapter is a revised version of an article published in *Journal of Education Policy* 26(1): 61–81..

12 Questing for Entrepreneurial Universities in East Asia

1. Academic ranking of world universities, http://www.shanghairanking.com/ARWU-Statistics-2012.html#1.
2. Trends in International Mathematics and Science Study (TIMSS), 1995, 1999, 2003, 2007 and 2011; OECD Programme for International Student Assessment.
3. National Science Board, Science and Engineering Indicators 2012, http://www.nsf.gov/statistics/seind12/pdf/at.pdf.
4. National Science Board, 2012, "Science and Engineering Indicators 2012," http://www.nsf.gov/statistics/seind12/pdf/at.pdf.

Conclusion

1. Jonathan Adams and David Smith, 2003, "Funding Research Diversity: The Impact of Further Concentration on University Research Performance and Regional Research Capacity," United Kingdom, Universities UK, http://www.universitiesuk.ac.uk/highereducation/Documents/2003/FundingResearch.pdf.

References

Abdul Razak, Ahmad. 2008. "The University's Governance in Malaysia: Re-examining the Role of the State." Paper presented at the symposium on Positioning University in the Globalized World: Changing Governance and Coping Strategies in Asia, University of Hong Kong, Hong Kong, 10–11 December.

Adams, Jonathan, and Smith, David. 2004. *Research and the Regions: An Overview of the Distribution of Research in UK Regions, Regional Research Capacity and Links between Strategic Research Partners.* Oxford: Higher Education Policy Institute.

Ahmad, Abd Rahman; Farley, Alan; and Naidoo, Moonsamy. 2012. "Funding Crisis in Higher Education Institutions: Rationale for Change." *Asian Economic and Financial Review* 2(4): 562–576.

Almedia, Rita K. 2010. "Openness and Technological Innovation in East Asia." World Bank Policy Research Working Paper 5272.

Altbach, Philip G. 1989. "The New Internationalism: Foreign Students and Scholars." *Studies in Higher Education* 14(2): 125–136.

Altbach, Philip G. 2004. "Globalization and the University: Myths and Realities in an Unequal World." *Tertiary Education and Management* 1:1–20.

Altbach, Philip G. 2010. *Leadership for World-Class Universities: Challenges for Developing Countries.* New York and London: Routledge.

Altbach, Philip G., and Levy, Daniel C. 2005. *Private Higher Education: A Global Revolution.* Rotterdam: Sense Publishers.

Anderseck, Klaus. 2004. "Institutional and Academic Entrepreneurship: Implications for University Governance and Management." *Higher Education in Europe* 29(2): 193–200.

Applied Science and Technology Research Institute. 2011. *ASTRI Annual Report 2010/2011.* Hong Kong: Hong Kong Applied Science and Technology Research Institute.

Aronowitz, Stanley. 2000. *The Knowledge Factory: Dismantling the Corporate University and Creating True Higher Learning.* Boston: Beacon Press.

Asian Development Bank. 2008. *Education and Skills: Strategies for Accelerated Development in Asia and the Pacific.* Manila: Asian Development Bank.

Baark, Erik, and Sharif, Naubahar. 2006. "Hong Kong's Innovation System in Transition: Challenges of Regional Integration and Promotion of High Technology." In *Asia's Innovation Systems in Transition*, ed. Bengt-Ake Lundvall et al. (pp. 123–147). Northampton, MA: Edward Elgar.

Baark, Erik, and So, Alvin Y. 2006. "The Political Economy of Hong Kong's Quest for High Technology Innovation." *Journal of Contemporary Asia* 36(1): 102–120.

Baer, Werner, et al. 1999. "The End of the Asian Myth: Why Were the Experts Fooled?" *World Development* 27(10): 735–1747.

Ball, Stephen J. 2007. *Education Plc: Understanding Private Sector Participation in Public Sector Education*. London: Routledge.
Ball, Stephen J. 2009. "Global Education, Heterarchies and Hybrid Organizations." Paper presented at the 2009 Asian-Pacific forum on Sociology of Education: Social Change and Educational Reform, National University of Tainan, Taiwan, 6–8 May.
Batra, Geeta, and Stone, Andrew H. W. 2004. "Investment Climate, Capabilities and Firm Performance: Evidence from the World Business Environment Survey." http://info.worldbank.org/etools/docs/library/206523/Investment%20climate%20capabilities%20and%20firm%20performance.pdf.
Bauhinia Foundation Research Centre. 2009. "Hong Kong-Shenzhen Education Cooperation" (in Chinese). http://www.bauhinia.org/publications/tchi_HK-SZ_EducationCooperation_MainReport.pdf.
Bayliss, John, and Smith, Steve. 2001. *The Globalization of World Politics: An Introduction to International Relations*. Oxford: Oxford University Press.
Blackmore, Jill. 2000. "Warning Signals or Dangerous Opportunities? Globalization, Gender, and Educational Policy Shifts." *Educational Theory* 50(4): 467–486.
Bray, Mark, and Lee, Wing On. 2001. *Education and Political Transition: Implications of Hong Kong's Change of Sovereignty* (2nd ed.). Hong Kong: Comparative Education Research Centre, University of Hong Kong.
Brehony, Kelvin J., and Deem, Rosemary. 2005. "Challenging the Post-Fordist/Flexible Organization Thesis: The Case of Reformed Educational Organizations." *British Journal of Sociology of Education* 26(3): 395–414.
Brown, Philip; Lauder, Hugh; and Ashton, David. 2011. *The Global Auction: The Broken Promises of Education, Jobs and Incomes*. Oxford: Oxford University Press.
Burbules, Nicolas C., and Torres, Carlos Alberto. 2000. *Globalization and Education: Critical Perspectives*. London: Routledge.
Burke, Kelly. 2005. "University Plays Down Fears about Singapore Offshoot." *Sydney Morning Herald*, 26 October 2005.
Castells, Manuel. 2000. *The Rise of the Network Society* (2nd ed.). Oxford: Blackwell.
Central Policy Unit, HKSAR Government. 2011. "Case Study of Hong Kong-Guangdong Cooperation in Education and Science and Technology in Nansha" (in Chinese). http://www.cpu.gov.hk/english/documents/new/press/2nd%20special%20report.pdf.
Cerny, Philip G. 1990. *The Changing Architecture of Politics: Structure, Agency, and the Future of the State*. London: Sage.
Cerny, Philip G. 1997. "Paradoxes of the Competition State: The Dynamics of Political Globalization." *Government and Opposition* 32:251–274.
Chan, David Kin Keung. 2007. "Global Agenda, Local Response: Changing Education Governance in Hong Kong's Higher Education." *Globalization, Societies & Education* 5(1): 109–124.
Chan, David Kin Keung. 2008. "Global Agenda, Local Response: Changing University Governance and Academic Reflections in Hong Kong's Higher Education." Paper presented at the symposium on Positioning University in the Globalized World: Changing Governance and Coping Strategies in Asia, University of Hong Kong, Hong Kong, 10–11 December.
Chan, David Kin Keung, and Lo, Yat Wai. 2007. "Running Universities as Enterprises: University Governance Changes in Hong Kong." *Asia Pacific Journal of Education* 27(3): 305–322.

Chan, David Kin Keung, and Ng, P. T. 2008. "Developing Transnational Higher Education: Comparing the Approaches of Hong Kong and Singapore." *International Journal of Educational Reform* 17(3): 291–307.
Chan, David, and Tan, Jason. 2006. "Privatization and the Rise of Direct Subsidy Scheme Schools and Independent Schools in Hong Kong and Singapore." Paper presented at the Asia Pacific Educational Research Association 2006 International Conference, Hong Kong, 28–30 November.
Chapman, David W.; Cummings, William K.; and Postiglione, Gerard A. 2010. *Crossing Borders in East Asian Higher Education*. Dordrecht: Springer.
Chen, Dorothy I. R., and Lo, Yat Wai. 2007. "Critical Reflections of the Approaches to Quality in Taiwan's Higher Education." *Journal of Comparative Asian Development* 6(1): 165–186.
Chen, Shin Horng. 1997. "Decision-Making in Research and Development Collaboration." *Research Policy* 26(1): 121–135.
Cheng, David X. 2013. "Assessing Student Exchange Programmes: Putting Students at the Centre of Internationalization Efforts." In *Going Global: Identifying Trends and Drivers of International Education*, ed. Mary Stiasny and Tim Gore (pp. 183–192). UK: Emerald Group Publishing.
Cheng, Tun Jen. 2001. "Transforming Taiwan's Economic Structure in the 20th Century." *China Quarterly* 165:19–36.
Cheng, Yin Cheong; Ng, Shun Wing; Cheung, Alan Chi Keung; et al. 2009. *A Technical Research Report on the Development of Hong Kong as a Regional Education Hub*. Hong Kong: Hong Kong Institute of Education.
Chesbrough, Henry William. 2003. "The Era of Open Innovation." *MIT Sloan Management Review*, Spring, 35–41.
Chinese University of Hong Kong. 2011. *Annual Report on Recurrent Funding for Knowledge Transfer in the 2009/10 to 2011/12 Triennium for the Period 1 July 2010–30 June 2011*.
Choi, Sang Duk, 2010. *Lessons from Economic Growth and Human Capital Formation Policies in South Korea*. Seoul: Korean Educational Development Institute.
Chou, Prudence. 2006. "Taiwan's Higher Education at the Crossroad: Implications for China." Paper presented at the senior seminar, Education for 2020 Project of East-West Center, Hawaii, US, 6–12 September.
Christensen, Clayton M., and Eyring, Henry J. 2011. *The Innovative University: Changing the DNA of Higher Education from the Inside Out*. San Francisco: Jossey-Bass.
Civic Exchange. 2009. "The Outline of the Plan for the Reform and Development of the Pearl River Delta (2008–2020)." http://www.civic-exchange.org/eng/upload/files/NDRC.pdf.
Clark, Burton Robert. 1998. *Creating Entrepreneurial Universities: Organizational Pathways of Transformation*. New York: Pergamon Press.
Clark, Burton Robert. 2004. *Sustaining Change in Universities: Continuities in Case Studies and Concepts*. Maidenhead, England: Society for Research into Higher Education and Open University Press.
Currie, Jan et al. 2003. *Globalizing Practices and University Responses: European and Anglo-American Differences*. Westport, CT: Praeger/Greenwood Press.
Currie, Jan, and Newson, Janice. 1998. *Universities and Globalization: Critical Perspectives*. Thousand Oaks, CA: Sage.

Currie, Jan; Peterson, Carole J.; and Mok, Ka Ho. 2005. *Academic Freedom in Hong Kong*. Lanham, MD: Lexington Books.

Dale, Roger. 2000. "Globalization and Education: Demonstrating a Common World Educational Culture or Locating a Globally Structured Educational Agenda?" *Education Theory* 50(4): 427–448.

Deem, Rosemary. 2001. "Globalization, New Managerialism, Academic Capitalism and Entrepreneurialism in Universities: Is the Local Dimension Still Important?" *Comparative Education* 37(1): 7–20.

Dill, David D., and Soo, Maarja. 2005. "Academic Quality, League Tables and Public Policy: A Cross-National Analysis of Universities Ranking System." *Higher Education* 49:495–533.

DiMaggio, Paul J., and Powell, Walter W. 1983. "The Iron Cage Revisited: Institutional Isomorphism and Collective Rationality in Organizational Fields." *American Sociological Review* 48:147–60.

Drahos, Peter, and Joseph, Richard A. 1995. "The Telecommunications and Investment in the Great Supranational Regulatory Game." *Telecommunications Policy* 19(8): 619–635.

East-West Centre. 2010. "The IFE 2020 Tool Kit." Paper presented at the International Forum for Education 2010 Leadership Institute, Bangkok, Thailand, 13–24 September.

Ebuchi, Kazuhiro. 1997. *Study of the Internationalization of Universities*. Tokyo: Tamagawa University Press.

Editor. 2010. "Reflections on Reforms in Shenzhen by Hu-Wen Administration." *Mingpao*, 7 September 2010.

Edquist, Charles, and Hommen, Leif. 2008. *Small Country Innovation Systems*. Cheltenham, England: Edward Elgar.

Etzkowitz, Henry. 2008. *The Triple Helix: University-Industry-Government Innovation in Action*. New York: Routledge.

Evans, Gillian R., and Packham, David E. 2003. "Ethical Issues at the University-Industry Interface: A Way Forward." *Science and Engineering Ethics* 9(1): 3–16.

Executive Yuan, Taiwan. 1998. "Action Plan for Building a Technologically Advanced Nation." http://web1.nsc.gov.tw/public/data/4714107571.htm.

Fetters, Michael L., et al. 2010. *The Development of University-Based Entrepreneurship Ecosystems: Global Practices*. Cheltenham, UK; Northampton, MA: Edward Elgar.

Florida, Richard L. 2005. *The Flight of the Creative Class: The New Global Competition for Talent*. New York: HarperBusiness.

Forss, Pearl. 2007. "University of New South Wales Singapore Campus to Shut in June." *Channel NewsAsia*, 23 May 2007.

Fraenkel, Ernst. 1941. *The Dual State: A Contribution to the Theory of Dictatorship*. New York: Octagon Book.

French, Nigel J. 1999. "Transnational Education: Competition or Complementarity: The Case of Hong Kong." *Higher Education in Europe* 24(2): 219–223.

Fukuyama, Francis. 1992. *The End of History*. New York: Penguin.

Fukayama, Francis. 2005. *State Capacity*. London: Profile Books.

Fukuyama, Francis. 2006. *The End of History and the Last Man*. New York: Free Press.

Furushiro, Norio. 2006. *Final Report of Developing Evaluation Criteria to Assess the Internationalization of Universities*. Kwansei: Osaka University.

Gallagher, Michael, et al. 2009. *OECD Reviews of Tertiary Education: China.* Paris: OECD.
Garrett, Richard. 2005. "The Rise and Fall of Transnational Higher Education in Singapore." *International Higher Education* 39:9–10.
Gill, Stephen. 1995. "Globalization, Market Civilization and Disciplinary Neoliberalism." *Millennium* 24(3): 399–423.
Giroux, Henry A. 2003. "Selling out Higher Education." *Policy Futures in Education* 1(1): 179–200.
Giroux, Henry A. 2005. "Academic Entrepreneurs: The Corporate Takeover of Higher Education." *Tikkun* 20(2): 18–22.
Goh, Andrew L. S. 2005. "Promoting Innovation in Aid of Industrial Development: The Singaporean Experience." *International Journal of Public Sector Management* 18(3): 216–240.
Gopinathan, Saravanan. 2001. "Globalization, the State and Education Policy in Singapore." In *Education and Political Transition: Implications of Hong Kong's Change of Sovereignty*, ed. Mark Bray and Wing On Lee. Hong Kong: Comparative Education Research Centre, University of Hong Kong.
Green, A. 2012. "Youth Crisis in Europe after Massification of Higher Education." Paper presented at the WUN Ideas and Universities Conference, October 2012, Zhejiang University, China.
Guarino, Cassandra; Ridgeway, Greg; Chun, Marc; and Buddin, Richard. 2005. "A New Approach to University Rankings Using Latent Variable Analysis." *Higher Education in Europe* 30(2): 147–165.
Gumport, Patricia J. 2000. "Academic Restructuring: Organizational Change and Institutional Imperatives." *Higher Education* 36(1): 67–91.
Hawkins, John N. 2000. "Centralization, Decentralization and Recentralization: Education Reform in China." *Educational Administration* 38(5): 442–455.
Hawkins, John N. 2005. "Some Trends in Public Higher Education: Asia and the U.S." *Chung Cheng Educational Studies* (special issue): 45–62.
Hawkins, John N. 2007. "Public Good, Commodification and Higher Education Reform: Some Trends in Japan and California." *University Studies* 35 (August 2007): 27–51.
Held, David. 1991. *Political Theory Today.* Stanford, CA: Stanford University Press.
Held, David. 2004. *Global Covenant.* Cambridge: Polity.
Held, David, and McGrew, A. 2000. *The Global Transformations Reader.* Cambridge: Polity.
Held, David; McGrew, Anthony; Goldblatt, David; and Perration, Jonathan. 1999. *Global Transformations.* Cambridge: Polity.
Hemmert, Martin, et al. 2008. "An Inquiry into the Status and Nature of University-Industry Research Collaborations in Japan and Korea." *Hitotsubashi Journal of Economics* 49:163–180.
Hirst, Paul; Thompson, Grahame; and Bromley, Simon. 1999. *Globalization in Question.* Cambridge: Polity.
Hobday, Michael. 1995a. "East Asian Latecomer Firms: Learning the Technology of Electronics." *World Development* 23(7): 1172–1193.
Hobday, Michael. 1995b. *Innovation in East Asia: The Challenge to Japan.* Aldershot, Hants, England: Edward Elgar.
Hong Kong Council for Accreditation of Academic and Vocational Qualifications [HKCAAVQ]. 2007. *Code of Practice for Non-local Courses Recommended by the*

Hong Kong Council for Accreditation of Academic and Vocational Qualifications. Hong Kong: Author.
Hong Kong Information Services Department. 2009. "Three-Year Action Plan on Shenzhen/Hong Kong Co-operation in Innovation and Technology." http://www.info.gov.hk/gia/general/200903/31/P200903300269.htm.
Hong Kong Science and Technology Parks Corporation. 2011. *Annual Report 2010/2011*. Hong Kong: Hong Kong Science and Technology Parks Corporation.
Hou, Y.C. (2008) "The 2005 and 2006 Carnegie Classification in U.S. and its Impact on Higher Education Institutions in Taiwan", Evaluation in Higher Education, Vol.2, No.1, pp. 107–142.
Hong Kong University of Science and Technology. 2009 *Annual Report 2008–2009*. Hong Kong: Author.
Hong Kong University of Science and Technology. 2010. *Annual Report on Research Activities 2009–10*. http://research.ust.hk/report1.pdf.
Hong Kong University of Science and Technology. 2011. *Knowledge Transfer Annual Report 2010/11*.
Hou, Y.C. 2008. "The 2005 and 2006 Carnegie Classification in U.S. and its Impact on Higher Education Institutions in Taiwan." *Evaluation in Higher Education* 2(1): 107–142.
Hsu, Chiung Wen, and Chiang, Hsueh Chiao. 2001. "The Government Strategy for the Upgrading of Industrial Technology in Taiwan." *Technovation* 21(2): 123–132.
Hu, Mei Chih, and Mathews, John A. 2005. "National Innovative Capacity in East Asia." *Research Policy* 34(9): 1322–1349.
Hu, Mei Chih, and Mathews, John. A. 2007. "Enhancing the Role of Universities in Building National Innovative Capacity in Asia: The Case of Taiwan." *World Development* 25:245–264.
Hu, Mei Chih, and Mathews, John A. 2009. "Estimating the Innovation Effects of University-Industry-Government Linkages: The Case of Taiwan." *Journal of Management & Organization* 15(2): 138–154.
Huang, Fu Tao. 2005. "The Growth and Development of Transnational Higher Education in China." In *Globalization and Higher Education in East Asia*, ed. Ka Ho Mok and Richard James (pp. 170–184). New York and Singapore: Marshall Cavendish Academic.
Huang, Fu Tao. 2006a. "Transnational Higher Education in Mainland China: A Focus on Foreign Degree-Conferring Programs." *RIHE International Publication Series* 10:21–34.
Huang, Fu Tao. 2006b. "Difference in the Context of Internationalization by Region: China." In *Final Report of Developing Evaluation Criteria to Assess the Internationalization of Universities*, ed. Norio Furushiro (pp. 41–50). Kwansei, Japan: Osaka University.
International Labor Organization [ILO]. 1998. "Guild to ILO Recommendation No. 189: Job Creation in Small and Medium-sized Enterprises." http://www.ilo.org/wcmsp5/groups/public/@ed_emp/@emp_ent/@ifp_seed/documents/publication/wcms_127673.pdf.
Jarrar, Yasar F., and Mohamed, Zairi. 2001. *Becoming World Class through a Culture of Measurement*. Bradford: Bradford University Management Centre.

Jayasuriya, Kanishka. 2000. "Authoritarian Liberalism, Governance and the Emergence of the Regulatory State in Post-crisis East Asia." In *Politics and Markets in the Wake of the Asian Crisis*, ed. Richard Robinson, Mark Beeson, Kanishka Jayasuriya, and Hyuk Rae Kim (pp. 315–330). London: Routledge.
Jessop, Bob. 2002. *The Future of the Capitalist State*. Cambridge: Polity.
Jordana, Jacint, and Levi-Faur, David. 2005. "Preface: The Making of a New Regulatory Order." *Annals of the American Academy of Political and Social Science* 598 (March 2005): 1–6.
Kao, John J. 2007. *Innovation Nation: How America Is Losing Its Innovation Edge, Why It Matters, and What We Can Do to Get It Back*. New York: Free Press.
Keck, Margaret E., and Sikkink, Kathryn. 1998. *Activists beyond Borders: Advocacy Networks in International Politics*. Ithaca, NY: Cornell University Press.
Keller, William W., and Richard J. Samuels, eds. 2002. *Crisis and Innovation in Asian Technology*. Cambridge: Cambridge University Press.
Kenway, Jane; Bullen, Elizabeth; and Robb, Simon. 2004. "The Knowledge Economy, the Technopreneur and the Problematic Future of the University." *Policy Futures in Education* 2(2): 330–348.
Kim, Haknoh. 2007. "Regional Innovation Policy of South Korea, Compared with, and Learning from, the European Union." http://www.europeanstudiesalliance.org/calendar/sp07events/Kim_Paper.pdf.
Kim, Linsu, and Nelson, Richard R. 2000. *Technology, Learning, and Innovation: Experiences of Newly Industrializing Economies*. Cambridge; New York: Cambridge University Press.
Kim, Terri. 2006. "The Academic Profession in East Asian Private Higher Education." Paper presented at the International Workshop "Frontier of Private Higher Education Research in East Asia," Hotel Arcadia Ichigaya, Tokyo, Japan, 14–15 December.
Knight, Jane. 2002. "Trade Talk: An Analysis of the Impact of Trade Liberalization and the General Agreement on Trade in Services on Higher Education." *Journal of Studies in International Education* 6(3): 209–229.
Know about Business [KAB], (China) Promotion Office. 2012. "Promotion Plan of KAB (China) Entrepreneurship Education Program." http://www.kab.org.cn/content/201 1-09/15/content_ 4894576.htm.
Koh, Winston T. H. 2006. "Singapore's Transition to Innovation-Based Economic Growth: Infrastructure, Institutions and Government's Role." *R&D Management* 36(2): 143–160.
Kooiman, Jan. 1993. "Socio-Political Governance: Introduction." In *Modern Governance: New Government-Society Interactions*, ed. Jan Kooiman (pp. 1–8). London: Sage.
Korean Educational Development Institute [KEDI]. 2010. *Brief Understanding of Korean Educational Policy* 25.
Krugman, Paul. 1994. "The Myth of Asia's Miracle." *Foreign Affairs* 27(6): 62–78.
Kwiek, Marek. 2004. "The Emergent Educational Policies under Scrutiny: The Bologna Process from a Central European Perspective." *European Educational Research Journal* 3(4): 1–24.Lee, Hiu Hong, and Gopinathan, Saravanan. 2005. "Reforming University Education in Hong Kong and Singapore." In *Globalization and Higher Education in East Asia*, ed. Ka Ho Mok and Richard James (pp. 56–98.) Singapore: Marshall Cavendish Academic.

Lee, Hiu Hong, and Gopinathan, Saravanan. 2007. "University Restructuring in Singapore: Amazing! Or a Maze?" *Journal of Comparative Asian Development* 6(1): 107–141.
Lee, Hock Guan. 2005. "Affirmative Action in Malaysia." *Southeast Asian Affairs*: 211–228. Singapore: Institute of Southeast Asian Studies.
Lee, Kong Rae. 2006. "Performance and Sources of Industrial Innovation in Korea's Innovation System." In *Asia's Innovation Systems in Transition*, ed. Bengt-Ake Lundvall, **Patarapong Intarakumnerd, and Jan Vang** (pp. 178–199). Cheltenham, Northampton, MA: Edward Elgar.
Lee, Michael H. 2005. "Major Issues of University Education Policy in Hong Kong." *Asia Pacific Education Review* 6(2): 103–112.
Lee, Michael H., and Gopinathan, Saravanan. 2008. "University Restructuring in Singapore: Amazing or a Maze?" *Policy Futures in Education* 6(5): 569–588.
Lee, Molly N. N. 2004. *Restructuring Higher Education in Malaysia*. Penang, Malaysia: School of Educational Studies, Universiti Sains Malaysia.
Legislative Council, Panel on Commerce and Industry, HKSAR. 2007. "Improvements to the Small Entrepreneur Research Assistance Programme and the University-Industry Collaboration Programme under the Innovation and Technology Fund." LC Paper No. CB(1)549/07–08(04). http://www.legco.gov.hk/yr07–08/english/panels/ci/papers/ci0115cb1–549–4-e.pdf.
Legislative Council, Panel on Commerce and Industry, HKSAR. 2011a. "Comprehensive Review of R&D Centres Set up under the Innovation and Technology Fund." LC Paper No. CB(1)624/11–12(05). http://www.legco.gov.hk/yr11–12/english/panels/ci/papers/ci1220cb1–624–5-e.pdf.
Legislative Council, Panel on Commerce and Industry, HKSAR. 2011b. "Updated Background Brief on Research and Development Centres Set up under the Innovation and Technology Fund." LC Paper No. CB(1)624/11–12(06). http://www.legco.gov.hk/yr11–12/english/panels/ci/papers/ci1220cb1–624–6-e.pdf.
Leung, Chi Kin, and Wu, Chung Tong. 1994. "Innovation Environment, R&D Linkages and Technology Development in Hong Kong." *Regional Studies* 29(6): 533–546.
Leung, C. Y. 2012. *Policy Address of 2012*. Hong Kong Government Printer.
Levi-Faur, David. 1998. "The Competition State as a Neo-mercantalist State: Understanding the Restructuring of National and Global Telecommunications." *Journal of Socio-Economics* 27(6): 655–686.
Leydesdorff, Loet, and Etzkowitz, Henry. 2001. "The Transformation of University-Industry-Government Relations." *Electronic Journal of Sociology*. http://sociology.org/content/vol005.004/th.html.
Lim, Chaisung. 2008. "Towards Knowledge Generation with Bipolarized NSI: Korea." In *Small Country Innovation Systems: Globalization, Change and Policy in Asia and Europe*, ed. Charles Edquist and Leif Hommen (pp. 113–155). Northampton, MA: Edward Elgar.
Lin, Jing; Zhang, Yu; Gao, Lan; and Liu, Yan. 2005. "Trust, Ownership and Autonomy: Challenges Facing Private Higher Education in China." *China Review* 5(1): 61–82.
Lingard, Bob, and Rizvi, Fazal. 2009. *Globalizing Education Policy*. New York: Routledge.
Liu, Nian Cai, and Cheng, Ying. 2005. "Academic Ranking of World Universities." *Higher Education in Europe* 30(2): 127–136.

Lundvall, Bengt-Ake; Intarakumnerd, Patarapong; Vang, Jan; et al. 2006. *Asia's Innovation Systems in Transition*. Cheltenham, UK; Northampton, MA: Edward Elgar.
Lo, Yat Wai, and Chan, David. 2006. "The Impact of Globalization on Higher Education in Taiwan and Mainland China." Paper presented at the International Conference on GDPism and Risk: Challenges for Social Development and Governance in East Asia, Bristol, UK, 12–13 July.
Lo, Yat Wai, and Weng, Fwu Yuan. 2005. "Taiwan's Responses to Globalization: Decentralization and Internationalization of Higher Education." In *Globalization and Higher Education in East Asia*, ed. Ka Ho Mok and Richard James (pp. 137–156). Singapore: Marshall Cavendish Academic.
Lu, Mu Lin. 2004. "The Blueprint and Competitiveness of Taiwan's Higher Education." Paper presented at Cross Strait Seminar on Review and Prospect of the Policy of University Excellence held at Taipei, Taiwan, 25–26 March.
Lucas, Lisa. 2006. *The Research Game in Academic Life*. Maidenhead: Open University Press/Society for Research into Higher Education (SRHE).
Mahbubani, Kishore. 2008. *New Asian Hemisphere: The Irresistible Shift of Global Power to the East*. New York: Public Affairs.
Mahmood, Ishtiaq P., and Singh, Jasjit. 2003. "Technological Dynamism in Asia." *Research Policy* 32(6): 1031–1054.
Marginson, Simon. 2006. "The Dynamics of National and Global Competition in Higher Education." *Higher Education* 52(1): 1–39.
Marginson, Simon, and Considine, Mark. 2000. *The Enterprise University: Power, Governance and Reinvention in Australia*. Cambridge: Cambridge University Press.
Marginson, Simon, and Sawir, Erlenawati. 2005. "Interrogating Global Flows in Higher Education." *Globalization, Societies and Education* 3(3): 281–310.
Marinetto, Mike. 2003. "Governing beyond the Centre: A Critique of the Anglo-governance School." *Political Studies* 51(3): 592–608.
Mathews, John A. 1997. "A Silicon Valley of the East: Creating Taiwan's Semiconductor Industry." *California Management Review* 39(4): 26–54.
Matlay, Harry. 2001. "Strategic Issues in Vocational Education and Training in Central and Eastern Europe." *Education + Training* 43(8/9): 395–404.
McBurnie, Grant, and Ziguras, Christopher. 2001. "The Regulation of Transnational Higher Education in Southeast Asia: Case Studies of Hong Kong, Malaysia and Australia." *Higher Education* 42:85–105.
Meek, V. Lynn, and Suwanwela, Charas. 2006. *Higher Education Research and Knowledge in the Asia Pacific Region*. New York: Palgrave Macmillan.
Merisotis, Jamie, and Sadlak, Jan. 2005. "Higher Education Ranking: Evolution, Acceptance and Dialogue." *Higher Education in Europe* 30(2): 97–101.
MEST, South Korea. 2007. "Summary of BK21 and NURI Projects." http://english.mest.go.kr.
MEST, South Korea. 2008. "Major Policies and Plans for 2009." http://english.mest.go.kr.
MEST, South Korea. 2009a "Major Policies to Enhance the Competitive Strength of Korean Higher Education." http://english.mest.go.kr.
MEST, South Korea. 2009b. "Major Policies and Plans for 2010." http://english.mest.go.kr.
Min, Wei Fang. 2004. "Chinese Higher Education: The Legacy of the Past and the Context of the Future." In *Asian Universities: Historical Perspectives and*

Contemporary Challenges, ed. Philip G. Altbach and Toru Umakoshi (pp. 53–84.) Baltimore and London: Johns Hopkins University Press.
Ming Pao Daily, 7 September 2010.
Ministry of Economic Affairs, Republic of China. 2008. *Small and Medium Enterprises in Taiwan*. Taipei: Ministry of Economic Affairs, Republic of China.
MOE, Taiwan. 2000. *List of Projects for the First Round of the Program for Promoting Academic Excellence of Universities*. Taipei: Ministry of Education.
MOE, Taiwan. 2007a. "Industry-Academia Partnerships a Win-Win Strategy." http://english.moe.gov.tw/ct.asp?xItem=7232&ctNode=504&mp=1.
MOE, Taiwan. 2007b. "The Ministry of Education Passed Rules Governing Industry-Academia Collaboration." http://english.moe.gov.tw/ct.asp?xItem=7232&ctNode=504&mp=1.
MOE, Taiwan. 2009. "Directions Governing Evaluations of Ministry of Education Subsidies for Colleges and Universities to Recruit Research Talents Program." http://english.moe.gov.tw.
MOE, Taiwan. 2011a. "Study-in-Taiwan Enhancement Program." http://english.moe.gov.tw.
MOE, Taiwan. 2011b. "2011 Educational Statistical Indicators." http://english.moe.gov.tw.
Mohrman, Kathryn. 2008. "The Emerging Global Model with Chinese Characteristics." *Higher Education Policy* 21(1): 29–48.
Mok, Ka Ho. 2003. *Centralization and Decentralization: Educational Reforms and Changing Governance in Chinese Societies*. Hong Kong: Comparative Education Research Centre, University of Hong Kong.
Mok, Ka Ho. 2005a. "Globalization and New Governance: Changing Policy Instruments and Regulatory Arrangements in Education." *International Review of Education* 51(4): 1–22.
Mok, Ka Ho. 2005b. "Fostering Entrepreneurship: Changing Role of Government and Higher Education Governance in Hong Kong." *Research Policy* 34:537–554.
Mok, Ka Ho. 2005c. "The Quest for World Class University: Quality Assurance and International Benchmarking." *Quality Assurance in Education* 13(4): 277–304.
Mok, Ka Ho. 2006a. "Varieties of Regulatory Regimes in Asia: The Liberalization of the Higher Education Market in Hong Kong, Singapore and Malaysia." Paper presented at the Asia Pacific Educational Research Association 2006 International Conference, Hong Kong Institute of Education, Hong Kong, 28–30 November.
Mok, Ka Ho. 2006b. "The Search for New Governance: Corporatization and Privatization Experiences in Singapore and Malaysia." Paper presented at the International Workshop on University Restructuring in Asia, Research Institute for Higher Education, Hiroshima University, 16 January.
Mok, Ka Ho. 2006c. "One Country, Diverse Systems: Politics of Educational Decentralization in Post-Mao China." Paper presented at the Contemporary China Seminar Series, Institute of Oriental Studies, University of Oxford, February.
Mok, Ka Ho. 2006d. *Education Reform and Education Policy in East Asia*. London: Routledge.
Mok, Ka Ho. 2007. "The Search for New Governance: Corporatization and Privatization of Public Universities in Malaysia and Thailand." *Asia Pacific Journal of Education* 27(3): 271–290.
Mok, Ka Ho. 2007a. "The Search for New Governance: Corporatization and Privatization of Public Universities in Malaysia and Thailand." *Asia Pacific Journal of Education* 27(3): 271–290.

Mok, Ka Ho. 2007b. "Questing for Internationalization of Universities in Asia: Critical Reflections." *Journal of Studies in International Education* 11(3–4): 433–454.
Mok, Ka Ho. 2008a "Varieties of Regulatory Regimes in Asia: The Liberalization of the Higher Education Market and Changing Governance in Hong Kong, Singapore and Malaysia." *Pacific Review* 21(2): 147–170.
Mok, Ka Ho. 2008b "Positioning as Regional Hub of Higher Education: Changing Governance and Regulatory Reforms in Singapore and Malaysia." *International Journal of Education Reform* 17(3): 230–250.
Mok, Ka Ho. 2008c "Varieties of Regulatory Regimes in Asia: The Liberalization of the Higher Education Market and Changing Governance in Hong Kong, Singapore and Malaysia." *Pacific Review* 21(2): 147–170.
Mok, Ka Ho. 2009. "The Growing Importance of the Privateness in Education: Challenges for Higher Education Governance in China." *Compare* 39(1): 35–49.
Mok, Ka Ho. 2010. "The Changing Role of University in Promoting Entrepreneurship and Innovation: A Comparative Study of Selected Asian Economies." www.undp.org.
Mok, Ka Ho. 2011. "The Quest for Regional Hub of Education: Growing Hierarchies, Organizational Hybridization, and New Governance in Singapore and Malaysia." *Journal of Education Policy* 26(1): 61–81.
Mok, Ka Ho. 2012a. "Bringing the State Back In: Restoring the Role of the State in Chinese Higher Education." *European Journal of Education* 47(2): 228–241.
Mok, Ka Ho. 2012b. "International Benchmarking with the Best: The Varied Role of the State in the Quest for Regional Education Hubs in Malaysia and Hong Kong." In *Policy Borrowing and Learning in Education*, ed. G. Steiner-Khamsi and F. Waldow. London: Routledge.
Mok, Ka Ho, and Chan, David Kin Keung. 2012. "Challenges of Transnational Higher Education in China." In *The Orientation of Higher Education: Challenging the East-West Dichotomy*, ed. Bob Adamson, Jon Nixon, and Feng Su. New York: Springer.
Mok, Ka Ho, and Cheung, Bing Leung Anthony. 2011. "Global Aspirations and Strategizing for World-Class Status: New Forms of Politics in Higher Education Governance in Hong Kong." *Journal of Higher Education Policy and Management* 33(3): 231–251.
Mok, Ka Ho; Deem, Rosemary; and Lisa Lucas. 2008. "Transforming Higher Education in Whose Image? Exploring the Concept of the World-Class University in Europe and Asia." *Higher Education Policy* 21:83–97.
Mok, Ka Ho, and Green, Andy. 2013. "Expansion of Higher Education, Changing Labor Market Needs and Social Mobility: A Dialogue between Europe and East Asia." Paper presented at the Hong Kong Educational Research Association Annual Conference 2012–13, Hong Kong Institute of Education, 22 February.
Mok, Ka Ho, and Hawkins, John N. 2010. "The Quest for World-Class Status: Globalisation and Higher Education in East Asia." In *Higher Education and Equality of Opportunities*, ed. Fred Lazin, Matt Evans, and N. Jayaram. Lanham, MD: Rowan & Littlefield.
Mok, Kan Ho, and Kan, Y. 2013. "Promoting Entrepreneurship and Innovation in China: Enhancing Research and Transforming University Curriculum." *Frontiers of Education in China* 8(1): 173–197.
Mok, Ka Ho, and Lee, Michael H. 2003. "Globalization or Glocalization? Higher Education Reforms in Singapore." *Asia Pacific Journal of Education* 23(1): 15–42.
Mok, Ka Ho, and Ong, Kok Chung. 2011. "Transforming from Economic Power to Soft Power: Transnationalization and Internationalization of Higher Education in

China." In *The Emergent Knowledge Society and the Future of Higher Education: Asian Perspectives*, ed. D. Neubauer. London: Routledge.
Mok, Ka Ho, and Ong, Kok Chung. 2012. "Asserting Brain Power and Expanding Education Services: Searching for New Governance and Regulatory Regimes in Singapore, Hong Kong and Malaysia." In *The Emerging Knowledge Economy and the Future of Higher Education: Asian Perspectives*, ed. Deane E. Neubauer. London: Routledge.
Mok, Ka Ho, and Tan, Jason. 2004. *Globalization and Marketization in Education: A Comparative Analysis of Hong Kong and Singapore*. Cheltenham, UK: Edward Elgar.
Mok, Ka Ho, and Welch, Anthony. 2003. *Globalization and Educational Restructuring in the Asia Pacific Region*. Basingstoke, Hampshire: Palgrave Macmillan.
Mok, Ka Ho, and Yu, Kar Ming. 2012. *Managing Human Capital in East Asia: Internationalization, Student Mobility and Educational Governance*. London: Routledge.
Mok, Ka Ho; Yu, Kar Ming; and Ku, Y. W. 2013. "After Massification of Higher Education: The Quest for Entrepreneurial University and Technological Advancement in Taiwan." *Journal of Higher Education Policy and Management*, in press.
Moon, Mugyeong, and Kim, Ki Seok. 2001. "A Case of Korean Higher Education Reform: The Brain Korea 21 Project." *Asia Pacific Education Review* 2(2): 96–105.
Moran, Michael. 2002. "Review Article: Understanding the Regulatory State." *British Journal of Political Science* 32:391–413.
Morshidi, Sirat. 2009a. "Internationalization and the Commercialization of Research Output of Universities: Emerging Issues in Malaysian Higher Education 2006–2010." Paper presented at the Regional Conference on Comparative Education and Development in Asia, National Chung Cheng University, Taiwan, 24–25 September.
Morshidi, Sirat. 2009b. "Strategic Planning Directions of Malaysia's Higher Education: University Autonomy in the Midst of Political Uncertainties." *Higher Education* 59(4): 461–473.
Morshidi, Sirat, and Abdul Razak, Ahmad. 2009. "University Governance Structure in Challenging Times: The Case of Malaysia's first APEX University (Universiti Sains Malaysia)." In *The Search for New Higher Education Governance in Asia*, ed. K. H. Mok. New York: Palgrave.
MOST and MOE. 2011. "The Outline of the Twelfth Five-Year Plan for National University Science Park." http://www.most.gov.cn/tztg/201108/ t20110817_89091.htm.
Nanyang Technological University. 2007. "Annual Report 2007." http://www.ntu.edu.sg/AboutNTU/Documents/NTU_AR_07_full_report.pdf.
Nanyang Technological University. 2008. "Annual Report 2008." http://www.ntu.edu.sg/AboutNTU/Documents/annual_report_2008.pdf.
Nanyang Technological University. 2009a "Annual Report 2009." http://www.ntu.edu.sg/AboutNTU/Documents/NTU%20Annual%20Report%202009.pdf.
Nanyang Technological University. 2009b. "Research Report 2009." http://research.ntu.edu.sg/News/Documents/Research%20Report/Research%20Report%20 2009.pdf.
National Science Foundation. 2007. "Asia's Rising Science and Technology Strength: Comparative Indicators for Asia, the European Union, and the United States." http://www.nsf.gov/statistics/nsf07319/pdf/nsf07319.pdf.

Nelson, Richard R. 1993. *National Innovation Systems: A Comparative Analysis.* New York: Oxford University Press.
Nelson, Richard R. 2012. "Introduction." In *The Global University,* ed. Adam R. Nelson and Ian. P. Wei. New York: Palgrave Macmillan.
Nelson, Adam R., and Wei, Ian. P. 2012. *The Global University: Past, Present and Future Perspectives.* New York: Palgrave Macmillan.
Neubauer, Deane E. 2006. "On the Public Good." Paper presented at the senior seminar, Education for 2020 Project of East-West Center, Hawaii, US, 6–12 September.
Neubauer, Deane E. 2013. "Introduction." In *Dynamics of Higher Education Development,* ed. Deane E. Neubauer, Jung Cheol Shin, and John N. Hawkins. New York: Palgrave Macmillan.
Newson, Janice. 1998. "The Corporate-Linked University: From Social Project to Market Force." *Canadian Journal of Communication* 23(1). http://www.cjc-online. ca/index.php/journal/article/viewArticle/1026/932.
Ng, Pak Tee, and Chan, David. 2006. "A Comparative Study of Singapore's School Excellence Model with Hong Kong's School-Based Management." Paper presented at the Asia Pacific Educational Research Association 2006 International Conference, Hong Kong, 28–30 November.
Ngok, King Lun, and Guo, Wei Qing. 2007. "The Quest for World Class Universities in China: Critical Reflections." *Journal of Comparative Asian Development* 6(1): 21–44.
NSC, Republic of China. 2001. *Abstract of National Science and Technology Development Plan (2001–2004).* Taipei: Author.
NSC, Republic of China. 2003. *White Paper on Science and Technology: Visions and Strategies for the Development of Science and Technology (2003–2006) (Executive Summary).* Taipei: Author.
NSC, Republic of China. 2005. *National Science and Technology Plan (2005 to 2008).* Taipei: Author.
Oba, Jun. 2006. "Incorporation of National Universities in Japan and Its Impact upon Institutional Governance." Paper presented at the International Workshop on University Restructuring in Asia, Hiroshima, Japan, 16 January 2006.
OECD. 1998. "Technology, Productivity and Job Creation: Best Policy Practices." http://www.oecd.org/industry/ind/2759012.pdf.
OECD. 1999. "Managing National Innovation Systems." http://echo.iat.sfu.ca/library/ oecd99_managing_National_IS.pdf.
OECD. 2009. *Education at a Glance.* Paris: OECD.
OECD. 2010. "Ministerial Report on the OECD Innovation Strategy." http://ebook-browse.com/ministerial-report-on-oecd-innovation-strategy-pdf-d158985533.
Olsen, Johan P., and Gornitzka, Ase. 2006. "Making Sense of Change in University Governance." *IAU Horizons* 11.4–12.1: 1–3.
Olssen, Mark, and Peters, Michael A. 2005. "Neoliberalism, Higher Education and the Knowledge Economy: From the Free Market to Knowledge Capitalism." *Journal of Education Policy* 20(3): 313–345.
Organization for Economic Cooperation and Development [OECD]. 1998. "Technology, Productivity and Job Creation: Best Policy Practices." http://www. oecd.org/industry/ind/2759012.pdf.
Pal, Leslie Alexander. 1997. *Beyond Policy Analysis: Public Issue Management in Turbulent Times.* Scarborough: International Thomson.

Perkmann, Markus, and Walsh, Kathryn. 2007. "University-Industry Relationships and Open Innovation: Towards a Research Agenda." *International Journal of Management Reviews* 9(4): 259–280.

Peterson, Carole J., and Currie, Jan. 2007. "Higher Education Restructuring and Academic Freedom in Hong Kong." *Journal of Comparative Asian Development* 6(1): 1–21.

Polanyi, Michael. 1975. *Personal Knowledge towards a Post-Critical Philosophy*. Chicago: University of Chicago Press.

Porter, Michael. 2008. "Why America Needs an Economic Strategy." *Bloomberg Businessweek*. http://www.businessweek.com/magazine/content/08_45/b41070382 17112.htm.

Research Center of Chinese Scientific Evaluation of Wuhan University. 2005. *How Do We Rank the Scientific Research Competition of the World Universities?* Wuhan: China, Research Center of Chinese Scientific Evaluation of Wuhan University.

Research Grants Council. 2009. "Postgraduate Research Fellowship Scheme." *Research Frontiers*, no. 16. http://cerg1.ugc.edu.hk/hkpfs/rgc.news.090216en.pdf.

Research Institute of Higher Education and University Evaluation. 2005. *University Rankings in Taiwan*. Taipei: Tamkang University.

Rivza, Baiba, and Teichler, Ulrich. 2007. "The Changing Role of Student Mobility." *Higher Education Policy* 20(4): 457–475.

Robertson, Susan L. 2010. "Critical Response to Special Section: International Academic Mobility." *Discourse* 31(5): 641–647.

Rodrigo, G. Chris. 2001. *Technology, Economic Growth and Crises in East Asia*. Northampton, MA: Edward Elgar.

Rodrik, Dani. 1997. *Has Globalization Gone Too Far?* Washington, DC: Institute for International Economics.

Sagintayeva Aida and Kurakbayev Kairat. 2013. "Internationalization of Higher Education in Central Asia: The Case of Kazakhstan." In *Going Global: Identifying Trends and Drivers of International Education*, ed. Mary Stiasny and Tim Gore (pp. 17–27). UK: Emerald Group Publishing.

Schirato, Tony, and Webb, Jen. 2003. *Understanding Globalization*. London: Sage.

Science and Technology Commission of Shanghai Municipality [STCSM]. 2005. "The Regulation on Shanghai Technology Entrepreneurship Foundation for Graduates (Trial)." http://www.stcsm.gov.cn/structure/x xgk/zcfg/gfxwj_info_zwzy3681_ 1.htm.

Scott, Colin. 2004. "Regulation in the Age of Governance: The Rise of the Post-regulatory State." In *The Politics of Regulation: Institutions and Regulatory Reforms for the Age of Governance*, ed. Jacint Jordana and David Levi-Faur (pp. 145–176). Cheltenham: Edward Elgar.

Segal, A. 2003. *Digital Dragon: High-technology Enterprises in China*. Ithaca, NY: Cornell University Press.

Shanghai Technology Entrepreneurship Foundation for Graduates [STEFG]. 2012. "Statistics." http://www.stefg.org.

Shapiro, Matthew. 2007. "The Triple Helix Paradigm in Korea: A Test for New Forms of Capital." *International Journal of Technology Management and Sustainable Development* 6(3): 171–191.

Sharif, Naubahar, and Baark, Erik. 2008. "Mobilizing Technology Transfer from University to Industry." *Journal of Technology Management in China* 3(1): 47–65.

Shields, Robin, and Edwards, Rebecca M. 2010. "Student Mobility and Emerging Hubs in Global Higher Education." In *Higher Education, Policy, and the Global Competition Phenomenon*, ed. Laura M. Portnoi, Val D. Rust, and Sylvia S. Bagley (pp. 235–248). New York: Palgrave Macmillan.
Singapore Economic Development Board. 2003. *Annual Report 2002/03*. Singapore: Economic Development Board.
Singapore Economic Development Board. 2004. *Annual Report 2003/04*. Singapore: Economic Development Board.
Singapore Economic Development Board. 2006. *Annual Report 2005/06*. Singapore: Economic Development Board.
Singapore Management University [SMU]. 2009. SMU Launches Institute of Innovation and Entrepreneurship. http://www.smu.edu.sg/news_room/smuhub/oct2009/academe4.asp.
Singapore Management University [SMU]. 2010. SMU Reports to Stakeholders 2009–2010. http://www.docstoc.com/docs/107456416/SINGAPORE-MAN-A-GEMENT-UNIVERSITY-Rep-ort-to-Stakeh-old-ers-2009–2010.
Skelcher, Chris; Navdeep, Mathur; and Smith, Mike. 2004. *Effective Partnership and Good Governance: Lessons for Policy and Practice*. Birmingham: School of Public Policy, University of Birmingham.
Slaughter, Sheila, and Leslie, Larry L. 1997. *Academic Capitalism: Politics, Policies, and the Entrepreneurial University*. Baltimore, MD: Johns Hopkins University Press.
Slaughter, Sheila, and Rhodes, Gary. 2004. *Academic Capitalism and the New Economy: Markets, State, and Higher Education*. Baltimore, MD: Johns Hopkins University Press.
Small and Medium Business Association, South Korea. 2009. *SMBA Annual Report*. South Korea: Seoul Regional Small and Medium Business Association.
Song, Mei Mei, and Tai, Hsiou Hsia. 2007. "Taiwan's Responses to Globalization: Internationalization and Questing for World Glass Universities." *Asia Pacific Journal of Education* 27(3): 323–340.
State Council, People's Republic of China. 2003. Regulations of the People's Republic of China on Chinese-Foreign Cooperation in Running Schools. http://www.jsj.edu.cn.
State Council, People's Republic of China. 2010. *Outline for National Educational Development*. Beijing: State Council.
State Education Commission [SEC]. 1995. Interim Provisions for Chinese-Foreign Cooperation in Running Schools. http://www.jsj.edu.cn.
Stiglitz, Joseph E. 1996. "Some Lessons from the East Asian Miracle." *World Bank Research Observer* 11(2): 151–177.
Stiglitz, Joseph E. 2002. *Globalization and Its Discontents*. New York: Norton.
Stiglitz, Joseph E., and Yusuf, Shahid. 2001. *Rethinking the East Asian Miracle*. Washington, DC: World Bank; New York: Oxford University Press.
Tan, Charlene, and Ng, Pak Tee. 2007. "Dynamics of Change: Decentralized Centralism of Education in Singapore." *Journal of Educational Change* 8(2): 155–168.
Tsang, Donald Yam Kuen, 2007. *The 2007–2008 Policy Address: A New Direction for Hong Kong*. Hong Kong: Government Printer.
Tsang, Donald Yam Kuen. 2009. *The 2008–09 Policy Address*. Hong Kong: Hong Kong SAR Government.
Tsui-Auch, Lai Si. 1998. "Has the Hong Kong Model Worked? Industrial Policy in Retrospect and Prospect." *Development and Change* 29(1): 55–79.

Turk, James. 2000. *The Corporate Campus: Commercialization and the Dangers to Canadas Colleges and University*. Toronto: Lorimer.
UNESCO. 1998. "Higher Education in the Twenty-First Century: Vision and Action." Declaration adopted at the World Conference on Higher Education, Paris, 5–9 October.
UNESCO. 2009. "2009 World Conference on Higher Education: The New Dynamics of Higher Education and Research for Societal Change and Development." Communiqué adopted at the World Conference on Higher Education, Paris, 5–8 July.
UNESCO/Council of Europe. 2001. *Code of Good Practice in the Provision of Transnational Education*. Riga, Latvia: UNESCO-CEPES.
University of Hong Kong. 2011. *Recurrent Funding for Knowledge Transfer in the 2009/10 to 2011/12 Triennium, Annual Report 2010/11*. Hong Kong: University of Hong Kong.
Viale, Riccardo, and Etzkowitz, Henry. 2010. *The Capitalization of Knowledge: A Triple Helix of University-Industry-Government*. Cheltenham: Edward Elgar.
Vogel, Ezra F. 1991. *The Four Little Dragons: The Spread of Industrialization in East Asia*. Cambridge, MA: Harvard University Press.
Wade, Robert. 2004. *Governing the Market: Economic Theory and the Role of Government in East Asian Industrialization*. Princeton, NJ: Princeton University Press.
Walters, Colin. 2013. "Australian International Education in 2012: A Focus on Quality and a Long-Term Strategy." In *Going Global: Identifying Trends and Drivers of International Education*, ed. Mary Stiasny and Tim Gore (pp. 29–39). UK: Emerald Group Publishing.
Wan Abdul Manan, Wan Muda. 2008. "The Malaysian National Higher Education Action Plan: Redefining Autonomy and Academic Freedom under the APEX Experiment." Paper presented at the ASAIHL Conference – University Autonomy: Interpretation and Variation, Universiti Sains Malaysia, Penang, Malaysia, 12–14 December.
Wang, D. G., and Liu, X. 2010. *Achievements of Higher Education Development in China in the Last Three Decades*. Beijing: Beijing Normal University Press.
Wang, Jian Bo. 2005. *Transnational Higher Education and SFCRS* (in Chinese). Jinan City: Shandong Education Press.
Washburn, Jennifer. 2005. *University, Inc.: The Corporate Corruption of American Higher Education*. New York: Basic Books.
Watson, David. 2006. "UK Higher Education: The Truth about the Student Market." *Higher Education Review* 38(3): 3–16.
Welch, Anthony. 2007. "Governance Issues in South East Asian Higher Education: Finance, Devolution and Transparency in the Global Era." *Asia Pacific Journal of Education* 27(3): 237–254.
Welch, Anthony, and Mok, Ka Ho. 2003. "Conclusion: Deep Development or Deep Division?" In *Globalization and Educational Restructuring in the Asia Pacific Region*, ed. Ka Ho Mok and Anthony Welch (pp. 333–356). Basingstoke: Palgrave Macmillan.
White, Geoffry D, and Hauck, Flannery C. 2000. *Campus, Inc.: Corporate Power in the Ivory Tower*. Amherst, NY: Prometheus Books.
Wong, Poh Kam. 2011. *Academic Entrepreneurship in Asia: The Role and Impact of Universities in National Innovation Systems*. Cheltenham: Edward Elgar.

Wong, Poh Kam, et al. 2007. "Towards an Entrepreneurial University Model to Support Knowledge-Based Economic Development: The Case of the National University of Singapore." *World Development* 35(6): 941–958.
Wong, Poh Kam; Ho, Yuen Ping; and Singh, Annette. 2011. "Towards a Global Knowledge Enterprise: The Entrepreneurial University Model of National University of Singapore." In *Academic Entrepreneurship in Asia: The Role and Impact of Universities in National Innovation Systems*, ed. Poh Kam Wong. UK: Edward Elgar.
World Bank. 2002a. *Building Knowledge Societies: Opportunities and Challenges for EU Accession Countries*. Washington, DC: World Bank.
World Bank. 2002b. *Constructing Knowledge Economies: New Challenges for Tertiary Education*. Washington, DC: World Bank.
World Bank. 2007. *Malaysia and the Knowledge Economy: Building a World-Class Higher Education System (Report No. 40397-MY)*. New York: Human Development Sector, East Asia and Pacific Region, the World Bank.
World Bank. 2009. *Accelerating Catch-Up: Tertiary Education for Growth in Sub-Saharan Africa*. Washington, DC: World Bank.
World Bank. 2012. *Putting Higher Education to Work: Skills and Research for Growth in East Asia*. Washington, DC: World Bank.
World Economic Forum [WEF]. 2009. *Educating the Next Wave of Entrepreneurs: Unlocking Entrepreneurial Capabilities to Meet the Global Challenges of the 21st Century: A Report of the Global Education Initiative*. Geneva: WEF.
Wride, Alison. 2008. "A Career in Higher Education: Inspiration, Opportunity, Strategy, Luck?" *Engage* 15 (Autumn): 6–7.
Yang, Rui. 2002. *The Third Delight: Internationalization of Higher Education in China*. London: Routledge.
Yang, Rui. 2005. "Globalization and Higher Education Restructuring: Issues and Debates." In *Globalization and Higher Education in East Asia*, ed. Ka Ho Mok and Richard James. Singapore and New York: Marshall Cavendish Academic.
Yang, Rui. 2006. "Transnational Higher Education in Hong Kong: An Analysis." In *Transnational Higher Education in Asia and the Pacific Region*, ed. Futao Huang (pp. 41–67). Hiroshima, Japan: Research Institute for Higher Education, Hiroshima University.
Yeh, Anthony Gar On, and Ng, Mei Kam. 1994. "The Changing Role of the State in High-Tech Industrial Development: The Experience of Hong Kong." *Environment and Planning C: Government and Policy* 12(4): 449–472.
Yonezawa, Akiyoshi. 2006. "Japanese Flagship Universities at a Crossroads." In *Final Report of Developing Evaluation Criteria to Assess the Internationalization of Universities*, ed. Norio Furushiro (pp. 85–102). Kwansei, Japan: Osaka University.
Yonezawa, Akiyoshi. 2007. "Japanese Flagship Universities at a Crossroads." *Higher Education* 54(4): 483–499. http://link.springer.com/article/10.1007%2Fs10734-006-9028-2#.
Young, Alwyn. 1995. "The Tyranny of Numbers: Confronting the Statistical Realities of the East Asian Growth Experience." *Quarterly Journal of Economics* 110(3): 641–680.
Yusuf, Shahid, and Nabeshima, Kaoru. 2007. *How Universities Promote Economic Growth*. Washington, DC: World Bank.
Zaharia, Sorin E., and Gilbert, Ernest. 2005. "The Entrepreneurial University in the Knowledge Society." *Higher Education in Europe* 30(1): 31–40.

Zhang, Xiao Peng. 2005. "A Comparative Study of Mainland Chinese and Foreign Cooperation in Running Schools and Non-local Courses in Hong Kong Regulations" (in Chinese). *Education Journal* 33(1–2): 125–147.

Zhejiang University. 2006. *A Report on the First Session of the International Academic Advisory Committee for University Evaluation.* Hangzhou, China: Zhejiang University.

Zheng, Lin. 2009. "Chinese Universities' Motivations in Transnational Higher Education and Their Implications for Higher Education Marketisation." In *Internationalising the University: The Chinese Context*, ed. Tricia Coverdale-Jones and Paul Rastall. Basingstoke, England: Palgrave Macmillan.

Ziguras, Christopher. 2003. "The Impact of the GATS on Transnational Tertiary Education: Comparing Experiences of New Zealand, Australia, Singapore, and Malaysia." *Australian Educational Researcher* 30(3): 89–109.

ZUNSP. 2012. Annual Report of Zhjiang University National Science Park. Hangzhou: Zhejiang University.

About the Author

Professor Ka Ho Mok is chair professor of comparative policy, concurrently acting vice president (research and development) and associate vice president (research and international exchange) of the Hong Kong Institute of Education (HKIEd). From 2010, he has been appointed by the Ministry of Education, People's Republic of China, as Changjiang Chair Professor of Zhejiang University, a national chair professorship in China conferred to distinguished scholars.

Before joining the HKIEd, he was associate dean and professor of social policy, Faculty of Social Sciences, University of Hong Kong (HKU). Being appointed as founding chair professor in East Asian studies, Professor Mok established the Centre for East Asian Studies at the University of Bristol, UK, before taking the position at HKU. Professor Mok is no narrow disciplinary specialist but has worked creatively across the academic worlds of sociology, political science, and public and social policy while building up his wide knowledge of China and the region.

Professor Mok has published extensively in the fields of comparative education policy, comparative development and policy studies, and social development in contemporary China and East Asia. In particular, he has contributed to the field of social change and education in a variety of additional ways, not the least of which has been his leadership and entrepreneurial approach to the organization of the field. His memberships on numerous editorial boards and commissions and in key scholarly societies all contribute to the recognition that he is among the best in his field. He is a founding editor of the *Journal of Asian Public Policy* and the Comparative Development and Policy in Asia Book Series (published by Routledge, Taylor & Francis Group), as well as editor-in-chief of *Asian Education and Development Studies* (published by Emerald).

In the last few years, Professor Mok has also worked closely with the World Bank and UNICEF as international consultant for comparative development and policy studies projects. He was also a part-time member of the Central Policy Unit, the HKSAR government. He also serves as a member of the Research Grant Council and the Public Policy Research Committee of the Central Policy Unit of the HKSAR government.

Index

211 Project, 7, 11, 95, 96, 98, 158, 208
21st Century Frontier R&D Program, 48
577 Initiative, 50
836 Program, 93
863 Program, 99, 100
973 Program, 102
985 Project, 7, 95–8, 158, 211

Academia Sinica, 68
academic capitalism, 212, 213
academic consumerism, 213
Academic Degrees Committee of the State Council (ADCSC), 141
academic entrepreneurship, 2, 82, 213
Academic Excellence Project, 208
academic freedom, 11, 84, 211, 214, 215, 216
academic lifestyle in Asia, 210
academic research and knowledge creation hub in the Asia-Pacific region, 64
Accelerated Program for Excellence (APEX), 132
Action Plan for Building a Technologically Advanced Nation, 63
Adam Nelson, 221, 222
Adrian Yeo, 87
advanced RFIC Pte. Ltd., 86
Advanced Technology Service Enterprise, 106
Advanced technology, 3, 106
A*GA's Youth Science Program, 79

Agency for Science, Technology and Research (A*STAR), 78, 79, 88, 136
Agensi Kelayakan Malaysia, 131
agent institution, 172
agricultural preproduction, 101
agroproduct, 101
All China Youth Federation (ACYF), 113
Amendment of Basic Law, 215
America, 5, 13, 14, 20- 24, 27–9, 42, 57, 67, 72, 87, 110, 113, 146, 148, 153–6, 179, 202, 206, 207, 213, 219–21
American Purdue University, 57
American Society for Quality, 155
American students, 207
American University of Beirut, 206
Americanization, 220
Angel Investors Tax Deduction Scheme (AITD), 81
Anglo-American, 219
Anglo-Chinese School International, 129
Anglo-Saxon, 210, 217, 220, 222
Anhui University, 110
Anhui, 96, 99
Anti-Indian movement, 168
Areas of Excellence Scheme, 45
Asia Entrepreneur Center, 65
Asian countries, 13, 17, 20, 22, 24, 26, 27, 29, 67, 209, 210, 211, 219, 220
Asian financial crisis, 14, 15, 19, 33, 48, 50, 63, 64, 75, 76, 117, 125, 193, 215

Asian Four Little Dragons/Tigers, 24, 28
Asian governments, 6, 22, 23, 139, 209, 223
Asian Miracles, 75
Asian Scientist, 107
Asian societies, 2, 8, 12, 21, 121, 122, 125, 161, 162, 167, 193, 194, 196, 201, 208, 214, 220
Asian Traditions, 218, 220
Asian universities, 6, 12, 13, 14, 202, 208, 209, 210, 211, 212, 217, 218, 220, 221, 222
Asian University Ranking, 12
Asia-Pacific region, 14, 15, 17, 64, 121, 192
Assist Service Sector Technology Development Plan, 64
Associate Vice President for Research and Innovation (AVP-RI), 42
Association of Southeast Asian Nations (ASEAN), 167, 185
Australia, 6, 14, 72, 123, 124, 127, 129, 131, 140, 145, 154, 166, 168, 169, 172, 173, 208, 220
authoritarian liberalism, 5, 192
authoritarian mode of liberalism, 5
Automotive Parts and Accessory Systems R&D Centre (APAS), 37

Bangalore, 13
Bangladeshi, 175
Bar-Ilan University, 205
Bayh-Dole Act, 63
Beida-Harvard Exchange Camp, 147
Beihang University, 97
Beijing Institute of Technology, 97
Beijing Normal University, 97, 157, 164, 177, 178
Beijing Normal University-Hong Kong Baptist University United International College, 164, 177, 178
Beijing University, 11
Belgian, 173, 174, 175

Belgium, 72, 151, 174
Bertil Anderson, 87
big science, 50
Bilkent University, 204
Biomedical Sciences Accelerator (BSA), 80
Biopolis, 78
biotechnology, 35, 61, 62, 65, 69, 71, 76, 93
Boqazici University, 205
borderless world, 3, 13
borderless world economy, 3
Bosch Group, 86
Brain Korea 21 Project (BK21), 52–4
branch campus, 12, 83, 121, 123–5, 128, 136, 146, 156, 157, 166, 167, 178–82, 184–6, 193
brand name effect, 184, 185
Brendan Orner, 87
Britain, 24, 208
British colony, 20, 24
British Council, 14
British rulers, 34
Business Angel Scheme (BAS), 80
Business Corporation Model, 6
Business Plan Competition (BPC), 85, 111, 112, 113, 116, 231

C. Y. Leung, 127, 198
C9 League, 96, 98, 99
Cambodia, 27
Cambridge, 148
Campus for Research Excellence and Technological Enterprise (CREATE), 81
campus inc., 212
Canada, 10, 35, 127, 149, 155, 168, 172, 208
Cancer Science Institute Singapore (CSI), 82
capitalization of knowledge, 212
Carole Peterson, 215
Case Western Reserve University, 151
cash cow, 50

Index

The Center of Chinese and Japanese Studies (CCJS), 149
Center of Excellence program in Japan, 211
Central Committee of the Communist Young League (CCYL), 113
Central Communist Youth League, 111
Central Europe, 10, 218
Central South University, 97
Central Taiwan Science Park, 60, 61, 63
Centralized decentralization, 214
Centralized governance, 7, 214
Centre for Innovation and Technology (CINTEC), 41
Centre for Quantum Technologies (CQT), 82
chaebols (big corporations), 47, 50
The Challenge Cup, 110
Cheung Kong Graduate School of Business, 145
Chiba University, 206
China, 2, 7, 9, 10, 11, 14–17, 20, 24, 26–8, 33, 35, 36, 39, 42–5, 63, 64, 70, 85, 91–100, 102–5, 107, 109–17, 125–7, 139–43, 145–51, 155–68, 172, 177–81, 183–7, 189, 196, 203–8, 210–11
China Association of Science and Technology (CAST), 113
China Medical University, 206
China-UK Graduate Work Experience Programme, 111
Chinese Academy of Sciences (CAS), 44
Chinese Agricultural University, 97
Chinese Communist Party (CCP), 7, 115, 157
Chinese Fever, 151
Chinese government, 7, 11, 43–4, 91–2, 94–5, 104–6, 111–12, 114–17, 141–2, 146–7, 159–60
Chinese students, 39, 111, 146, 148, 179, 181, 207
Chinese University of Hong Kong (CUHK), 34–5, 41, 203–4
Chinese-Foreign Cooperation in Running Schools (CFCRS), 140, 141, 142, 143, 144, 145, 155, 156, 157, 158, 177, 178, 179, 180, 181, 182, 184, 186
Chongqing University, 98
Christopher Ngoi, 87
Chulalongkorn University, 206
Chung Yuan Christian University, 206
Chung-Ang University, 206
City University of Hong Kong (CityU), 39, 162, 187, 203–4
City-state, 6, 10, 12, 21, 34, 37–8, 45–6, 78, 82–3, 89, 125, 128–9, 135–6, 169, 185, 193, 198
Clearbridge BSA Pte. Ltd., 80
CLEVO, 72
Coe College, 151
coercive isomorphism, 222
cohort participation rate (CPR), 84
Cold War, 221–2
Collaborative Research Fund, 45
College of Education, 11
College of International Education, 164, 177, 183
Commercial spin-offs, 93, 201
Commercialization, 27, 33, 37, 38, 40, 42, 60, 77, 84–6, 89, 94, 118, 209, 217
Committee on University Expansion Pathways beyond 2015 (CUEP), 84
commodification, 216
Common World Education Culture (CWEC), 216
Communist Party, 7, 24, 115
competition states, 4
Competitive Research Program (CRP), 81
Contract Program, 56
Conventional Industry Technology Development Initiative, 64
Cornell University, 149
corporate campus, 212

Corporate University of LG Electronics, 56
corporate university, 52, 56
corporate-linked university, 212
corporatization, 4, 6–8, 118, 128, 132, 214–15, 217, 219
Cosmos Bank, 72
cost competition, 16, 17
credit bank system, 52
cross-border education, 122
cross-border higher education collaboration, 43
cross-university research centers, 10
CUHK Open Innovation Network (COIN), 41
cultural imperialism, 222
Cultural Revolution, 92, 151
Curtin University, 123
customer-focused business enterprises, 6
cyber-university, 52

Daegu Gyeongbuk Institute of Science and Technology (DGIST), 55
Dalian University of Technology, 97, 206
Dalian, 156
Dani Rodrik, 208
David Birch, 108
David Cheng, 187
DBS Bank, 72
decentralization in university governance, 214
decentralized centralism, 135
decolonized, 220
defensive modernization, 196
Deloitte Touche Tohmatsu Ltd., 72
Deng Xiaoping, 93, 99
Deng Yongqiang, 110
Denmark, 28
Department of Education and Skills (DfES), 111
dependency culture, 220
deregulation, 4, 8, 49, 192

developed economies, 14–15, 19–20, 24–5, 208–9
developing economies, 14, 208
Development Program of Industrialization for Agricultural Biotechnology, 69
Diamond Project, 71
DigiPen Institute of Technology, 128
Digital Taylorism, 16
disparity between universities, 209
Division of Intellectual Property and Technology Licensing, 72
divisions between the North and the South, 209
Donald Tsang, 126
Donghua University, 73
Drexel University, 155
dual degree, 121, 144, 154
dualistic state, 5
Duan Huaqia, 110
DuPont, 43
duty-free policy, 60

Eagle Scheme, 111
Earth Observatory of Singapore (EOS), 82
East Asia, 2, 4, 8, 10, 12–13, 15–17, 19, 21, 22, 25–9, 59–60, 114, 117–18, 191, 194, 199, 201–2, 207, 209, 216–19, 221
East Asian countries, 26, 219
East Asian financial crisis, 215
East Asian Miracle, 20, 25
East Asian States, 8, 19, 29, 219
East Asian students, 202, 207
East Asian Tigers, 9, 15, 19, 25, 28
East Asian universities, 217–18
East China Normal University (ECNU), 98, 164, 165, 177, 181
Eastern Europe, 78
EC Harris, 111
Eco-car, 87
economic determinism, 21–2

Economic Development Board (EDB), 77, 79, 83, 86, 128, 129, 167
economic globalization, 221
economic interdependence, 3
economic nationalism, 194
economic rationalism, 5, 7
economic savior, 3
Education Bureau (EDB), 127, 134
education factory, 89–90
education market, 128, 135, 139, 141, 175, 185
Education Reform Scheme, 51
education reforms, 51, 65
educational entrepreneurs, 195
educational services, 126, 133, 143, 195, 197
Egypt, 124
Eight UGC-funded Institutions, 134
emerging economies, 14
emerging global model, 22, 222
Engineering Index (EI), 71
England, 168, 218, 219
entrepreneurial activities, 2, 8, 9, 17, 27, 28, 38, 40, 41, 47, 48, 71, 84, 111, 201
entrepreneurial institutions, 7
Entrepreneurial Universities, 9, 19, 22, 31, 59, 65, 68, 71, 75, 118, 201, 202, 212, 216
entrepreneurialism, 91, 113, 115, 116, 217
Entrepreneurship Academy, 40
entrepreneurship education, 40, 73, 87, 88, 108, 109, 110, 111, 112, 114, 116
ESSEC Business School of France, 166
ESSEC IRENE Business School, 129
EU27, 16
Europe (EU), 10, 13, 14, 15–17, 20, 22, 27, 28, 29, 35, 43, 67, 78, 149, 167, 202, 218, 220, 221
European Aeronautic Defence and Space Company, 86
European Commission, 218

European universities, 218
Eurozone, 16
Ewing Marion Kauffman Foundation, 87
Ex-colonies of the United Kingdom, 21
Executive Yuan, 10, 60, 63, 67
Expand Your Business (EYB), 112
experiential learning, 57, 89, 111
Expert Park, 57
Eyas Scheme, 111

Feng Chia University, 206
Finance College, 65
finance-centered economy, 33
financial capital, 22, 142
Finland, 28
firm-led approach, 21
First and Second World Wars, 20, 24
Five-Year Plan, 44, 88, 95, 99, 100, 101, 102, 105, 106, 160
Five-Year S&T Principal Plan, 48
Flagship Project, 208
Flagship University, 8
Fok Ying Tung Graduate School, 44
foreign direct investment (FDI), 25, 27, 60, 75
Foreign R&D Human Resource Development Program, 49
foreign students, 17, 39, 68, 83, 127, 130, 131, 147, 148, 151, 166, 184, 185
foreign-invested companies, 105
foreign-invested enterprises, 92, 106
Formula Grant Project for Enhanced Higher Education Capacity, 54
Fort Hays State University of Kansas, 156
Foshan, 44
Four East Asian Tigers, 9, 19
Four Little Dragons, 12, 24, 27, 28, 82, 117, 202
France, 15, 72, 151, 155, 166, 181, 208

free market, 5, 24, 25, 133, 134, 176, 193
free trade, 4
French Trade Commission, 72
Fudan University, 96, 97, 99, 204
Fundamental Science and Technology Act, 63
Funding Research Diversity, 218
Fusionopolis, 78

General Agreement on Trade in Services (GATS), 135, 141, 191
General Knowledge College, 65
General Research Fund (GRF), 45
Generate Your Business (GYB), 112
Geneva, 87
George Mason University, 155
Georgia Institute of Technology, 83
German "grammar+career" two-track system, 89
Germany, 15, 29, 149, 208, 218
global auction, 16, 17
global cities, 222, 223
Global Climate Solution Award, 87
global competitiveness indexes, 19, 21, 28, 29
global competitiveness, 4, 10, 13, 19, 20, 21, 28, 29, 58, 73, 95, 201
global development, 221
global economic crisis, 15, 75
global economic integration, 3
global economic system, 2
global economy, 1–3, 114
global financial crisis, 13, 15, 17, 23, 26, 29, 33, 36, 60, 67, 117
global financial tsunami, 126
The Global Institute of Technology, 73
global model of a university, 222
global reform measures, 220
Global Schoolhouse, 83, 84, 125, 128, 135, 137, 192, 194
Global Thin Film Photovoltaic Business/R&D Center, 43

global trendy strategies, 220
global university league, 10–12, 21, 202, 208, 209, 211, 219
global university ranking, 10, 132, 207, 209, 212
globalism, 2
globalization, 1–4, 7, 8, 10, 15, 17, 23, 50, 83, 89, 114, 121, 142, 148, 191, 192, 194, 196, 197, 201, 208, 209, 216, 217, 219, 221, 222
globalizing economy, 2, 17
governed education market, 135
governed market, 141
government-led regime, 21
government-university-industry cooperation centers, 37
Greece, 16
green growth industry, 55
Gross Expenditures on R&D (GERD), 29, 50
Guangdong, 43, 44, 157, 164, 165, 166
Guangzhou Institute of Biomedicine and Health (GIBH), 44
Guangzhou, 15, 43, 44
Gwangju Institute of Science and Technology (GIST), 55

halal foods, 172
Halatuju Report, 123
Hangzhou, 99
Hanyang University, 206
Harbin Institute of Technology, 96, 97, 99, 205
Harbin Normal University (HRBNU), 163, 165, 177
Harbin University of Science and Technology (HUST), 156, 163, 177
Harbin, 99, 156, 157, 163, 166, 177
Harvard, 108, 147, 148
Hebrew University of Jerusalem, 204
Hefei, 99
Heilongjiang, 96, 99, 163, 165, 166
Henan, 164–6, 240
HHT Tech Co., 109

Index

High New Technology Enterprise, 106
High technology, 20, 28, 34, 44, 64, 78, 92, 92
Higher Education Governance, 114, 115, 133, 146, 155, 195
Higher Education Institutions (HEIs), 6, 9, 10, 11, 22, 34, 38–40, 43–6, 52, 54, 67, 83, 89, 95, 98, 108, 109, 112–14, 116, 123–6, 131, 140–2, 144, 157, 158, 160, 162, 165–7, 169–87, 194, 201, 208, 209, 218, 220, 231
higher education systems, 2, 4, 15, 16, 17, 29, 114, 194, 214, 218, 219, 223
high-income countries, 27
high-skill but low-paid jobs, 17
high-skilled labor, 15, 17
high-skilled professional jobs, 16, 17
high-tech enterprises, 104
high-tech manufacturing, 39, 75, 76
high-tech products, 28, 94
Hiroshima University, 205
HKUST LED-FPD Technology R&D Center, 44
HKUST R and D Corporation Ltd., 41, 42
Hokkaido University, 205
Holmes Colleges Australia, 145
Hong Kong Academy for Performing Arts, 38
Hong Kong Applied Science and Technology Research Institute (ASTRI), 35–37, 44
Hong Kong Baptist University (HKBU), 157, 162, 164, 175, 177, 178, 181, 205
Hong Kong Business Angel Network (HKBAN), 35
Hong Kong Council for Academic Accreditation (HKCAA), 133
Hong Kong Council for Accreditation of Academic and Vocational Qualifications (HKCAAVQ), 127, 133, 134
Hong Kong Government, 33, 34, 36–8, 44, 45, 125, 127, 133, 134, 193, 194
Hong Kong (HK), 2, 6, 7, 9–15, 19–21, 24, 25, 27–9, 33–47, 64, 78, 117, 121, 122, 125–8, 131, 133–5, 137, 139, 145, 151, 157, 160–2, 164–6, 169, 175–8, 181, 183, 184, 186–9, 191, 193–8, 202–5, 208, 212, 215, 221, 222
Hong Kong Jockey Club Institute of Chinese Medicine, 37
Hong Kong parents, 188
Hong Kong PhD Fellowship Scheme, 39
The Hong Kong Polytechnic University (PolyU or HKPU), 35, 204
Hong Kong Productivity Council, 36
Hong Kong R&D Centre for Information and Communications Technologies under the Hong Kong Applied Science and Technology Research Institute (ASTRI), 37
Hong Kong R&D Centre for Information and Communications Technologies, 37
Hong Kong R&D Centre for Logistics and Supply Chain Management Enabling Technologies (LSCM), 37
Hong Kong Research Institute of Textiles and Apparel (HKRITA), 37
Hong Kong Science Park, 34, 35, 43
Hong Kong Shue Yan University, 126
Hong Kong University of Science and Technology (HKUST), 13, 35, 41, 42, 44, 203, 204
Hong Kong Venture Capital and Private Equity Association, 35
Hong Kong-Guangdong Stem Cell and Regenerative Medicine Research Centre, 44
Hong Kong-Shenzhen Institute of Research and Innovation, 44

270 INDEX

Hongik University, 57
hot product, 9
HSBC Holdings plc, 72
Hsinchu Science Park, 60, 61, 63, 71
Hsinchu Science-Based Industrial Park, 60
Huawei-HKUST Innovation Laboratory, 42
Huazhong University of Science and Technology, 97, 206
Hub of Technopreneurs, 79
human capital, 23, 39, 52, 55, 68, 87, 109, 115, 142, 187, 201, 213
Human Resource College, 65
Human Resources Development Plan, 49
Hunan University, 98
The Hwaying Education and Culture Foundation, 150
Hynix, 57
hyperglobalists, 2, 3
hyperliberalism, 216

imbalanced tension between research and teaching, 211
incorporatizing, 8
incubated companies, 70
incubated enterprises, 70
Incubation Center Knowledge Service Environment Construction Project, 65
incubator centers, 68
Incubator Development Programme (IDP), 81
India, 9, 13, 15, 72, 85, 86, 125, 167, 168, 169, 172, 173, 204, 205
Indian Institute of Technology Kharagpur, 71
Indian Institute of Technology, Bombay, 204
Indian Institute of Technology, Roorkee, 205
Indian problem, 168
Indonesia, 9, 125, 175, 209

Industrial Technology Development Plan, 64
Industrial Technology Research Institute (ITRI), 60
Industrialization, 20, 24, 25, 47, 59, 60, 69, 75, 94, 100, 101
Industrialization, 20, 24, 25, 47, 59, 60, 69, 75, 94, 100, 101
Industry Collaborative Project scheme, 35
industry-academia cooperation, 68
industry-University Collaboration, 34
information provision/accreditation, 194
Information Technology College, 65
information technology, 1, 36, 44, 65, 71, 76, 77, 78, 103, 124, 129
informatization, 101
Inha University, 206
inno-biz, 49
Innovation and Entrepreneurial Universities, 19, 59, 75
innovation and research development, 33, 34, 46, 59, 60, 201
Innovation and Technology Commission (ITC), 35, 36
Innovation and Technology Fund (ITF), 36, 37, 42
innovation capital, 22
Innovation Incubation Program, 70
innovation system, 1, 27, 34, 36, 38, 39, 42, 47, 48, 64, 77, 79, 91, 117, 243
innovation-oriented country, 94
Innovative Incubation Center, 71
Innovative Local Enterprise Achievement Development (iLEAD) program, 85
Innovative Technology Applications and Services Program, 64
innovative university, 22
Institut Européen d'Administration des Affaires (INSEAD), 83, 128
Institute of Innovation and Entrepreneurship (IIE), 87, 88

Index

The Institute of International Education, 151
Institute of Technical Education, 78, 130
Institutions of the Chinese-Foreign Cooperation in Running Schools (CFCRS), 141–5, 155–8, 177–82, 184, 186
international academic exchanges, 150, 155
International Academic Symposium of Hiromatu Wataru and Marxist Philosophy, 149
International Air Transport Association (IATA), 87
international college, 156, 158
international competitiveness, 11, 66, 100, 101, 202
The International Cultural Festival, 147
International Enterprise Singapore, 129
international exchanges, 103, 220
International Labor Organization (ILO), 108, 109, 113
International Medical University (IMU), 163, 169, 170, 172
International Medical University (IMU), 163, 169, 170, 172, 173, 174
International Monetary Fund (IMF), 216
International Patent Registration (IPR), 100
international standard tests, 202
International Student Exchanges, 140, 146, 187
international student market, 14
international student, 14, 15, 67, 68, 78, 83, 123, 124, 126, 129, 130, 140, 146–8, 150, 172, 173, 185, 187, 192–4
international university ranking, 202, 207, 210
international/world-class standard of universities, 14
internationalization and transnationalization of higher education, 119, 201
internationalization, 12, 60, 94, 119, 121, 122, 142, 172, 181, 187, 189, 201, 207, 216, 220–2
Internationalizing Higher Education, 13, 159, 160
irresistible shift of global power, 13, 24
Isfahan University of Technology, 206
Israel, 85, 204, 205
Istanbul Technical University, 205
ITC internship program, 36
Ivy League, 99

James Cook University (JCU), 163, 167
Jan Currie, 215
Janssen Pharmaceutica, 72
Japan, 7, 8, 9, 12, 13, 17, 24, 26, 27, 28, 29, 147, 149, 151, 202, 203, 204, 205, 206, 207, 208, 211, 214, 215
Japanese government, 7, 12, 25, 214, 215
Japanese students, 207
Japanese-led East Asian developmental model, 25
Jiang Zemin, 95
Jiangsu, 96, 99, 142, 163, 165, 166
Jilin University, 97
Jinan University, 127
Johns Hopkins University, 83, 148
The Johns Hopkins University-Nanjing University Center for Chinese and American Studies, 148
Joint Research Schemes, 45
Jordan, 124
Joseph Stiglitz, 208
JPMorgan, 111
Jun Oba, 214
Juntendo University, 205

Kanazawa University, 206
Kansei University, 208

Kauffman Global Scholars
  Program, 87
Kauffman, 87
Kazakhstan, 57, 58
Kazuhiro Ebuchi, 220
Keio University, 205
King Abdulaziz University, 205
King Fahd University of Petroleum
  and Minerals, 205
King Mongkut's University of
  Technology, Thonburi, 205
King Saud University, 206
Klang Valley, 123
Know about Business (KAB), 112, 113
knowledge capitalism, 212
knowledge economy, 1, 2, 20, 21, 29,
  33, 51, 76, 83
knowledge exchange (KE), 40
knowledge factory, 212
Knowledge Transfer Fund, 41
knowledge transfer, 2, 17, 20–2, 27,
  34, 39–42, 45, 47, 88, 103, 201
Kobe University, 206
Koc University, 204
Konkuk University, 206
Korea Advanced Institute of
  Science and Technology
  (KAIST), 13, 55, 203, 204
Korea Research Foundation, 48, 53
Korean Educational Development
  Institute (KEDI), 53
Kuala Lumpur, 123, 163
Kyoto University, 13, 203, 204
Kyung Hee University, 205
Kyungpook National University,
  57, 206
Kyushu University, 205

La Roche College, 155
laissez-faire, 141–3, 192
land-based capital, 22
Lanzhou University, 98
Lao PDR, 27
leapfrog development, 100

Lee Hsien Loong, 84
Lee Kong Chian School of
  Business, 88
Lee Myung Bak, 50, 57
Lembaga Akreditasi Negara (LAN),
  124, 131
less-developed economies, 14
LG, 56, 57
Li Da Yong, 157
Li Ka Shing, 145
Liaoning Normal University, 156
liberal market economy, 5
Lifelong Education Law, 52
LNU-MSU College of International
  Business, 156
local cultures and traditions, 196, 218
local-global dualism, 198
London, 72, 219
L'Oréal Group, 72
low-cost innovation, 17
lower-wage countries, 16
low-income economies, 27
low-tax policy, 125
low-technology clusters, 27
Lung Yen Group, 72
Luoyang, 164, 166

Ma Ying-jeou, 64
Macao, 43, 151
Macquarie Capital Securities, 72
macroeconomic environment, 28, 75
mahathir administration, 122
Mahidol University, 205
Mainland Chinese, 39, 126, 178,
  179, 180, 184
Malay Muslims, 172
Malaysia, 8, 9, 12–14, 26, 92, 121–6,
  131–5, 137, 139, 146, 157, 161–3,
  165, 166, 168–75, 183, 185–7,
  189, 191–7, 206, 209, 211
Malaysia's master plan of Vision
  2020, 194
Malaysian government, 122, 125, 131,
  132, 133, 171, 185, 187, 193

Malaysian Qualifications Agency
   (MQA), 125, 131–4, 175
The Malaysian Qualifications Agency
   (MQA), 124, 125, 131–4, 175
Malaysian Qualifications Framework
   (MQF), 125, 131
Maldivian student, 172
managerialism, 7
Mandarin, 148, 168, 170
Mao Zedong, 144
market economy, 5, 7, 134, 194, 198
market facilitator, 134, 193
market generator, 134, 193
market multilateralism, 197
market-accelerationist state, 5, 23, 131,
   191–4, 196, 197
market-facilitating state, 133, 191,
   192, 194, 197
Marketing and Channel Management
   College, 65
marketization, 8, 118, 121, 214, 216, 219
market-oriented, 6, 158, 214, 215
Marxists, 159
Mass Transit Railway (MTR), 42
Massachusetts Institute of Technology
   (MIT) of Asia, 71
Massachusetts Institute of Technology
   (MIT), 83, 108, 129
massification of higher education, 9,
   15, 16, 59, 73, 114
Mechano-Biology Institute (MBI), 82
Michael Lee, 215
Michael Polanyi, 209
Middle East Technical University, 204
Middle East, 13, 78, 125, 167, 185, 204
middle-income countries, 27
Minban, 7, 98, 114, 143, 156, 181, 184
mineral resources, 102
Ministry of Commerce, Industry and
   Energy, 49
Ministry of Economic Affairs, 64, 70
Ministry of Education and
   Human Resources Development
   (MOEHRD), 52

Ministry of Education (MOE), 6–8,
   10, 52, 53, 55–7, 65–8, 70, 79, 83,
   84, 95, 96, 104, 109–13, 123, 124,
   128, 129, 132, 135, 136, 140, 141,
   146, 150, 155, 156, 158–60, 195,
   211, 212
Ministry of Education, Science and
   Technology (MEST), 52–5
Ministry of Employment and Labor
   (MOEL), 56
Ministry of Labor, 57
Ministry of Science and Technology
   (MOST), 44, 52, 55, 56, 93, 112
Ministry of Trade and Industry
   (MTI), 79
Minzu University of China, 98
Missouri State University, 156
modernization, 58, 100, 102, 142,
   196, 220
Monash University, 123, 124
mongolian students, 151
Morgan Stanley Private Wealth
   Management, 72
Morshidi, 132, 133
multinational companies (MNCs), 75,
   76, 105
Myanmar, 168, 173
Myles Mace, 108

Nagoya University, 204
Nanjing University, 96, 97, 99, 148,
   149, 150, 205
Nankai University, 97
Nano and Advanced Materials
   Institute (NAMI), 37
nanotechnology, 16, 48, 65, 71, 103
Nansha Information Technology
   Park, 44
Nanyang Technological University, 8,
   78, 79, 84–7, 129, 153, 203, 204
Nanyang Technology University
   (NTU), 13, 72, 78, 83, 85–7
National Central University, 205
National Cheng Kung University, 205

National Chiao Tung University (NCTU), 71, 203, 204
National Chung Cheng University, 206
National Chung Hsing University, 206
National College Entrance Examination (gaokao), 182
national competitiveness, 2, 4, 15, 17, 59, 65, 66, 88, 113, 139, 159, 223
National Development and Reform Commission of the Chinese government, 43
National Framework for Innovation and Enterprise (NFIE), 82
National Healthcare Group (NHG), 87
National Higher Education Action Plan, 122, 211
National Higher Education Action Plan 2007–2010 in Malaysia, 211
National Higher Education Strategic Plan, 122, 123, 211
National Higher Education Strategic Plan beyond 2020, 211
National Innovation Framework for Action (NIFA), 77
national innovation system (NIS), 1, 27, 38, 47, 48, 64, 77, 79, 91, 117
National Natural Science Foundation, 102, 211
national political systems, 2
national professional education, 69
National Program for Intelligent Electronics, 69
National Program on Nano Technology, 69
National Research Laboratories (NRL), 53
National Research Program for Genomic Medicine, 69
National Science and Technology Board (NSTB), 76, 77, 88
National Science and Technology Center for Disaster Reduction, 69
National Science and Technology Development Plan, 63, 70
National Science and Technology Program for Biotechnology and Pharmaceuticals, 69
National Science and Technology Program for Telecommunications, 69
National Science and Technology Program—Energy, 69
National Science Council (NSC), 10, 60, 63, 66, 68, 70, 72
National Science Council (NSC), 10, 60, 63, 66, 70, 72
National Strategic Plan for Educational Development (The Plan), 142
National Students' Federation, 111
National Sun Yat-sen University, 205
National Taipei University of Technology, 206
National Taiwan Normal University, 205
National Taiwan Ocean University, 206
National Taiwan University (NTU), 72, 73, 203, 204, 205
National Taiwan University of Science and Technology, 205
National Tsing Hua University (NTHU), 71, 72, 203, 204
national universities, 6–8
national university corporations, 8
National University Hospital, 78
National University of Defence Technology, 98
National University of Singapore (NUS), 8, 13, 78, 81, 83–5, 129, 202–4
National University of Singapore Enterprise (NUS ETP), 84
National Yang-Ming University, 206
Nationalist Party, 24
Natural Science Foundation of China, 211

INDEX

natural sciences, 207
Negeri Sembilan, 123, 163
neoinstitutionalism, 222
neoliberal opportunity bargains, 16, 17
neoliberal reforms, 8
neoliberalism, 3–5, 7, 12, 141, 209, 214, 217
neoliberalist ideologies and practices, 219
Nepal, 151
Netherlands, 16, 218
Network Governance, 195, 197
Networked Communications Program, 69
Neusoft, 103
New Era College (NEC), 163, 169
New Technology Training Scheme, 36
New York University's Tisch School of the Arts, 83, 128
New Zealand, 28, 124, 172, 173
Nilai University College (NUC), 163, 169, 170, 171, 172, 173, 237, 240
Ningbo, 145, 146, 157, 164, 166, 177, 178, 181
Nongovernment Funding, 69
noninterventionist, 37
nonlocal academic staff, 222
non-local students, 126
nordic countries, 28, 29
North America, 14, 20
Northeast China, 99
Northeastern University, 98
Northern Ireland, 218
Northwest A&F University, 98
Northwestern Polytechnic University, 98, 151
Norway, 28
NRF, 81, 82
NTHU incubation center, 72
NTU Innovation Incubation Center, 72
Nursultan Nazarbayev, 57
NUS Enterprise Incubator (NEI), 85
NUS Entrepreneurship Centre (NEC), 84, 85

NUS Extension, 84
NUS Industry Liaison Office, 84, 85
NUS Overseas Colleges, 84, 85
NUS Press, 84
NUS Technology Holdings Pte. Ltd., 85
NUS Technology Holdings, 84, 85

Ocean University of China, 98
OECD countries, 17, 24, 26
Office of University-Industry Collaboration, 71
offshore campuses, 13
offshore programs, 13
Ohio State University, 151
Okayama University, 206
One-North Project, 78
Online Talent Pool Career Platform, 35
Open Distance Learning (ODL), 9
open innovation, 1, 41
Open University of Hong Kong, 134
open-door policy, 142
Operations Center for Industry Collaboration, 71
Organization for Economic Cooperation and Development (OECD), 17, 24, 26, 114, 202
Organizational Hybridization, 195
Osaka City University, 206
Osaka University, 204
Outstanding Achievement in Science and Technology Award, 68
Outstanding Industry-University Cooperation Award, 68
Outstanding Technology Licensing Center Award, 72
Over the counter (OTC), 70
overcentralization, 7
overseas learning experiences, 14
overseas students, 125, 146, 148, 169, 175, 179, 185, 194
Oxford, 40, 127, 148

Pakistan, 14, 151, 172
Park Geun-hye, 51
Patent Application Fund, 41, 77
Pearl River Delta (PRD), 37, 43, 44
Peking Globalist, 147
Peking University, 11, 95–7, 99, 103, 104, 126, 147, 148, 203, 204
periphery, 14, 209
PhD Entrepreneur-in-Training (PET) program, 86
Philippines, 9, 209
Photodynamic Therapy (PDT), 85
Pohang University of Science and Technology, 13, 202–4
poisoned chalice, 209
policy copying, 117, 219, 220, 221
policy implications, 189, 199, 217
policy learning, 117, 219, 220
policy yo-yo, 133
political economy, 16, 198
political influence, 115, 137
political-economic, 4
polytechnics, 128, 130
post-Mao era, 7
post-Mao period, 94
Presidential Science Prize, 68
private education institutions, 9, 129
private higher education, 9, 69, 122, 124, 132
private professional education, 69
private-driven national innovation system, 47
private-public mix, 9
Private-Public R&D partnerships, 36
privatization, 4, 6, 8, 118, 121, 216, 219
Proctor & Gamble, 72
Productivity and Innovation Credit (PIC), 79, 82
Program for Cultivating Science and Engineering Talents at Universities, 66
Program for Expanding Overseas Student Recruitment, 66
Program for Improving Basic Education in Universities, 66
Program for Improving Research University Infrastructure, 66
Program for International Student Assessment (PISA), 202
Program for Promoting Academic Excellence of Universities, 66
Program for Promoting Teaching Excellence of Universities, 66
Program for Rewarding Teaching Excellence of Universities, 66
Program to Promote International Competitiveness of Universities, 66
Programme for Promoting Academic Excellence of Universities, 10
Project for Developing Top-Notch Universities, 66
Project HOPE—Health Opportunity for People Everywhere, 155
promote entrepreneurship and innovation, 41, 82, 115
Proof-of-Concept Fund, 42
public higher education systems, 218
publicly owned organizations, 8
public-private distinction, 9, 197
Publish or Perish, 10, 210
Pusan National University, 56, 206

Qidihoude Co., 110
Qin Shi Huang, 151
Qing dynasty, 151
Qingdao University, 145
qualifications framework (QF), 125, 131, 133, 134, 194
qualifications register (QR), 124, 131, 133
The quest for world-class university status, 11, 209, 222, 223

R&D competition, 27
R&D expenditures, 34, 36, 48–50, 64
Raffles Education, 129, 130

Index

Recolonialization of Higher Education, 221
recolonization, 220
red capitalist, 44
Regency Steel Asia Pte. Ltd., 86
regional ecology, 102
Regional Education Hub, 13, 14, 38, 121, 122, 128, 137, 193
regional financial crisis, 15
Regional Hub of Education, 83, 122, 128, 135, 137, 171, 192, 196, 198
regional hub of higher education, 10, 12
regional hub status, 137, 139, 194
regional innovation systems (RISs), 47, 91
regional technology service hub, 37
Regional University Researchers Program, 49
Regionalization of Asian universities, 221
reinvention of the state, 195
Renmin University of China, 97, 205
Renminbi (RMB), 95, 96, 106, 107, 145, 146
Research and Development (R&D) 1, 9, 20, 24–9, 33–40, 42–51, 53, 54, 59, 60, 63–72, 75–82, 84, 86, 87, 92–4, 99–101, 105–8, 117, 158, 201, 209, 214
Research and Development Assistance Scheme, 77
Research and Development Cash Rebate Scheme, 36
research assessment exercise (RAE), 10, 218, 219
Research Endowment Fund (REF), 45, 46
Research Grants Council (RGC), 39, 45, 46
Research Incentive Scheme for Companies, 77
Research Talent Recruitment Program, 67
Research to Market (R2M) Platform, 85

Research University Integration Project, 66
Research, Innovation and Enterprise (RIE) 2015 Plan, 80
Research, Innovation and Enterprise Council (RIEC), 79
research-led universities, 209
Richard Garrett, 128
The rise of academic capitalism, 213
Rise of China, 148
Robert Chung Affair, 215
Rolls Royce, 86
Russia, 78, 151

S. P. Jain Center of Management, 128
Samsung Electronics Company Ltd., 55
Samsung, 55–7
Saravanan Gopinathan, 215
SAS Enterprise Intelligence Laboratory, 88
Savannah College of Arts and Design, 127
scarcity of natural resources, 75
School of Continuing Education, Hong Kong Baptist University (HKBU-SCE), 162, 175
Schoolhouse, 83, 84, 125, 128, 135, 137, 192, 194
Science and Technology (S&T), 13, 27, 38- 41, 47–55, 60, 63–8, 76–9, 84, 85, 87, 88, 92- 94, 99–103, 107, 127, 142, 150, 152, 202, 207, 221
Science and Technology Commission of Shanghai Municipality (STCSM), 111
Science and Technology Framework Law, 48
Science Citation Index (SCI), 10, 11
Sciences and Engineering (S&E), 78, 129, 153, 154, 207, 210
Scotland, 218
Second World War, 20, 24, 220
Second-tier College, 156

second-tier students, 185
Sector Specific Accelerators (SSA), 80
selective decentralization, 133
self-funded programs, 215
Semenyih, 123
Semiconductor Systems Engineering Program, 55, 56
semi-periphery, 14
Seoul National University, 13, 203, 204
Seton Hall University, 155
Shaanxi Province, 99
Shandong Entrepreneurship Foundation for Graduates (SEFG), 112
Shandong University, 97
Shandong, 112, 142, 145
Shanghai Jiao Tong University, 13, 83, 96, 97, 99, 145, 147, 148, 164, 177, 179, 181, 202, 205, 210
Shanghai Jiao Tong University's Academic Ranking, 13, 202
Shanghai Municipal Education Commission (SMEC), 111
Shanghai Normal University (SHNU), 164, 177
Shanghai Technology Entrepreneurship Foundation for Graduates (STEFG), 111
Shanghai, 11, 13, 33, 96, 99, 111, 142, 163–6, 177
Sharif University of Technology, 205
Shawn Chen, 156
Shenzhen, 33, 43, 44, 115
Shenzhen-Hong Kong Industry-University-Research Base, 43
Shenzhen-Hong Kong Innovation Circle cooperation agreement, 43
Sias Group, 156
Sias International University, 155, 156
Sichuan University, 97
Silicon Valley of the East, 59
Singapore, 2, 8, 9, 12–14, 19–21, 24–9, 33, 72, 75–84, 86, 88–90, 92, 117, 121, 122, 125, 128–30, 135–7, 139, 153, 161–3, 165–70, 172–5, 183–7, 189, 191, 193–7, 202–4, 207, 208, 215, 222
Singapore Centre on Environmental Life Sciences Engineering (SCELSE), 82
Singapore Economic Development Board, 79, 83, 86
Singapore Government, 8, 9, 75, 76, 78, 79, 82, 84, 89, 128–30, 135, 169, 193, 194
Singapore Institute of Technology (SIT), 84
Singapore International Graduate Award (SINGA), 78
Singapore Management University (SMU), 8, 78, 83, 84, 87, 88
Singapore Medtech Accelerator Pte. Ltd., 80
Singapore Polytechnic, 78
Singapore Productivity and Standards Board, 77
Singapore Scholarship, 129
Singapore Science Centre, 79
Singapore Science Park, 75
Singapore University of Technology and Design (SUTD), 84
Singapore's Global Schoolhouse project, 194
Singaporean students, 207
Singapore-MIT Alliance (SMA), 129
Sino-British College, University of Shanghai for Science and Technology (SBC-USST), 163, 165, 177
Sino-Canadian College, 149
Sino-Dutch International Business Center of Nanjing University, 149
Sino-German College of Applied Sciences, Tongji University (CDHAW-Tongji), 163, 177, 180
Sino-German Institute for Legal Studies, 149

INDEX

Siti Hamisah, 125
Small and Medium Business Administration (SMBA), 49, 50
Small and Medium Enterprise Administration (SMEA), 64, 65, 70
Small and Medium-Sized Enterprise (SME) Master Plan, 76
Small and Medium-Sized Enterprises (SMEs), 36, 47–51, 55, 57, 59, 64, 65, 70, 77, 79, 86, 87
Small Business Innovation Research Program, 64
Small Entrepreneur Research Assistance Program, 36
small government, 176, 197
small government, big market, 197
SME e-Learning Project, 65
social institution, 213
social Mobility, 15
Social Science Citation Index (SSCI), 10, 11
socioeconomic changes, 6
soft power, 115, 137, 139, 160
Sogang University, 206
Somerset County Council, 111
South China University of Technology, 98
South China, 44
South Korea, 2, 9, 12–14, 17, 19–21, 24–9, 34, 38, 40, 47–58, 64, 78, 92, 117, 151, 202–8, 210, 211
South Korean students, 207
Southeast Asia, 8, 12, 67, 192, 209
Southeast University, 97, 150
Southern Sunshine Scholarship Program, 67
Southern Taiwan Science Park, 60–3
Southern Taiwan University, 73
Soviet Union, 92
Spain, 16
Special Tax Treatment Control Act, 51
spin-off companies, 1, 40, 85, 86
spin-off enterprises, 93
SPRING SEEDS Capital (SSC), 80

SPRING Start-up Enterprise Development Scheme (SPRING SEEDS), 80
Sri Lanka, 169, 172, 173
Standard Chartered Bank, 111
Standard Chartered plc, 72
Standards, Productivity and Innovation Board (SPRING Singapore), 79–81, 129
Stanford University, 40, 83
Stanford University, 40, 83, 148
Start and Improve Your Business (SIYB), 112
Start-up Enterprise Development Scheme (SEEDS), 80
Start-up, 23, 35, 51, 64, 65, 79–82, 85–7, 104, 110, 111, 152–4
State Capacity, 192–5
State Education Commission (SEC), 140, 143
state intervention, 93, 132, 191, 192, 194, 197
state universities, 6–8, 214, 215
state-guided market, 141
state-oriented, 6
state-owned industries, 4, 8
The Straits Times, 130
Structural Reform, 7, 104, 105, 115, 117, 159
Student Learning, 90, 119, 160, 161, 166, 183, 187, 196, 212
Student Mobility, 13, 14
Students' International Communication Association (SICA), 147
study destinations, 14
study overseas, 14, 90, 148, 220
Sun Wei, 181–3
Sun Yat-sen University, 97, 205
Sung Kyun Kwan University, 55, 57, 204
Sunway Group, 124
supranational organizations, 216
Sweden, 28, 85

Swinburne University of Technology, 124
Swinburne University of Technology, 124

Taipei, 15
Taiwan, 2, 7, 9–12, 14, 16, 17, 19–21, 24, 25, 27–29, 34, 38, 40, 47, 59, 60, 63–73, 78, 92, 117, 133, 151, 160, 168, 172, 202–206, 208, 210, 212
Taiwan Government, 7, 59, 60, 63–5, 68, 73, 212
Taiwan International Graduate Program, 68
Taiwan Semiconductor Manufacturing Company, 63
Taiwan Social Science Citation Index (TSSCI), 11
Taiwan Stock Exchange, 70
Taiwan's SME Online University, 65
Taiwanese students, 207
Tamkang University, 11
Tan Nguan Soon, 87
Ta-You Wu Memorial Award, 68
teaching and learning, 89, 122, 136, 141, 146, 174, 178, 210–12, 217
Teaching Excellence Project, 212
technical and vocational education, 89, 90
Technical University of Eindhoven, 83
Technical University of Munich, 83
Technion Israel Institute of Technology, 204
technoglobalist country, 117
technologically advanced economies, 68
technologically advanced nation, 63, 94
Technology and Business Development Fund, 41
technology commercialization, 77
Technology Enterprise Commercialization Scheme (TECS), 80
Technology Licensing Office, 71

technology licensing, 59, 68, 71, 72, 85, 106, 201
Technology Transfer Center, 41, 42
Technology Transfer Office, 40, 41
Technology Transfer Promotion Act, 48
technonationalist countries, 117
technopreneurship, 85, 86, 88
techno-scientists, 214
Tehran University of Medical Sciences, 205
Tel Aviv University, 204
Tengku Dato' Shamsul Bahrin, 171
terra-cotta warriors and horses, 151
Terri Kim, 208
Tertiary students, 14, 126
Tesco, 111
Texas A&M University, 155
Thailand, 9, 205, 206, 209
Theme-Based Research Scheme, 45
Third International Mathematics and Science Study (TIMSS), 202
TI Food and Nutrition Publication Prize, 87
Tianjin University, 97
Times Higher Education Supplement, 210
Times Higher Education University Ranking, 12, 202, 203
Times Higher Education World University Rankings, 204
Tohoku University, 204
Tokyo Institute of Technology, 13, 203, 204
Tokyo Medical and Dental University, 205
Tokyo Metropolitan University, 205
Tokyo University of Agriculture and Technology, 206
Tokyo, 13, 147, 149, 202–6
Tongji University, 97, 163, 177, 180
Top University Project Phase II, 67
Top University Project, 66
top-tier universities, 67

Index

Tourism Board, 129
Toward World Class Universities Project, 69
Traditional Chinese medicine (TCM), 102
Traditional Keynesian welfare state regimes, 215
Transformation of Higher Education Document, 123
transformation of higher education, 123, 213
transformationists, 2, 3
transnational corporations (TNCs), 2, 16, 197
transnational education enterprises, 195
transnational education programs, 124, 182, 194, 195
transnational education, 23, 121–4, 126, 128–30, 134, 140, 141, 143, 159, 182, 191, 192, 194–8
transnational financial and political formations, 3
Transnational Higher Education (TNHE), 13, 14, 114, 121, 123, 125–33, 135–7, 139, 141–3, 146, 147, 155, 159–62, 165, 189, 191–4, 196, 197
Transnationalization of Higher Education, 119, 139, 155, 160, 161, 201
Transnationalizing Higher Education, 121, 140
trend of academic entrepreneurship, 213
Trimble Navigation Limited, 151
Tsinghua Tongfang, 103
Tsinghua University, 11, 95–7, 99, 104, 109–11, 113, 126, 148, 203, 204
TSMC (the world's first semiconductor foundry, founded in Taiwan), 72
Twelfth Five-Year Plan (2011–2015) on National Intellectual Property Development, 105

Twelfth Five-Year Plan on Patents, 105
twinning programs, 123, 124, 126, 144–6, 170
two-way travel, 14

U.S. News & World Report, 210
UK's Patent Law, 63
Ulsan National Institute of Science and Technology (UNIST), 55
Unilever, 72
Union University, 73
United Arab Emirates University, 206
United International College (UIC), 157, 164, 177, 178, 181, 182
United Kingdom (UK), 10, 14, 15, 17, 21, 111, 121, 124, 127, 140, 145, 155, 172, 173, 182, 202, 208, 218, 220
United Microelectronics Corporation, 63
United Nations Educational, Scientific and Cultural Organization (UNESCO), 108, 121, 216
United Overseas Bank Ltd. (UOB), 87, 88
United States (US)/USA, 13, 15–17, 21–5, 28, 29, 35, 42, 43, 52, 53, 59, 63, 72, 85–7, 99, 107, 109, 110, 124, 127, 130, 140, 148, 151, 156, 172, 202, 207, 208, 210, 213, 220, 221
United States Air Force Academy, 86
universalization, 52
Universiti Kebangsaan Malaysia, 206
Universiti Sains Malaysia (USM), 132
universities/research institutes (URIs), 93
The University Board for Christian Higher Education in Asia, 151
university bureaucracy, 213
University Governance, 4, 6, 8, 17, 115, 122, 139, 140, 159, 195, 199, 201, 202, 207, 209, 212, 214–16
University Grant Committee (UGC), 6, 38–41, 45, 125, 134, 183

university law, 214
university league tables, 10–12, 202, 208, 209
university national science parks (UNSP), 112
University of Arizona, 155
University of Auckland, 173
University of British Columbia, 127
University of California, 155
University of Chicago, 83, 128, 155
University of Edinburgh, 173
University of Electronic Science and Technology, 98
University of Glasgow, 173
University of Göttingen, 149
University of Hawaii System, 155
The University of Hong Kong (HKU), 13, 35, 40, 41, 44, 126, 135, 202
The University of Hong Kong School of Professional and Continuing Education (HKU SPACE), 126
university of Illinois, 151
University of Leeds, 40
University of Manchester, 173, 182
University of Massachusetts Medical School, 151
University of Miami, 155
University of Michigan, 155, 164, 177, 179
University of Michigan-Shanghai Jiao Tong University Joint Institute (UM-SJTU Joint Institute), 164, 177, 179
University of Middlesex, 127
University of New South Wales, 83, 127, 154, 173
University of North Carolina at Charlotte, 155
University of North Carolina at Greensboro, 151
University of Nottingham, 123, 145, 146, 157, 164, 177, 178, 181
University of Nottingham-Ningbo (UNN), 145, 157, 164, 177, 178, 181
University of Ontario Institute of Technology, 35
University of Oxford, 127
University of Pennsylvania's Wharton School, 83
University of Pittsburgh, 155
University of Science and Technology of China, 96, 97, 99, 204
University of Scranton, 155
University of Shanghai for Science and Technology, 163, 165, 177
University of Tennessee-Knoxville, 151
University of Tokyo, 13, 147, 202–4
University of Tsukuba, 205
University of Ulster, 127
University of Warwick, 84, 127
University of Waterloo (UW), 127, 149, 154
University of Wisconsin, 153, 155, 221
University Performance, 10, 199, 210, 222
University Ranking, 6, 10–13, 132, 202–10, 212, 214, 216
University Restructuring, 6, 95, 215
university spin-off companies, 1
University Transformations, 17, 20
university-affiliated enterprises, 92
university-based entrepreneurship ecosystem, 1, 2
university-enterprise cooperation, 55–7, 73, 75, 103
university-industry cooperation, 20, 37, 56, 68, 104, 111
university-industry linkages, 47, 70
university-industry partnership, 40, 111, 213
university-industry relationships, 213
University-Industry-Business cooperation, 19, 20, 23, 29
university-owned enterprises, 104, 105

Index

university-run enterprises, 103–5, 217
UOB-SMU Entrepreneurship Alliance (USEA) Centre, 87, 88

value for money, 174
venture businesses, 49
vice-ministerial universities, 96, 97
vietnam, 27, 151, 168, 170, 171, 173, 175, 209
vision 2025 plan, 48
Vocational Training Council (VTC), 36

Wales, 83, 127, 164, 173, 218, 219
Wan Hai Lines, 72
Wang Hao, 109
Waseda University, 205
Washington, 4, 25, 125
Water resource, 102
Watermark Award, 87
Wawasan 2020 (Vision 2020), 122, 194
Western China, 99
western developed economies, 15
western graduates, 16
western managerial-oriented doctrines, 219
western model, 22, 222
western university model, 222
westernization, 220
White Paper on Science and Technology, 63
Wiki Partnership Fund, 71
Wilhelm Exner Medal, 87
Women Scientists Program, 49
Work Pass for Foreign Entrepreneur (EntrePass), 80
World Bank, 9, 25–8, 123, 216
World Business Environment Survey, 26
World Class University (WCU) project, 54
World Conference on Higher Education (WCHE), 108

World Economic Forum (WEF), 109, 116
world factory, 91
World Trade Organization (WTO), 139–41, 143
world university ranking league tables, 208
world-class status, 10, 12, 60, 118, 132, 142, 158, 215, 216, 218, 219, 221, 222
world-class universities, 7, 8, 11–13, 83, 91, 95, 99, 148, 207, 208, 216, 220
world-class university status, 6, 11, 209, 222, 223
world-renowned universities, 209
Wuhan University of Technology, 205
Wuhan University, 11, 97, 151–5, 205

Xiamen University, 97
Xi'an Jiaotong University, 96, 97, 150, 151, 206
Xi'an Jiaotong-Liverpool University, 145, 157

Yale, 84, 147, 148
Yangtze River Delta region, 99
Yayasan Sarawak, 124
Yeungjin College, 57
Yokohama National University, 206
Yonsei University, 204
Young Entrepreneurs Scheme for Schools (YES! Schools), 81
youth unemployment, 16
Yu Chi Chung, 150
Yuan Ze University, 73, 206

Zhang Li, 146
Zhang Shensheng, 181
Zhejiang Foundation for Youth Entrepreneurship and Employment (ZFYEE), 112
Zhejiang University National Science Park (ZUNSP), 112

Zhejiang University, 11, 96, 97, 99, 112, 205
Zhejiang Wanli Education Group, 157
Zhejiang, 96, 99, 112, 164–6
Zhengzhou University, 156
Zhongshan University, 73
Zhongwai Hezuo Banxue, 140
Zhongyuan University of Technology (ZUT), 164, 177, 182, 183
Zhongyuan University of Technology (ZUT), 164, 177, 182, 183
Zhuhai, 43, 157, 164, 166, 177, 181

GPSR Compliance

The European Union's (EU) General Product Safety Regulation (GPSR) is a set of rules that requires consumer products to be safe and our obligations to ensure this.

If you have any concerns about our products, you can contact us on

ProductSafety@springernature.com

In case Publisher is established outside the EU, the EU authorized representative is:

Springer Nature Customer Service Center GmbH
Europaplatz 3
69115 Heidelberg, Germany

www.ingramcontent.com/pod-product-compliance
Lightning Source LLC
LaVergne TN
LVHW011801060526
838200LV00053B/3653